STRATEGIC ASIA 2014–15

STRATEGIC ASIA 2014–15

U.S. ALLIANCES AND PARTNERSHIPS

at the Center of Global Power

Edited by

Ashley J. Tellis, Abraham M. Denmark, and Greg Chaffin

With contributions from

Catharin Dalpino, Bates Gill, Sheena Chestnut Greitens,
Russell Hsiao, Van Jackson, Ann Marie Murphy,
Nguyen Manh Hung, Scott Snyder, Matthew Shannon Stumpf,
Nicholas Szechenyi, Ashley J. Tellis, and Daniel Twining

 THE NATIONAL BUREAU *of* **ASIAN RESEARCH**
Seattle and Washington, D.C.

THE NATIONAL BUREAU *of* ASIAN RESEARCH

Published in the United States of America by
The National Bureau of Asian Research, Seattle, WA, and Washington, D.C.
www.nbr.org

Copyright © 2014 by The National Bureau of Asian Research

ISBN (print): 978-1-939131-34-8
ISBN (electronic): 978-1-939131-35-5

Cover images

Front: Highly detailed planet Earth at night, lit by the rising sun, illuminated by light of cities. Earth is surrounded by a luminous network, representing the major air routes based on real data © Shutterstock

Back (left to right): Barack Obama during a state visit to Tokyo, Japan, on April 24, 2014 [State Department photo by William Ng/public domain/U.S. government work]; Ships transit the Pacific Ocean during RIMPAC [U.S. Navy photo by Chief Mass Communication Specialist Mark C. Schultz (Released), 140711-N-FE250-324, licensed under creative commons BY]; Commercial container port in Hong Kong © Shutterstock; and Secretary of Defense Chuck Hagel meets with the Prime Minister of India Narendra Modi at the Blair House in Washington D.C., Sept. 30, 2014 [DoD Photo by Master Sgt. Adrian Cadiz (Released), licensed under creative commons BY]

Design and publishing services by The National Bureau of Asian Research

Cover design by Stefanie Choi

Publisher's Cataloging-In-Publication Data
(Prepared by The Donohue Group, Inc.)

U.S. alliances and partnerships at the center of global power / edited by

Ashley J. Tellis, Abraham M. Denmark, and Greg Chaffin ; with

contributions from Catharin Dalpino [and 11 others].

pages ; cm. -- (Strategic Asia, 1933-6462 ; 2014-15)

Issued also as an ebook.

Includes bibliographical references and index.

ISBN: 978-1-939131-34-8

1. United States--Foreign relations--Asia. 2. Asia--Foreign relations--United States. 3. United States--Military relations--Asia. 4. Asia--Military relations--United States. 5. United States--Foreign relations--2009- 6. Security, International--Asia. 7. Security, International--Pacific Area. 8. Alliances. I. Tellis, Ashley J. II. Denmark, Abraham. III. Chaffin, Greg. IV. Dalpino, Catharin E. V. National Bureau of Asian Research (U.S.) VI. Series: Strategic Asia ; 2014-15.

JZ1480.A55 U55 2014

327.7305

Printed in Canada

The paper used in this publication meets the minimum requirement of the American National Standard for Information Sciences—Permanence of Paper for Printed Library Materials, ANSI Z39.48-1992.

Contents

> A review of how the United States came to treat alliances and
> partnerships as essential instruments of its quest for hegemony,
> what tasks U.S. alliances performed in the past, and how their
> functions promise to mutate in the future.

U.S. Allies

> An examination of Japan's emerging foreign policy strategy and
> efforts to strengthen the U.S.-Japan alliance.

> An analysis of the current status and future prospects of the alliance
> between the United States and the Republic of Korea.

Strategic Partners

Special Study

Preface

Richard J. Ellings

2014 marks the one hundredth anniversary of World War I. The Great War's centenary has prompted many to reflect on the circumstances that led up to one of the most devastating wars in history and, inevitably, compare the state of the world then with that of today. Some of the prevailing trends of the early 1900s included swelling nationalism, significant military expansion among great powers, heightened economic interdependence, and a system of binding alliances within the context of a shifting international strategic environment centered around the rise of a new great power. And while important differences exist between 1914 and 2014—U.S. leadership and the deterrent effects of nuclear weapons, for example—the early 1900s offer a cautionary history. Is the Asia-Pacific, in fact, reaching a modern day tipping point similar to that of 1914? Are there parallels as well to the 1930s, when dissatisfied, rising powers sought once again to overturn the prevailing world order?

The balance of power and locus of economic activity continue to shift toward and within the Asia-Pacific. Largely as a consequence, the region is undergoing other dramatic changes. In Japan, the Shinzo Abe administration's policies, including the decision to reinterpret the constitution and allow a broader exercise of military power, have brought meaningful change to a decades-old foreign policy, yet have spawned accusations from some in neighboring states of Japanese remilitarization. In what may be a historic turn, India has elected a new, pro-business prime minister who seeks to reinvigorate the nation's economy and revitalize its approach to foreign policy. South Korea has responded as well by joining a free trade agreement with the United States and expanding defense preparations, largely as a result of increasing unease with Chinese intentions and rising power and the growing nuclear threat posed by North Korea. Other countries across the Asia-Pacific, such as Vietnam, Indonesia, and

Australia, are also expanding their investments in military power out of similar concerns.

At the center of attention is the People's Republic of China (PRC), whose leader Xi Jinping has consolidated power in a way not seen since Mao Zedong, while projecting China's power abroad. In the South China Sea, the PRC has accelerated its aggressive maritime strategy, using fishing boats, paramilitary ships, and naval and air forces in an effort to bolster territorial claims and excise the presence of its rivals. Over the past year, China stepped up its harassment of Japanese forces defending the Senkaku/Diaoyu Islands and of U.S. surveillance aircraft patrolling in international airspace in accordance with well-established international law and practice. This behavior has deepened fear and distrust of Beijing in many Asian countries, as well as in the United States, despite China's growing centrality to the regional economy.

For nearly 70 years, the United States has led the international order. It has done this based on enormous power, U.S. leaders' belief in the rule of law and economic and political liberalism, and the promotion of U.S. interests in stability and prosperity. This has been especially true in the Asia-Pacific, where American military might, economic strength, and political commitments have sustained a relatively peaceful regional environment, allowing Asian countries to focus on economic and, in many cases, political development while serving to provide the United States with an environment of relative peace and a tremendous economic opportunity. The cumulative effects of China's rise are being increasingly felt throughout the region, however, particularly as Beijing has become more assertive along the country's periphery. The PRC seems intent on supplanting the United States as the dominant power in the western Pacific and challenging some of the foundational aspects of the existing regional order. As China continues to build its national power, other Asian states are seeking to expand their own power and influence within the region and beyond. Whether this is simply designed to counteract China's growing strength or is also the result of the natural tendencies of states to maximize their own power and influence within the international system, a more multipolar Asia-Pacific is emerging, and it is becoming more contentious. States are seeking to manage frequently shifting interests, power dynamics, and potential threats posed by a larger number of growing powers. Indeed, states must interpret the intentions of a wider array of more powerful and capable actors, each replete with expanding interests and motivations, and thus face heightening uncertainty in state-to-state interactions. Most eyes, of course, are on China, and much of the diplomatic jockeying boils down to coalition-building as a hedge.

In addition to the core, structural factors, the region is beset with myriad other challenges: a belligerent North Korea consumed with developing nuclear weapons, transnational terrorism, natural disasters, and resource scarcity. Moreover, the United States continues to be hampered by significant constraints. Persistent war in the Middle East, intensifying problems in Eastern Europe, growing popular distrust of foreign military entanglements, and constricted defense budgets signal to Asians that the United States' will and ability to meet the demands of maintaining the regional order may be diminishing. The severity of these and other challenges, all resting on the foundation of Asia's shifting geopolitical structure, will place greater strain on the United States and the international and regional arrangements built since World War II.

The parallels with the early and mid-twentieth century cannot be dismissed. The international economy is highly integrated again, but to date has been an ineffective brake on Chinese as well as Russian behavior. The principal rising power, China, is resentful, highly nationalistic, authoritarian, and increasingly aggressive. Due to China's extraordinary economic success and an equally extraordinary military buildup, the balance of power is changing rapidly, yet the alliances from the Cold War, aimed mostly at deterring the Soviet Union, remain intact. And international leadership is not what it was during most of the post–World War II period. Although the United States is fully engaged and vastly experienced in foreign affairs today, it is weary and losing its clear preeminence. In sum, economic integration is no more a panacea for world peace today than it ever was; the Asia-Pacific contains potentially dangerous actors, and the fast-changing balance of power is increasingly ambiguous. The sources of instability—such as the possibility of miscalculation (or successful calculation) by all actors or of the failure of coalition adjustment before aggression takes place—are increasing, as they were in the early and mid-twentieth century.

The differences with these earlier periods are significant too. The United States remains the most powerful nation militarily, shows resilience economically, and retains the will to respond to threats it deems vital. Unlike Germany, Italy, and Japan of the 1930s, China does not currently define its mission as imperial, and to the extent that Russia does, it is a modest imperialism in comparison with that of the twentieth century's Soviet Union and fascist powers. Making all major powers think twice before directly attacking one another today is the fact of nuclear proliferation. The world today is a multipolar (albeit asymmetrical), nuclear one. No one knows the extent of deterrence achieved in this complex nuclear environment, but countries that have already acquired or are trying to acquire nuclear weapons believe in their deterrent or even compellent effects.

Perhaps the most critical variable determining the prospects for peace in the decades ahead will be the diplomatic opportunities either grasped or allowed to slip through America's fingers. Dexterity at building and reshaping coalitions as exigencies are ascertained and keeping opposing coalitions from forming will be the measure of international leadership. The United States will increasingly need to coordinate with its allies and partners with specific goals in mind, including preventing Russia from entering into an alliance with China.

Which countries can Washington call on to assist, and with which responsibilities? Who has the potential capacity? Who has the relevant experience? Who has the willingness to assist? Policymakers must decide where to make investments to deepen capacity, where to shift responsibility, and where to accept greater risk. Regional concerns over entrapment and abandonment, as well as potential political disputes among partner states, must all be considered and, to the degree possible, addressed and mitigated. This will require an accurate assessment of our existing and developing relationships in the region, as well as these countries' abilities, willingness, and capacity to support the United States in the Asia-Pacific.

This year's volume of *Strategic Asia* offers just such an assessment. *Strategic Asia 2014–15: U.S. Alliances and Partnerships at the Center of Global Power* analyzes the current state and likely future trajectory of U.S. alliances and partnerships in the Asia-Pacific in light of the region's shifting strategic and geopolitical landscape. By providing new insight into these relationships, this volume will enable the United States to strengthen its existing alliances, breathe fresh life into relationships, and seek out new and influential regional partners in order to respond to current and emerging challenges.

The nature and escalating pace of events in the Asia-Pacific mark this as a moment full of opportunities for progress and advancement in the region, while being simultaneously rife with threats to the "long peace." The United States and its allies and partners must adapt and closely coordinate to ensure that pivotal changes do not undermine U.S. vested interests in stability and prosperity in the Asia-Pacific.

Acknowledgments

This year's *Strategic Asia* volume forms the intellectual foundation of a two-year project entitled "Strengthening the Asia-Pacific Order: The Future of U.S. Alliances and Partnerships." The volume will therefore not only contribute to the wealth of scholarly research contained in the *Strategic Asia* series; it will also support the broader goals of the Future of Alliances project by crafting new strategies to build and enhance U.S. relations with key Asian partners in order to sustain the health of the liberal international order.

The volume relied on the contributions of many individuals. We are once again grateful for the ongoing support of the program's senior adviser, Aaron Friedberg, who is professor of politics at Princeton University and former deputy national security adviser to the vice president. For the past eleven years, Ashley Tellis has served as research director of the Strategic Asia program, and we are thankful for his strong leadership. NBR vice president for political and security affairs Abraham Denmark likewise deserves major credit for his role in ensuring the overall success of the program. Joining the editorial team after two years of working behind the scenes on this series is Greg Chaffin, whose hard work and adroit eye greatly contributed to the high quality of analysis found in this year's edition.

Alison Szalwinski provided essential research and logistical support for the production of the book and the planning of launch events surrounding its release. NBR's publications team—led by Joshua Ziemkowski and with the able assistance of Jessica Keough, Jonathan Walton, Craig Scanlan, and Hannah Haegeland—was responsible for the technical editing, layout, and proofreading of the entire volume. We all wish Jonathan well as he departs for a PhD program at the University of California, San Diego. Behind the scenes, the program has relied on NBR fellows and interns to bring this volume to publication. They provided thorough research assistance to scholars and contributed in many other essential ways, notably by helping produce the "Strategic Asia Trends and Indicators" section.

NBR senior vice president Michael Wills has been involved with the Strategic Asia program since its inception in 2000 and remains indispensable to its success. Likewise, NBR senior adviser Roy Kamphausen continues to provide expert guidance to this and many other NBR programs.

This year's scholars have done an extraordinary job in assessing Asia's geopolitical environment and how current trends are likely to shape U.S. alliances and partnerships in the future. We want to extend special thanks for their diligence in adhering to a very tight production schedule while still producing high-quality research. These authors join a community of over one hundred leading specialists who have written for the series. Their work was aided significantly by anonymous reviewers, whose prompt and thorough evaluations of the draft chapters were essential to ensuring the volume's accuracy and policy relevance.

Finally, I would like to acknowledge the continued support of the Lynde and Harry Bradley Foundation. The Bradley Foundation has been a core sponsor of the Strategic Asia program since its inception and remains a critical partner. I would also like to express my sincere thanks to the

Smith Richardson Foundation, whose sponsorship of a major project on this subject provided support for the research of several of the chapters in this year's volume. That project will produce NBR's forthcoming monograph by Abraham Denmark examining strategies for the United States to encourage and enable its Asian allies and partners to contribute more to regional stability and prosperity. I am deeply grateful to our colleagues at these organizations for their ongoing commitment to NBR's mission of informing and strengthening policy toward the Asia-Pacific.

As I like to say, NBR's "niche" is the truth (as best it can be ascertained). They may not always be comfortable to read, but quality, objective assessments are increasingly vital in this complex period. Last year's history of the origin of World War I by Christopher Clark, *The Sleepwalkers*, detailed the events and relationships that led Europe's leaders into an unintended cataclysm. It is our hope that, armed with the truth, today's leaders can avoid the tragedies of the past.

Richard J. Ellings
President
The National Bureau of Asian Research

STRATEGIC ASIA 2014–15

OVERVIEW

EXECUTIVE SUMMARY

This chapter reviews how the U.S. came to treat alliances and partnerships as essential instruments of its quest for hegemony over time, what tasks U.S. alliances performed in the past, and how their functions promise to mutate in the future.

MAIN ARGUMENT:
Despite frequent references to the U.S.'s early isolationist past, the country has consistently rejected both isolationism and multilateralism as instruments for meeting its highest strategic ambitions, instead utilizing a dialectical relationship between confederationism and unilateralism to achieve hegemony. U.S. power, no matter how formidable, benefits from the presence of partners, thanks to both their capacity to supplement American resources and their ability to bestow legitimacy to various U.S. policies. Even when these are not at issue, however, the company of confederates is undoubtedly valuable because it enhances the freedom that the U.S. enjoys to undertake unilateral actions whenever these are demanded by its global interests.

POLICY IMPLICATIONS:
- Confederationism, as a constituent element of U.S. grand strategy, is here to stay. As Washington focuses on national rejuvenation, it does not have the luxury of jettisoning its alliances because no matter what their infirmities currently may be, they are essential to preserving U.S. global hegemony.

- In an environment characterized by both deepening interdependence and rising Chinese power, Washington's quest for partnerships in the Indo-Pacific region is eased by the fact that a large number of nations therein value the U.S. and its protective presence because of the positive externalities accruing to them.

- The cohesion between the U.S. and its many partners is likely to be greatest when U.S. power is at its most durable and resolute. The ultimate value of confederationism as an anchor of grand strategy, thus, hinges fundamentally on the vitality of U.S. power.

Seeking Alliances and Partnerships: The Long Road to Confederationism in U.S. Grand Strategy

Ashley J. Tellis

Although it is widely believed that the United States pursued an isolationist foreign policy for much of its early political life, the truth of the matter is more complex. The argument that the United States should remain isolationist—shunning alliances on grounds of both principle and pragmatism—certainly did not lack for advocates, as Thomas Paine's celebrated pamphlet *Common Sense* illustrated. And isolationism's appeal was certainly enhanced by the ostensible exhortations of the United States' founding fathers. George Washington, the nation's first president, for example, would in his oft-quoted farewell address urge his fellow citizens to remember that "the great rule of conduct for us, in regard to foreign nations, is in extending our commercial relations, to have with them as little political connection as possible."[1] The third president, Thomas Jefferson, would reinforce this theme in his inaugural address by admonishing the polity to pursue "peace, commerce, and honest friendship with all nations, entangling alliances with none."[2]

Ashley J. Tellis is a Senior Associate at the Carnegie Endowment for International Peace and Research Director of the Strategic Asia Program at the National Bureau of Asian Research. He can be reached at <atellis@carnegieendowment.org>.

[1] George Washington, "Washington's Farewell Address," 1796, Avalon Project, http://avalon.law.yale.edu/18th_century/washing.asp.

[2] Thomas Jefferson, "Inaugural Address," March 4, 1801, American Presidency Project, http://www.presidency.ucsb.edu/ws/?pid=25803.

This chapter reviews how the United States came to treat alliances and partnerships as essential instruments of its quest for hegemony over time. It thus complements the rest of the volume, which focuses on how key nations in the Indo-Pacific region view their association with U.S. policy as serving their own particular national security interests. Toward that end, this chapter is divided into four major sections. The first section examines the logic of the founding fathers' injunction against "entangling alliances." The second section reviews why the United States was compelled to return to confederationism in the early twentieth century and how collective defense served the nation's strategic aims until the end of the Cold War. The third section assesses how the logic of alliances has changed as a result of the transformations witnessed in international politics in the post–Cold War era. The fourth section previews how the various Asian countries examined in this edition of *Strategic Asia* approach the question of affiliating with the United States. Finally, the brief conclusion emphasizes the paradoxical insight that the United States' alliances and partnerships are most effective when U.S. power is indeed robust.

The Misunderstood Founders on Alliances

If early U.S. foreign policy were to be described solely by the literal content of the founders' remonstrations against alliances, it would be profoundly misleading. For even as Washington was beseeching his countrymen in 1796 (at the end of his second term in office) to have "as little political connection as possible" with Europe, he—more than most Americans—had every reason to remember that the birth of his country was owed greatly to the alliance that the infant United States had forged with France in the war of independence against Great Britain. In fact, not only French but also Spanish and Dutch contributions were critical to American success: beyond the supplies, weapons, and ammunition offered, the land and sea power mustered by these European allies was vital to enabling the Continental Army's victories both through their local warfighting contributions and by tying down British power outside North America.[3]

If Washington's accomplishments were thus aided by the partnerships forged with various European powers—the purported variance with his later advice to eschew political connections notwithstanding—Jefferson's great successes a few decades later, in fact soon after his famous inaugural address decrying entangling alliances, suggest that the absence of such confederations was actually a key factor this time around in producing territorial gains

---

[3] Howard Jones, *Crucible of Power: A History of American Foreign Relations to 1913*, 2nd ed. (Lanham: Rowman and Littlefield, 2009), 1–29.

for the United States. The termination of the alliance with France after the Revolutionary War and the conclusion of John Jay's Treaty with Great Britain, which secured the withdrawal of British military units from the Northwest Territory of the United States, found the country engaged with the two major European powers but without any formal affiliation with either.

This fact, materializing against the backdrop of renewed conflict between Britain and France in Europe, soon provided Jefferson with the golden opportunity to consummate the purchase of the Louisiana Territory, a diplomatic feat that instantaneously doubled the size of the then United States. This achievement, which counts among Jefferson's greatest contributions to the consolidation of U.S. power on the continent, became possible because the United States, having no pact with either of the European rivals, could play one off against the other. By accentuating French fears that the United States might make up with Great Britain at a time when Napoleon was preparing to invade the British Isles, while at the same time keeping the English guessing as to whether negotiations for a rapprochement might occur, Jefferson skillfully induced the cash-strapped French dictator to sell a vast territory to the United States at a fire-sale price.[4]

Although the differences in Washington's and Jefferson's actions might seem dramatic—the former nurturing strategic partnerships, the latter avoiding them, even as they both uniformly decried geopolitical alliances—the convergence is far greater than is apparent: both statesmen approached the issue of confederating with other nations entirely instrumentally. Binding affiliations with foreign countries were thus acceptable when pressed by necessity, but then only if they helped to advance some fundamental national aims. This approach to international engagement would become the leitmotif that defined U.S. strategic policy at the time of the nation's founding, and the residues of this approach survive today. Because an alliance with France was essential for attaining success during the Revolutionary War, the Continental Congress grudgingly accepted such a partnership when it became apparent that independence could not be achieved without it and other, lesser partnerships with countries such as Spain and the Dutch Republic.

Once the aim of independence was achieved, however, the United States slowly jettisoned the Treaty of Alliance with France, using the uncertainties created subsequently by the French Revolution to assert neutrality and thereby escape the military obligations of that accord. When Washington in his farewell address a few years later warned his citizens to maintain "as little political connection as possible" with other nations, he could therefore do so without the slightest fear of inconsistency, because confederations

---

[4] Charles Cerami, *Jefferson's Great Gamble: The Remarkable Story of Jefferson, Napoleon and the Men behind the Louisiana Purchase* (Naperville: Sourcebooks, 2004).

with others were valuable only to the degree that they enabled the United States to better achieve its own geopolitical objectives. What served the country's interests well in securing liberty from Great Britain thus became a handicap afterward because continued strategic partnerships with the fractious European countries threatened to undermine the fundamental post-independence objective of the United States: the westward conquest and expansion of national territory to its natural limits at a time when the young nation was opposed by indigenous inhabitants as well as European great powers that often supported the natives in their struggles against the new American settlers.[5]

Because avoiding the diversion of American energies from this new task was critical, the United States consciously chose to turn its back on its wider strategic rear—the European promontory—in the hope that escaping the geopolitical quarrels in the Old World would enable it to singularly focus on, as Washington phrased it, "laying the foundation of a great Empire" in the New World.[6] After all, Washington had astutely perceived that maintaining an appropriate distance from Europe's relentless struggle for power would be good for the United States:

> Europe has a set of primary interests, which to us have none, or a very remote relation. Hence she must be engaged in frequent controversies, the causes of which are essentially foreign to our concerns. Hence, therefore, it must be unwise in us to implicate ourselves, by artificial ties, in the ordinary vicissitudes of her politics, or the ordinary combinations and collisions of her friendships or enmities.[7]

The ability of the United States to create for itself the great territorial and commercial empire envisaged by its first president—initially in North America and eventually even beyond—would depend, however, on its capacity to first secure local hegemony: that is, to acquire and maintain preeminent power over the many rivals in its immediate surroundings. This aim was undoubtedly ambitious in 1776, but it ultimately proved viable because, for all of the United States' limitations, its immediate adversaries—both American Indians and the European colonial outposts—were weaker than the fledgling country. Moreover, the European powers were consumed, as Washington and others of his generation rightly perceived, in internecine wars that distracted them from the growing upstart across the Atlantic. And,

---

[5] Fred Anderson and Andrew Cayton, *The Dominion of War: Empire and Liberty in North America, 1500–2000* (New York: Penguin Books, 2005).

[6] George Washington, "General Orders to John Stark," April 18, 1783, in *The Writings of George Washington from the Original Manuscript Sources*, vol. 26, ed. John C. Fitzpatrick (Washington, D.C.: U.S. Government Printing Office, 1931), 335.

[7] Washington, "Washington's Farewell Address."

finally, the North American continent itself was huge, with great strategic depth, and surrounded by oceans on both sides, which prevented even the major European powers of the day from being able to project overwhelming force against or across it.[8]

Under these circumstances, the counsel of the founding fathers to refrain from entangling alliances was indeed wise insofar as it freed the young republic to concentrate on amassing the hegemony that would be required for the success of its empire-building in North America. But the advice to avoid alliances was not a directive to become isolationist. Isolationism, in the ordinary meaning of the word, connotes either disengagement from international politics or abdication from commercial intercourse, or both. The United States was never isolationist in this sense. On the contrary, from the moment of the country's founding, American leaders, realizing the importance of actively participating in foreign diplomacy, maintained strong links with the outside world and were constantly attuned to how developments abroad affected their imperial enterprise at home (if for no other reason than to mitigate the deleterious consequences of any external events on their interests). As George C. Herring succinctly summarized it, "the enduring idea of an isolationist America is a myth often conveniently used to safeguard the nation's self-image of its innocence."[9]

As part of this active involvement with the world, John Adams's "plan of treaties" soon came to define how the new union conceived of its relations with other governments: an open trading system was central and it was to be fostered because such a system was vital for the material prosperity of the American nation.[10] Animated by this "spirit of commerce," as Montesquieu phrased it in his great work *The Spirit of the Laws*, the United States in fact constantly sought access to European markets for the export of cotton, rice, and tobacco. Moreover, to bolster its domestic economy, the United States articulated a doctrine of free trade that actually ran counter to the mercantilist fashion of the times. As Eliga H. Gould described it, Adams's "Model Treaty, as the plan came to be known, stipulated that any agreement be fully reciprocal, with trade on the freest possible terms in peacetime and a liberal definition of the goods that American ships could carry in times of war."[11] Although it

---

[8] Peter Maslowski, "To the Edge of Greatness: the United States 1783–1865," in *The Making of Strategy: Rules States, and War*, ed. Williamson Murray, Alvin Bernstein, and MacGregor Knox (New York: Cambridge University Press, 1994), 207.

[9] George C. Herring, *From Colony to Superpower: U.S. Foreign Relations since 1776* (New York: Oxford University Press, 2011), 1.

[10] John E. Hill, *Democracy, Equality, and Justice: John Adams, Adam Smith, and Political Economy* (Lanham: Lexington Books, 2007), 198–204.

[11] Eliga H. Gould, *Among the Powers of the Earth: The American Revolution and the Making of a New World Empire* (Cambridge: Harvard University Press, 2012), 1.

would be a long time before this vision materialized in practice, it nonetheless demonstrates that the United States never viewed its hesitation about alliances as deriving from any conventional form of isolationism.

If the choices facing the United States since its birth are thus arrayed across a spectrum defined by the alternatives of isolationism, unilateralism, confederationism, and multilateralism—where isolationism implies a hermetic distance from other states or the international system; unilateralism, the readiness to act alone in pursuit of certain strategic goals; confederationism, the willingness to seek or accept international allies when required; and multilateralism, the acceptance of "international governance of the 'many'" through formal institutions as a means of securing critical interests—the country has consistently rejected both isolationism and multilateralism as instruments for meeting its highest strategic ambitions.[12] Neither of these two approaches has been seen to accord with either the United States' objective circumstances or its exceptional sense of self. Isolationism prevented the United States from prospering materially, while simultaneously denying it the opportunity to prevent the wider world from undermining U.S. interests close to home. Multilateralism, similarly, represented an abdication of responsibility: it relied on international collective action to protect U.S. equities and, in the process, created opportunities for bruising disputes over burden-sharing, reciprocity, and the division of benefits, all of which could produce either inaction or misdirected initiatives that harm the nation.[13]

In contrast, unilateralism and confederationism invariably proved far more attractive for U.S. leaders, with the choice between them being dictated largely by circumstances. Of the two, unilateralism was always to be preferred. It protected the United States' freedom to secure its interests in whatever way it pleased, without having to worry about making the compromises that are always necessary to sustain alliances in international politics. As long as the republic's attention was focused mainly on expanding its own territory within North America, the disparities in power between itself and its local rivals implied that few partners, if any, were necessary for the success of that objective.

The great accomplishments of Manifest Destiny and, later on, the victory of the Union in the U.S. Civil War finally created a state that

---

[12] Miles Kahler, "Multilateralism with Small and Large Numbers," *International Organization* 46, no. 3 (1992): 681.

[13] Bradley F. Podliska, *Acting Alone: A Scientific Study of American Hegemony and Unilateral Use-of-Force Decision Making* (Lanham: Lexington Books, 2010). For an excellent systematic treatment of how U.S. choices between unilateralist and confederationist solutions hinged on the character of the economics of joint security production, the expected costs of opportunism, and the relative burdens of governance, see David A. Lake, *Entangling Relations: American Foreign Policy in Its Century* (Princeton: Princeton University Press, 1999).

was not only powerful vis-à-vis its own society but also superior to all its immediate neighbors on the continent. These conditions, accordingly, made the unilateralist approach to strategy and foreign policy not only effective but also incredibly rational. After the end of the Civil War in 1865, this unilateralism, which had succeeded in creating a vast empire in North America from the United States' humble origins in thirteen small colonies along the east coast, would only incur further gains. By driving the nation to its westward limit, the United States would soon enjoy control of land from the Atlantic to the Pacific Ocean. This process of political consolidation resulted in the reorganization of the vast U.S. territories lying between the Mississippi and California into new states.[14]

The Long and Hard Road to Collective Defense

The United States' success in achieving dominance and creating a stable hegemony within North America only opened the door to realizing the founders' old dream of conclusively eliminating all rival geopolitical influences in and around the continent for good. Dramatic industrialization, which began in the early 1800s and continued through the Civil War, had made the United States the world's largest economy by 1900, thus enabling it to pursue the next stage of its hegemonic ascendancy—the closure of the Western Hemisphere—again through unilateralist strategies.[15] If protecting the American political experiment required the domination of the North American heartland for its success, shielding the unified nation that emerged after its continental consolidation required the isolation of the Western Hemisphere from all pernicious extraregional influences. Whether the enforcement of the Monroe Doctrine promulgated toward this end was necessitated by the demands of security or merely remained an expression of imperialism is beside the point: what is pertinent is that preserving the unique position of the United States as the predominant power without any rival in its geographic theater marked the evolutionary culmination of the country's success in attaining hegemony within North America. As Jay Sexton concludes, "the [doctrine] proclaimed American opposition to European colonialism, but within it lurked the imperial ambitions of the expansionist United States."[16]

---

[14] Bruce Cumings, *Dominion from Sea to Sea: Pacific Ascendancy and American Power* (New Haven: Yale University Press, 2009).

[15] Angus Maddison, "Historical Statistics of the World Economy: 1–2008 A.D.," 2008, http://www.ggdc.net/maddison/Historical_Statistics/horizontal-file_02-2010.xls.

[16] Jay Sexton, *The Monroe Doctrine: Empire and Nation in Nineteenth-Century America* (New York: Hill & Wang, 2012), 3.

This achievement of continental hegemony was realized entirely through unilateralist strategies, except for the initial phase, which required a global confederacy to produce American independence. Since that time, however, the superiority of U.S. capabilities relative to both the country's rivals and the strategic tasks at hand ensured that unilateralism would suffice to produce the local primacy that would ensure durable security for the United States. The continued expansion of this material power into the late nineteenth and early twentieth centuries further ensured that when the United States finally sought to eject the last remnants of the European empires in the Western Hemisphere—through the Spanish-American War of 1898, for example—it would still be able to enforce hemispheric closure entirely by unilateral means rather than by seeking the help of other nations.

The desire to sanitize the Western Hemisphere of all European military presence was anchored in the recognition that no local entity was powerful enough to challenge the hegemony of the United States unless it was aided by confederates from the Old World. Such assistance, at least in any meaningful terms, was unlikely to be forthcoming as long as the European continent was riven by internal struggles for mastery. As long as no local European state was powerful enough to control the entire resources of its continent, the United States' imperial enterprise in its own hemisphere would be safe from the depredations of any external interlopers. In such circumstances, the United States could afford to ignore Europe, which functioned as its strategic rear when it was expanding westward and as its strategic flank when it was enforcing hemispheric closure. Washington's recommendation that his country maintain "as little political connection as possible" with Europe "in the ordinary vicissitudes of her politics, or the ordinary combinations and collisions of her friendships or enmities,"[17] thus made sense, but only when there was little danger that the Old World might be subjugated either by one of its own constituents or by some other foreign power. In other words, the United States could afford to be indifferent to the reality of European rivalries but not to their outcome—especially one that portended continental domination by a single power.

As long as this hazard was remote—as it was in the early phase of U.S. history—the notion of avoiding alliances with European partners was eminently sensible. But by the time the United States had successfully crowned its continental hegemony with hemispheric dominance, its luck had run its course. For now at the center of Europe, a newly unified nation, Germany, appeared to be on the cusp of amassing sufficient capabilities so as to be able to dominate not only its own surroundings but lands much

---

[17] Washington, "Washington's Farewell Address."

farther afield—in time acquiring the capacity "to look across the sea for conquest without fear of being menaced at the center of its power, that is, in Europe itself."[18] Although the United States had generally eschewed foreign partnerships so long as there were no stark dangers to its own power—a clear reflection of its unilateralist preferences—it was, by the same token, always sensitive to perturbations in the larger balance of power, especially insofar as these affected its own hegemony. This was a trenchant confirmation of its more fundamental rejection of isolationism.

Not surprisingly, then, U.S. diplomacy, even when remaining distant from entangling alliances, continually pursued policies aimed at maintaining a local balance of power in Europe. Hans J. Morgenthau succinctly summarized this point:

> [American statecraft] opposed whatever European nation— be it Great Britain, France, Germany, or Russia—seemed to be likely to gain that ascendancy over its European competitors which would have jeopardized the hemispheric predominance and eventually the very independence of the United States. Conversely, it has supported whatever European nation seemed to be most likely to restore the balance of power by offering successful resistance to the would-be conqueror. While it is hard to imagine a greater contrast in the way of thinking about matters political than that which separates Alexander Hamilton from Woodrow Wilson, in this concern for the maintenance of the balance of power in Europe—for whatever different reasons—they are one. It is by virtue of this concern that the United States has intervened in both World Wars on the side of the initially weaker coalition and that its European policies have… invariably pursued one single objective in Europe: the maintenance of the [regional] balance of power.[19]

It is entirely possible that American hegemony might have had to cope with expanding German power unilaterally if circumstances had warranted it, but the vicissitudes of history ensured that the United States did so as part of a confederacy in both world wars. By the time of the first global conflict, however, the previously instrumental rejection of alliances advocated by the founding fathers had unfortunately congealed into something resembling a substantive opposition to them, leading the United States to enter the Great War as an "associated power" rather than as a formal ally of the Triple Entente. World War II eliminated this fiction entirely, but the legacy of avoiding entangling alliances died hard. Despite the recognition of farsighted leaders, such as President Franklin D. Roosevelt, that the United States' entry into the war as part of an Allied coalition was essential for the preservation of American primacy in its own hemisphere, if not globally,

---

[18] Hans Morgenthau, "The Mainsprings of American Foreign Policy: The National Interest vs. Moral Abstractions," *American Political Science Review* 44, no. 4 (1950): 835.

[19] Ibid.

the country was able to intervene only after the Japanese attack on Pearl Harbor conclusively forced its hand.

Although a decisive victory in World War II was eventually procured after many years of carnage, this grinding conflict highlighted a reality that the United States did not have to confront when it was preoccupied with either continental or hemispheric hegemony: despite its wartime triumph and its material superiority, maintaining global primacy would require sturdy allies who, while not substituting for unilateralism, were nonetheless essential for preserving an international order that protected U.S. interests and thereby economized on the need for independent action continuously. The culmination of the worldwide struggle in 1945 had thus brought U.S. strategy full circle: a nation that was born through the activity of a confederation would now be able to preserve its position at the universal apex only through an alliance. The coming Cold War era would in fact corroborate the proposition that although American power was indeed formidable—compared both with previous hegemonies and with the past demands imposed by continental and hemispheric domination—it was still insufficient by itself to assure global supremacy under all circumstances.

In part this was because the United States now confronted, for the first time since its founding, a genuine peer competitor. Unlike its European rivals of the past, the Soviet Union was a large, continental-sized entity, with vast natural resources, a high level of technological capability, a battle-hardened military, and, thanks to its revolutionary Communist ideology, a willingness to confront the United States in a global struggle for power and influence. Although Soviet Russia fell short of being a comprehensive equal—mainly because its own ideology prevented it from nurturing the market economy that might have made it an even bigger threat than it finally was—it nonetheless proved to be a formidable opponent of the United States for many decades, largely because it continually assembled deadly military capabilities and demonstrated a willingness to use these around the world in support of its political ambitions.[20]

Although the Soviet challenge was manifested most strongly by its military threats to the United States, to nations lying within the European and Asian "shatter belts," and occasionally to countries farther afield, Washington feared encompassing dangers that prompted it to embark on an ambitious strategy called "containment." As Melvyn P. Leffler succinctly describes the approach, "the key goals of containment were to limit the spread of Soviet power and Communist ideology. Yet containment was

---

[20] John Lewis Gaddis, *The Cold War: A New History* (New York: Penguin Books, 2006).

never a defensive strategy; it was conceived as an instrument to achieve victory in the Cold War."[21]

Consistent with the older American tradition of preserving security through hegemony, the United States now pursued "a preponderance of power,"[22] anchoring its containment policy through the instrument about which it had historically felt most ambivalent: alliances. Integrating elements of the coalition it had inherited from World War II, as well as defeated adversaries who were now threatened by Soviet power, the United States returned to confederationism with a vengeance, building up a network of partnerships that extended well beyond Western Europe and East Asia to span new, far-flung areas of the world. The willingness to entertain alliances as part of the strategy for confronting Moscow proved that the traditional U.S. opposition to this mechanism was more instrumental than it often appears. When faced with catalyzing threats and the realization that U.S. power alone was insufficient for victory, American statecraft could be adroit enough to not only orchestrate effective confederations but also integrate new and quite diverse elements of policy aimed at humbling its adversary.

Toward this end, the United States first promoted several, and sometimes overlapping, mutual security agreements and formal alliances, such as the Inter-American Treaty of Reciprocal Assistance, the Western European Union, the Southeast Asia Treaty Organization (SEATO), and the Central Treaty Organization (CENTO). Additionally, in Asia the United States forged a hub-and-spoke system of discrete pacts with the Republic of Korea, the Republic of China (Taiwan), Japan, and the Philippines, all united by the objective of resisting Soviet power through coordinated actions between Washington and the allied capitals.[23]

Second, Washington led the development of collective defense strategies through military institutions such as the North Atlantic Treaty Organization (NATO) in Europe and the combined forces commands in key Asian states. In some instances, extended deterrence guarantees substituted for the absence of formal combined commands. All these instruments were developed to apportion the combat capabilities available to the United States and its partners in order to defeat Communist expansion. These aims, in turn, spawned a vast global network of military bases that supported U.S. forward-deployed or forward-operating forces, whose mission was to execute

---

[21] Melvyn P. Leffler, "Containment," in *A Dictionary of 20th-Century Communism*, ed. Silvio Pons and Robert Service (Princeton: Princeton University Press, 2012), 236.

[22] Melvyn P. Leffler, *A Preponderance of Power: National Security, the Truman Administration, and the Cold War* (Stanford: Stanford University Press, 1992).

[23] For a comprehensive list of all the agreements entered into by the United States, see U.S. Congress, House Committee on Foreign Affairs, *Collective Defense Treaties, with Maps, Texts of Treaties, a Chronology, Status of Forces Agreements, and Comparative Chart* (Washington, D.C., 1967).

the warfighting plans developed in concert with the allies under the protective cover of strategic nuclear deterrence.[24]

Third, the United States and its partners made special efforts to deliberately limit Soviet economic connectivity with the major centers of power, thus ensuring that the critical engines of growth internationally were tied only to the United States and to one another. This policy of encouraging deep economic integration among the Western partners but limiting commercial intercourse with the Soviet bloc was aided initially by Moscow's own opposition to the liberal international economic order fostered by the United States. Later on, however, the policy acquired a life and logic of its own and was consciously intended to constrain access to capital, technology, and markets as a way of enervating and eventually defeating Soviet Russia decisively.[25]

Fourth, the United States redoubled its efforts to preserve the scientific and industrial supremacy that it had so painstakingly established during World War II. The nation maintained an unswerving commitment to preserving a free-market economy domestically, while also avoiding the creation of a garrison state. Nonetheless, it incorporated sufficient state direction—through federal policies and fiscal subventions—to sustain the economic growth and technological innovation required to maintain the requisite combat capabilities in various strategic locales, sustain a globe-girding military infrastructure, and underwrite an open international economic system where trade and aid would combine to reinvigorate the capabilities of its war-torn allies.[26]

Fifth, and finally, the United States complemented these material elements of the containment strategy with a vigorous worldwide ideological campaign aimed at delegitimizing the Soviet state, its worldview, its occupation of Eastern Europe, its efforts at spreading Communism worldwide, and its opposition to free markets, liberal democracy, and religious freedom. This crusade involved huge democracy-promotion efforts, vast foreign-aid programs, and lengthy public-diplomacy campaigns, all intended to bolster public resolve at home, strengthen liberal forces globally (with the battleground states of the Cold

---

[24] A broad overview can be found in Allan R. Millet and Peter Maslowski, *For the Common Defense* (New York: Free Press, 1984), 471–541.

[25] The logic of restricting trade during the Cold War is perceptively examined in Joanne Gowa, *Allies, Adversaries, and International Trade* (Princeton: Princeton University Press, 1994).

[26] See Audra J. Wolfe, *Competing with the Soviets: Science, Technology, and the State in Cold War America* (Baltimore: Johns Hopkins University Press, 2013); and Aaron L. Friedberg, *In the Shadow of the Garrison State* (Princeton: Princeton University Press, 2000).

War receiving the most attention), and constrain the Soviet Union's ability to project influence beyond its borders.[27]

Although there are still disagreements about whether concerted containment in the form described above comported with George Kennan's original conception, just as there were persistent debates throughout the Cold War about how it was to be operationalized at any given point in time, the strategy nonetheless proved extraordinarily fruitful insofar as it contributed toward the bloodless defeat of Soviet power and the peaceful disintegration of the Warsaw Pact as an opposing bloc. With the demise of the Soviet Union in 1991, the United States had indeed secured global primacy in a universally perceptible form for the first time in its history—even though it had already acquired the world's largest economy almost a hundred years earlier and had maintained greater comprehensive power than its rival throughout the Cold War.

The Cold War victory, which accrued from containment through alliances, gave confederationism a unique cast that in time came to constitute a desirable template for how the United States ought to conduct itself in the international system. Its alliances never deprived Washington of the ability to prosecute unilateral actions. To the contrary, they only enhanced it by conveying unity of purpose, providing additive contributions to U.S. power and strengthening the legitimacy of U.S. actions internationally. These alliances thus came to be seen as the indispensable accoutrements of U.S. hegemony in the postwar order. Three characteristics of the Cold War alliance system made them especially so.

To begin, the strength and robustness of the alliances nurtured by the United States vis-à-vis the Soviet Union derived their bonding glue from the intensity and the singularity of the threat perceived by the participating states.[28] Although, as noted earlier, Washington created a global network of anti-Communist confederations, not all survived successfully; the ones that did, such as the Western European Union, NATO, and the East Asian pacts with South Korea and Japan, thrived because the intense military dangers emanating from the Soviet Union, its proxies, or other local challengers created powerful incentives for the partners to stay united.

The persistence of external threats (and sometimes internal perils that fed off external sources of support) thus made for very tight alliances with a high degree of reciprocity internally and conspicuous levels of self-sufficiency externally. Although in every instance the United States remained the superior

---

[27] See Nicholas J. Cull, *The Cold War and the United States Information Agency: American Propaganda and Public Diplomacy, 1945–1989* (Cambridge: Cambridge University Press, 2009).

[28] For a conceptual overview of this issue, see Stephen M. Walt, "Why Alliances Collapse or Endure," *Survival* 39, no. 1 (1997): 156–79.

partner, the common commitment to collective defense (meaning the recognition that a threat to any one would evoke a response by all) and the functional benefits of strong economic interdependence within the alliance (thereby implying autarky with respect to adversaries) became the attributes by which the worth of all confederations would be judged, even though these principles in their fullness were enshrined in NATO alone.[29]

Further, the commitments required by U.S. alliances—the extended security guarantees offered by Washington in exchange for either explicit or implicit pledges by the protectees to contribute to their own defense, if not actually to aid the United States reciprocally—did not in any way abridge the United States' freedom to undertake unilateral action when its interests so demanded. The alliances, in fact, liberated Washington to pursue independent policies in many areas and on many issues that did not implicate its partners' equities directly.

The postwar coalitions underwritten by U.S. power, therefore, were emphatically not partnerships of equals. They were instruments of hegemonic power that served multiple objectives simultaneously. Beyond protecting U.S. allies and partners, they helped dampen intra-alliance security competition that might have otherwise become distracting. To the degree that they served as expressions of political solidarity, these coalitions legitimated the United States' exercise of power globally, even when its allies might not have been directly involved. And by pooling national resources to deal with the direct threats to their security, they augmented U.S. power while simultaneously emancipating the United States to advance its wider interests globally.

Finally, the United States' superiority in wealth and power relative to both its own allies and even its adversaries created a favorable strategic environment that enabled U.S. confederations to function very effectively. Given the disparity in resources between the United States and the rest of the world, Washington was able, throughout the Cold War, to play the role of the "privileged" provider who bore the costs of supplying global public goods precisely because of the disproportionate benefits accruing specifically to U.S. interests. Thus, for example, the United States invested heavily in securing nuclear deterrence at every level of conflict, protecting the global commons, and creating an institutional regime that enabled orderly trade and commerce, first among its friends and eventually globally. The United States did this not out of altruism but because these investments reinforced its hegemony and thereby buttressed its security.

Although the allies undoubtedly supplemented these efforts, their contributions paled in significance because, in comparison, the United States'

---

[29] Kenneth A. Myers, *NATO, the Next Thirty Years: The Changing Political, Economic, and Military Setting* (Boulder: Westview Press, 1981).

resources were larger, its private interests more dominant, and its ability to disregard the costs far more significant. As a result, the U.S. alliances during the Cold War came to represent the components of a hegemonic strategy that, though first manifested in the desire for continental control, had now reached its apotheosis in global involvement.

The Challenges to Confederationism in the Post–Cold War Era

The virtuous interaction between unilateralism and confederationism that reached its high point during the Cold War—a dynamic that was evident at the beginning of the republic, went into remission during the United States' continental and hemispheric expansion, but made a comeback as the struggle for mastery in Europe resolved itself into the potential rise of local threats that could eventually endanger the United States—could have persisted in this unique form to further entrench American hegemony well into the distant future were it not for three developments that the United States struggles with to this day.

First, the demise of the Soviet Union as a singular threat has removed the glue that kept the United States' most successful alliances, such as NATO, functioning as cohesive entities. Those alliances that did not feel the brunt of Soviet dangers as vividly—CENTO and SEATO being good examples—atrophied much earlier. The broad realist insight that the weaker the threat, the more infirm the alliance, therefore, seems to have been borne out. Not surprisingly, then, NATO has struggled since the end of the Cold War to find a mission that could substitute for its previous raison d'être.[30] It has attempted to find new meaning by focusing on managing everything from challenges on its periphery to becoming a provider of collective security, even as its principal underwriter, the United States, has slowly shifted its gaze from Europe to new security demands in Asia. Whether the recent Russian political resurgence under Vladimir Putin will reanimate NATO's sense of purpose remains to be seen. But what seems clear in the interim is that the absence of riveting geopolitical dangers has weakened the unity of purpose and the vitality of what was once the United States' most successful multilateral coalition.

Other U.S. compacts, such as the ones with South Korea and Japan, have proved more durable because the absence of the Soviet Union has, unfortunately, been substituted by newer dangers in Asia: North Korea for

---

[30] For further discussion, see Mark Webber, James Sperling, and Martin A. Smith, *NATO's Post–Cold War Trajectory: Decline or Regeneration?* (New York: Palgrave Macmillan, 2012).

starters, but increasingly China over the longer term. Many traditional U.S. alliances have thus survived partly out of institutional inertia, but often at the cost of losing their original momentum. They continue to serve a variety of important purposes, often demonstrating their greatest utility where cooperative intelligence collection, diplomatic consultation and coordination, and the pooling of military resources in crises are concerned. Many of these functions are of special benefit to the United States' weaker partners insofar as the legacy alliances provide them with the advantages of bandwagoning that might have otherwise been lost. But the singular preeminence of these partnerships has undoubtedly diminished in the absence of a common overarching strategic threat.[31]

Moreover, all of the United States' core alliances are now hobbled by a problem that was previously suppressed: the disappearance of an absorbing global danger has prompted populations in allied countries (and in the United States as well) to refocus on domestic issues, thus weakening support for strong defense budgets and extended military involvements abroad. As a result, Washington has had to allocate resources for supporting alliance capabilities (particularly in NATO) from its own diminishing defense spending in greater measure than might otherwise have been necessary. Compensating for these deficits is something Washington has done with equanimity thus far, but that does not alter the fact that the combined military power available to the United States is still smaller than it could have been if domestic pressures had not constrained allied defense budgets.[32] At any rate, the continued U.S. subventions for collective defense only prove that Washington still values all of its alliances and partnerships immensely, if for no other reason than the legitimacy they provide through collaboration; yet the challenges of preserving both allied capabilities and allied cohesion have undoubtedly increased in ways that were not the case during the high tide of the Soviet threat.

Second, although new challengers to U.S. power have emerged since the ending of the Cold War, these rivals are for the most part regional entities who do not, at least for the moment, pose a worldwide threat to both the United States and its partners uniformly. The tight reciprocity and coordination that U.S. alliances previously produced, accordingly, become harder to achieve,

---

[31] For more on this issue in the Asian context, see Carl W. Baker and Brad Glosserman, eds., "Doing More and Expecting Less: The Future of U.S. Alliances in the Asia Pacific," Pacific Forum CSIS, Issues & Insights, January 2013.

[32] For specific trends in declining U.S. defense budgets, see Dinah Walker, "Trends in U.S. Military Spending," Council on Foreign Relations, July 2014. For analysis on declining NATO and U.S. defense budgets, see Nora Bensahel and Jacob Stokes, "The U.S. Defense Budget and the Future of Alliance Burden-Sharing," German Marshall Fund of the United States, Transatlantic Security Task Force Series, November 2013.

even though they may be entirely desirable. To complicate matters further, China, the one country that holds the potential of becoming a dangerous global rival, is already deeply entwined economically with the United States as well as with the economies of all U.S. allies—including those who are otherwise Beijing's natural rivals. This fundamental transformation of the situation prevailing during the Cold War—when economic integration characterized intra-allied relations but did not extend to rivals—complicates the maintenance of future American hegemony immensely.[33]

International interdependence has undoubtedly been among the most significant fruits of U.S. primacy. But its fecundity and depth imply that the United States and its allies today contribute toward enhancing the prosperity and the material capabilities of countries that will one day become their rivals. Because Washington and its partners also profit from such economic intercourse, they end up in the awkward situation where their quest for absolute gains (the benefits each derives from trade) collides with the problem of relative gains (the reality that some of their cohort, especially competitors like China, have gained more from trade than they have). This tension is made all the more acute due to the disproportionate costs borne by Washington in upholding the liberal order, while rivals such as Beijing not only free ride en route to harvesting incommensurate benefits from this regime but also use these gains to develop military capabilities that are intended to threaten the guardian of the system, the United States itself.[34]

Because interdependence has now engendered "global codependency" on a massive scale, neither the United States and its allies nor its competitors appear eager to limit their trading relations. This is the case even though Washington and its partners are well aware that Beijing's assertiveness, which leaves them all vulnerable, is underwritten substantially by the larger web of cooperative economic activities. What complicates matters fundamentally, however, is that the dangers posed by China's ambitions do not affect the United States and its allies symmetrically. Rather, the differences in the intensity of the threat perceptions enable Beijing to exploit the benefits of interdependence by deepening its economic and technological ties with those alliance members less threatened by China in order to accumulate the very capabilities necessary to intimidate other, more vulnerable partners.

Because China is not yet viewed as the Soviet Union previously was—as a clear and present danger to all—the tight reciprocity and cohesion that underwrote the alliance denial regimes of yesteryear do not exist where

---

[33] Ashley J. Tellis, "Power Shift: How the West Can Adapt and Thrive in an Asian Century," German Marshall Fund of the United States, Asian Paper Series, January 2010.

[34] Ashley J. Tellis, "Balancing without Containment: An American Strategy for Managing China," Carnegie Endowment for International Peace, 2014.

Beijing is concerned. In such a situation, China cannot only exploit the pervasiveness of economic interdependence to grow even more rapidly, but it can also play alliance members against each another. Thanks to their common desire for uninterrupted absolute gains, partners are often inclined to trade strategic technologies with China for fear of losing out to other states (including those outside the alliance) who might be less reticent. The net result of this competition is to make both the United States and its allies more complicit in aiding the growth of Chinese power at exactly the time when Beijing promises to become at least Washington's principal competitor, if not that of others eventually. There is no easy exit from this conundrum, but that makes the task of maintaining American hegemony, both through the U.S. alliance network and unilaterally, all the more challenging.

Third, the liberal international order created by the United States against the backdrop of its conflict with the Soviet Union contributed greatly to resuscitating its war-devastated allies—a vital necessity in the effort to defeat Soviet expansionism—but in the process accelerated the relative decline of U.S. power as well. So long as Washington's own allies were being strengthened, however, U.S. relative decline had little geopolitical significance. But the crucial decisions made by the United States during the last years of the Cold War and after, decisions that included integrating potential rivals such as China into the world trading system, have hastened its decline in relative power compared with where it stood in 1945.[35]

To be sure, that standing was in some ways artificial and would have eroded inevitably as the European and Asian states destroyed by World War II slowly made a comeback. But the shift in the center of gravity to Asia occurring thanks to the new economic integration of countries that are not U.S. allies—the paradoxical result of the success of American internationalism—implies that the United States' relative power could decline even further, and perhaps more consequentially, in the years ahead. This contraction in comparative capabilities does not necessarily have momentous strategic implications right now, because the United States will still remain the most powerful nation globally for some time to come. But if competitors, such as China, continue to successfully accumulate national power, while the capacity of the United States to protect its hegemony weakens, relative decline, which is but a statistical artifact today, could well become politically fateful.[36]

---

[35] Ashley J. Tellis, "U.S.-China Relations in a Realist World," in *Tangled Titans: The United States and China*, ed. David Shambaugh (Lanham: Rowman and Littlefield, 2013), 75–100.

[36] For a useful discussion, see Geir Lundestad, *The Rise and Decline of the American "Empire"* (Oxford: Oxford University Press, 2012); and Stuart S. Brown, *The Future of U.S. Global Power: Delusions of Decline* (New York: Palgrave Macmillan, 2013).

These concerns have grown in importance because the global financial crisis of 2007–8 exacted a greater toll on the U.S. economy than it did on rivals like China. Even more problematically, it ruptured the United States' self-confidence and sense of exceptionalism, a development that in recent years has been manifested in profound geopolitical diffidence and diminished U.S. contributions to the production of global public goods, such as international stability and order. The economic recession resulting from the crisis also exacerbated the problems of U.S. public finance and has led to dangerous reductions in defense spending, which are likely to persist for some time.[37] If these trends gather steam, U.S. primacy could be dangerously eroded and the larger global order itself could be at heightened risk, particularly because U.S. allies today appear unable to make increased compensating contributions. The United States' reluctance to deploy a vigorous unilateralism has thus materialized at exactly the time when its absence has proved to be quite costly.

There is no reason, however, that the current American despondency should become the new normal. The U.S. economy could be on the cusp of experiencing another major round of growth in productivity thanks to emerging breakthroughs in energy, manufacturing, and digitization. An economic rebound stimulated by a new wave of Schumpeterian revolutions could help arrest the United States' relative decline significantly, a prospect that can never be ruled out given the vitality of its national innovation system.[38] What will be required, however, is inspired leadership in Washington—leadership that is willing to squarely confront the nation's economic difficulties, build the foundations for future economic growth, and reinvest in a set of disruptive military capabilities that will enable the U.S. armed forces to successfully execute their global power-projection missions, whatever the opposition. To the degree that the United States can effectively undertake these tasks, it will be able to make those "supernormal" contributions to the production of global public goods and, by so doing, buttress its own hegemony for another long cycle in world politics.

As the United States prepares to manage these three challenges that have arisen in this current "interwar period"[39]—the weakening of alliance

---

[37] Ashley J. Tellis, "The Global Economic Crisis and U.S. Power," in *Strategic Asia 2009–10: Economic Meltdown and Geopolitical Stability*, ed. Ashley J. Tellis, Andrew Marble, and Travis Tanner (Seattle: National Bureau of Asian Research, 2009), 3–35.

[38] For further information on economic innovations, see James Manyika et al., "Disruptive Technologies: Advances That Will Transform Life, Business, and the Global Economy," McKinsey Global Institute, 2013, http://www.mckinsey.com/insights/business_technology/disruptive_technologies; and Susan Lund et al., "Game Changers: Five Opportunities for U.S. Growth and Renewal," McKinsey Global Institute, July 2013, 2.

[39] Colin Gray, "How Has War Changed Since the End of the Cold War?" *Parameters* 35 (2005): 14.

unity and capabilities in an era where serious threats seem distant, the strengthening of competitors' power due to economic interdependence, and the possibility of a real (as opposed to nominal) relative decline that hinders the United States' ability to underwrite global order—it is obvious that revitalizing U.S. national power remains the foundation on which American hegemony will ultimately be preserved.[40] The effectiveness of this renewal will determine both the latitude for and the potency of unilateralism as a means of protecting U.S. interests. As Washington focuses on national rejuvenation, however, it does not have the luxury of jettisoning its alliances because no matter what their infirmities currently may be, the history of the twentieth century has sufficiently proved three propositions: global hegemony can be best preserved through the additive power provided by allies and friends; the presence of effective confederations enables unilateralism whenever necessary and thus acts as its natural complement; and there is no better device for according "a decent respect to the opinions of mankind" than a healthy set of strategic partnerships.

For all these reasons—and especially in the face of a rising China—the challenge before the United States, both around the world and, most importantly, in Asia, consists of how to recast its approach to its geopolitical associations in order to advance vital U.S. interests. This task takes on a special urgency because China's ascendency in Asia is now assured, the likelihood of its evolving into a global rival of the United States is also very high, and China's assertiveness vis-à-vis its neighbors and U.S. power more generally will only further increase in intensity. But the challenge of revamping U.S. geostrategic partnerships also involves a certain delicacy because, thanks to economic interdependence, neither the United States nor its European and Asian partners seek to break ties with China for fear of losing the common gains arising from mutual commerce. Therefore, developing confederations that are simultaneously capable of deterring China without unnerving it, reassuring allies without exacerbating either their own mutual security dilemmas or their common problems with Beijing, and strengthening the web of interdependence in the Indo-Pacific when the future of U.S. power globally appears uncertain will remain quite a challenge.

At the very least, achieving these multiple aims will require what Elizabeth Sherwood-Randall describes as "[a new] alliance strategy that is multifaceted, multilayered, and multi-yeared":

> This would entail a four-pronged approach: First, to build upon existing bilateral and multilateral alliance institutions, relationships, and capabilities; second, to promote the establishment of stronger ties that might become enduring alliances (both bilaterally and multilaterally) with several key countries and regions; third,

---

[40] Tellis, "Balancing without Containment," 67–84.

to invest in peacetime security cooperation with countries that can be coaxed toward partnership and may in the future be capable of sustaining an alliance relationship; and fourth, to utilize the full spectrum of cooperative international arrangements that complement alliances.[41]

Since the end of the Cold War, the United States has set about these diverse tasks. Even as it has pursued the larger goal of broadening its strategic partnerships, however, the aims underlying these associations have also subtly mutated. During the Cold War, U.S. alliances were oriented primarily toward collective defense, protecting the partners from any external threat by communicating the indivisibility of their armed response. Toward this end, the tightly knit pacts focused equally on dampening intra-alliance rivalries, weakening incentives for free-riding, and mitigating temptations for excessive self-reliance. By so doing, the United States preserved its alliances as instruments that protected both the common security and its own hegemony.

The Asian partnerships that the United States must foster in the future will have to do all this and more. The core of collective defense (or extended deterrence where relevant) will remain unchanged, at least for all the formal alliances involving countries that rely on Washington directly for their security. Because any deterioration in the regional balance of power to the United States' disadvantage cannot be beneficial to its interests, however, the United States will have to countenance the possibility of coming to the defense of some key Asian states *in extremis*, even though these nations may not be bound *a priori* by any agreement that commits Washington to their defense. From Korea to Kuwait, the United States, historically, ended up creating a variety of new strategic partnerships under conditions of adversity, and it is very possible that such contingencies could recur.

Beyond this fundamental responsibility for protecting critical states because of their value for U.S. interests, the United States may also on occasion need the support of various Asian countries in what are otherwise unilateral actions undertaken in the face of necessity. As one analysis stated pointedly,

> The United States has fought in five major wars during the 20th century. In each of these conflicts U.S. forces found themselves operating as part of an alliance, or coalition. Even today, when U.S. military superiority has reached a level rarely matched in history, the United States retains its affinity for combined military operations. Recent military actions in Bosnia, Haiti, Iraq, Somalia, and Yugoslavia all were conducted in conjunction with forces from other nations.[42]

---

[41] Elizabeth Sherwood-Randall, *Alliances and American National Security* (Carlisle: Strategic Studies Institute, 2006), viii.

[42] Andrew F. Krepinevich Jr., "Transforming America's Alliances," Center for Strategic and Budgetary Assessments, February 2000, 1.

The need for partners to populate the "coalitions of the willing," both for reasons of capability and legitimacy, especially in situations where the United States pursues military operations without United Nations Security Council authorization, remains another reason for thinking about confederates beyond simply collective defense.

Contributing to the continued provision of global public goods remains an equally important motive for seeking more partners, even outside formal political associations.[43] Because the cost of U.S. contributions toward such collective goods may become more burdensome over time, accepting increased contributions by friends and allies remains an attractive solution. In fact, any potential reduction in U.S. contributions need not be catastrophic if the helping hands of capable powers friendly to the United States can compensate for the decrease. These contributors need not be formal U.S. allies. So long as their political aims fundamentally cohere with Washington's, anything they do to augment the supply of global public goods serves U.S., their own, and other common interests. Given this calculus, developing partnerships with friendly states for purposes of strengthening the liberal international order becomes one more reason for thinking beyond collective defense.

Finally, a critical impetus for developing new strategic ties with countries that may not need U.S. resources strictly for their security is preserving "the balance of power that favors freedom" in Asia.[44] In an environment where many states may be uncomfortable with becoming part of a formal U.S. alliance—either because of their domestic politics, their historical traditions, or their economic ties with China, or even because of a desire to avoid entering into an entangling relationship with the United States or provoking Beijing—it may still be in Washington's interest to develop strong political relations with some key nations. These ties, which are often encompassed by the euphemism "strategic partnerships," are valuable not because they produce active assistance for the United States vis-à-vis China. If they do, so much the better. But even if they do not, such strategic partnerships will still be extremely worthwhile if, having strengthened the partner involved, they serve the purpose of limiting China's ability to dominate its wider periphery and thereby mount more consequential challenges to U.S. interests in Asia and globally. The quest for even passive benefits of this kind, therefore, becomes an important driver of the widening of U.S. strategic ties beyond collective defense.

---

[43] The clearest official statement of this goal can be found in U.S. Department of Defense, *Sustaining U.S. Global Leadership: Priorities for 21st Century Defense* (Washington, D.C., January 2012), http://www.defense.gov/news/defense_strategic_guidance.pdf.

[44] Condoleezza Rice, "Remarks by National Security Advisor Condoleezza Rice on Terrorism and Foreign Policy" (speech given at the Paul H. Nitze School of Advanced International Studies at Johns Hopkins University, Washington, D.C., April 29, 2002).

Seeking the United States: Perspectives from Asia

The diverse chapters in this *Strategic Asia* volume examine the interest, capacity, and willingness of key Asian countries to partner with the United States in the emerging strategic environment. The contributions gathered here, therefore, complement the analysis in this introductory chapter. Whereas this overview focuses on how the United States came to enshrine confederations as part of its grand strategy, what tasks U.S. alliances performed in the past, and how their functions promise to mutate in the future, the individual chapters that follow examine how a variety of Asian counterparts assess the utility, importance, and benefits of their specific associations with the United States and what the impact of such partnerships might be for regional and global security.

Toward this end, each country study broadly takes the following form. To begin, it assesses how the country in question views its external environment in the context of its own strategic priorities, national ambitions, and vision of a desirable international order. By integrating both the pressures emanating from the country's domestic politics and its judgments about perceived threats against the larger backdrop of economic realities as well as the evolving strategic competition between Beijing and Washington, each chapter elucidates how these myriad factors drive the country's approach to working with the United States on a range of economic, political, and security issues.

From this foundation, the analysis then proceeds to the heart of the matter: identifying key priorities for the country being investigated, issues that are also important for the international order, and areas where shared interests with the United States open the possibilities for practical cooperation. Where specific initiatives and mechanisms to build partner capability are relevant to deeper collaboration with the United States, each chapter provides such recommendations as well.

Finally, each investigation evaluates the potential impact of the country's cooperation with the United States along three concrete dimensions: its domestic politics, regional prosperity and stability, and the strength of the international order writ large. By so doing, each chapter describes how national security managers envisage their country's ties with the United States as improving that country's own external environment, while at the same time assessing how each specific partnership advances core U.S. national interests in Asia and beyond. As might be imagined, given the diversity of U.S. associations in Asia, the strength of the relationships and the aims of the various partners involved vary considerably.

The chapter on Japan, authored by Nicholas Szechenyi, abundantly confirms the proposition that Tokyo remains Washington's most capable partner in Northeast Asia. The Japanese economy today is the second-largest in Asia, but its technological capacities remain preeminent. Unfortunately, however, the stasis of the last two decades has taken a toll on Japanese self-confidence, but Szechenyi emphasizes that Shinzo Abe's government remains determined to revitalize the economy, pursue vigorous diplomatic engagement, and upgrade Japanese defense capabilities to undertake new roles and missions. Success on these counts is by no means complete. Yet if accompanied by a concerted effort at outreach to neighbors who have been previously victims of Japanese aggression, Tokyo's emerging capabilities will serve Washington's core objective of preserving a favorable regional balance of power, even as Japan's contributions to the production of global public goods and possibly even to future coalitions of the willing come to enjoy the approbation of the region at large. What is clear from Szechenyi's analysis, however, is that even as this strategic evolution takes place, Japan remains firmly committed to its alliance with the United States as the principal instrument for advancing its political aims.

The transformation in Japanese security policy is mirrored by the changes occurring in the other critical U.S. partnership in Northeast Asia: the alliance with South Korea. Scott Snyder's chapter on South Korea argues that what was previously a fundamentally asymmetrical relationship of super- and sub-ordination between Washington and Seoul is now slowly changing in the direction of greater equality and a more wide-ranging partnership. South Korea's dramatic economic achievements and its steady consolidation of democracy at home have made this evolution possible, leading to the country's growing desire for more responsibility for its own defense. Seoul's increasing willingness to play on a larger canvas than simply Northeast Asia—in collaboration with the United States—and its rejection of Beijing's effort to limit its alliance relationship merely to peninsular matters subtly aids the balancing of China while creating opportunities for greater South Korean contributions toward regional and global stability. The ongoing changes in the U.S.–South Korean partnership thus reflect the new realities of the post–Cold War order in Asia.

The U.S.-Australian alliance remains the quietest of the major bilateral compacts enjoyed by the United States in Asia, partly because of geography and partly because many of the partnership's most valuable activities, such as intelligence collection, occur entirely outside the public eye. Australia has long been a steadfast partner, contributing troops to every U.S. campaign since World War II. Bates Gill's chapter captures the strength of this relationship eloquently while highlighting how Australia, like other U.S. partners such as Japan and South Korea, is now torn between the challenges of balancing China and remaining economically integrated with it. Because Australia maintains a highly proficient military and because its strategic ties with the United States run far deeper than those with other states, Australian capabilities will remain valued in diverse arenas, such as protecting the commons, humanitarian assistance, and counterproliferation. This is the case even as Canberra's tightrope walk between Washington and Beijing remains emblematic of the challenges facing many other U.S. partners in the region.

The U.S. alliance with the Philippines is unique because of the colonial bonds that tied the two nations together. After its independence in 1946, the country remained a sturdy, but dependent, ally throughout the Cold War. The Philippines finally rejected the decades-long U.S. military presence on its territories at the end of that epoch as domestic politics took a decisive turn in the direction of democracy. Sheena Chestnut Greitens's chapter on the U.S.-Philippines alliance documents how Manila's discomfort with the memories of U.S. military presence has now slowly been subordinated to its growing fears of China because of the latter's claims over offshore islands in the South China Sea. Unlike many other U.S. allies, however, the Philippines remains a militarily weak state, something its recent military modernization will not alter, at least vis-à-vis China. The Philippines will thus persist as a consumer of the security produced by U.S. military power in the region, yet because of its colonial history and the ferment in its domestic politics, it will also remain an example of a country that cannot fully embrace the United States as it once did. Greitens nonetheless persuasively argues that strengthening the Philippines will aid in deterring China, but that the partnership must be broadened beyond security cooperation in order to satisfy the larger aspirations of the Filipino people.

The U.S.-Thailand alliance is another example of a relationship that has been transformed by the end of the Cold War. With Thailand having actively sought a credible, but informal, security relationship with the United States in order to defend against regional Communist threats—thereby perpetuating the independence that Thailand had atypically enjoyed during the colonial period—the end of the Vietnam War and finally the defeat of Communism eroded the foundations of this partnership. But as Catharin Dalpino notes in her chapter, the country's salience paradoxically increased as Southeast Asia gradually grew more prosperous, new forms of engagement with China materialized, and Thailand's location as a land bridge made it the fulcrum for increased connectivity throughout continental Southeast Asia. Bangkok's return to an older diplomatic practice of seeking flexibility in foreign relations has changed the character of its ties with Washington considerably. For the foreseeable future, however, Thailand's importance in regard to permitting the United States access through the region will protect its significance. The convulsions in Thai domestic politics, as evidenced by the recurring coups, have stressed bilateral relations periodically, but even when these troubles are finally behind both countries, Thailand's importance as an ally will likely derive from somewhat narrow considerations: providing access for U.S. military movements and hosting major regional training exercises. To that degree, however, this partnership contributes toward preserving peace and stability in the wider region.

In contrast with the countries discussed thus far, the next country assessed in this volume is the first of several that are not allies of the United States. In fact, India, which is the subject of Daniel Twining's chapter, is unlikely to ever become Washington's formal ally, even though it has enjoyed unprecedented U.S. attention in recent years. In what remains a great example of how the evolving post–Cold War environment has demanded new kinds of strategic partnerships, the United States has developed close ties with this large, formally nonaligned democracy in Asia because of the values shared by the two countries. Even more importantly, India's emerging capabilities and extant rivalry with China have made it a desirable object of U.S. engagement. Unlike the ties that bind traditional U.S. alliances, however—which are defined by different types of reciprocity—the transformation of U.S.-Indian relations in recent years has been driven by a unique, calculating detachment on the part of Washington. In an effort to build objective constraints on the misuse of Chinese power in Asia, the United States has sought to aid India's rise on the global stage. It has done so not with the expectation that New Delhi will repay this generosity in specific ways but rather with the expectation that India will preserve a regional balance of power that constrains China's capacity to dominate Asia merely by the fact of India's own developmental and strategic success, thereby advancing U.S. interests in the process. Although any Indian strategic cooperation with the United States would undoubtedly be welcome, the fact that the country's effective rise becomes the true measure of the success of the strategy indicates how the complexities of economic interdependence have now compelled Washington to think of "alliances" in new ways if the fundamental objective of preserving American hegemony globally is to be achieved.

Like India, Indonesia is an important state situated in a critical locale in Asia. Like India again, Indonesia was historically a nonaligned polity that unfortunately subsisted for many decades under military rule. As Ann Marie Murphy emphasizes in her chapter, Indonesia's strategic location at the crossroads of the Pacific and Indian Oceans, its ongoing but largely successful democratic transition, and its status as the world's largest Muslim country all combine to bequeath it with special relevance to the United States. Although Indonesia continues to pursue its external engagements primarily through the Association of Southeast Asian Nations (ASEAN), the importance ASEAN accords to a strong partnership with the United States as part of its own efforts to avoid being dominated by China inevitably enhances U.S.-Indonesian ties as well. In recent years, the latter have intensified as a new generation of democratic leaders in Jakarta has, according to Murphy, "demonstrated a willingness to invest [their] diplomatic energies to support the current international order in a manner consistent with U.S. interests." In ways similar to those adopted vis-à-vis India, the United States seeks to shore up Indonesian capacities to deal with a wide range of challenges, including terrorism, natural disasters, and maritime security, thus enabling Jakarta to protect its core interests in the face of both internal dangers and Chinese threats. Washington thereby seeks to ensure that Indonesia thrives as a regional center of power in ways that ultimately enhance U.S. security.

The new post–Cold War effort to build resilient partnerships with states that nonetheless eschew the option of a formal alliance with Washington finds no better example than Singapore, the focus of Matthew Shannon Stumpf's chapter. A small island-state, Singapore has sought to maintain the deepest possible strategic ties with the United States—in fact, reaching the point where it has developed physical infrastructure specifically to support U.S. naval vessels deploying to the country—while consistently rejecting the formalities of an alliance. Given Singapore's location and history, its grand strategy has focused on maintaining close links with both Beijing and Washington, resolutely avoiding any temptation to decisively choose between the two. Yet Singaporean leaders, astutely recognizing the dangers of proximity to an increasingly assertive China, have doubled down on strengthening their partnership with the United States, betting on the fact that U.S. economic and military superiority will ultimately suffice to protect the regional order even in the face of growing Chinese power. To ensure this outcome, Singapore has sought to contribute tangibly by hosting U.S. naval assets, acquiring various U.S. military technologies, and training extensively with the U.S. armed forces—even as it maintains close economic and diplomatic ties with China. For Washington, the U.S.-Singaporean model of engagement remains in many ways the exemplar of what new "alliances" in the post–Cold War order might look like: allies maintaining robust practical cooperation with the United States on the most important strategic issues, while pursuing their interests with other regional countries so long as these do not undermine the larger common objective of preserving an Asia free of Chinese domination.

This principle applies to Taiwan in a most unique way. Although Taipei was Washington's formal partner through the mutual defense treaty signed in 1954, the U.S.-China rapprochement that occurred after President Richard Nixon's historic visit to Beijing slowly left Taipei in a geopolitical netherworld.

Today, the U.S. commitment to Taiwan's security is ensured not by an official bilateral treaty but rather by domestic U.S. law—the Taiwan Relations Act—which requires the United States to aid Taiwan through both defensive arms transfers and maintenance of a capacity to intervene in case it becomes a victim of strategic coercion or attack. In an environment defined by tight economic interdependence between China and the United States, on the one hand, and by Beijing's growing global ascendency, on the other, Washington has walked a tightrope for many years struggling to protect Taiwan politically while avoiding conclusively alienating China. This balancing act has been most effective when dyadic relations among the three states involved have enjoyed equipoise. But the longer-term future remains highly uncertain. For the moment, however, Taiwan's growing economic links with China and the stability of their bilateral relations offer welcome respite. Nonetheless, the key to the continued success of the exceptional extended deterrence relationship that exists between the United States and Taiwan will require, as Russell Hsiao highlights in his chapter, a steady strengthening of Taiwan's military capabilities, a willingness on Washington's part to reconsider its traditional policy of "strategic ambiguity," and deliberate efforts to redress what Hsiao calls the "sovereignty gap" in China-Taiwan relations. A failure to do so could not only subvert the security of a steadfast U.S. ally but also undermine the United States' credibility in the face of rising Chinese power in Asia.

On the face of it, Vietnam might appear as an odd inclusion in a volume on U.S. allies and partners in Asia. After all, Washington and Hanoi were locked in a bitter conflict for some twenty-odd years, a domestically divisive war in the United States that ultimately ended in defeat and the loss of over 58,000 American lives. Yet in a remarkable testament to the enduring importance of interests in international politics, Nguyen Manh Hung's chapter succinctly demonstrates that "U.S.-Vietnam relations have come a long way, from enmity to partnership, thanks to two major geopolitical shifts that have created a convergence of strategic interests between both sides: Vietnam beginning to overcome its mistrust of U.S. intentions and commitment, and the rise of China and assertive Chinese behavior in the South China Sea driving worries in both Washington and Hanoi." The steadily intensifying engagement between what remains formally a Communist regime in Vietnam and the anti-Communist paragon par excellence, the United States, indicates the importance to both sides of preserving an Asia that is free from Chinese control. Although Vietnam, like India, Indonesia, and Singapore, will never become a formal ally, U.S. investments in assisting Vietnam to preserve its independence, even if not reciprocated, serve vital U.S. interests. Consequently, Nguyen argues that supporting Vietnam's domestic evolution without threatening its ruling regime, strengthening its economy through continued investment, and integrating the country eventually into the Trans-Pacific Partnership remain important ways in which Washington and Hanoi can collaborate to achieve their common core strategic interests.

The country chapters in this edition of *Strategic Asia* are supplemented—as they always are in this series—by a special study. In this volume, the special study focuses on understanding an important attribute of interstate competition in the era of economic interdependence: the persistence of strategic hedging. The conventional argument for strategic hedging—that is, the desire of states to avoid either balancing or bandwagoning vis-à-vis China and the United States—is rooted in either uncertainty about the future character of the power hierarchy or ambiguity about state intentions amid diffuse threats. Van Jackson's special study of this issue offers a third perspective. Drawing insights from the literature on network analysis and complex interdependence, he argues that hedging in the Indo-Pacific region is likely to be a permanent—not transient—condition (as is usually supposed) because of the multiple and cross-cutting cleavages that the regional states have to contend with in the evolving international system. This insight has powerful consequences: among other things, it validates the fundamental shift in U.S. regional strategy witnessed since the end of the Cold War—namely, the desire to nurture diverse kinds of strategic partnerships of the type detailed in this volume as a means of preserving a favorable continental balance of power. Jackson argues that these efforts should be supplemented by continued engagement with Asia's multilateral institutions because "consensual multilateralism may be the only acceptable or functional model of security governance in Asia" in the years to come.

Conclusion

The studies gathered in this volume on alliances and partnerships illustrate the central argument of this overview: confederationism, as a constituent element of U.S. grand strategy, is here to stay. U.S. power, no matter how formidable, benefits from the presence of partners thanks to both their capacity to supplement American resources and their ability to bestow legitimacy to various U.S. policies. Even when these are not at issue, however, the company of confederates is undoubtedly valuable because it enhances the freedom the United States enjoys to undertake unilateral actions whenever these are demanded by its global interests. Washington's quest for partnerships in the Indo-Pacific region, at any rate, is only eased by the fact that a large number of nations therein value the United States and its protective presence—in fact, demand it, even if they are not formal allies—because of the positive externalities accruing to them specifically in an environment characterized by both deepening interdependence and rising Chinese power.

The dialectical relationship between confederationism and unilateralism, coupled with the Asian desire for a strong U.S. regional presence even when formal alliances are not particularly favored, highlights an important paradox that ought not to be forgotten by U.S. policymakers: the cohesion between the United States and its many partners, formal and informal, is likely to be greatest when U.S. power is at its most durable and resolute—in other words, when associates may be least needed. If U.S. power atrophies, however, due to either poor policies at home or a failure to lead in the manner appropriate to U.S. interests, the collaborators necessary for success are unlikely to be enthusiastic partners when they are most desirable. The ultimate value of confederationism as an anchor of U.S. grand strategy thus hinges fundamentally on the vitality of U.S. power.

STRATEGIC ASIA 2014–15

U.S. ALLIES

EXECUTIVE SUMMARY

This chapter examines Japan's emerging foreign policy strategy, including efforts to strengthen the U.S.-Japan alliance, and posits that the alignment of strategic objectives enhances the prospects for the alliance to shape the economic and security architecture of the Asia-Pacific.

MAIN ARGUMENT:

Japan has unveiled a comprehensive strategy centered on economic revitalization, diplomacy in support of international rules and norms, and investments in defense capabilities to strengthen deterrence against emerging threats and enhance cooperation with like-minded countries. The U.S.-Japan alliance, as the cornerstone of Japanese foreign policy, has a central role to play in realizing this strategic vision for Japan's future. Japan's emerging economic, diplomatic, and security initiatives mirror the objectives of the U.S. strategic rebalance to the Asia-Pacific, and the convergence of these two strategies presents an opportunity for joint leadership in strengthening the regional order.

POLICY IMPLICATIONS:

- Economic power is the foundation of Japan's strategy to enhance its leadership role in international affairs, and the U.S. has a strategic interest in supporting Japan's path toward sustainable growth and in strengthening bilateral economic cooperation as a catalyst for shaping the rules and norms of Asia-Pacific economic integration.

- The introduction of defense reforms, including measures that would allow Japan to exercise the right of collective self-defense, suggests the potential to expand the parameters for U.S.-Japan defense cooperation, enhance coordination with like-minded countries in the Asia-Pacific, and establish a balance of power that favors regional stability.

- Sustaining bilateral strategic dialogue at senior levels will be critical to ensuring that the diplomatic, economic, and security strategies of the two governments remain complementary and ultimately help shape the regional order.

The U.S.-Japan Alliance: Prospects to Strengthen the Asia-Pacific Order

Nicholas Szechenyi

After two decades of anemic economic growth and a period of political paralysis that tested its capacity for leadership, Japan has introduced a policy framework to enhance its economic and strategic weight and to work with the United States and other partners in order to help shape the Asia-Pacific order. Beset by multiple domestic challenges such as deflation, public debt, an aging population, and a declining birthrate, the political leadership is focused on economic revitalization tied to a process of regional economic integration. In the face of multiple security challenges, including instability on the Korean Peninsula and Chinese assertiveness in the maritime domain, the government also has taken measures to reorganize national security policy, strengthen the U.S.-Japan alliance, and further enhance Japan's contributions to international security. These initiatives are buttressed by a robust diplomatic agenda to amplify Japan's strategic priorities and explore opportunities for economic and security cooperation with like-minded countries. The realization of this policy agenda will require sustained political leadership that begins with projecting confidence in Japan's leadership credentials, as evidenced by recent efforts to reassure the Japanese people and the international community that Japan "is not and will never be a tier-two country."[1]

As a treaty ally with a shared interest in fostering stability and prosperity in the Asia-Pacific region, the United States has a stake in Japan sustaining its leadership role in diplomatic, economic, and security affairs. The cornerstone

---

Nicholas Szechenyi is a Senior Fellow and Deputy Director of the Japan Chair at the Center for Strategic and International Studies (CSIS). He can be reached at <nszechenyi@csis.org>.

---

[1] Shinzo Abe, "Japan is Back" (speech given at the CSIS Statesman's Forum, Washington, D.C., February 22, 2013), http://csis.org/files/attachments/132202_PM_Abe_TS.pdf.

of U.S. strategy in the region is the alliance with Japan, which is based on a bilateral security treaty that commits the United States to defend Japan and enables U.S. access to bases for forward deployments and operational capacity to maintain regional peace and security.[2] This core strategic bargain has remained in place for over 50 years, although the alliance has evolved in response to changes in the international security environment. The security treaty also includes clauses referencing economic cooperation and support for international institutions, which are two important elements of alliance cooperation that still resonate.[3] The United States and Japan are the first- and third-largest economies in the world, respectively, and leading contributors to multilateral institutions that have governed the international order. Japan's efforts to support the economic and security architecture of the Asia-Pacific region are based first and foremost on strengthening the U.S.-Japan alliance and coincide with a U.S. strategy also based fundamentally on robust alliance relationships. The alignment of these respective policies, anchored by the bilateral security treaty, presents a unique opportunity for the U.S.-Japan alliance to shape the regional order.

This chapter first summarizes the evolution of U.S.-Japan alliance cooperation as context for recent developments in Japanese policy and the bilateral agenda. Japan's perceptions of the external security environment are then examined to explain the rationale behind a nascent national security strategy designed to strengthen Japan's leadership role in the region. An analysis of the synergies between Japanese and U.S. strategies segues into potential opportunities to enhance alliance cooperation across a range of issue areas. The chapter concludes with a discussion of key variables and recommendations for realizing Japan's strategic objectives and an expanded framework for alliance cooperation.

An Evolving Alliance

The U.S.-Japan alliance is the cornerstone of Japanese foreign policy but has undergone a process of adjustment over six decades in response to new security challenges and political developments in both countries. Japan's emerging national security strategy, centered on enhancing defense capabilities and furthering security cooperation with the United States and

---

[2] Articles V and VI of the treaty refer to the U.S. commitment to defend Japan and to permission for the United States to use bases for regional security, respectively. For more on this treaty, see Ministry of Foreign Affairs of Japan, *Treaty of Mutual Cooperation and Security between Japan and the United States of America* (Tokyo, January 19, 1960), http://www.mofa.go.jp/region/n-america/us/q&a/ref/1.html.

[3] Michael J. Green and Nicholas Szechenyi, "Japan-U.S. Relations," in *The Routledge Handbook of Japanese Politics*, ed. Alisa Gaunder (Abington: Routledge, 2011).

other partners, marks the beginning of a new chapter in this process of adjustment and contrasts sharply with the outset of the Cold War when Japan's strategic culture emphasized economic development over defense cooperation with the United States. At that time, Prime Minister Shigeru Yoshida outlined foreign policy principles, later dubbed the Yoshida Doctrine, designed to facilitate Japan's economic development while utilizing Article 9 of the postwar constitution (which renounces war as a sovereign right of the nation and prohibits the threat or use of force as a means of settling international disputes) to engage in security cooperation with the United States at the minimum level necessary to demonstrate a commitment to the alliance. A desire both for increased sovereignty and a U.S. security umbrella created an "entrapment versus abandonment" dilemma, in which excessive reliance on the United States could draw Japan into Cold War conflicts, while increased demands for autonomy—or, conversely, failure to pull its weight in the alliance—could drive the United States away and leave Japan vulnerable to external threats.[4] This dilemma has featured prominently in Japan's foreign policy debate ever since. Throughout the postwar era, governments have reinterpreted Article 9 to allow the limited use of force for self-defense and revised security policy incrementally as developments in the security environment warranted.

Japanese political leaders placed strict limits on bilateral defense cooperation in the 1960s to avoid entanglement in the Vietnam War. However, the parameters were expanded a decade later with the introduction of bilateral guidelines for defense cooperation in 1978 that focused on sea lane defense and joint exercises for the defense of Japan to contain Soviet expansion in the Far East. In the 1980s, Japan's increased economic clout and the relative decline in U.S. competitiveness created tension in the alliance, which led to a period of drift after the collapse of the Soviet Union in 1991. This trend was highlighted by Japan's failure to dispatch forces to support military operations during the Persian Gulf War. The subsequent collapse of Japan's economy weakened its diplomatic clout just as Japanese strategic thinkers began to favor multilateral diplomacy over defense cooperation with the United States, both of which raised doubts about the relevance of the alliance in the post–Cold War era.[5]

Concerns about drift prompted U.S. officials to initiate a bilateral dialogue on the future of the alliance known as the "Nye initiative," named after Joseph Nye, the former assistant secretary of defense for international

---

[4] For a detailed review of the evolution of alliance cooperation, see Michael J. Green, "Balance of Power," in *U.S.-Japan Relations in a Changing World*, ed. Steven K. Vogel (Washington, D.C.: Brookings University Press, 2002).

[5] Green and Szechenyi, "Japan-U.S. Relations."

security affairs. Two crises—the 1995 rape of an Okinawan schoolgirl by U.S. servicemen, which stoked opposition in Japan to the U.S. military presence, and Chinese missile tests around Taiwan to discourage calls for the island's independence—added urgency to the bilateral dialogue. In 1996, Japan and the United States issued a joint security declaration reaffirming a commitment to the U.S. force presence in Japan, establishing the Special Action Committee on Okinawa to explore means of reducing the U.S. military footprint, and announcing plans to revise the guidelines for bilateral defense cooperation. New guidelines were issued in 1997 that introduced plans for bilateral security cooperation in "situations surrounding Japan," signaling a greater commitment to regional security and a departure from Japan's exclusive focus on homeland defense during the Cold War.

Alliance cooperation evolved further in the aftermath of the terrorist attacks of September 11, 2001. Under the leadership of Prime Minister Junichiro Koizumi, Japan passed special legislation enabling the Self-Defense Forces (SDF) to participate in refueling activities in the Indian Ocean during Operation Enduring Freedom in Afghanistan, and the SDF was later dispatched to support reconstruction activities in Iraq as part of Operation Iraqi Freedom. Japan's security contributions were no longer confined to "situations surrounding Japan." This increased commitment to global security was documented in the new defense strategy issued in 2004, emphasizing "international peace cooperation activities" where Japan should "voluntarily and actively participate in activities that nations of the world cooperatively undertake to enhance the international security environment."[6] The parameters for bilateral security cooperation in the post–September 11 era were defined further in 2005 when the bilateral Security Consultative Committee released common strategic objectives (regional and global) along with a review of the roles, missions, and capabilities of Japan's SDF and the U.S. military to enhance interoperability and the capacity to respond to diverse challenges, including the North Korean nuclear and missile threat, terrorism, and China's military rise.[7]

Koizumi stepped down in 2006 and his Liberal Democratic Party (LDP) failed to connect with the public, creating an opportunity for the opposition Democratic Party of Japan (DPJ) to assume power in 2009 for the first time ever. The DPJ election platform advocated a "close but equal"

[6] Yuki Tatsumi, *Japan's National Security Policy Infrastructure* (Washington, D.C.: Henry L. Stimson Center, 2008), chap 1; and Japan Ministry of Defense, *National Defense Program Guidelines, FY 2005* (Tokyo, December 10, 2004), 5, http://www.mod.go.jp/e/d_act/d_policy/pdf/national_guidelines.pdf.

[7] U.S.-Japan Security Consultative Committee, "Joint Statements of the U.S.-Japan Security Consultative Committee," February 19, 2005; and U.S.-Japan Security Consultative Committee, "U.S.-Japan Alliance: Transformation and Realignment for the Future," October 29, 2005, http://www.mofa.go.jp/region/n-america/us/security/scc/pdfs/doc0510.pdf.

U.S.-Japan alliance, though U.S. observers were unsure whether "equal" meant Japan assuming a greater leadership role on security or taking a more defiant approach to the alliance. The latter prevailed under Yukio Hatoyama, the first DPJ prime minister, who precipitated a crisis in the alliance by promising to relocate U.S. Marine Corps Air Station Futenma, located in a densely populated area in central Okinawa, outside the prefecture. This pledge disregarded previously agreed-upon plans to build a replacement facility in a less-populated area of Okinawa. Hatoyama resigned after one year in office due mainly to the controversy over Futenma, and his successors sought to repair relations with Washington. Hatoyama's departure created space for Japan to refine its own defense strategy and coordinate with the United States on the broader strategic objectives of alliance cooperation. A natural disaster of monumental proportions then put the operational capacity of the alliance to the test.

The events following the 3.11 disaster highlighted the enduring importance of the alliance. On March 11, 2011, a 9.0-magnitude earthquake rocked the Tohoku region and triggered a massive tsunami that covered over five hundred square kilometers along the northeast coast of Honshu. The desperate situation in northeast Japan was compounded when the combined effects of the earthquake and tsunami precipitated a nuclear meltdown at the Fukushima Daiichi nuclear power plant and the release of significant quantities of nuclear radiation into the surrounding countryside.[8] The United States and Japan undertook a massive whole-of-government response effort to aid those affected by the triple disaster, the defense component of which was named Operation Tomodachi ("friends" in Japanese).[9] Operation Tomodachi was a watershed moment in the alliance in that it was the "first time that full scale bilateral cooperation was carried out from decision-making to the implementation of response under the existing Japan-U.S. security arrangements."[10]

In demonstrating the continued utility of the U.S.-Japan alliance, these combined efforts undoubtedly saved innumerable lives and prevented a horrific tragedy from becoming even worse.[11] As then secretary of state Hillary Clinton observed in a March 2011 interview with Japanese television network NHK, "this unprecedented disaster has produced unprecedented cooperation between our countries. Our alliance, which was already strong and enduring,

---

[8] "Strategic Assistance: Disaster Relief and Asia-Pacific Stability," National Bureau of Asian Research (NBR), 2014, 13–14, http://nbr.org/downloads/pdfs/psa/HADR_report_081114.pdf.

[9] Ibid.

[10] Akihisa Nagashima, "Genpatsu taisho: Nichi-Bei kyoryoku no butaiura" [Response to the Nuclear Accident: Behind the Scenes of Japan-U.S. Cooperation], *Voice*, July 2011.

[11] "Strategic Assistance," 14–16.

has become even more so."[12] Indeed, in the weeks and months following the 3.11 disaster, Japanese public perceptions of the United States and of the alliance improved dramatically, with a 2011 Pew Research poll indicating that 85% of Japanese viewed the United States favorably.[13] The triple disaster brought into relief a broad range of areas, in addition to defense, in which to potentially enhance bilateral cooperation, including disaster response and recovery, health, energy security, and civil society linkages.[14]

The LDP returned to power in 2012 under the leadership of Shinzo Abe. Since then, Japan has embarked on an ambitious policy agenda to revitalize the economy and strengthen the country's defense capabilities in order to reaffirm its influence both in Asia and globally and address an external security environment that Tokyo views as "increasingly severe."[15] Consistent with the pattern established over the history of the alliance, Japan is once again poised to expand the parameters for cooperation while keeping the core strategic bargain of the alliance intact. The two governments are pursuing complementary security strategies to maintain stability in the Asia-Pacific region.

The Regional Security Environment

Japan is confronted by an increasingly complex and demanding external security environment, in which a number of "challenges and destabilizing factors are becoming more tangible and acute."[16] As Asia's strategic landscape continues to evolve, Japan, for the first time since the start of the Cold War, now faces what one prominent U.S. scholar has described as a "security deficit," wherein the challenges confronting Japan are greater than its capacity to address them.[17] These challenges range from more recent and unconventional

---

[12] "Interview with Kaho Izumitani of NHK," U.S. Department of State website, March 22, 2011, http://www.state.gov/secretary/20092013clinton/rm/2011/03/158840.htm.

[13] Pew Research Center, "Global Indicators Database: Opinion of the United States," Global Attitudes Project, 2014, http://www.pewglobal.org/database/indicator/1/country/109.

[14] *Partnership for Recovery and a Stronger Future: Standing with Japan after 3-11* (Washington, D.C.: CSIS, 2011), http://csis.org/files/publication/111026_Green_PartnershipforRecovery_Web.pdf.

[15] Japan Ministry of Defense, *In Defense of Japan 2014* (Tokyo, 2014), http://www.mod.go.jp/e/publ/w_paper/pdf/2014/DOJ2014_1-1-0_1st_0730.pdf. For more on Tokyo's external security views, see Richard J. Samuels, "Securing Japan: The Current Discourse," *Journal of Japanese Studies* 33, no. 1 (2007): 128, 142–46; and Kenneth B. Pyle, "The Sea Change in Japanese Foreign Policy," NBR, NBR Analysis Brief, June 17, 2014, http://www.nbr.org/publications/analysis/pdf/Brief/061714_Pyle_JapanSeaChange.pdf.

[16] Japan Ministry of Defense, *In Defense of Japan 2014*.

[17] James L. Schoff, "Realigning Priorities: The U.S.-Japan Alliance & the Future of Extended Deterrence," Institute for Foreign Policy Analysis, Report, March 2009, x, 7–15, http://www.ifpa.org/pdf/RealignPriorities.pdf.

threats, such as those posed by the increasing interconnectedness of the international system, the diffusion of hard-power capabilities to weak state and nonstate actors as a result of globalization, and so-called "gray-zone situations" involving subconventional contingencies primarily over "territory, sovereignty, and maritime economic interests," to more traditional concerns over the proliferation of weapons of mass destruction and arms build-ups by potential adversary nations.[18] Punctuating these broad-based threats are the specific challenges posed by China's ongoing military expansion and increasingly assertive behavior in and around its periphery as well as by North Korea's steady stream of provocative rhetoric and actions, matched by its slow march toward an operational nuclear capability.[19]

Meanwhile, Japanese strategists frequently express a creeping anxiety over the long-term capabilities and commitment of the United States to the Asia-Pacific generally and the defense of Japan specifically. Japan's concerns mainly involve the United States' ongoing fiscal difficulties and are focused on the potential that the two allies may have diverging strategic interests and priorities, particularly regarding regional territorial disputes. Moreover, the perception exists in Japan that despite Washington's declaration of its intent to rebalance toward the Asia-Pacific, the United States has become distracted by exigent events in the Middle East and Eastern Europe and allowed the rebalance to languish.[20] Such anxieties are exacerbated by Tokyo's intensifying concerns about the rising power and increasing assertiveness of China.

Growing Anxiety over China

Although Japan's 2014 defense white paper raises the expectation that China will "recognize its responsibility in the international community, accept and stick to international norms, and play a more active and cooperative role in regional and global issues," defense planners and strategists in Tokyo view China with growing anxiety and apprehension.[21] Indeed, concerns over China have risen sharply in the past several years as Beijing has adopted more assertive policies along its immediate periphery and as Chinese influence has extended further throughout the region. While remaining opaque regarding its intentions, China has expanded defense spending considerably as it continues to build up and modernize its military capabilities, particularly those designed to prevent the United States from

---

[18] Japan Ministry of Defense, *In Defense of Japan 2014*, 1–6.

[19] Ibid., chap. 1, 1–8.

[20] Ibid., chap. 1.

[21] Ibid., 4–5.

deploying or operating military assets in the western Pacific (so-called anti-access/area-denial capabilities).[22]

The latest adjustment in Japanese strategic thinking has been prompted by China's assertiveness in the East China Sea over the last several years. Coercive activities to support China's sovereignty claims over the Senkaku Islands—depicted most vividly in a video posted online in 2010 showing a Chinese trawler colliding with a Japan Coast Guard vessel in the surrounding waters—have increased tensions and frozen diplomatic ties between Tokyo and Beijing.[23] The defense policy debate in Japan refocused on the country's immediate neighborhood, and specialists began to emphasize maritime security and surveillance capabilities in the East China Sea.[24] In December 2010, Japan issued a defense strategy, known in Japan as the National Defense Program Guidelines (NDPG), which introduced the concept of "dynamic defense" focused on improving the capability to defend the Nansei island chain.[25] The document also called attention to the challenges posed by gray-zone incidents over sovereignty, territorial disputes, or economic interests that fall short of military conflict, reflecting concerns about the potential for accidents to escalate into a military confrontation with China. The 2010 NDPG departed from Cold War–era principles centered on homeland defense and signaled an interest in reallocating resources toward improving Japan's capabilities in the maritime domain and taking a more proactive approach to maintaining security in the Asia-Pacific. That trend has continued under the Abe government as Japan seeks to manage China's rise and fashion a rules-based regional order together with the United States and other partners in the region.

The deterioration in Japan-China ties has hardened public opinion in both countries and complicated efforts to maintain the strong economic ties that have heretofore stabilized the bilateral relationship. One recent survey found that 93% of the Japanese public has a negative impression of China, while 86% of the Chinese public shares the same sentiment toward

---

[22] Japan Ministry of Defense, *In Defense of Japan 2014*, 4–5.

[23] Located in the East China Sea, the sovereignty of the Senkaku Islands (referred to as the Diaoyu Islands by China and the Diaoyutai Islands by Taiwan) is the subject of a long-standing dispute between Japan, China, and Taiwan. The uninhabited islands are administered by Japan and are thought to be surrounded by undersea energy reserves. Japan claims sovereignty over the Senkaku Islands and does not acknowledge the existence of a territorial dispute with China. The United States does not take a position on the question of sovereignty but recognizes Japan's administrative control of the islands and their applicability under Article V of the U.S.-Japan Security Treaty, which stipulates that the United States will defend Japan and the territories under its administrative control.

[24] For more on Japan's maritime refocus, see Tokyo Foundation, "New Security Strategy of Japan: Multilayered and Cooperative Security Strategy," October 8, 2008, http://www.risingpowersinitiative. org/wp-content/uploads/tokyofoundation1.pdf.

[25] Japan Ministry of Defense, *National Defense Program Guidelines for FY 2011 and Beyond* (Tokyo, December 17, 2010), http://www.mod.go.jp/e/d_act/d_policy/pdf/guidelinesFY2011.pdf.

Japan. Public opinion in both countries points to territorial issues as the biggest obstacle to improving bilateral relations.[26] In addition, neither country's public trusts the political leadership of the other country: just 6% of Japanese have confidence in Chinese president Xi Jinping to do the right thing in international affairs, and only 15% of Chinese have confidence in Abe.[27] Nonetheless, recent discussions on maritime security and bilateral engagement by business leaders suggest that the potential exists to gradually reopen channels for official dialogue and foster stability in the relationship.[28] Japanese strategic elites remain skeptical of China's long-term military ambitions, however, and the balance between deterrence and engagement will likely remain a central theme in the policy debate in Japan going forward.[29]

The North Korean Threat

While many Japanese observers see China as a rising threat, North Korea remains at the top of the list in terms of immediate security challenges confronting Japan. The succession of Kim Jong-un and the subsequent and sudden personnel shuffles within the highest echelons of the leadership in Pyongyang have only served to reinforce the pervasive sense of uncertainty that surrounds the future trajectory of the reclusive North. Moreover, North Korea has advanced both its nuclear weapons and ballistic missile programs and appears to be making progress toward realizing its goal of fielding an operational nuclear weapons capability that would severely threaten Japan. Meanwhile, North Korea has continued to behave provocatively toward its neighbors, going so far as to threaten specific Japanese cities with missile attacks in early 2013. Finally, Japan seeks a resolution to the long-standing issue of Japanese nationals abducted by North Korea.[30]

Efforts to deter aggression by Pyongyang have combined multilateral initiatives such as the six-party talks, which have been dormant since 2008, with initiatives to strengthen deterrence through bilateral cooperation with the United States on ballistic missile defense and trilateral coordination with

---

[26] Genron NPO, "The 10th Japan-China Opinion Poll: Analysis Report on the Comparative Data," September 9, 2014, http://www.genron-npo.net/en/pp/archives/5153.html.

[27] Pew Research Center, "Global Opposition to U.S. Surveillance and Drones, but Limited Harm to America's Image," July 2014, http://www.pewglobal.org/files/2014/07/2014-07-14-Balance-of-Power.pdf.

[28] Toko Sekiguchi and Chun Han Wong, "China-Japan Relations Ease Back from the Brink," *Wall Street Journal*, September 25, 2014, http://online.wsj.com/articles/china-japan-relations-ease-back-from-brink-1411650347.

[29] Just 2% of Japanese strategic elites believe that China's impact on regional security is positive. For more on this issue, see Michael J. Green and Nicholas Szechenyi, *Power and Order in Asia: A Survey of Regional Expectations* (Washington, D.C.: CSIS, 2014), http://csis.org/files/publication/140605_Green_PowerandOrder_WEB.pdf.

[30] Japan Ministry of Defense, *In Defense of Japan 2014*, 3–4.

the United States and South Korea. Japan and the United States continue to enhance missile defense capabilities through measures such as the SM-3 Block IIA cooperative development program and the deployment of the X-band radar system in Japan.[31] Japan also included plans to procure more Aegis-equipped destroyers in the five-year defense spending outline that was released with its new defense strategy white paper in December 2013. However, in addition to these defensive modernizations, as the North Korean missile threat has advanced, a new debate has emerged among Japanese strategic thinkers on whether Japan needs to acquire a limited strike capability that could target North Korean missile launch sites and preempt an attack. The 2013 defense strategy listed this as an issue for further study, but earlier drafts had placed greater emphasis on this theme. That the desire for offensive capabilities continues to animate the strategic debate in Japan could suggest the country's unease about the U.S. commitment to defend Japan against the North Korean threat.[32] Depending on how this debate develops in the future, it could have dramatic implications for the alliance and for cooperation between the United States and Japan on North Korea.

Humanitarian concerns over the fate of Japanese citizens abducted by North Korea in the 1970s and 1980s, another priority issue for the Abe administration, necessitate careful consideration of the balance between deterrence and engagement with Pyongyang. Japanese and North Korean officials have met several times over the past year on the abduction issue. Following an official meeting in July 2014, Pyongyang announced that it would conduct an investigation into the matter under a special mandate from the National Defense Commission. In return, Japan relaxed a number of the unilateral sanctions it had in place against North Korea. However, with Pyongyang claiming as of this writing that its investigation is still in an "initial stage," it appears that current efforts on this front have stalled.[33] While this latest episode is indicative of the difficulty in engaging North Korea, it also demonstrates an area where the United States and Japan may be acting at cross-purposes as each pursues its own interests. Although these actions are unlikely to cause major perturbations in U.S.-Japan cooperation on the North Korean problem, they do provide Pyongyang with a small opportunity

---

[31] U.S.-Japan Security Consultative Committee, "Joint Statement of the Security Consultative Committee: Toward a More Robust Alliance and Greater Shared Responsibilities," October 3, 2013, http://www. defense.gov/pubs/U.S.-Japan-Joint-Statement-of-the-Security-Consultative-Committee.pdf.

[32] Nobuhiro Kubo, "Exclusive: Japan, U.S. Discussing Offensive Military Capability for Tokyo—Japan Officials," Reuters, September 10, 2014, http://uk.reuters.com/article/2014/09/10/uk-japan-usa-military-idUKKBN0H500L20140910.

[33] "N. Korea Refuses to Say When It Will Deliver Abduction Report," Kyodo News, September 29, 2014, http://www.japantimes.co.jp/news/2014/09/29/national/politics-diplomacy/japan-envoy-urges-n-korea-end-delay-report-abductees/.

to drive a wedge between the allies, a tactic it has sought to use before. By remaining in close consultation over any likely policy shifts, the United States and Japan can sustain a more concerted approach toward North Korean denuclearization while also exploring avenues for engagement.

Japan's policy debate centers mainly on deterring North Korean aggression and Chinese attempts at coercion in the maritime domain, concerns shared by the United States. Over the long term, however, the greatest challenge for Japan and the United States in the region is to manage China's rise by shaping Beijing's choices in ways that favor regional stability. Overall, Japan's emerging foreign policy doctrine toward the region under Abe has stressed the rule of law and the importance of respecting long-standing international norms, particularly involving peaceful dispute and conflict resolution. The essence of Japan's perspective on the regional order is best illustrated in the keynote address Abe delivered to the Shangri-La Dialogue in May 2014. He denounced attempts to use coercion in support of maritime sovereignty claims, hailed Asia's potential as a center of growth and economic integration, declared support for the Association of Southeast Asian Nations (ASEAN) and the East Asia Summit as key forums to address regional politics and security, and vowed that Japan would champion the rule of law and be a force for peace.[34] The three pillars of economy, diplomacy, and security also undergird the national security strategy introduced by the Abe government in 2013 and indicate a renewed commitment to shaping a rules-based order in collaboration with the United States and other partners in the region.

The Recent Evolution of Japan's Economic and Security Policy

Abe first served as prime minister in 2006–7 but resigned suddenly for health reasons and was subsequently criticized for not paying proper attention to Japan's economic woes. His resignation initiated a period of political paralysis in which Japan produced six leaders in six years, the last three under the leadership of the relatively inexperienced DPJ. Abe mounted a remarkable political comeback in 2012 by leading the LDP to a landslide victory in the Lower House election, a feat that was repeated in the Upper House election in 2013. He benefits from a relatively stable political environment with a weak opposition and no parliamentary elections scheduled before summer 2016.

---

[34] "The 13th IISS Asian Security Summit—The Shangri-La Dialogue—Keynote Address by Prime Minister Abe," Prime Minister of Japan and His Cabinet website, May 30, 2014, http://japan.kantei. go.jp/96_abe/statement/201405/0530kichokoen.html.

This presents a window of opportunity for Abe to develop and implement a policy agenda that, if successful, could keep him in office for several years.

During a visit to the United States in February 2013, Abe announced that "Japan is back" and outlined his strategic vision for the nation centered on revitalizing the Japanese economy, upholding the rules and norms that govern the international system, promoting maritime security and freedom of navigation, strengthening the U.S.-Japan alliance, and cooperating with Australia, South Korea, and other like-minded states in the region.[35] Later that year, Abe expanded further on his prescription for Japan's global leadership role in international security by pledging in an address to the United Nations General Assembly that Japan would make a "proactive contribution to peace" in the Asia-Pacific region and globally.[36] The Abe government also introduced measures to enhance national security policy by submitting legislation to establish a National Security Council that would centralize foreign policy decision-making in the prime minister's office and formulate strategy. Abe has repeatedly projected confidence in Japan's capacity for sustained leadership in international affairs, a first step in drawing the attention of the international community after a period of political turmoil. His first task, however, was to renew the confidence of the Japanese public in his ability to resuscitate the domestic economy.

Economic Policy

Abe has launched a three-pronged economic strategy, dubbed "Abenomics," featuring fiscal stimulus to boost GDP growth, monetary easing to combat deflation, and structural reforms to improve Japan's economic competitiveness. Japan's economy grew at an annual rate of 5.9% in the first quarter of 2014, and price increases have moved toward the Bank of Japan's target of 2% inflation.[37] Abe was forced, however, to strike a balance between providing fiscal stimulus and reducing Japan's chronic public debt, and he approved the first of a two-stage increase in the consumption tax that took effect on April 1, 2014, under legislation passed before he assumed office. GDP growth decreased at an annualized rate of 6.8% in the second quarter of 2014 as a result of the sales tax increase,[38] and Abe must decide by the

---

[35] Abe, "Japan is Back."

[36] "Address by Prime Minister Shinzo Abe at the Sixty-Eighth Session of the General Assembly of the United Nations," Prime Minister of Japan and His Cabinet website, September 26, 2013, http://japan. kantei.go.jp/96_abe/statement/201309/26generaldebate_e.html.

[37] "Japan's Economy Grows at Fastest Rate in Three Years," Associated Press, May 15, 2014, http://www. nytimes.com/2014/05/16/business/international/japans-economy-grows-at-fastest-rate-in-3-years.html.

[38] Charles Riley, "Japan GDP Growth Collapses amid Sales Tax Shock," CNN, August 13, 2014, http:// money.cnn.com/2014/08/12/news/economy/japan-gdp.

end of 2014 whether to implement a second consumption tax increase of 8%–10% in 2015.

In the long run, the success of Abenomics will depend on the extent to which Abe is willing to expend political capital on structural reforms. His government has released two packages of reforms thus far—an expansive blueprint in June 2013 that was widely criticized for a dearth of details and a revised strategy a year later that contained more concrete initiatives, including measures to gradually reduce the corporate tax rate, increase female labor force participation and promote other labor market reforms, strengthen agricultural competitiveness, promote deregulation in designated special economic zones, and reform Japan's healthcare system.[39] Demography also poses a significant challenge, as the proportion of Japanese who are 65 or older is expected to reach 39% by 2050, necessitating measures to increase the participation of women in the labor force or introduce immigration reform to stem the decline of the population.[40] The other potential avenue for structural reform is Japan's participation in the Trans-Pacific Partnership (TPP) trade negotiations. Abe announced Japan's decision to formally enter this multilateral initiative in March 2013, declaring that enhancing Japan's competitiveness is in the national interest.[41] However, bilateral negotiations with the United States under the rubric of the TPP negotiations have been bogged down by market access issues and the politics of trade in both capitals. Such delays risk an opportunity to strengthen the economic pillar of the U.S.-Japan alliance and demonstrate joint leadership in setting the norms for trade liberalization and economic integration in the Asia-Pacific. Ultimately, domestic reforms and trade liberalization under the TPP will maximize the prospects for sustainable growth as a foundation for Japan's broader leadership ambitions.

Diplomacy

Abe's regional diplomatic agenda thus far has focused primarily on shoring up Japan's relationships with countries in ASEAN and exploring avenues for cooperation with other like-minded states in the Asia-Pacific. Abe visited Indonesia, Thailand, and Vietnam in January 2013, the first foreign

---

[39] Prime Minister of Japan and His Cabinet, *Japan is Back: Japan Revitalization Strategy* (Tokyo, June 14, 2013), http://www.kantei.go.jp/jp/singi/keizaisaisei/pdf/en_saikou_jpn_hon.pdf; and Prime Minister of Japan and His Cabinet, *Japan Revitalization Strategy: Japan's Challenge for the Future* (Tokyo, June 24, 2014), http://www.kantei.go.jp/jp/singi/keizaisaisei/pdf/honbunEN.pdf.

[40] Richard Jackson, "Japan's Demographic End Game," CSIS, Japan Chair Platform, November 21, 2013, http://csis.org/files/publication/131121_Jackson_JapansDemographicEndGame_JapanPlatform.pdf.

[41] "Press Conference by Prime Minister Shinzo Abe," Prime Minister of Japan and His Cabinet website, March 15, 2013, http://japan.kantei.go.jp/96_abe/statement/201303/15kaiken_e.html.

trip of his second term, and unveiled his "five new principles for Japanese diplomacy" that represent Japan's core foreign policy objectives in Southeast Asia: protecting freedom of thought, expression, and speech; establishing rules and norms for the maritime domain; promoting economic integration; fostering intercultural ties throughout the region; and promoting youth exchanges between Japan and Southeast Asian countries.[42] Abe has since hosted a Japan-ASEAN summit and visited all ten ASEAN member states. His efforts build on a solid foundation of economic diplomacy initiated by former prime minister Takeo Fukuda in 1977 (the Fukuda Doctrine) but add particular emphasis to maritime security and the rule of law in a subtle reference to Chinese assertiveness in the East and South China Seas.[43]

The Abe government has also moved to further economic and security partnerships with Australia and India. Japan signed a joint security declaration with Australia in 2007 identifying areas for cooperation, including counterterrorism, maritime and aviation security, and humanitarian assistance and disaster relief (HADR).[44] The two countries later signed an acquisition and cross-servicing agreement in 2010 that facilitates the reciprocal provision of supplies and services for activities such as exercises and joint training, and in 2012 they concluded an information-sharing agreement for the protection of classified information. In addition, Abe and Australian prime minister Tony Abbott signed an agreement on the transfer of defense equipment and technology in July 2014, and the two countries have initiated a marine hydrodynamics project, which reflects Australia's interest in Japanese submarine technology.[45] The two leaders also signed into force a bilateral economic partnership agreement, and both countries are parties to the TPP negotiations.

With respect to Japan's diplomacy toward India, the countries signed a joint security declaration in 2008 and have explored avenues for bilateral defense cooperation.[46] The Indian Navy and Japan Maritime SDF have

---

[42] Shinzo Abe, "The Bounty of the Open Seas: Five New Principles for Japanese Diplomacy" (address, Jakarta, January 18, 2013), http://www.mofa.go.jp/announce/pm/abe/abe_0118e.html.

[43] Association of Southeast Asian Nations, "Joint Statement of the ASEAN-Japan Commemorative Summit," December 14, 2013, http://www.mofa.go.jp/files/000022451.pdf.

[44] Shinzo Abe and John Howard, "Japan-Australia Joint Declaration on Security Cooperation," March 13, 2007, http://www.mofa.go.jp/region/asia-paci/australia/joint0703.html. For further discussion, see Michael J. Green and Nicholas Szechenyi, "U.S.-Japan Relations: Big Steps, Big Surprises," CSIS, Comparative Connections, January 2014.

[45] "Defence Minister David Johnston Hails Defense Science and Technology Accord with Japan," Australian Government Department of Defence, Press Release, July 8, 2014, http://www.minister. defence.gov.au/2014/07/08/minister-for-defence-defence-minister-david-johnston-hails-defence-science-and-technology-accord-with-japan/.

[46] Taro Aso and Manmohan Singh, "Joint Declaration on Security Cooperation between Japan and India," October 22, 2008, http://www.mofa.go.jp/region/asia-paci/india/pmv0810/joint_d.html.

conducted two bilateral defense exercises, and India has invited Japan to participate in the Malabar exercises with the United States three times, most recently in 2014. [47] On the economic front, the two countries signed an economic partnership agreement into force in 2011, and Japan continues to provide development aid. The latter is aimed primarily at next-generation infrastructure projects, such as building "smart cities," in support of what Abe has described as India's "bold and ambitious vision for accelerating inclusive development" under new prime minister Narendra Modi.[48] Abe visited India in January 2014 to further develop economic and security ties, and in September 2014 he reaffirmed the importance of this bilateral relationship during a summit with Modi, at which the two leaders issued a joint declaration outlining a strategic partnership between Asia's two largest democracies.[49] The declaration contained five agreements covering "defense exchanges, cooperation in clean energy, roads and highways, healthcare, and women."[50] With relations between Japan and India on the rise, the September summit demonstrated Japan's commitment to this emerging strategic partnership.

In addition to promoting closer ties with Australia and India, Abe has advocated for a quadrilateral dialogue that would include the United States, which is motivated ostensibly by a desire to address uncertainties associated with China's rise. His 2006–7 initiative did not survive because of concerns, primarily in Australia, about the potentially adverse impact on diplomatic relations with China, and at the time of writing the prospects for reviving the quadrilateral are uncertain. There is no question, however, that enhanced cooperation with Asia's maritime democracies remains a diplomatic priority for Abe in order to reaffirm a shared commitment to international rules and norms and shape Chinese behavior in a manner that favors regional stability.

National Defense Policy

Japanese defense policy has advanced considerably during Abe's second term in office. In 2013 the Diet approved legislation establishing Japan's first National Security Council, to be housed in the Prime Minister's Office, for the purpose of centralizing policy coordination and facilitating communication with the United States and other partners. Toward that end, the Abe

---

[47] Akhilesh Pillalamarri, "India, Japan, and the U.S. Hold Joint Naval Exercises," *Diplomat*, July 25, 2014, http://thediplomat.com/2014/07/india-japan-and-the-us-hold-joint-naval-exercises.

[48] "India to Get 35 Billion Dollars from Japan for Infrastructure Projects," Press Trust of India, September 1, 2014, http://www.newindianexpress.com/nation/India-to-Get-35-Billion-Dollars-From-Japan-for-Infrastructure-Projects/2014/09/01/article2409374.ece.

[49] Shinzo Abe and Narendra Modi, "Tokyo Declaration for Japan-India Special Strategic and Global Partnership," September 1, 2014, http://www.mofa.go.jp/files/000050532.pdf.

[50] "India to Get 35 Billion Dollars from Japan."

government pushed through a bill on the protection of classified information that was widely criticized as a retreat from transparency in government but deemed vital to furthering coordination with foreign governments. The Abe government also introduced Japan's first national security strategy, which outlined priorities for strengthening Japan's own security, the U.S.-Japan alliance, cooperation with other regional partners, and Japan's leadership globally.[51] The strategy dictates that as a "proactive contributor to peace" Japan would seek to achieve three core national security objectives: strengthening deterrence to reduce threats against Japan; improving the security environment of the Asia-Pacific region by strengthening the U.S.-Japan alliance and promoting cooperation with partners within and outside the region; and improving the global security environment and strengthening the international order based on universal values and norms. The document identifies a range of global and regional security challenges, such as the proliferation of weapons of mass destruction; international terrorism; the potential to deny access to the global commons, including the sea, space, and cyberspace; North Korea's nuclear weapons and missile programs; and the opaque nature of China's military buildup and attempts to change the status quo through coercion in the East and South China Seas and the airspace above. (The latter challenge was highlighted by China's unilateral establishment in November 2013 of an air defense identification zone over the East China Sea.)

The Abe cabinet also issued a new defense strategy. The document further developed the plans for the defense of Japan's southwest islands that were outlined under the rubric of "dynamic defense" in the previous NDPG of December 2010 and promoted the integration of Japan's SDF to build a more dynamic defense force, as well as encourage jointness and interoperability with U.S. forces. In addition, the new defense strategy identified priorities such as the development of amphibious capabilities; intelligence, surveillance, and reconnaissance (ISR); command, control, communications, and intelligence; ballistic missile defense; and space and cyber defense.[52] The NDPG was accompanied by the Medium Term Defense Program outlining procurement priorities, which included primarily air and naval assets, and a 5% increase in defense spending over the next five years.[53] The spending plan was designed

---

[51] Japan National Security Council and the Cabinet, *National Security Strategy* (Tokyo, December 17, 2013), http://www.cas.go.jp/jp/siryou/131217anzenhoshou/nss-e.pdf.

[52] Japan Ministry of Defense, *National Defense Program Guidelines for JFY 2014 and Beyond* (Tokyo, December 17, 2013), http://www.mod.go.jp/j/approach/agenda/guideline/2014/pdf/20131217_e2.pdf.

[53] Japan National Security Council and the Cabinet, "Medium Term Defense Program (FY2014–FY2018)," December 17, 2013, http://www.mod.go.jp/j/approach/agenda/guideline/2014/pdf/Defense_Program.pdf.

to enhance SDF capabilities to respond to attacks on remote islands, ballistic missile attacks, outer space and cyberspace threats, and large-scale disasters, as well to participate in international initiatives such as HADR efforts and UN peacekeeping operations. The Abe government also replaced long-standing restrictions on arms exports with a set of principles for the transfer of defense equipment and technology to promote defense industrial cooperation with the United States and other countries.[54]

Another significant development occurred in July 2014, when the Abe cabinet announced defense policy reforms based on a reinterpretation of Article 9 of the Japanese constitution that would allow the SDF to exercise the right of collective self-defense and come to the aid of allies under attack.[55] These measures resulted from a government review of the legal basis for security policy and were informed by recommendations submitted by an advisory panel in May 2014.[56] The decision builds on the interpretations of previous governments by stating that measures of self-defense are permitted under Article 9 when an armed attack against Japan occurs and no other means are available to repel the attack and ensure national security. The use of force, however, must be limited to the minimum extent necessary. Although Japan has an inherent right to collective self-defense under international law, legal specialists in the government have repeatedly concluded that exercising that right would violate the constitutional provision to use force to the minimum extent necessary. Following the recommendations of the advisory panel, the Abe cabinet reinterpreted Article 9 by arguing that measures of collective self-defense are also permitted when an attack on a country with a close relationship with Japan occurs and as a result threatens Japan's security. The details of this policy are subject to debate in the Diet, and the Abe government is expected to submit the requisite legislation in 2015.

The decision to reinterpret the constitution to allow the exercise of collective self-defense generated controversy and was met with public protests decrying a perceived departure from Japan's pacifist principles.[57] Abe's public approval rating dropped below 50% in some surveys immediately after the cabinet decision, and he acknowledged insufficient public understanding

---

[54] "The Three Principles on Transfer of Defense Equipment and Technology," Ministry of Foreign Affairs of Japan, Press Release, April 1, 2014, http://www.mofa.go.jp/press/release/press22e_000010.html.

[55] Prime Minister of Japan and His Cabinet, "Cabinet Decision on Development of Seamless Security Legislation to Ensure Japan's Survival and Protect Its People," July 1, 2014, http://japan.kantei.go.jp/96_abe/decisions/2014/__icsFiles/afieldfile/2014/07/03/anpohosei_eng.pdf.

[56] Advisory Panel on Reconstruction of the Legal Basis for Security (Japan), "Report of the Advisory Panel on Reconstruction of the Legal Basis for Security," May 15, 2014, http://www.kantei.go.jp/jp/singi/anzenhosyou2/dai7/houkoku_en.pdf.

[57] Andrew L. Oros, "Japan's Cabinet Seeks Changes to Its Peace Constitution—Issues New 'Interpretation' of Article Nine," East-West Center, Asia Pacific Bulletin, no. 270, July 1, 2014.

of the policy in media interviews.[58] A potential alternative to the current approach would be to engage the public on revising rather than reinterpreting Article 9, but that would require two-thirds support in both houses of the Diet and majority support in a public referendum. (The Abe government at one point floated the notion of first revising Article 96 of the constitution to require support by only a simple majority of both houses to revise the constitution but abandoned the proposal in the face of public opposition.) While reinterpreting Article 9 is consistent with previous attempts to refine security policy and is not unusual in that context,[59] it will nonetheless be important for Abe to explain the objectives, technical details, and implications fully to the public. Indeed, he has already begun to expand on the rationale for collective self-defense in commentaries and can be expected to further amplify his views in advance of parliamentary debate on this issue.[60] With the submission of the advisory panel report, the cabinet decision, and subsequent legislative procedures in the Diet, a transparent process has been established to thoroughly debate this proposed change in security policy and explain it to the Japanese public and the international community.

The U.S. government welcomed the Abe cabinet's decision on collective self-defense as a means of enhancing Japan's role in the U.S.-Japan alliance. Though the implications of the policy in operational terms are dependent on the outcome of the Diet debate in 2015, the decision provides context for a review of the guidelines for bilateral defense cooperation due at the end of 2014. Much of the commentary on collective self-defense in Japan has centered on the potential to expand the parameters for the use of force by the SDF, but U.S. officials have stressed the prospects for improved information sharing and coordination that can strengthen interoperability between the two militaries.[61] The cabinet decision should lead to looser restrictions on SDF "integration in the use of force" with the U.S. military, which would facilitate joint exercises and operational planning for future contingencies, as well as cooperation with other allies and partners.[62]

---

[58] Yuka Hayashi, "Abe's Constitutional Reform Push Slows," *Wall Street Journal*, July 8, 2014, http://online.wsj.com/articles/abe-slows-constitutional-reform-push-1404818542.

[59] Pyle, "The Sea Change in Japanese Foreign Policy."

[60] Shinzo Abe, "Enabling Japan to Further Contribute to the Peace and Stability of the Region and the International Community," Association of Japanese Institutes of Strategic Studies, Commentary, July 31, 2014, http://www2.jiia.or.jp/en_commentary/201407/31-1.html.

[61] Michael J. Green and Nicholas Szechenyi, "Japan Takes a Step Forward on Defense Policy Reform," CSIS, Critical Questions, July 2, 2014, http://csis.org/publication/japan-takes-step-forward-defense-policy-reform.

[62] Ibid.

Implications for U.S.-Japan Cooperation

Japan's emerging strategy dovetails nicely with the U.S. strategic rebalance to the Asia-Pacific, which is centered fundamentally on robust alliance relationships. The Abe agenda includes the core elements of U.S. strategy—bilateral alliances, coordination with like-minded partners, multilateral diplomacy, support for regional institutions, and economic engagement—articulated when the "pivot" or rebalance was first introduced.[63] The alignment of the two strategies was evident in a joint statement issued during President Barack Obama's state visit to Japan in April 2014.[64] The United States thus has in Japan an ally willing to assume a greater leadership role in areas that support U.S. interests.

Less certain is the pace at which the pillars of an emerging alliance agenda can be implemented. The United States has already endorsed Japan's decision on collective self-defense, but details will not emerge until 2015. Both governments have a strategic interest in concluding bilateral trade negotiations that will feed into the larger TPP framework and set high standards for regional trade, but the process could be prolonged by resistance to trade liberalization by agricultural interests in Japan and concerns in Tokyo over whether the Obama administration will expend the political capital necessary to obtain trade promotion authority from Congress (which limits members to an up-or-down vote on trade agreements). Despite great interest in Abenomics and the prospects for sustainable growth in Japan, detailed blueprints for structural reform have yet to emerge and could develop incrementally over a long-term time horizon.

There are also concerns in Japan about the sustainability of the U.S. rebalance amid constraints on defense spending, multiple crises in other regions that command urgent attention, and confusing signals—such as U.S. endorsement of a "new model of major power relations" with China in 2013—that generate anxiety about U.S. commitment to alliances.[65] Bilateral coordination at senior levels can best alleviate any concerns and reinforce a shared interest in maintaining a secure and prosperous Asia-Pacific region.

Japan's efforts to refine security policy bode well for advancing bilateral defense ties. The 2014 U.S. Department of Defense Quadrennial Defense Review

---

[63] Hillary Clinton, "America's Pacific Century," *Foreign Policy*, October 11, 2011, http://www.foreignpolicy.com/articles/2011/10/11/americas_pacific_century.

[64] "U.S.-Japan Joint Statement: The United States and Japan: Shaping the Future of the Asia-Pacific and Beyond," White House Office of the Press Secretary, Press Release, April 25, 2014, http://www.whitehouse.gov/the-press-office/2014/04/25/us-japan-joint-statement-united-states-and-japan-shaping-future-asia-pac.

[65] Susan E. Rice, "America's Future in Asia" (remarks at Georgetown University, Washington, D.C., November 20, 2013), http://www.whitehouse.gov/the-press-office/2013/11/21/remarks-prepared-delivery-national-security-advisor-susan-e-rice.

calls on allies to optimize contributions to their own security and combined activities, and U.S.-Japan defense cooperation is advancing toward that end.[66] In October 2013 the bilateral Security Consultative Committee called for a review of the guidelines for bilateral defense cooperation with a wide range of objectives. These include ensuring the capacity of the U.S.-Japan alliance to respond to an armed attack against Japan; expanding the scope of bilateral defense cooperation to include areas such as counterterrorism, counterpiracy, peacekeeping, capacity building, and HADR; and promoting cooperation with other regional partners in support of shared values and interests.[67] Priorities for bilateral security and defense cooperation were highlighted in that context and include ballistic missile defense cooperation, space and cyberspace, and joint ISR activities. Regional engagement to increase security capacity and develop patterns of cooperation with other like-minded countries also features prominently. Such engagement emphasizes maritime security, HADR, trilateral cooperation with Australia and South Korea, and joint efforts to strengthen regional institutions, including the East Asia Summit, the ASEAN Regional Forum, and the ASEAN Defence Ministers' Meeting-Plus.

Maritime security, regional capacity building, and HADR are examples of potential areas for enhanced bilateral defense cooperation. Japan's strategic imperative to defend the Nansei island chain creates opportunities to coordinate on maritime strategy and cooperate in areas such as ISR, antisubmarine warfare, and the development of amphibious capabilities.[68] Strengthening maritime security capacity in Southeast Asia is another priority for Japan, as evidenced by the country's increased participation in joint military exercises such as Cobra Gold and Balikatan and its interest in using official development assistance to improve the maritime domain awareness of countries in the South China Sea.[69] The collective experience of Japan and the United States in HADR, from the 2004 Indian Ocean tsunami to the Great East Japan Earthquake of 2011 and Typhoon Haiyan in 2013, also favors joint leadership consistent with alliance objectives to ensure peace and stability in the Asia-Pacific.[70]

---

[66] U.S. Department of Defense, *Quadrennial Defense Review 2014* (Washington, D.C., March 2014), vi, http://www.defense.gov/pubs/2014_Quadrennial_Defense_Review.pdf.

[67] U.S.-Japan Security Consultative Committee, "Joint Statement of the Security Consultative Committee," October 3, 2013.

[68] Tetsuo Kotani, "U.S.-Japan Allied Maritime Strategy: Balancing the Rise of Maritime China," CSIS, April 2014, http://csis.org/files/publication/140422_Kotani_USJapanAlliance.pdf.

[69] Ken Jimbo, "Japan and Southeast Asia: Three Pillars of a New Strategic Relationship," Tokyo Foundation, May 30, 2013, http://www.tokyofoundation.org/en/articles/2013/japan-and-southeast-asia.

[70] Andrew L. Oros and Weston S. Konishi, "Beyond Haiyan: Toward Greater U.S.-Japan Cooperation in HADR," NBR, NBR Analysis Brief, February 6, 2014, http://nbr.org/publications/analysis/pdf/brief/020614_Kinoshi-Oros_US-Japan_HADR.pdf.

The United States and Japan therefore stand ready to embark on an ambitious combined agenda to reinforce their bilateral bond and to further contribute to the security and stability of the region. While they face a number of difficult challenges and variables, the opportunities before the allies are similarly plentiful. Through deft management, the United States and Japan can better position the alliance to realize their shared goals in the Asia-Pacific.

Realizing Japan's Strategy: Key Variables and Recommendations

Japan's strategy to help shape the economic and security architecture of the Asia-Pacific region is promising but could depend on several factors. The first is the extent to which Japan pursues economic reforms, triggered either by domestic initiatives or international trade agreements such as the TPP, to generate economic power as a foundation for increasing its strategic and diplomatic weight. The significance of the economic revitalization project cannot be overstated, and much will hinge on how forcefully Abe and his successors confront the structural and political obstacles to enhanced competitiveness. Concluding bilateral trade negotiations linked to the TPP would facilitate joint leadership in setting high standards for regional economic integration and strengthen the economic pillar of the U.S.-Japan alliance, but doing so will require political will in both capitals. For the Abe government, this means liberalizing the agricultural sector, while the Obama administration could alleviate concerns in Japan about the staying power of any agreement by obtaining trade promotion authority from Congress. Both governments should also do more to rally support for the agreement domestically by reiterating the economic and strategic importance of the TPP to the alliance in terms of strengthening their respective economies and developing high standards for regional economic integration.

Ensuring an open, peaceful, and prosperous Asia-Pacific rests fundamentally on managing the rise of China. Recent developments in Japanese defense policy focused on remote island defense understandably reflect the need to strengthen deterrence in response to Chinese coercion in the maritime domain. Abe's approach to the rise of China centers on strengthening Japan's military capabilities (internal balancing) and developing ties with other states similarly threatened by China's assertiveness (external balancing).[71] Yet maintaining channels for dialogue and cooperation where

---

[71] Michael J. Green, "Japan is Back: Unbundling Abe's Grand Strategy," Lowy Institute for International Policy Analysis, December 17, 2013, http://www.lowyinstitute.org/publications/japan-back-unbundling-abes-grand-strategy.

possible also has a place in a strategy designed ultimately to shape China's choices in favor of the rules and norms that govern the international system. Balancing without containing—a necessity given the degree of economic interdependence with China—will require close coordination among Japan, the United States, and other partners in the region.[72] Japan and the United States have a shared interest in China's peaceful rise, and Japan has stated that it does not wish to stand against China and is working to welcome China as a responsible contributor to regional peace and stability.[73] In the near term, however, China's assertiveness in the East China Sea necessitates alliance cooperation to dissuade coercive behavior that is a source of tension and instability. The Obama administration can assure Japan about the U.S. commitment to its defense by continuing to explain that the Senkaku Islands are covered by the bilateral security treaty and declaring opposition to any unilateral attempts at changing the status quo through coercion. The two governments should also facilitate operational planning for gray-zone contingencies, a probable outcome of the bilateral defense guidelines review.

Japan's relationship with South Korea is critical in terms of facilitating cooperation with like-minded countries in the region. Historical sensitivities surrounding the issue of comfort women; Abe's December 2013 visit to the Yasukuni Shrine, where Japan's war dead, including Class A war criminals, are enshrined; and territorial disputes over the Liancourt Rocks (known as Takeshima in Japan and Dokdo in Korea) have nearly frozen diplomatic ties and created a foundation of distrust between the two countries.[74] Tense bilateral ties have not precluded trilateral coordination with the United States—a trilateral leaders' summit at the April 2014 Nuclear Security Summit, subsequent consultations on North Korea, and trilateral defense talks serve as examples—but the trend line is not positive. Although both South Korean president Park Geun-hye and Abe have expressed an interest in pursuing a future-oriented relationship, historical issues loom large in 2015, with the 70th anniversary of the end of World War II and the 65th anniversary of bilateral diplomatic ties between Japan and South Korea. Estrangement between Tokyo and Seoul could invite North Korea or China to drive a wedge between these two important U.S. allies in the region. The United States should not weigh

---

[72] Ashley J. Tellis, "Balancing without Containment: A U.S. Strategy for Confronting China's Rise," *Washington Quarterly* 36, no. 4, 109–24.

[73] Itsunori Onodera, "Japan's New Security and Defense Policy: An Enduring Partnership in the U.S.-Japan Alliance" (remarks at CSIS, Washington, D.C., July 11, 2014), http://csis.org/files/attachments/140711_TS_Itsunori_Onodera.pdf.

[74] A public opinion survey published jointly by Genron NPO and the East Asian Institute in July 2014 found that 54% of the Japanese public had an unfavorable impression of South Korea and 70% of South Koreans had the same impression of Japan. For the full survey, see Genron NPO, "The 2nd Joint Japan–South Korea Public Opinion Poll (2014) Analysis Report on Comparative Data," July 2014, http://www.genron-npo.net/en/pp/archives/5142.html.

in on sensitive historical issues but continue to engage in diplomacy that focuses the attention of its close allies on shared national security interests.[75] All three countries recognize that trilateral defense cooperation is critical to deterring the nuclear weapon and missile threat from North Korea. Trilateral dialogues can open lines of communication and establish priorities for defense cooperation, diplomacy, and economic engagement as a foundation for future Japan–South Korea ties.

The realignment of the U.S. military footprint on Okinawa will be an important factor in measuring the vitality of the U.S.-Japan alliance. The two governments remain committed to a plan first unveiled in 1996 to relocate the Marine Corps Air Station Futenma from a heavily populated neighborhood in central Okinawa to a less-developed area in the prefecture. Progress has been glacial, however, amid local opposition to the U.S. military presence. Reducing the burden on the local population while preserving the U.S. military's capacity to deter or respond to future threats and challenges in the region will help maintain public support for the U.S.-Japan alliance and facilitate new avenues of defense cooperation. The two governments should continue to pursue the existing realignment plan in the absence of more promising alternatives. However, it also will be important for the United States to maintain funding for the relocation of U.S. Marines from Okinawa to Guam as evidence of progress in reducing the burden of the U.S. military presence on Okinawa. Japan's financial support for infrastructure development on Guam, as outlined in bilateral agreements, is also a critical means toward that end.[76]

The success of Japan's emerging strategy will in large part be determined by domestic political winds. With no elections required before summer 2016, the current political environment favors stability. Moreover, some of the core elements of the Abe government's strategy—Japanese participation in the TPP negotiations, the dynamic defense concept focused on maritime security, and the relaxing of restrictions on arms exports—emerged under the previous government led by the DPJ. This suggests broad consensus on Japan's strategic trajectory, though animated debates on the modalities of trade liberalization or collective self-defense are to be expected. Further, there is no evidence to suggest that support for the U.S.-Japan alliance as the cornerstone of Japanese

---

[75] Richard L. Armitage and Joseph S. Nye, *The U.S.-Japan Alliance: Anchoring Stability in Asia* (Washington, D.C.: CSIS, 2012), 8, http://csis.org/files/publication/120810_Armitage_USJapanAlliance_Web.pdf.

[76] "Agreement between the Government of Japan and the Government of the United States of America Concerning the Implementation of the Relocation of III Marine Expeditionary Force Personnel and Their Dependents from Okinawa to Guam," February 17, 2009, http://www.mofa.go.jp/region/n-america/us/security/agree0902.pdf; and U.S.-Japan, Security Consultative Committee, "Joint Statement of the Security Consultative Committee," April 27, 2012, http://www.mofa.go.jp/region/n-america/us/security/scc/pdfs/joint_120427_en.pdf.

foreign policy is in jeopardy among either mainstream political leaders or the general public.

Indeed, the bilateral agenda spanning the diplomatic, economic, and security realms rests on a solid foundation of public support for the alliance in both countries. The latest public opinion survey on diplomacy issued by the Cabinet Office of Japan found that 83% of the Japanese public has feelings of friendship toward the United States and that the same percentage considered U.S.-Japan relations to be in good condition.[77] Another poll by Yomiuri/Gallup revealed that 55% of Americans think China will become more important politically for the United States than Japan, whereas only 40% chose Japan, but 65% said that Japan can be trusted, compared with 32% who said the same about China. In the same poll, respondents in the United States and Japan expressed great confidence in their militaries (91% and 78%, respectively), and the U.S. military and Japan SDF were the most trusted institutions in both countries.[78] This survey data shows that the alliance relationship is currently on very solid ground. Moreover, it suggests that despite the great uncertainty surrounding the future of the strategic environment in the Asia-Pacific, the alliance relationship between the United States and Japan will be an enduring feature.

The United States has a part to play in helping Japan realize an emerging economic and security strategy with the potential to further enhance the role of the U.S.-Japan alliance in preserving regional peace and prosperity. Concluding bilateral trade negotiations that will shape the outcome of the broader TPP negotiations would demonstrate the leadership credentials of the two countries in shaping the evolution of regional economic architecture. Strengthening deterrence to counter Chinese coercion in the maritime domain and facilitating close ties among the United States, Japan, and South Korea in the face of the North Korean missile and nuclear threat will help maintain a balance of power in the region. That objective is also served by maintaining the U.S. forward military presence on Okinawa while realigning force posture to reduce the burden on the local population and sustain the popular support for the alliance that is evident in both countries.

---

[77] "Gaiko ni kansuru Yoron Chosa" [Public Opinion Survey on Diplomacy], Cabinet Office of Japan website, November 25, 2013, http://survey.gov-online.go.jp/h25/h25-gaiko/2-1.html.

[78] Michael J. Green, "New Poll Shows Underlying Strength of U.S.-Japan Alliance, Need for Greater Confidence," CSIS, cogitASIA web log, December 16, 2013, http://cogitasia.com/new-poll-shows-underlying-strength-of-u-s-japan-alliance-need-for-greater-confidence.

Conclusion

Japan's emerging foreign policy strategy reflects a pragmatic approach to shaping the economic and security dynamics of the Asia-Pacific and is fundamentally in U.S. interests. The prospects for domestic economic reform and Japan's joint leadership with the United States on trans-Pacific trade liberalization can reinforce the economic pillar of the U.S.-Japan alliance as a critical instrument for regional prosperity. Likewise, regional diplomacy based on promoting rules and norms for economic and security architecture—both unilaterally and in multilateral institutions in coordination with the United States and other partners—furthers Japan's potential leadership role in shaping the regional order. Proposed investments in defense capabilities are also welcome amid U.S. fiscal pressures and strategic doctrine calling on allies to assume a greater role in their own defense and increase security cooperation with the United States. Japan's potential to exercise the right of collective self-defense, in particular, reflects a pragmatic response to changes in the regional security environment. If implemented, this policy could facilitate bilateral information sharing, exercises, and planning to address potential contingencies and promote cooperation with other allies and partners.

Successful implementation of this emerging strategy, however, is fundamentally contingent on political leadership to confront structural impediments to sustainable growth and project economic power as the foundation for advancing Japan's diplomatic and national security objectives. In addition, an apparent domestic political consensus on the general principles of Japan's new strategy does not guarantee uniform views on specific policy initiatives, which may evolve over time. Nonetheless, the alignment of strategic priorities across the economic, diplomatic, and security realms presents a unique opportunity for the U.S.-Japan alliance to not only maintain regional peace and stability but also spearhead a new order for the world's most dynamic region.

EXECUTIVE SUMMARY

This chapter examines the current status and future prospects of the alliance between the U.S. and the Republic of Korea (ROK).

MAIN ARGUMENT:
The U.S.-ROK relationship, once focused solely on deterrence of North Korean aggression, has developed into a comprehensive security alliance as a result of South Korea's economic, democratic, and military transformation. The alliance contributes to the foundation of the U.S. rebalance to Asia and has the potential to be an important component of this policy going forward. Factors likely to influence the future contributions of the alliance to broader U.S. strategies in Asia include the sustainability of a combined command structure, the continued interoperability of U.S. and ROK systems in areas such as missile defense, the deepening of defense cooperation to deter expanding North Korean asymmetric capabilities, strengthened relations between South Korea and other U.S. security partners, a sophisticated response to China's efforts to bound the alliance's applicability, and sustained support from both the U.S. and South Korean publics.

POLICY IMPLICATIONS:
- The U.S. and South Korea should maintain a combined approach to existing and emerging security challenges in order to ensure close security cooperation and interoperability and to increase efficiency in use of defense resources.

- With U.S. support, South Korea should prioritize defense diplomacy, development assistance, and other forms of security cooperation with other U.S. allies both as a viable hedge against China's rise and to reinforce regional and global security interests.

- The U.S. should attempt to frame the alliance in ways that reduce pressure on South Korea to choose between the U.S. and China and that expose China's efforts to force such a choice as detrimental to South Korea's security.

The U.S.-ROK Alliance
and the U.S. Rebalance to Asia

Scott Snyder

On January 12, 1950, Secretary of State Dean Acheson gave a speech at the National Press Club in which he excluded the Korean Peninsula from the defensive perimeter that the United States committed to defend against Communist expansion. Less than six months later, North Korean president Kim Il-sung invaded the Republic of Korea (ROK) and almost succeeded in forcibly unifying the Korean Peninsula under Communist rule, necessitating the mobilization of a costly U.S.-led international coalition under United Nations command to reverse Kim's aggression. To this day, Acheson's speech and the war that followed serve as cogent illustrations of South Korea's geostrategic value to U.S. security interests in the Asia-Pacific.[1]

Following the Korean War, the United States established security alliances with South Korea and Japan as the central components of its strategy to contain Communist expansion in Asia. While the primary objective of the U.S.-ROK alliance was to deter renewed aggression from North Korea, it also had the broader regional benefit (in combination with the U.S.-Japan alliance) of preserving the regional stability necessary for both Japan's and South Korea's remarkable economic development, enabling both countries to emerge as economic dynamos in their own right with close economic and political partnerships with the United States. Although the end of the

Scott Snyder is a Senior Fellow for Korea Studies and Director of the Program on U.S.-Korea Policy at the Council on Foreign Relations. He can be reached at <ssnyder@cfr.org>.

The author would like to acknowledge the research contributions to this chapter of Darcie Draudt, a research associate at the Council on Foreign Relations.

[1] Sheila Miyoshi Jager, *Brothers at War: The Unending Conflict in Korea* (New York: W.W. Norton, 2013), 59.

Cold War changed the Korean Peninsula from a flashpoint for potential global conflict to a flashpoint for conflict with primarily regional implications, the inter-Korean stalemate has persisted, as has the need for a U.S. force presence to support both peninsular and regional stability in Northeast Asia.

Since the end of the Cold War, the combination of enhanced South Korean capabilities and a broader vision for South Korea's security role in the international community has enabled the ROK both to contribute to its own defense and to work alongside the United States on global stability issues.[2] North Korea's provocative behavior and continued nuclear weapons development have necessitated and enabled ever-deeper levels of coordination between Washington and Seoul. As a result, the value of the U.S.-ROK alliance has increased in the context of the U.S. rebalance to Asia to become a foundational element (alongside the U.S.-Japan alliance) in the United States' security policy toward Asia. The alliance has also grown in importance as a result of its expanded capability to contribute to U.S. security interests beyond the peninsula over the past decade.

Amid these developments, a more complex threat environment has emerged. China's rising influence could put at risk the regional order and underlying conditions that have enabled South Korea's stability and economic success. Thus, the United States has a strategic interest in blocking Chinese efforts to expand its influence on the Korean Peninsula in ways that might be detrimental to South Korean or Japanese autonomy or that would threaten the credibility of the U.S. alliance framework for preserving South Korean and Japanese security. In addition, a weakening North Korea has invested in a wide range of asymmetric capabilities that threaten U.S. allies in the region and potentially the American homeland. The United States maintains a deep interest in blocking North Korea's ongoing challenge to the global nuclear nonproliferation regime through its pursuit of nuclear and missile-delivery capabilities. Finally, the United States has acknowledged that it shares with South Korea the objective of realizing Korean reunification in a fashion that extends human freedom on the peninsula to the North and establishes a democratic, economically modernized, and unified Korea in place of the current inter-Korean confrontation. Washington remains committed to working through its alliance with South Korea as well as international organizations toward such an end.

This chapter will review the evolution and development of the U.S.-ROK alliance against the backdrop of this increasingly complex and multidimensional threat environment. The first section will examine the

---

[2] For a wider discussion of South Korea's contributions to regional and global security operations, see Scott Snyder, ed., *Global Korea: South Korea's Contributions to International Security* (Washington, D.C.: Council on Foreign Relations, 2012).

security impact of South Korea's economic modernization, which has enabled the evolution of the U.S.-ROK alliance from a patron-client relationship in which the United States had an obligation to provide for the security of its South Korean client to a mutual relationship in which both the United States and South Korea are able to pursue common interests and objectives on the basis of shared contributions to international stability. The second and third sections will describe the evolution of South Korea's threat environment and the emergence of tensions between U.S. and South Korean priorities. Previously the environment was straightforward: North Korea was South Korea's primary security concern, and South Korea and the United States were aligned on peninsular and global threats. However, the situation has become more complex. South Korea has a growing stake in a secure global environment, while China's rise is challenging U.S. hegemony within East Asia. In short, South Korea's economic modernization and cultivation of enhanced security capabilities have provided Seoul with greater capabilities for self-defense. These enhanced capabilities have enabled South Korea to broaden its own thinking about security needs both on and beyond the peninsula. Following a discussion of public perceptions of the U.S.-ROK alliance, the chapter will conclude with a discussion of the strategic challenges facing South Korea and their implications for the alliance.

The Evolution of the U.S.-ROK Alliance: From Patron-Client to a Global Security Partnership

The origins of the U.S.-ROK security alliance lie clearly in the intersection of U.S. global strategy and South Korea's dire security need. These factors were relatively constant until the end of the Cold War. But since then, the evolution of the alliance has been influenced by the interaction of a variety of factors, including changes in U.S. global strategy, South Korea's growing capabilities, shifts in the respective orientations of political leadership in both countries, and other domestic factors. On balance, South Korea's economic modernization, its democratic transformation, and its interest in a stable global system led by the United States have resulted in a convergence of interests between the two sides. This not only has made South Korea an increasingly attractive and influential partner for the United States on the peninsula, but has also enabled the alliance to encompass cooperation on regional and global issues. This is a surprising and positive development given that the alliance has at many points in its history been characterized by tensions resulting from mutual distrust and from South Korean inability to independently provide for its own defense.

South Korea's Security Dependence on the United States

Following the Korean War, the South Korean security equation was simple. South Korea did not have the capacity to defend itself from renewed aggression from North Korea, so it had no choice but to rely on the United States as its main security guarantor.

Subsequently, the ROK's overarching security concern through the first three decades of statehood was the possibility of U.S. abandonment. The country's foreign policy universe was thus defined by its relationship with the United States. For this reason, President Richard Nixon's announcement in the late 1960s of the withdrawal of troops from South Korea despite a significant commitment of South Korean forces to support U.S.-led efforts in Vietnam was a shock to President Park Chung-hee.[3] Likewise, President Jimmy Carter's efforts in the 1970s to fulfill a campaign promise to withdraw all U.S. forces from South Korea on the basis of human rights concerns about Park Chung-hee's authoritarian rule posed another serious challenge to the alliance.[4] A further complication arose in the context of Chun Doo-hwan's coup d'état in May 1980, at a time when United States Forces Korea (USFK) was widely perceived by South Koreans as complicit with, if not supportive of, Chun's suppression of South Korea's pro-democracy movement. This event sowed the seeds for widespread Korean resentment of USFK, especially among young pro-democracy activists who later became known as the "386 generation" because they were in their thirties, attended university in the 1980s, and were born in the sixties.[5]

The Post–Cold War Decoupling of U.S. Global and South Korean Regional Priorities

Along with the end of the Cold War, South Korea's rapid economic development and its political transition to democracy revealed, and in some cases triggered, severe differences in U.S.-ROK relations that generated tension in the alliance. First, the conflict between North and South Korea was transformed from a flashpoint for potential confrontation between superpowers to yet another regional conflict alongside all the others that needed to be managed. The United States began to reduce its troop levels to take advantage of a prospective peace dividend from the end of the Cold

---

[3] Min Yong Lee, "The Vietnam War: South Korea's Search for National Security," in *The Park Chung Hee Era: The Transformation of South Korea*, ed. Byung-Kook Kim and Ezra F. Vogel (Cambridge: Harvard University Press, 2011), 421.

[4] Yong-Jick Kim, "The Security, Political, and Human Rights Conundrum, 1974–1979," in Kim and Vogel, *The Park Chung Hee Era*.

[5] Don Oberdorfer, *The Two Koreas: A Contemporary History* (Reading: Addison-Wesley Press, 1997).

War. Efforts to further reduce U.S. forces and transfer key roles and missions to South Korea in 1990 under the Strategic Framework for the Asian Pacific Rim, also known as the East Asia Strategy Initiative, faced opposition from the South Korean government.[6] U.S. moves to reduce forces despite the continuation of inter-Korean confrontation engendered South Korean fears of abandonment.[7] Efforts at reduction under the East Asia Strategy Initiative had come to a halt by 1992, however, as a result of rising tensions over North Korea's nuclear development program, thereby easing South Korean abandonment concerns.[8]

Second, as a result of normalization of relations with Russia and China, South Korea's dominant foreign policy framework came to be concerned not only with fostering the U.S.-ROK alliance but also with maintaining good relations with each of the peninsula's great-power neighbors (namely, China, Russia, and Japan). As a result, South Korea was no longer wholly dependent on the United States politically, despite the continuation of the U.S.-ROK alliance. This evolution in South Korea's conduct of foreign affairs raised public expectations for the country to pave its own way in global affairs while lessening its reliance on the United States.

At the same time, democratization allowed the emergence for the first time of an active public debate over the extent to which South Korean foreign policy should be tied solely to that of the United States. One such example can be seen in increased domestic pressure on Seoul to address local basing arrangements with the U.S. military. These arrangements were a long-standing source of friction at the local level. South Korea had become an industrialized economy, and U.S. bases that had once been located in the countryside were now surrounded by cities. Despite the dramatic changes in South Korea and the international environment, most of the changes in the U.S.-ROK alliance were gradual. In the late 1990s the Clinton administration negotiated initial steps in a land partnership plan under which USFK prepared to vacate and return bases and land to South Korea. The terms of the Status of Forces Agreement were also revised to provide greater Korean autonomy and responsibility in handling off-duty offenses by U.S. military personnel.[9]

---

[6] U.S. Department of Defense, *A Strategic Framework for the Asian Pacific Rim: Report to Congress: Looking Toward the 21st Century* (Washington, D.C., 1990).

[7] For a comprehensive assessment of U.S. military policy and operations in the Asia-Pacific in the early 1990s in the context of the restructuring of U.S. forces in the region, see James A. Winnefeld, Jonathan D. Pollack, Kevin N. Lewis, Lynn D. Pullen, John Y. Schrader, and Michael D. Swaine, *A New Strategy and Fewer Forces: The Pacific Dimension* (Santa Monica: RAND Corporation, 1992).

[8] For more on alliance adaptation following the Cold War, see Scott Snyder, "Strengthening the U.S.-ROK Alliance," Asia Foundation, February 2009, 4–5.

[9] Center for Strategic and International Studies (CSIS), "Path to an Agreement: The U.S.–Republic of Korea Status of Forces Agreement Revision Process," CSIS International Security Program, July 2001, http://csis.org/files/media/csis/pubs/pathtoanagreement.pdf.

But these measures lagged behind changes in the strategic environment, the structure of South Korean domestic politics, and the political economy between U.S. bases and the broader Korean population.

Democratic Shifts in Political Power and Their Impact on the U.S.-ROK Alliance

Coinciding with the end of the Cold War and the U.S. repositioning in the region, democratization required an evolution in the management of the U.S.-ROK alliance to accommodate new voices in South Korea's political process. For instance, as a result of its first democratic change in political power, South Korea changed its approach toward North Korea under President Kim Dae-jung's Sunshine Policy, most dramatically represented by the June 2000 inter-Korean summit. Kim Dae-jung's trip to Pyongyang and the first-ever meeting between North and South Korean leaders was a historic event that had powerful reverberations for South Korean perceptions of security on the Korean Peninsula. Upon returning from the North, Kim Dae-jung declared that his visit had forestalled the possibility of war.[10] Although this statement was widely regarded as overly optimistic, it both served to validate and facilitate a transformation of South Korean public perceptions of the North from an enemy to a brother in need.

A subtle implication of this transformation was a shift in public perceptions of the U.S. force presence on the peninsula from a necessity to a luxury or even a legacy of the past era of inter-Korean conflict.[11] The 2000 inter-Korean summit coincided with an uptick in public incidents involving USFK personnel that was partially reflective of this shift in perceptions among South Koreans. One high-profile incident was a traffic accident in 2002, when a U.S. army vehicle returning from exercises hit and killed two middle-school girls. The public response to the incident revealed an underlying feeling by South Koreans that USFK had not updated its perceptions of South Korea as a partner in line with the country's economic and political accomplishments in recent decades.[12] The fallout from this incident was merely a symptom of a much deeper problem, however: the U.S.-ROK alliance remained on autopilot, guided by Cold War premises, structures, and patterns of interaction, and no serious effort had been made to review and update the strategic framework

---

[10] "2 Koreas Pledge Nonaggression; Seoul to Activate Task Force," *Korea Herald*, June 16, 2000.

[11] Scott Snyder, "North Korean Nuclear Factor and Changing Asia-Pacific Alliances," in *Asia-Pacific Alliances in the 21st Century: Waxing or Waning?* ed. In-Taek Hyun, Kyudok Hong, and Sung-han Kim (Seoul: Oruem Publishing House, 2007), 221–39.

[12] Robert Marquand, "Anti-U.S. Voices Surge in Streets of a Major Asian Ally," *Christian Science Monitor*, December 16, 2002.

underlying the alliance in a manner similar to the process that led to the reaffirmation of the U.S.-Japan alliance.[13]

Kim Dae-jung's engagement policy toward North Korea received support from the Clinton administration, which in the mid-1990s had negotiated a politically controversial framework agreement with North Korea to freeze its nuclear development.[14] The election of George W. Bush in 2000 resulted in a much more skeptical U.S. policy toward North Korea, one that created tension with South Korea. Kim Dae-jung pressed for an early meeting with President Bush in March 2001 to explain his engagement policy toward the North and win continued U.S. support, but those efforts only engendered more political friction between the two allies.

The tension between the Bush administration and Korean progressives was further heightened following the election of Roh Moo-hyun in 2002. While wishing to maintain the alliance, the Roh administration entered office seeking greater independence and equality in its relations with the United States through the concept of "cooperative, self-reliant defense."[15] South Korea's quest for greater recognition in the relationship coincided with the United States' preoccupation with the war on terrorism in Afghanistan and Iraq. That preoccupation made the extent of South Korea's "out of area" contributions a primary focus of the alliance and revealed a perception gap between Washington and Seoul regarding how to respond to challengers in the international system, including North Korea. For example, President Bush was vocal on North Korea's human rights abuses, even insinuating that regime change is necessary, while President Roh reportedly asked him to keep such chastisements private, worrying that such a tactic would undermine progress on resolving the nuclear dispute.[16]

During this period, it sometimes appeared that the United States and South Korea had divergent interests that might result in the dissolution of the alliance. The United States reviewed and updated its global force posture to respond to new threats following September 11 as well as to the increasing need for troops to serve in Iraq and prosecute the global war on terrorism, further exacerbating the gap between the U.S. and South Korean policies toward North Korea.[17]

---

[13] Jonathan D. Pollack, Asia Eyes America: Regional Perspectives on U.S. Asia-Pacific Strategy in the Twenty-First Century (Newport: Naval War College Press, 2007), 140.

[14] Lally Weymouth, "Questioning the Korea Deal," Washington Post, January 25, 1995.

[15] Blue House (Republic of Korea), "National Security Strategy of the Republic of Korea," 2003. See also Scott Snyder, "A Comparison of U.S. and South Korean National Security Strategies: Implications for Alliance Coordination toward North Korea," in North Korea: 2005 and Beyond, ed. Philip W. Yun and Gi-Wook Shin (Stanford: Walter H. Shorenstein Asia-Pacific Research Center, 2006), 149–66.

[16] David E. Sanger, "U.S. Is Shaping Plan to Pressure North Koreans," New York Times, February 14, 2005.

[17] Stacie L. Pettyjohn, U.S. Global Defense Posture, 1783–2011 (Santa Monica: RAND Corporation, 2012), 92–96.

Despite such differences in the countries' priorities and approaches, there were areas of overlap in their underlying political interests across a broad range of issue-specific areas, including counterterrorism, a coordinated response to pandemics, and even a common desire to stabilize post-conflict situations so as to buttress global stability. The Roh administration continued to work with the Bush administration on sensitive alliance issues such as setting a timetable for replacing the ROK-U.S. Combined Forces Command (CFC) with separate command arrangements in which the United States would play a supporting role, dispatching troops to Iraq, and negotiating a potentially strategically significant bilateral free trade agreement.[18]

The Reconvergence of U.S.-ROK Strategic Interests and the Evolution of the Alliance

Lee Myung-bak's election as president in 2008 revived a more traditional South Korean policy approach in which the alliance with the United States played a central role. The day after his election in January 2008, Lee affirmed his intent to "restore the U.S.-ROK alliance based on the established friendship" as a primary anchor of South Korea's foreign policy.[19] This statement suggested that a decade of progressive rule had aimed at making South Korea more independent at the expense of its ties with the United States. During his first stop in the United States in April 2008, Lee declared that the "politicization of alliance relations will be behind us" and pledged that the alliance going forward should be based on the principles of "common values, trust, and peace."[20]

The 2009 U.S.-ROK Joint Vision Statement provided a framework by which to expand alliance cooperation beyond the Korean Peninsula and enable South Korea to contribute to new dimensions of international security. Many of these forms of cooperation are not new in the context of NATO or even the U.S. alliance with Japan, where security cooperation is also grounded in common democratic values.[21] However, they do represent a significant step forward in the U.S.-ROK alliance relationship, one that could

---

[18] Snyder, "Strengthening the U.S.-ROK Alliance," 9.

[19] "President Elect Vows Creative Diplomacy," *Korea Times*, December 19, 2007.

[20] Lee Myung-bak (address to the Korea Society 2008 Annual Dinner, New York, April 15, 2008), http://www.koreasociety.org/dmdocuments/20080415-LeeMyungBak-English.pdf. For more on the realignment of foreign policies of the United States and ROK, see Snyder, "Strengthening the U.S.-ROK Alliance," 9.

[21] "Joint Vision for the Alliance of the United States and the Republic of Korea," White House, June 16, 2009, http://www.whitehouse.gov/the_press_office/Joint-vision-for-the-alliance-of-the-United-States-of-America-and-the-Republic-of-Korea. See also Scott Snyder, "Expanding the U.S.-ROK Security Alliance," in *The U.S.–South Korea Alliance: Meeting New Security Challenges*, ed. Scott Snyder (Boulder: Lynne Rienner, 2012), 10–11.

enable the realization of untapped potential resulting from enhanced South Korean capabilities and aspirations to make a more sustained international contribution. In addition, a key lesson that can be drawn from comparisons with NATO and the U.S.-Japan alliance is that the U.S.-ROK alliance must maintain not only a strategic but also an operational rationale. Whereas a clear rationale supported the structural transition to the post–Cold War period in the case of NATO, the relative lack of one has impeded the evolution of the U.S.-Japan alliance.[22] Such lessons underscore the importance of an assessment of the prospects for operationalizing expanded cooperation on security issues off the peninsula in the context of a new strategic vision for the alliance, South Korea's growing international interests and capabilities, and U.S. efforts to upgrade its role in Asia and secure international stability together with like-minded partners.

Under conservative president Lee Myung-bak, South Korean foreign policy evolved further under the rubric of the catchphrase "global Korea."[23] Lee's foreign policy sought to raise South Korea's profile on the international stage by hosting international gatherings such as the G-20 and Nuclear Security Summit and by touting the country's role as a "middle power."[24] While North Korean provocations reminded South Koreans that peninsular stability is critical to prosperity, Lee pursued an internationalized response to these provocations that illustrated the evolution of South Korean foreign policy from one consumed by security on the peninsula to one that links peninsular security to global stability. This shift can also be seen in South Korea's nascent contributions to international security, reflecting both the country's economic success and its dependence on international trade.

A critical factor that has enabled South Korea to increase its defense contributions has been the systematic expansion of its military capacity to perform off-peninsula roles. For instance, the development of a blue water naval capability has enabled South Korea to participate in multilateral antipiracy operations.[25] Joint exercises with the United States in the face of the North Korean threat have also contributed to the maturation of the ROK military. Greater interoperability with U.S. systems provides a strong basis for South Korea to participate in international operations, such as post-conflict

---

[22] Michael Finnegan, "Benchmarking America's Military Alliances: NATO, Japan, and the Republic of Korea," Asia Foundation, February 2009, 20.

[23] Kim Yon-se, "Lee Pledges to Build a Global Korea," *Korea Times*, December 20, 2007, http://www.koreatimes.co.kr/www/news/nation/2007/12/116_15904.html.

[24] Kim Sung-han, "Global Governance and Middle Powers: South Korea's Role in the G20," Council on Foreign Relations, February 2013.

[25] Bruce Klingner, "Enhancing South Korean–U.S. Naval Capabilities Is Critical to American Interests," Heritage Foundation, Backgrounder, no. 2829, July 24, 2013, http://www.heritage.org/research/reports/2013/07/enhancing-south-koreanus-naval-capabilities-is-critical-to-american-interests.

stabilization in Iraq and Afghanistan. Moreover, South Korea's development of indigenous systems, such as tanks and air trainers, has enabled it to utilize defense exports as a tool in its efforts to strengthen political and security cooperation with new partners as well as to contribute to global peacekeeping operations under the United Nations.[26]

South Korea has continued to make steady contributions to peninsular and global security under the leadership of President Park Geun-hye. During her first visit abroad, she joined with President Barack Obama in reaffirming the U.S.-ROK Joint Vision Statement with a new vision statement on the occasion of the 60th anniversary of the U.S.-ROK alliance, signaling the continuity of her approach to the alliance with that of her predecessor.[27] Yet while reaffirming the U.S.-ROK alliance as a central pillar of South Korea's foreign policy, Park has proposed a further delay in the timetable agreed on during the Roh administration for adjusting operational control arrangements within the alliance. She has also attempted to strengthen South Korean capacity to respond to North Korea's development of asymmetric capabilities and grappled with the implications for the alliance of a deteriorating East Asian security environment. Each of these issues will be addressed in greater detail below.

The U.S.-ROK Alliance: Issues at Stake

Through the 2009 U.S.-ROK Joint Vision Statement and the 2013 U.S.-ROK Joint Declaration in Commemoration of the 60th Anniversary of the U.S.-ROK Alliance, the United States and South Korea have established a solid framework for advancing common interests through peninsular, regional, and global cooperation. Moreover, alliance coordination continues to evolve in the context of a complex threat environment that has been made more difficult by the development of North Korean asymmetric capabilities as well as new sources of instability in the regional security environment. While the U.S.-ROK alliance has been made stronger as a result of South Korea's acquisition of new capabilities that have enabled it to make contributions to international stability operations, whether these capabilities should be channeled through the alliance or should be reserved exclusively for South Korea's own self-defense has become an important consideration that is also related to the relative costs and contributions that each partner is expected

---

[26] Richard A. Bitzinger and Mikyoung Kim, "Why Do Small States Produce Arms? The Case of South Korea," *Korean Journal of Defense Analysis* 17, no. 2 (2005): 183–205.

[27] "Joint Declaration in Commemoration of the 60th Anniversary of the Alliance between the Republic of Korea and the United States of America," White House, May 7, 2013, http://www.whitehouse.gov/the-press-office/2013/05/07/joint-declaration-commemoration-60th-anniversary-alliance-between-republ.

to contribute toward the alliance. Put differently, the question is the extent to which the ROK should pursue an internal balancing strategy or channel its resources to support external balancing. The emergence of tension between the pursuit of self-defense and the use of new capabilities to bolster alliance objectives is common within alliances. But in the case of the U.S.-ROK alliance, this tension has manifested itself in two important debates that will shape the alliance's future.

The first debate is over the question of how and when to restructure operational control arrangements on the Korean Peninsula in ways that would provide South Korea with greater autonomy and responsibility in managing its own defense while reducing the U.S. profile and role in securing South Korea. Such an arrangement would replace the current arrangement, in which command responsibility during wartime is centered in the U.S.-ROK Combined Forces Command, which is led by a U.S. four-star general with a South Korean general as his deputy. Under this arrangement, the United States automatically takes the lead in providing for South Korea's defense in wartime with support provided by ROK forces. Under the new arrangement, a South Korean commander would take the lead in executing operations with support from U.S. assets dedicated to the defense of the peninsula, including U.S. air and intelligence resources.[28] The shift from the current to new arrangement has implications for the respective roles and missions of U.S. and ROK forces in the defense of South Korea.

The second debate involves the question of whether South Korea or the United States should acquire a mid-tier Theater High Altitude Area Defense (THAAD) capability in response to North Korea's growing missile capabilities. This debate is important both because THAAD acquisition would reinforce U.S.-ROK interoperability through enhanced capabilities and because China has opposed South Korea's acquisition of THAAD, despite North Korea's growing missile capabilities, out of concerns that such capabilities might also have uses beyond the Korean Peninsula.

These two debates have proceeded against the backdrop of a complex threat environment in which capabilities are being calibrated to address both the near-term development of the North Korean nuclear and missile programs and longer-term questions about the implications of China's rise for South Korean security and the U.S.-ROK alliance.

---

[28] Mark E. Manyin et al., "U.S.–South Korea Relations," Congressional Research Service, CRS Report for Congress, R41481, June 24, 2014, 17, http://fas.org/sgp/crs/row/R41481.pdf.

*The Significance and Implications of the Debate
over Wartime Operational Control*

One effect of South Korea's growing capabilities and confidence in contributing to its own self-defense was demonstrated in the mid-2000s when Roh Moo-hyun proposed that South Korea retain operational control over its armed forces during wartime rather than ROK forces supporting the Combined Forces Command that operates under the command and control of a U.S. general. Although in practice South Korea has exercised control over its own armed forces, the Combined Forces Command formally relinquished authority to exercise peacetime control over South Korean forces in 1992. When the Roh administration made its request to revise the command and control arrangement in the mid-2000s, Secretary of Defense Donald Rumsfeld reportedly responded that South Korea was "knocking on an open door," and negotiations to revise the wartime command relationship commenced through Security Policy Initiative talks.[29] These negotiations reached an agreement that envisioned South Korea taking a leading role in directing a joint operation against the North, with the United States committing to a continued supporting role in certain areas, including air and intelligence support. Under this arrangement, the Combined Forces Command would be dissolved and replaced by the new arrangements, including a U.S. Korea Command with the mission of supporting South Korea in taking a leading role in its own defense by October 31, 2012.

However, in the wake of North Korea's sinking of the *Cheonan* in March 2010, doubts arose regarding South Korea's readiness to take the lead in the envisioned command arrangements. In light of these concerns, Presidents Obama and Lee Myung-bak jointly announced in June 2010 that the implementation of revised command arrangements would be delayed until December 31, 2015.[30] North Korea's shelling of Yeonpyeong Island in November 2010 raised further questions about South Korea's readiness to assume the leading role in responding to North Korean provocations and whether North Korea might misinterpret the transition in the U.S.-ROK command structure as a sign of weakness or as a prelude to U.S. withdrawal of forces from the Korean Peninsula. Yet another factor that encouraged Washington and Seoul to reconsider the timing of the transition was North Korea's continuing development of its nuclear weapons program.

After coming into office in February 2013, the Park Geun-hye administration subjected the revised timetable to further review and decided

---

[29] "U.S. Defence Chief to Visit South Korea for Security Talks," Yonhap News Agency, November 4, 2007.

[30] "Remarks by President Obama and President Lee Myung-Bak of the Republic of Korea after Bilateral Meeting," White House, June 26, 2010, http://www.whitehouse.gov/the-press-office/remarks-president-obama-and-president-lee-myung-bak-republic-korea-after-bilateral-.

to seek a further delay in the timing of the implementation of revised command and control arrangements from the target date of December 31, 2015. This request for delay appears to have been tied to continuing doubts about the advisability of going forward with new arrangements in the context of North Korea's ongoing expansion of its nuclear weapons program. In October 2014, the Obama administration agreed to delay the timing for implementation of revised command arrangements to a future date.[31]

With the passage of time since the negotiation of the original agreement on revised U.S.-ROK command and control arrangements in the mid-2000s and in light of both the revitalization of the alliance and the new challenges North Korea has posed through its asymmetric approach to combined U.S.-ROK deterrence at both the low and high ends of the spectrum, the United States and South Korea have gradually re-evaluated how best to implement a revised command and control arrangement. Both allies appear to have set aside the concept of replacing the Combined Forces Command with the separate but parallel command structures that were envisioned under the Roh administration as a means to demonstrate publicly that South Korea retained full sovereignty over its armed forces. The joint Strategic Alliance 2015 strategy, adopted at a historic joint meeting of U.S. and South Korean defense and foreign ministers in 2012, envisaged that the South Korean Joint Chiefs of Staff would lead warfighting with support from a U.S. Korea Command rather than the Combined Forces Command.[32] But as a result of North Korea's recent provocations, both sides have returned to a concept that envisions the continuation of a combined command component through which both sides simultaneously report to their respective national authorities.[33] The maintenance of a combined warfighting capability with commands fused together would preserve coherence and efficiency in undertaking a combat operation; at the same time, it is politically impossible to imagine that either the United States or South Korea would undertake a military operation in the absence of an agreement to do so by the national command authorities in both countries.

These twists and turns in the debate over revised wartime operational control arrangements illustrate the tensions between South Korea's desire for greater autonomy and continuing dependence on the alliance to deter North Korean aggression. They also illustrate the necessity of coordinating a revised

---

[31] "Joint Fact Sheet: The United States–Republic of Korea Alliance: A Global Partnership," White House, April 25, 2014, http://www.whitehouse.gov/the-press-office/2014/04/25/joint-fact-sheet-united-states-republic-korea-alliance-global-partnershi.

[32] "Fact Sheet on the U.S.-ROK Alliance," U.S. Department of Defense, October 13, 2011, http://www.defense.gov/pubs/pdfs/KoreaStateVisitFactSheetforNSS(JSJ5input)_F9E9.pdf.

[33] Jun Ji-hye, "Joint Korea-U.S. Army Unit to Be Launched," Korea Times, September 4, 2014, http://www.koreatimesus.com/joint-u-s-south-korea-army-division-to-be-launched.

understanding of roles, missions, and accompanying mechanisms for ensuring close coordination in tandem with the transition to new arrangements. The evolution of the debate reflects the extent to which both the United States and South Korea have recognized the value of a combined military approach for dealing with an increasingly complex regional threat environment.

As the two allies have coordinated closely on the structure of operational control arrangements, they have also enhanced coordination through the addition of two new mechanisms for consultation on policy issues. First, the Korea-U.S. Integrated Defense Dialogue was established as a senior-level policy consultation co-chaired by the deputy minister for policy in the ROK Ministry of National Defense and the undersecretary for policy in the U.S. Office of the Secretary of Defense in order to coordinate alliance issues and directions for future security cooperation.[34] This dialogue operates alongside the Extended Deterrence Policy Committee, which was established in 2010 to discuss how the United States plans to execute its capability to defend and deter North Korea's nuclear capabilities.[35]

The Significance and Implications of South Korea's Missile Defense Debate

A second debate over the introduction of missile defense capabilities highlights tensions between South Korean desires to develop indigenous capabilities and the need for interoperability within the U.S. alliance framework. This debate reveals the complexity of a threat environment that includes both North Korean efforts to develop longer-range missiles and China's long-standing opposition to South Korea's participation in higher-tier defense systems that are necessary to defend against North Korea's expanded missile threat but that also could be used as a defense against Chinese missile capabilities. However, China's objections to the ROK's involvement in the U.S.-Japan missile defense project have been weakened considerably by North Korea's development of new capabilities.[36]

There are two components to the South Korean debate over missile defense. The first is related to the adequacy of South Korea's own indigenous response to North Korea's nuclear and missile threats. South Korean efforts have focused on the development of an indigenous missile defense

---

[34] "Joint Statement of the Korea-U.S. Integrated Defense Dialogue," U.S. Department of Defense, February 22, 2013, http://www.defense.gov/releases/release.aspx?releaseid=15831.

[35] Ministry of Defense (ROK), *2012 Defense White Paper* (Seoul, 2012), 75–76.

[36] "U.S. Missile Defense on Korean Soil Not Related to China: Seoul," Yonhap News Agency, July 21, 2014.

capability known as Korean Air and Missile Defense[37] and on planning for a preemptive strike capability, referred to as a "kill chain" system, that could be deployed in the event that South Korea detects North Korean preparations to use nuclear weapons.[38] South Korea's current capabilities consist of a ground-based early-detection Green Pine radar system, sea-based KDX-III radars on Aegis ships, and PAC-2 or Cheongung-2 missiles, with plans to upgrade to PAC-3 by 2016. However, questions remain about whether the current system is adequate to defend South Korea against incoming North Korean missiles. North Korea has recently made overtures toward developing battlefield or tactical weapons to be fitted on Scud missiles that can strike targets in South Korea.[39] The ROK would understandably like to promote the indigenous development of its own missile defense system, but the easiest pathways for development of an adequate system require U.S. support and equipment in critical areas.[40]

Second, South Korea has been reticent to integrate its low-level missile defense efforts with the U.S. Japan combined mid- and long-range missile defense systems that have already been deployed, primarily out of concern over alienating China. A spokesperson from China's Ministry of Foreign Affairs has stated that "the deployment of antimissile systems in this region will not help maintain stability and strategic balance in this region."[41] But now that North Korea is testing missiles with ranges that outstrip South Korea's indigenous capabilities, there is greater pressure to consider deployment of THAAD, even as President Park Geun-hye has made an improved relationship with China a centerpiece of her foreign policy. THAAD could be deployed either by USFK to protect U.S. bases or as part of a combined alliance approach to the broader defense of South Korea against the North Korean missile threat. As a result, at the time of writing in summer 2014 the terms of this second debate appear to be shifting as the Park government re-evaluates its options.

---

[37] Karen Montague, "A Review of South Korean Missile Defense Programs," George C. Marshall Institute, March 2014, http://marshall.org/wp-content/uploads/2014/03/South-Korean-BMD-Mar-14.pdf.

[38] "S. Korea Sets Out 'Active Deterrence' against N. Korea's Nuke Threats," Yonhap News Agency, April 1, 2013.

[39] Patrick M. Cronin, "If Deterrence Fails: Rethinking Conflict on the Korean Peninsula," Center for a New American Security, March 2014, 10, http://www.cnas.org/sites/default/files/publications-pdf/CNAS_IfDeterrenceFails_report_Cronin.pdf.

[40] Patrick M. Cronin and Moon-young Kim Jun, "A Window of Vulnerability: Rethinking the Defense of the Korean Peninsula" (presented at Council on U.S.-Korean Security Studies conference, Columbia University, New York, August 20, 2014).

[41] Te-Ping Chen and Alastair Gale, "China Warns on Proposed New Missile Defense System for Seoul," *Wall Street Journal*, May 29, 2014.

The Impact of North Korean Provocations on
U.S.-ROK Alliance Capabilities

These debates are occurring in the context of an evolving threat from North Korea. Recent provocations, including the sinking of the *Cheonan* and the shelling of Yeonpyeong Island in 2010, have induced an intensive effort within the U.S.-ROK alliance to strengthen coordination in anticipation of future North Korean aggression that may be designed to take tactical and political advantage of the alliance without escalating conflict into a full-scale war. Alongside the ROK's domestic review of its policies for responding to North Korean provocations, the United States and South Korea have conducted an intensive series of discussions on how to respond to North Korean provocations. This dialogue reviewed the process of consultations that would occur between USFK and the ROK Ministry of National Defense to handle future North Korean "gray zone" provocations that might require a military response without precipitating a potential military escalation of a crisis. The result was the adoption in March 2013 of a new joint counter-provocation plan, which is designed to enhance the capability of the United States and ROK to effectively respond to future low-level military provocations from North Korea.[42]

The other component of North Korea's asymmetric capabilities that has necessitated closer coordination within the alliance is Pyongyang's ongoing commitment to nuclear weapons development. To deal with this threat, the 2009 U.S.-ROK Joint Vision Statement explicitly reiterates the U.S. commitment to extended deterrence against North Korea's nuclear weapons capabilities. In addition, the Extended Deterrence Policy Committee, discussed above, is an ongoing component of regular alliance consultations to provide South Korea with assurances regarding U.S. extended deterrence commitments to South Korea. The dialogue discusses in detail how the United States would fulfill its commitment to South Korea's defense in the event that North Korea were to use nuclear weapons.[43] North Korea's nuclear capabilities have also required revisions of joint U.S.-ROK war planning to take into account scenarios involving North Korea's use of nuclear weapons in the event of renewed hostilities on the Korean Peninsula.

North Korea's successive nuclear tests have prompted a more active debate in South Korea on measures available to counter its vulnerability to North Korean brinkmanship. These debates have played into Washington's efforts

---

[42] Choe Sang-hun, "South Korea and U.S. Make Plans for Defense," *New York Times*, March 25, 2013, http://www.nytimes.com/2013/03/26/world/asia/us-and-south-korea-sign-plan-to-counter-north.html.

[43] Cheon Seong Whun, "The Significance of Forming a ROK-U.S. Extended Deterrence Policy Committee," Korea Institute for National Unification, Online Series, November 2, 2010, https://www.kinu.or.kr/upload/neoboard/DATA01/co10-39(E)1.pdf.

following each nuclear test to reassure Seoul regarding the credibility of U.S. extended deterrence commitments to South Korea. The South Korean debate over whether the ROK should take steps to acquire nuclear weapons has revolved around three main schools of thought. First, a small but growing group of conservative nationalists has argued that South Korea must match North Korea by acquiring its own nuclear capability.[44] Second, Chung Mong-joon, a long-time member of the National Assembly, has led calls for the reintroduction of U.S. tactical nuclear weapons to the peninsula to deter North Korea's nuclear capabilities.[45] Third, the majority of South Koreans still hold that the economic costs of defying the Nuclear Non-Proliferation Treaty and pursuing nuclear weapons would far outweigh the benefits of acquiring a nuclear capability and prefer to place their faith in U.S. extended nuclear deterrence commitments as being sufficient to meet South Korea's defense needs.

The U.S.-ROK Alliance and the Regional Environment

The U.S. rebalance toward Asia shows how the United States' regional strategy and policies toward Asia are important contextual factors that increasingly may influence the development of the U.S.-ROK alliance, beyond the management of the specific operational issues in the alliance or the deterrence of North Korea.[46] Aspects of this policy may serve either as a source of opportunity or constraint on the development of the U.S.-ROK alliance. On the one hand, South Koreans have largely welcomed the renewed attention to Asia signified by the Obama administration's rebalancing strategy, at least to the extent that U.S. prioritization of Asia in general terms supports stability and prosperity in the region. President Park stated her clear support for the rebalance in a joint press conference with President Obama during his visit to Seoul in April 2014.[47] On the other hand, as the rebalancing strategy unfolds, issues such as the relative importance of the North Korean threat and the right balance between cooperation with China and hedging against the negative effects of China's rise could produce different priorities in the United States and South Korea.

---

[44] "Interview with Ambassador Park: We Should Withdraw from NPT and Build Own Nuclear Arsenal," Chogabje.com, March 12, 2007, https://www.chogabje.com/board/view.asp?C_IDX=17092&C_CC=BB.

[45] "Rep. Chung Mong-joon Argues for Reintroduction of Tactical Nuclear Weapons," YTN, June 25, 2013, http://www.ytn.co.kr/_ln/0104_201306250533180145.

[46] This section draws from material covered in Scott A. Snyder, "U.S. Policy toward the Korean Peninsula: Accomplishments and Future Challenges," *Kokusaimondai*, no. 614, September 2012, http://www2.jiia.or.jp/en/pdf/publication/2012-09_003-kokusaimondai.pdf.

[47] "Press Conference with President Obama and President Park of the Republic of Korea," White House, April 25, 2014, http://www.whitehouse.gov/the-press-office/2014/04/25/press-conference-president-obama-and-president-park-republic-korea.

The first area in which the two countries' priorities could diverge as a result of the rebalancing strategy is related to the United States' emphasis on a broader geographic distribution of its forces, which might hypothetically draw U.S. attention and resources in the direction of Southeast Asia and the Indian Ocean at the expense of South Korea.[48] The broadening of the scope of U.S. operations and policy to cover the whole of the Asia-Pacific rather than a more geographically limited prioritization of Northeast Asia could create new stresses on the U.S.-ROK alliance, especially when combined with U.S. budget constraints. South Korean defense specialists have already expressed concerns that the United States will seek to extract greater financial support from South Korea to pay for costs related to the U.S. presence on the peninsula.[49]

Second, a broader U.S. strategy that encourages horizontal cooperation among alliance partners has run into some initial roadblocks as a result of South Korean reluctance to establish an agreement for intelligence sharing and pursue closer security cooperation with Japan, a country that would be called on to support U.S.-ROK military operations in the event of a conflict with North Korea. U.S. interests in strengthening the combined defense posture toward North Korea include promoting high levels of cooperation with South Korea but also with Japan on many rear-area support issues. More effective Japanese involvement in information sharing and logistical support for the United States and South Korea during a crisis would require that South Korea and Japan are able to cooperate with each other. The United States has made its need for and support of such cooperation clear through efforts to promote greater trilateral coordination, including through maritime exercises on humanitarian assistance and disaster relief. The United States has also encouraged South Korean involvement in U.S. and Japanese joint research on and implementation of advanced missile defense technologies.

In addition to U.S. pressure on South Korea to strengthen horizontal relationships with Japan, Washington may seek to work together with Seoul to enhance South Korea's role in providing security in the region based on its increasing capabilities. Thus far, U.S.-ROK off-peninsula cooperation has primarily supported global stability and has occurred outside the Asia-Pacific region. But there may also be possibilities to enhance the nontraditional and functional roles of the U.S.-ROK within East Asia as well—for instance, in maritime security cooperation.

---

[48] Robert G. Sutter et al., "Balancing Acts: The U.S. Rebalance and Asia-Pacific Stability," Sigur Center for Asian Studies, George Washington University, August 2013, http://www2.gwu.edu/~sigur/assets/docs/BalancingActs_Compiled1.pdf.

[49] Jun Ji-hye, "ROK, U.S's Defense Cost Sharing Pact Passed," *Korea Times*, April 15, 2014, http://www.koreatimes.co.kr/www/news/nation/2014/04/116_155431.html.

The U.S. Rebalance and South Korea's Management of Relations with China

Park Geun-hye's strong rhetorical support for the U.S. rebalancing policy reveals that her China engagement strategy is predicated on the existence of a strong U.S.-ROK alliance. But this positive-sum view of the relationship between the U.S.-ROK security alliance and a stronger Sino–South Korean relationship comes into conflict with Chinese perceptions that the U.S. rebalance may be aimed at containing China.[50] To the extent that Beijing is concerned that the U.S.-ROK alliance may one day become focused on China rather than North Korea, China will seek to persuade South Korea to marginalize the importance of the alliance or even to abandon the alliance with the United States. Thus, China has sought ways to limit the scope of the alliance with the United States and potentially to highlight costs South Korea may incur as a result of continuing the alliance. Chinese analysts have already stated that they are carefully examining the U.S.-ROK alliance because they do not want it to have a broader application beyond the mission of deterring North Korea. One example of this desire to constrain the scope of the U.S.-ROK alliance within the region was China's objection in late 2013 to South Korean exports of military equipment to the Philippines. China is likely to continue to criticize South Korean defense cooperation in the region with other U.S. allies in ways that might expand the applications of the U.S.-ROK alliance to missions within the broader Asia-Pacific region.

Such efforts to weaken and circumscribe the scope of the alliance by containing the application of U.S.-ROK joint cooperation to the Korean Peninsula pose a challenge to South Korea. Although the Park administration has tried to improve the tone and substance of China–South Korea relations, it has refused to do so at the expense of the U.S.-ROK alliance.[51] The task of improving relations is enormously difficult given the fact that China's views of its relationship with South Korea often seem to be mediated by China's views of its respective relationships with North Korea and the United States, in addition to its perception of the nature and state of inter-Korean relations. For relations to improve, China will have to perceive a direct strategic benefit from its relationship with South Korea, even as the latter continues to value its security relationship with the United States.

At this stage, there is little for the United States to be concerned about in Park's efforts to improve South Korea's relationship with China, especially

---

[50] Joseph A. Bosco, "Washington and Beijing Need Straight Talk on Containment," Pacific Forum CSIS, PacNet, February 12, 2012, http://csis.org/files/publication/Pac1212A.pdf.

[51] "Balancing Act: President Xi Goes to South Korea as China Looks to Increase Regional Clout," *Economist*, July 5, 2014, http://www.economist.com/news/china/21606320-president-xi-goes-south-korea-china-looks-increase-regional-clout-balancing-act.

since the strategic stakes for South Korea in getting its relationship with China right are much higher than the likely costs to the United States of any South Korean missteps. Yet over the long term, there is concern in some circles that Seoul's pursuit of a better relationship with Beijing—fueled in part by a shared distrust of Japan—might have the effect of weakening the U.S.-ROK alliance. Another concern is that South Korea's relatively small size and high dependency on China could make it vulnerable to Chinese pressure to limit the scope of Korean coordination with the United States. As discussed below, Korean reunification could be a game changer for the future of Korea's geopolitical preferences and orientation between China and the United States.

The Goal of Korean Reunification

The United States and South Korea stated a clear vision for Korean reunification in the June 2009 U.S.-ROK Joint Vision Statement, leading to a single democratic, market-based, unified Korean state that presumably would maintain alliance ties based on common values with the United States. For both countries, it is easy to agree to such an end state but potentially much more difficult to achieve a consensus on the process and division of labor necessary to achieve this goal. Even within South Korea, the debate over the desirability of reunification is colored by a generation gap between older Koreans who desire reunification regardless of cost and a younger generation that has grown increasingly wary of the impact of reunification costs on their potential tax burden and quality of life. President Park Geun-hye's description in her January 2014 New Year's press conference as a "jackpot" or "bonanza" was widely perceived to be directed at such sentiment.

The U.S.-ROK shared vision regarding the preferred end state of a reunified Korea is an area where U.S. and South Korean policies toward reunification might come into direct conflict with Chinese policy preferences regarding the Korean Peninsula. China's primary interest on the peninsula has been to support stability by shoring up a comprehensive relationship with North Korea. To the extent that China sees the Korean Peninsula in geostrategic terms as an object of rivalry with the United States, China's objective of promoting stability on the peninsula ultimately comes into conflict with the U.S.-ROK objective of achieving Korean reunification.

At the same time, broader regional stability in the Asia-Pacific is increasingly dependent on Sino-U.S. cooperation. Although conflict between U.S. policies toward South Korea and China is not inevitable, how the United States prioritizes the objective of Korean reunification in its respective policies toward South Korea and China will influence the scope, aspirations, and nature of U.S.-ROK cooperation within the alliance. While the United States must avoid an approach to Korean reunification that unnecessarily provokes conflict with China, the scope of U.S.-ROK alliance cooperation should not neglect the fact that both sides have identified unification essentially on South Korean terms as a main objective of the alliance. South Korean policymakers realize that Korean reunification is unlikely to be attained without regional cooperation, including with China. But they also realize that South Korea will have little leverage to influence China's stance toward Korean reunification outside the context of strong policy coordination with the United States.

Heightened tension surrounding North Korea has provided a moment of opportunity for the United States to press China for greater cooperation vis-à-vis North Korea, especially given that North Korean provocations are adversely affecting China's security environment and are detracting from the regional stability necessary for continued economic growth. But the United States also faces a paradox in its efforts to induce stronger cooperation from the Xi Jinping administration: to the extent that the United States takes advantage of North Korean provocations to press for increases in missile defense or stronger Chinese cooperation with the United States at a perceived cost to North Korean stability, Chinese leaders are reminded of their own geostrategic equities on the Korean Peninsula vis-à-vis the United States and distracted from focusing on North Korea as the original instigator and source of instability.

On the other hand, South Korea's perceived need for Chinese cooperation in order to achieve Korean reunification may provide the biggest temptation for South Korea to make compromises with China that could limit or damage the effectiveness of the U.S.-ROK alliance. In particular, the need for cooperation with China may inhibit South Korean cooperation with other U.S. allies such as Japan. South Korean progressives, for example, have often cited the emergence of a U.S.-Japan-ROK security triangle as a development that could result in a "second cold war."

Public Perceptions of the U.S.-ROK Alliance

The broadening and deepening of U.S.-ROK alliance cooperation has received increasing levels of South Korean public support over the course of the past decade. An annual global poll conducted by the Pew Research Global Attitudes Project shows a steady increase in favorable South Korean views of the United States from 46% in 2003 to 82% in 2014.[52] What accounts for the dramatic improvement in South Korean attitudes toward the United

---

[52] Pew Research Center, "South Korea: Opinion of the United States," Global Attitudes Project, Global Indicators Database, available at http://www.pewglobal.org/database/?indicator=1&country=116.

States, and to what extent is such support for the alliance sustainable? A variety of contextual factors help explain the recovery of South Korean perceptions of the United States. First, negative South Korean perceptions of U.S. policy have ameliorated as it has become clear that the United States has been and is currently a contributor to stability rather than a source of increased tensions on the Korean Peninsula. As North Korea has played the role of provocateur, the salience of the alliance as a deterrent against such aggression has increased.

Second, the United States has made extensive efforts to show respect for South Korea's achievements and to treat the country as a valued partner not only on the peninsula but also on the world stage. The Lee Myung-bak administration's emphasis on an alliance for peace and willingness to comprehensively cooperate with the United States on regional and global security issues through the 2009 U.S.-ROK Joint Vision Statement established a framework for the expansion of the alliance and positively influenced American perceptions of South Korea. In a 2010 joint press conference with Lee Myung-bak on the sidelines of the group of eight (G-8) meeting in Toronto, President Obama referred to the U.S.-ROK alliance as a linchpin of stability in the Asia-Pacific.[53]

Third, North Korea's aggression has reinforced the main purposes of the alliance and provided an occasion for extraordinarily close policy coordination to address both the security and political aspects of the response to North Korea. South Korean attitudes toward the North hardened following the *Cheonan* and Yeonpyeong incidents. According to the East Asia Institute's analysis of South Korean public opinion, an effect of the Yeonpyeong artillery shelling is that "the military option, which was unthinkable in the past, is now seriously considered as a reasonable response by the majority of the public."[54]

Fourth, South Korean support for the alliance with the United States has correlated with growing concern about the impact of China's rise on South Korea's security environment. In many respects, this development reinforces the primary rationale for a strong relationship with the United States: the United States is a powerful external balancer that provides security for South Korea. China opposes the expansion of this rationale for the U.S.-ROK alliance precisely because its rise would likely become the main threat that would propel alliance cooperation. A 2014 Asan Institute poll found that, in contrast with the relatively rosy South Korean view of China that had existed in the mid-2000s, almost two-thirds of South

---

[53] "Remarks by President Obama and President Lee Myung-Bak."

[54] Nae-young Lee and Han-wool Jeong, "Ambivalence toward North Korea: South Korean Public Perceptions Following the Attack on Yeonpyeong Island," East Asia Institute, Issue Briefing, January 17, 2011, 6.

Koreans now harbor apprehensions regarding China's influence. This trend of growing apprehension toward China tracks closely with rising levels of support within South Korea for the U.S.-ROK alliance.[55] Among respondents to a 2010 Asan Institute poll who described themselves as having an unfavorable attitude toward the United States, 73% saw a need for the continuation of the alliance.[56]

American public support for the U.S.-ROK alliance is likewise at its strongest in over a decade, despite a public mood that has been otherwise wary of expanded military entanglements abroad. According to the 2014 biennial poll of American views on foreign policy conducted by the Chicago Council on Global Affairs, over 60% of Americans continue to support a U.S. troop presence in South Korea. This strong support is primarily due to the perception that North Korea continues to pose a serious threat to U.S. interests as well as broader American coolness toward North Korea. Whereas the survey by the Chicago Council on Global Affairs shows that American attitudes toward South Korea have warmed significantly over the past decade—from a rating of 44 out of 100 in 2006 to 56 out of 100 in 2014—the same survey shows that American attitudes are coolest toward North Korea, which received a rating of 23 out of 100. While over 85% of Americans continue to favor the use of diplomacy toward North Korea over military options for dealing with the country, 66% of Americans support interdiction of North Korean ships suspected of trafficking in nuclear materials and arms but continue to regard use of force on the Korean Peninsula as a last resort. Most Americans surveyed oppose the use of airpower to strike North Korean military targets or suspected nuclear sites or sending in U.S. ground forces to take control over the country.[57]

Conclusion: The Future of the U.S.-ROK Alliance and South Korea's Strategic Challenges

The U.S. rebalance to Asia depends on the strength of existing alliances, buttressed by efforts to build new partnerships across the region. It anticipates greater lateral cooperation among U.S. allies so as to improve

---

[55] Asan Institute for Policy Studies, "South Koreans and Their Neighbors," April 19, 2014, http://en.asaninst.org/contents/south-koreans-and-their-neighbors-2014.

[56] Hahm Chaibong, Kim Ji-yoon, Lee Jongsoo, Paik Wooyeal, and Woo Jung-Yeop, "AIPS Opinion Survey 2010: Report on Korean Attitudes toward the U.S.," Asan Institute for Policy Studies, 2010.

[57] Dina Smeltz and Ivo Daalder, "Foreign Policy in the Age of Retrenchment: Results of the 2014 Chicago Council Survey of American Public Opinion and U.S. Foreign Policy," Chicago Council on Global Affairs, September 2014, http://www.thechicagocouncil.org/UserFiles/File/Task%20Force%20Reports/2014_CCS_Report.pdf.

efficiency and strengthen the interoperability of the alliances with each other as a means by which to shape and mitigate potential negative consequences from China's rise. While not focused on a specific threat, the U.S. alliances with South Korea and Japan build on common interests that result from shared values and priorities as like-minded capitalist economies that hold democratic values.

The U.S.-ROK alliance has developed as a model for this type of cooperation, especially through its framing as an alliance with peninsular, regional, and global dimensions and a high degree of interoperability. The latter is a direct benefit of decades of the United States and South Korea working together on the peninsula through a combined command structure. As one looks across the Pacific at countries that are able to bring resources to the table and share common interests with the United States, South Korea increasingly stands out as a like-minded nation in Asia that also has the capacity to contribute to global and regional stability. These elements have enabled South Korea to develop as a unique and valuable partner and critical component of U.S. strategy in the Asia-Pacific.

The U.S. rebalance promises expanded economic and political engagement with Asia alongside existing U.S. security commitments. In this regard, it is notable that U.S.-ROK security coordination is complemented by growing cooperation in other areas. For instance, the Korea-U.S. Free Trade Agreement (KORUS FTA) came into force in early 2013, establishing a formal foundation for trade liberalization between the two countries. Importantly, the ratification of the KORUS FTA helped jump-start the launch of the Trans-Pacific Partnership negotiations to establish a regional trade agreement among twelve negotiating partners, including Japan. South Korea has not been a part of these negotiations but is likely to apply for membership after the regime is established.

But the further development of the U.S.-ROK alliance faces potential challenges and obstacles in the coming years that must be managed well so that it can grow and be sustained. The first challenge requires the United States and South Korea to continue to grow their combined capabilities to promote joint defense both on and off the Korean Peninsula. This means that both sides must sustain and build interoperability, including through procurement of systems that enhance peninsular defense but are also able to contribute to security in situations that might require cooperation beyond the peninsula. It also requires both sides to be willing to sufficiently invest in combined alliance capabilities alongside efforts to strengthen capabilities for self-defense. The United States and South Korea should build greater capacity to operate together regionally off the peninsula. One opportunity to build such capacity is through conducting joint humanitarian assistance and disaster response operations off the peninsula—for instance, the United States and South Korea could build joint efforts to respond to the effects of typhoons such as Typhoon Haiyan, which struck the Philippines in 2013.

Second, the United States should encourage South Korea to build greater capacity to expand security cooperation with other U.S. allies and partners in the Asia-Pacific through the provision of equipment, regular staff exchanges and exercises, and the cultivation of joint training opportunities. These ties are beneficial to South Korea's relations with its neighbors and help promote networking within the alliance framework that the United States is cultivating as part of the rebalance.

Third, the United States should remain cognizant of South Korea's military relations with China and especially to China's efforts to pressure South Korea to make choices that could result in the weakening of the U.S.-ROK alliance. While not forcing South Korea to make a choice between the United States and China, the United States should attempt to frame alliance cooperation as part of a South Korean hedging strategy that is necessary to protect the ROK against potential negative consequences of China's rise. Although the United States should be prepared to counter Chinese pressures on South Korea to weaken the alliance, it must avoid doing so in an overbearing fashion and instead provide space for South Korea to independently make the choices that will most effectively meet the country's defense needs.

Fourth, regardless of how and when conditions are established for the adoption of alternative arrangements for administering operational control, the United States and South Korea should sustain and build greater combined capacity to address North Korean threats. The retention of combined command elements sends a clear political signal to North Korea and the region that the U.S.-ROK alliance cannot be divided, while providing an essential foundation for an enduring security alliance.

The U.S.-ROK alliance works in tandem with other U.S. alliances to provide a strong foundation for the U.S. rebalancing strategy; more generally, the strengthening of U.S. bilateral alliances will remain a critical ingredient in enabling an effective U.S. strategy in the Asia-Pacific. To the extent that South Korea continues to improve its defense capabilities in partnership with the United States, the U.S.-ROK alliance will play a critical role in peninsular, regional, and global security.

EXECUTIVE SUMMARY

This chapter assesses how Australian security perceptions and priorities mesh with those of the U.S. in the Asia-Pacific and examines the challenges and opportunities ahead for the alliance.

MAIN ARGUMENT:
Among the U.S. treaty alliances in Asia, the U.S.-Australia partnership is the closest and least problematic. Both sides appreciate that the strength of the alliance arises not just from the security pact but also from a growing array of common interests and challenges, and the two countries are well positioned to deepen their cooperation. However, challenges lie ahead. These include an expansive regional security environment characterized by rising powers, geopolitical rivalries, budgetary austerity, and increasingly complex nontraditional security problems. In particular, the two countries must grapple with balancing their economic relationships with China against their concerns about its emergence as a more assertive power.

POLICY IMPLICATIONS:
- Given their closely shared interests, the U.S. and Australia will deepen their security relationship in the years ahead. This will include a larger U.S. security-related presence at facilities in Australia and closer cooperation on defense procurement projects.

- As both countries increasingly engage the region with tighter budgets, they will jointly step up collaborations with third parties in areas such as humanitarian assistance and disaster relief, antipiracy, counterproliferation, security-force training, military exercises and exchanges, defense procurement, and institution building.

- With the Australian economy likely to remain heavily reliant on resource exports to Northeast Asia, Canberra will be highly sensitive to any significant and destabilizing deterioration in relations among the region's major players. Canberra does not wish to choose between its alliance relations and China, and will push back against efforts to make it to do so.

The U.S.-Australia Alliance: A Deepening Partnership in Emerging Asia

Bates Gill

During his visit to Australia in November 2011, U.S. president Barack Obama declared that "the United States of America has no stronger ally than Australia. We are bound by common values, the rights and the freedoms that we cherish. And for nearly a century, we've stood together in defense of these freedoms."[1] He added, in a speech to the Australian parliament, "today I can stand before you and say with confidence that the alliance between the United States and Australia has never been stronger."[2] Earlier that year, in a speech before the U.S. Congress, Australian prime minister Julia Gillard stated,

> You have an ally in Australia. An ally for war and peace. An ally for hardship and prosperity. An ally for the 60 years past and Australia is an ally for all the years to come. Geography and history alone could never explain the strength of the commitment between us. Rather, our values are shared and our people are friends. This is the heart of our alliance.[3]

These statements are emblematic of the strong alliance relationship between the United States and Australia. What is more, the strength of this relationship extends far beyond the military alliance. At the relationship's

---

Bates Gill is CEO of the United States Studies Centre at the University of Sydney. He can be reached at <bates.gill@sydney.edu.au>.

[1] "Remarks by President Obama and Prime Minister Gillard of Australia in Joint Press Conference," White House, November 16, 2011, http://www.whitehouse.gov/the-press-office/2011/11/16/remarks-president-obama-and-prime-minister-gillard-australia-joint-press.

[2] "Remarks by President Obama to the Australian Parliament," White House, November 17, 2011, http://www.whitehouse.gov/the-press-office/2011/11/17/remarks-president-obama-australian-parliament.

[3] "Julia Gillard's Speech to Congress," *Sydney Morning Herald*, March 10, 2011, http://www.smh.com.au/world/julia-gillards-speech-to-congress-20110310-1boee.html.

foundation, the countries share deeply held values in support of human dignity, democracy, and the rule of law. In addition, the United States is by far the largest investor in Australia and, in the words of the Australian foreign minister, Australia's "most important economic partner."[4] Australian investment in the United States—now totaling more than $400 million and far outpacing U.S. investment in Australia on a per capita basis—is an important but often unsung component of the relationship.[5] Polling data confirms the high value that is placed on the bilateral relationship by the peoples of both countries.[6] Americans and Australians vote with their feet as well: the bilateral exchange of visitors amounts to about 1.5 million persons per year.[7]

But in spite of the overall strength and depth of U.S.-Australia ties, challenges lie ahead. How will the two countries face an expansive Asia-Pacific security environment characterized by emerging powers, geopolitical rivalries, and an increasingly complex set of nontraditional security challenges, especially in more austere budgetary times? Must Australia choose between the benefits of its security relationship with the United States and the substantial benefits of its economic relationship with China?[8] Given these challenges, how can these long-time partners best work together to assure a stable, open, and rules-based international order at a time when this order is undergoing profound changes, not least in the Asia-Pacific?

To address these and related questions, this chapter will look closely at the role of Australia in the U.S.-Australia alliance relationship. First, the chapter will provide a brief history of the alliance and an overview of Australian perceptions of the international order and the country's external security environment. This section will also assess the impact of these perceptions on the role Australia seeks to play in Asia, Canberra's investments in defense, and its approach to cooperation with the United

---

[4] Christopher Joye, "Bishop Sees U.S., Not China, as Top Economic Partner," *Australian Financial Review*, January 25, 2014, http://www.afr.com/p/national/bishop_sees_us_not_china_as_top_nx5p89KwWyMAhw0M9RuI1L.

[5] U.S. Department of State, "2013 Investment Climate—Australia," Report, February 2013, http://www.state.gov/e/eb/rls/othr/ics/2013/204594.htm.

[6] Alex Oliver, "Lowy Institute Poll 2014," Lowy Institute, June 2014, 14–15, http://www.lowyinstitute.org/files/2014_lowy_institute_poll.pdf; and "Americans Give Record-High Ratings to Several U.S. Allies," Gallup, February 16, 2012, http://www.gallup.com/poll/152735/americans-give-record-high-ratings-several-allies.aspx.

[7] Over 500,000 Americans traveled to Australia in 2013, while over one million Australians traveled to the United States. See Tourism Australia, "December 2013: Highlights," http://www.tourism.australia.com/statistics/10455.aspx; and U.S. International Trade Administration, Office of Travel and Tourism Industries, "2012 Market Profile: Australia," http://travel.trade.gov/outreachpages/download_data_table/2012_Australia_Market_Profile.pdf.

[8] According to figures from the Australian Department of Foreign Affairs and Trade, China is Australia's largest import and export partner and accounted for 36.1% of Australia's merchandise exports in 2013. See Australian Department of Foreign Affairs and Trade, "China Fact Sheet," 2013, https://www.dfat.gov.au/geo/fs/chin.pdf.

States on regional and international issues. The chapter will then examine how domestic politics influence Australia's foreign and national security policies, with particular attention to the impact on cooperation with the United States. Finally, the chapter will spell out the policy implications and consequences of strengthened Australian cooperation with the United States and consider the opportunities and challenges that lie ahead for the alliance in the context of an emerging Asia.[9]

An Overview of the U.S.-Australia Alliance

It is important to understand the history of the U.S.-Australia alliance and recognize how the national interests of each country are served by it. During World War II, U.S. and Australian forces fought side by side to defend Australia from Japanese invasion. Since that time, Australian security interests have been protected by an alliance with the American superpower. With the onset of the Cold War, the Security Treaty between Australia, New Zealand, and the United States (the ANZUS Treaty) was formed. Following on those two important milestones in twentieth-century Australian history, Australia's great and powerful friend has been the United States. Likewise, in Australia the United States has found a reliable and capable ally, one willing and able to make serious contributions and sacrifices throughout the Cold War and post–Cold War eras.

The ANZUS Treaty arose from three principal concerns which evolved in the late 1940s following World War II. First, Australia and New Zealand sought greater security assurances to counter their perception that the United States and the United Kingdom were overly focused on developments in Europe (NATO was formed in 1949) and were unable and disinclined to commit resources toward security in the South Pacific. Second, with memories of the bitter Pacific war against Japan still fresh, both Australia and New Zealand were concerned with the ongoing U.S. effort to rebuild and rearm Japan in close alignment with it. Third, with rising tensions between the West and the Soviet Union, victory of Chinese Communist forces in 1949, and the outbreak of the Korean War in 1950, Washington, Canberra,

---

[9] For previous studies of Australia in the *Strategic Asia* series, see Andrew Shearer, "Southeast Asia and Australia: Case Studies in Responding to China's Military Power," in *Strategic Asia 2012–13: China's Military Challenge*, ed. Ashley J. Tellis and Travis Tanner (Seattle: National Bureau of Asian Research, 2012); Rory Medcalf, "Grand Stakes: Australia's Future between China and India," in *Strategic Asia 2011–12: Asia Responds to Its Rising Powers—China and India*, ed. Ashley J. Tellis, Travis Tanner, and Jessica Keough (Seattle: National Bureau of Asian Research, 2011); Rory Medcalf, "Australia: Allied in Transition," in *Strategic Asia 2008–09: Challenges and Choices*, ed. Ashley J. Tellis, Mercy Kuo, and Andrew Marble (Seattle: National Bureau of Asian Research, 2008); and Hugh White, "Australian Strategic Policy," in *Strategic Asia 2005–06: Military Modernization in an Era of Uncertainty*, ed. Ashley J. Tellis and Michael Wills (Seattle: National Bureau of Asian Research, 2005).

and Wellington all saw the need to form a more united front to prevent the spread of Communism in the region. The ANZUS Treaty was signed in San Francisco on September 1, 1951, just days before the U.S.-Japan alliance treaty was signed, and came into force on April 29, 1952, one day after the U.S.-Japan alliance treaty came into effect.

According to Article IV of the ANZUS Treaty, "each Party recognizes that an armed attack in the Pacific Area on any of the Parties would be dangerous to its own peace and safety and declares that it would act to meet the common danger in accordance with its constitutional processes." Article V states, "For the purpose of Article IV, an armed attack on any of the Parties is deemed to include an armed attack on the metropolitan territory of any of the Parties, or on the island territories under its jurisdiction in the Pacific or on its armed forces, public vessels or aircraft in the Pacific."[10]

Australia and the United States were also original signatories to the Southeast Asia Treaty Organization (SEATO) along with France, the United Kingdom, the Philippines, Thailand, and Pakistan. Formed in 1954 and disbanded in 1977, SEATO was primarily intended to counter growing Communist influence in the region. But the treaty had no formal mechanism for collective military action or intelligence-sharing and was vague as to what obligations the parties would have in response to a "common danger." Australia is also part of the Five-Power Defence Arrangements (FPDA) with the United Kingdom, New Zealand, Singapore, and Malaysia. Established in 1971, the FPDA was initially intended to provide a loose security coalition among Commonwealth partners in the region, particularly in the wake of declining British influence east of the Suez since the late 1960s. The arrangement does not provide formal alliance security assurances among the parties, but started as a way to establish viable air defenses for both Malaysia and Singapore—a capacity that continues to this day—and has since evolved to facilitate joint naval and air exercises among the parties.

Of all of these defense arrangements, Australia's alliance with the United States stands out as the most durable and robust. Since the formation of the ANZUS Treaty, Australian and U.S. forces have fought side by side in Korea, in Vietnam, in both wars against Iraq, and in Afghanistan. In 2014, Australia was among the first U.S. allies to commit air power and Special Forces to the fight against the Islamic State of Iraq and Syria (ISIS) in northern

---

[10] The ANZUS Treaty is available at https://www.dfat.gov.au/geo/new_zealand/documents/anzus.pdf. While originally a trilateral treaty, ANZUS today is best understood as a bilateral treaty between Australia and the United States and between Australia and New Zealand, but not between the United States and New Zealand. Following a dispute in the mid-1980s in which New Zealand prohibited U.S. nuclear-armed and nuclear-powered naval vessels from entering New Zealand waters and ports, the United States in 1986 suspended its security commitments to New Zealand under the ANZUS Treaty.

Iraq. (Indeed, prior to the ANZUS Treaty, U.S. and Australian forces fought together during the Boxer Rebellion and in World War I and World War II, and Australia sent forces to the Korean War under UN auspices before the ANZUS Treaty came into effect). However, while Australia has consistently committed troops alongside the United States since the treaty was established, the treaty provisions governing such commitments have only been invoked once—in the wake of the September 11, 2001, terrorist attacks on American soil. In the days following those attacks, then prime minister John Howard (who was in Washington, D.C., on an official visit on September 11) declared:

> The [Australian] Government has decided, in consultation with the United States, that Article IV of the ANZUS Treaty applies to the terrorist attacks on the United States.... The Australian Government will be in close consultation with the United States Administration in the period ahead to consider what actions Australia might take in support of the U.S. response to these attacks.[11]

The history of the Australia-U.S. security relationship is not without its controversies. As in other parts of the world, a large swath of the Australian public opposed the United States' war against Vietnam and Australia's involvement in it, as was also the case with Australia's involvement in the war against Iraq in 2003. The Labor government under Prime Minister Bob Hawke in 1985 brought an end to initial plans to use Australian territory for testing the U.S. MX intercontinental ballistic missile. In addition, in spite of Australia's clear willingness to provide military support to the United States, it is important to recognize that the treaty does not formally require either the United States or Australia to respond militarily if one of the partners is attacked, but rather states that they will "consult together" and "act to meet the common danger." In June 2014, during an extensive interview about security relations among Australia, Japan, the United States, and China, Australian defense minister David Johnston said he does not believe that the ANZUS Treaty necessarily commits Australia to join with the United States in a regional conflict.[12]

But understanding the past resilience and future prospects of the Australia-U.S. alliance requires looking beyond the specifics of the ANZUS Treaty itself and recognizing the shared values, similar cultures and histories, and deeply held common interests that are at the foundation of the overall relationship and drive its strategic motivations. Today, as a result

---

[11] Office of the Prime Minister (Australia), "Application of the ANZUS Treaty to Terrorist Attacks on the United States," September 14, 2001, http://parlinfo.aph.gov.au/parlInfo/download/media/pressrel/YFY46/upload_binary/yfy462.pdf;fileType=application%2Fpdf.

[12] For video and a transcript of the interview, see "Australia Supports Japan's Return to 'Normal Defence Posture,'" Australian Broadcasting Corporation, June 12, 2014, http://www.abc.net.au/lateline/content/2014/s4024426.htm.

of more than 60 years of close relations, security, defense, and intelligence cooperation between the two countries is extensive and deep, including common positions on most major international security issues, as well as ongoing support for one another in a variety of defense-related activities around the world, exchanges of personnel, joint training, access to Australian military bases, and joint operation of advanced surveillance and monitoring facilities such as Pine Gap. Moreover, in contrast with other U.S. allies in the region, such as Japan, the Philippines, and South Korea, Australia is not embroiled in tense and potentially explosive security relationships with its neighbors. For these reasons and more, the U.S.-Australia alliance will build on its past and move toward even deeper and more integrated forms of security and defense cooperation in the years ahead.

Australian Security Perceptions

In 2012 and 2013 the Australian government issued three high-profile assessments of the country's external environment: the white paper *Australia in the Asian Century* in October 2012, the first national security strategy white paper *Strong and Secure: A Strategy for Australia's National Security* in January 2013, and the *Defence White Paper 2013* in May 2013. The Labor government, now in opposition, issued these white papers prior to its defeat at the polls in September 2013, and the current government intends to publish a new defense white paper in 2015. While it is important to read the 2012 and 2013 white papers in this political context, they nevertheless provide useful background for understanding Australian security perceptions, particularly the increasing significance of Asia for Australia's security and well-being, the continuing importance of strong relations with the United States, the opening of new security relationships with other key partners, and a concern with nontraditional security challenges such as cybersecurity and irregular migration. At home, an unusual period of political turbulence between 2010 and 2013, combined with deepening economic dependence on Asian markets, contributed to sharpening some debates about foreign and security policy, including over military budgets and Australian relations with China.

External Environment

Australia's geostrategic circumstance—an island continent remote from likely traditional security threats, sparsely populated, highly developed, interdependent with the outside world, and increasingly integrated within a dynamic Asia-Pacific region—sharply defines its security perceptions. Stability in its regional neighborhood, and particularly in Southeast and

Northeast Asia where its primary trading routes and export markets lie, is of paramount importance for Australia's security and well-being. One of the key risks identified in the 2013 national security strategy white paper is "state-based conflict or coercion significantly affecting Australia's interests," which should be interpreted as a concern with traditional state-on-state rivalry or war rather than with the threat of an invasion directly impinging Australia's sovereignty and territorial integrity. As for the U.S.-China relationship, the white paper explicitly cited it as "the single most influential force in shaping the strategic environment" in the region and beyond.[13]

In assessing the future security outlook for Australia, the challenges and opportunities in the Asia-Pacific region come into sharpest focus across the white papers and within the broader strategic analyst community. Over the past 40 years and especially over the past decade, Australia has become ever more deeply a part of the Asia-Pacific—not only in terms of economic engagement but also demographically. Of the five million persons born overseas and now living in Australia, two million were born in Asia, while 10% of Australians claim Asian ancestry and approximately 40% of long-term temporary skilled migrants in Australia come from Asia. In 2011, for the first time in Australia's history, the United Kingdom was not the principal source of permanent residents moving to Australia. More new residents came from China that year, and during 2011–12, India was the leading source of permanent migrants to Australia. Today, more Asians live in Australia than ever before.[14]

In the words of *Australia in the Asian Century*, "the Asian century is an Australian opportunity. As the global centre of gravity shifts to our region, the tyranny of distance is being replaced by the prospects of proximity. Australia is located in the right place at the right time—in the Asian region in the Asian century."[15] The 2013 national security white paper similarly contends that a "shift in economic and strategic weight, and trade flows towards the Asia-Pacific region creat[e] new risks and opportunities for Australia."[16] To address these risks and opportunities, Australians increasingly recognize the need to sustain and develop indigenous defense capabilities; strengthen Australian businesses' capacity to engage successfully in Asia; assure and sustain stability in Asia through constructive ties with key bilateral and multilateral partnerships,

---

[13] Australian Government, *Strong and Secure: A Strategy for Australia's National Security* (Canberra, 2013), ii–iii, http://apo.org.au/files/Resource/dpmc_nationalsecuritystrategy_jan2013.pdf.

[14] These figures drawn from Australian Government, *Australia in the Asian Century* (Canberra, October 2012), section 3.4, http://pandora.nla.gov.au/pan/133850/20130914-0122/asiancentury.dpmc.gov.au/white-paper.html.

[15] Australian Government, *Australia in the Asian Century*, 1.

[16] Australian Government, *Strong and Secure*, iii.

particularly with the United States and China; and further deepen diplomatic, social, cultural, and people-to-people links across Asia so as to have a "deeper understanding of what is happening in Asia and [be] able to access the benefits of growth in [the] region."[17] Whereas in past eras Australians could believe they were far removed from the main arena of geopolitical dynamics, they are now far closer to it as part of the Asia-Pacific region.

This emphasis on the importance of Asia to Australia's security and prosperity will continue. In the run-up to the September 2013 election, Liberal Party leader Tony Abbott promised that his foreign policy would be "more Jakarta, less Geneva," and within his first month in office he made back-to-back trips to Indonesia for bilateral talks (his first foreign trip as prime minister) and the APEC (Asia-Pacific Economic Cooperation) meeting in Bali. His first major foreign trip in 2014 was to Japan, South Korea, and China in April; this trip preceded a third visit to Indonesia and his first visit to the United States in June. Another major plank in the Liberal Party's electoral platform was an ambitious initiative to send Australian university students to study and intern in Asia, a program that began in earnest in 2014. These and other plans signal a continuing recognition under the Abbott government of the Asia-Pacific's importance to Australia's long-term future.

Australia's geostrategic position leads to a clear and understandable security focus on Asia. The country's single most important bilateral relationship, however, is the alliance with the United States. For most Australian strategists, these two points are not in contradiction and ideally should be mutually reinforcing. Because of Australia's geographically remote location, small population, and lengthy coastline of some 60,000 kilometers, as well as its history as part of the British empire—for example, the Royal Australian Navy did not assume independent responsibility for the protection of Australia until 1913—the country has traditionally required a "great and powerful friend" to bolster its security.

As discussed below, the U.S.-Australia alliance faces some challenges, but it stands today as a strong and deeply intertwined relationship that in many respects is the closest of the United States' Asia-Pacific alliance partnerships. The 2013 Australian national security strategy states:

> The Australia–United States Alliance remains our most important security relationship [and] an important anchor for peace and security in our region.... [It] increases Australia's ability to protect itself and its interests by providing for: regular dialogue; joint training exercises; intelligence-sharing; access to defence technology; scope for complementary diplomacy; and research and development cooperation.[18]

---

[17] Australian Government, *Australia in the Asian Century*, 2–3.

[18] Australian Government, *Strong and Secure*, 22.

In addition to concerns over Asian stability and the importance of maintaining strong security ties with the United States, recent national security assessments also give significant attention to nontraditional challenges, including problems associated with fragile states, violent nonstate groups, malign cyber activity, climate change, and resource scarcity. These challenges pose a "low likelihood of major power war, but probable ongoing low-level instability in Australia's region."[19] To deal with these risks, the country prioritizes countering terrorism and espionage, assuring the integrity of its extensive maritime borders, mitigating and preventing serious criminal activity, and strengthening societal and infrastructural resilience. Increasingly, however, traditional concerns about geopolitical tensions and great-power rivalry—including, most importantly, potential problems related to China's rise and the resulting U.S.-China competition—are gaining a greater profile in Australian strategic circles. In particular, Australian observers are concerned with how and whether tensions between China and Japan and between China and its Southeast Asian neighbors, such as Vietnam and the Philippines, could disrupt Australia's economic ties to the region as well as bring greater instability and conflict to the Asia-Pacific, precipitating U.S. and possibly Australian military responses.

Domestic Perceptions

As in many mature democracies around the world, Australia's domestic politics are not strongly influenced by issues of foreign and security policy. One important reason for this may be that all Australians are required to vote—meaning that politicians must play to the moderate middle of the electorate on the issues that matter most to citizens, such as economic growth and jobs. That said, Australian politics went through an uncommonly turbulent phase between 2010 and 2013, and this turmoil provided opportunities for foreign policy differences to occasionally rise in profile.

For example, immigration—and particularly "irregular maritime immigration" associated with asylum seekers and human smuggling by sea—came to the fore during 2012–14 as several hundred persons lost their lives at sea attempting to reach Australian shores. To address this issue, Tony Abbott, the leader of the opposition at the time, pledged that if elected, his government would put in place policies and actions to "turn back the boats." The issue continues to stir controversy and remains a sore point between

---

[19] Australian Government, *Strong and Secure*, iii.

Australia and its close neighbor Indonesia, where many of these would-be immigrants begin the last leg of their journey to reach Australia.[20]

Defense spending was also the object of domestic political wrangling in 2012 and 2013, particularly in the run-up to the national election in September 2013. The Labor government under Prime Minister Gillard came under considerable criticism from the opposition, as well as political commentators, for putting forward defense budgets that by the 2012–13 fiscal year had fallen below 1.6% of GDP, the lowest level by that metric since 1938. The Gillard government, in issuing its *Defence White Paper 2013*, pledged to increase that figure to 2% of GDP but cautioned that this target would be a "long-term objective…implemented in an economically responsible manner as and when fiscal circumstances allow."[21] Of note, however, is that Australian defense expenditures have been in long-term decline since the end of the Cold War, and the last time the Australian defense budget amounted to 2% of GDP was in 1995.[22]

After the September elections, the newly elected government, headed by Liberal Party leader Tony Abbott, pledged to increase defense spending to 2% of GDP. According to newspaper accounts, the Abbott government aims to nearly double defense spending over the course of the next ten years to approximately A\$50 billion. In the first budget under the new government, which covers the fiscal year beginning July 2014, the defense budget was slated to rise to A\$29.3 billion, an increase of just over 6% from the previous fiscal year, accounting for approximately 1.7% of GDP.[23]

More broadly on the domestic front, the U.S.-Australia alliance occasionally generates political attention, but overall it enjoys strong domestic support and is not a matter of significant political dispute within the country. For the past six years, when asked how important the alliance relationship with the United States is for Australia's security, more than three-quarters of the respondents to the annual poll conducted by the Lowy

---

[20] According to the academic organization Border Crossing Observatory, more than 530 persons died at sea while attempting to reach Australia by boat between early 2012 and early 2014, representing more than 35% of the deaths associated with crossing Australian borders since January 2000. See the Border Crossing Observatory's Australian Border Deaths Database, available at http://artsonline. monash.edu.au/thebordercrossingobservatory/publications/australian-border-deaths-database. See also "Australia and Asylum-Seekers: Go North, Young Man," *Economist*, February 1, 2014, http:// www.economist.com/news/asia/21595509-tony-abbotts-draconian-approach-has-its-costs-go-north-young-man.

[21] Department of Defence (Australia), *Defence White Paper 2013* (Canberra, May 3, 2013), 72, http:// www.defence.gov.au/whitepaper2013/docs/WP_2013_web.pdf.

[22] David Watt and Alan Payne, "Trends in Defence Expenditure Since 1901: Budget Review 2013–2014 Index," Parliament of Australia, http://www.aph.gov.au/About_Parliament/Parliamentary_ Departments/Parliamentary_Library/pubs/rp/BudgetReview201314/DefenceExpenditure.

[23] Julian Kerr, "Australian Defence Spending to Rise by 6.1%," *IHS Jane's Defence Weekly*, May 12, 2014, http://www.janes.com/article/37831/australian-defence-spending-to-rise-by-6-1.

Institute for International Policy have said it is either "fairly important" or "very important." The polls in 2012 and 2013 marked the highest degree of support for the U.S. alliance since the poll was launched in 2005, with 87% and 82% of respondents, respectively, stating that the relationship was either fairly important or very important.[24] In the most recent Lowy poll, issued in June 2014, that figure declined slightly to 78%.[25] One potentially contentious issue, the rotation of U.S. marines through a base in Darwin in Australia's Northern Territory, found growing support among Australian respondents according to the poll: the percentage of respondents in favor of the marine rotation rose from 55% to 61% from 2011 to 2013.

However, while overall support for the bilateral security relationship remains strong, levels of support diminish when polling probes more specific scenarios. For example, in the 2013 Lowy Institute poll, a majority of Australians queried—51%—stated that the country should not join the United States in a military action in the Middle East and 60% disagreed with the statement "Australia should act in accordance with our security alliance with the United States even if it means supporting U.S. military action in Asia, for example, in a conflict between China and Japan." A large majority, 76%, said that Australia should not support U.S. military action that is not sanctioned by the United Nations.

For both economic and political reasons inside Australia, it is highly unlikely that any U.S. military presence in the country would expand in the foreseeable future to encompass large, formal bases such as Futenma in Japan. However, there is relatively strong support among political elites to expand other forms of military-to-military ties and security cooperation short of sizeable basing arrangements. For example, in addition to close intelligence cooperation, secondment of military and intelligence personnel, joint planning and exercises, and strategic consultations, Washington and Canberra are working to expand the sharing of facilities and pre-positioning of U.S. equipment on Australian soil. In addition to the annual rotation of Marines in Darwin, this includes the relocation of a C-band space surveillance radar and the transfer of an advanced space surveillance telescope, both to Western Australia, as well as increased U.S. access to Australian naval and airfield facilities. These issues, including the conclusion of a force posture agreement between the two countries, were key points of discussion during the White House meeting between President Obama and Prime Minister Abbott in

---

[24] This and other polling data is drawn from the Lowy Institute Poll 2013. See Alex Oliver, "Australia and the World: Public Opinion and Foreign Policy," Lowy Institute, June 2013.

[25] Oliver, "Lowy Institute Poll 2014."

June 2014.[26] At the conclusion of that meeting, President Obama noted "the security cooperation that is continuing to deepen between our two nations as treaty allies" and "additional agreements around force postures that will enhance the bilateral cooperation between our militaries and give us additional reach throughout this very important part of the world." Prime Minister Abbott added, "I'm here to thank the United States for its deepening engagement in our region. I'm here to further entrench our security and our economic cooperation. I'm here to celebrate the extraordinary friendship between the Australian and the American peoples."[27] Looking ahead, shared basing and facility-access arrangements will represent the next significant phase for bilateral defense cooperation.

China has increasingly become the single most important issue at the domestic level influencing how the U.S.-Australia alliance is viewed. As the polling cited above suggests, many Australians are concerned about being drawn into a confrontation with China as a result of the alliance, especially given the economic importance of China to Australia. But this concern, too often portrayed as a simplistic choice for Australia between either economic or security interests, is countered by the fact that the United States is far and away Australia's largest investment partner, not least in helping assure that resource exports continue to China and elsewhere in Asia.[28] Some commentators outline an argument that foresees an almost inevitable confrontation between the United States and China, at which point Australia must be prepared to make difficult choices about its alliance partnership with the United States.[29] China's growing importance to the Australian economy—and a long-standing though generally muted concern about over-dependence on the United States—helps explain calls for balancing relations between the United States and China. Kerry Stokes, an Australian billionaire with strong economic interests in China, made headlines in 2012 when, speaking of the presence of U.S. armed forces in Australia and its impact on relations with China, he said, "Apart from China, I may be the

---

[26] White House, "The United States and Australia: An Alliance for the Future," Fact Sheet, June 12, 2014, http://www.whitehouse.gov/the-press-office/2014/06/12/fact-sheet-united-states-and-australia-alliance-future.

[27] White House, "Remarks by President Obama and Prime Minister Abbott of Australia after Bilateral Meeting," June 12, 2014, http://www.whitehouse.gov/the-press-office/2014/06/12/remarks-president-obama-and-prime-minister-abbott-australia-after-bilate.

[28] On the importance of the United States as an investor in Australia, see Christopher Joye, "We're All the Way with the USA," *Australian Financial Review*, January 25, 2014, http://www.afr.com/f/free/national/we_re_all_the_way_with_usa_XxL9PlFv8NgRdGyWr46GGO.

[29] See, for example, Hugh White, *The China Choice: Why America Should Share Power* (Collingwood: Black, Inc., 2012); and Hugh White, "Australia's Choice: Will the Land Down Under Pick the United States or China?" *Foreign Affairs*, September 4, 2013, http://www.foreignaffairs.com/articles/139902/hugh-white/australias-choice.

only Australian in Australia who is physically repulsed by the thought of armed people on my soil not being under our command."[30] Going even further, former conservative prime minister Malcolm Fraser has argued for abandoning the alliance altogether.[31] By and large, however, these debates about the U.S.-China-Australia triangle unfold among political elites. Thus far, this issue has had little effect in diminishing broad domestic political support for the U.S.-Australia alliance and a continued strong U.S. leadership role in the Asia-Pacific.

Australian Security Priorities

Given these external and domestic factors shaping Australia's security perceptions, what are the country's highest-priority security policies for the immediate future? Some of its priorities can be gleaned from the three major white papers produced in 2012–13. While these documents were issued by the previous government, the overall strategic circumstances facing Australia and the security priorities those circumstances dictate have not changed in any significant way since their publication. As such, the priorities outlined in these white papers are unlikely to differ all that much at their core from the priorities of the newly elected government (which is expected to issue its own defense white paper in 2015). Achieving these priorities will be constrained by the realities of a slowing economy and likely limits on national security spending, including defense budgets. Hence, the cost-saving measures and efficiencies inherent in the diplomatic and economic engagement, partnerships, and joint security-related activities envisioned by these policy approaches are important.

Engaging More Effectively with the Indo-Pacific Region

Australian leaders recognize more clearly than ever that the country's destiny is strategically intertwined with the Indo-Pacific region. As noted in the national security strategy of 2013, one of the country's eight pillars of national security is "understanding and being influential in the world,

---

[30] Enda Curran, "Stokes Slams Canberra over U.S. Troops Decision," *Australian*, September 14, 2012, http://www.theaustralian.com.au/business/in-depth/australia-can-help-ease-regional-tensions-says-carr/story-fnekegrp-1226474070921.

[31] This argument is outlined in Malcolm Fraser and Cain Roberts, *Dangerous Allies* (Carlton: Melbourne University Press, 2014). See also "The American Influence: Malcolm Fraser on Australian Foreign Policy," *Economist*, May 30, 2014, http://www.economist.com/blogs/prospero/2014/05/malcolm-fraser-australian-foreign-policy; and Hugh White, "Strategic Overreach," *American Review*, August 2014, http://americanreviewmag.com/books/Strategic-overreach.

particularly the Asia-Pacific."[32] The 2013 defense white paper also stresses the importance of the region in Australia's strategic outlook: "Australia's defence policy continues to be based on four key strategic interests: a secure Australia; a secure South Pacific and Timor-Leste; a stable wider region, which we now conceptualise as the emerging Indo-Pacific; and a stable, rules-based global order."[33]

As a result, Australia—like the United States—will place increasingly greater emphasis on the importance of the Indo-Pacific to its national security. Canberra intends to step up its engagement with the region, both through more constructive and intensive relations with key countries and through support for regional institutions. This is in large measure a reflection of the region's economic importance to Australia but also reflects an increasing concern with the shifting security dynamics around the country. These include the rise of China, India's future importance as a security actor, the potential for state-on-state conflict given greater territorial tensions in Southeast and Northeast Asia, and persistent threats posed by nontraditional security challenges in the region such as human trafficking and cybersecurity.

For the United States, Australia's evolving relationships with China and Japan warrant special attention. The Gillard government was able to establish a "strategic partnership" with China in 2013 in an effort to give weight to political and security issues in a relationship dominated by economic ties. While perhaps more symbolic than substantive at the outset, the strategic partnership aims to ensure an annual summit meeting between Canberra and Beijing and signals to China and the world the importance of this relationship to Australia's future. Although he toned down use of the term strategic partnership, Prime Minister Abbott made a high-profile visit to China in April 2014, accompanied by a delegation of six hundred Australian business leaders, and heavily promoted a stronger Australia-China economic relationship, calling for the speedy completion of a free trade agreement (FTA) between the two countries. Importantly, Abbott's meetings in China also led to agreements to step up Sino-Australian defense cooperation, including "high-level meetings between the two militaries...staff exchanges and joint exercises, including multi-lateral exercises involving other countries."[34]

At the same time, and with important implications for both U.S.-Australia and China-Australia ties, Canberra is working to significantly step up its relations with Japan. The two sides officially refer to one another as strategic

---

[32] Australian Government, *Strong and Secure*, part 2.

[33] Department of Defence (Australia), *Defence White Paper 2013*, 24.

[34] David Crowe, "Abbott 'Confident' about Closer Defence Ties with China," *Australian*, April 12, 2014, http://www.theaustralian.com.au/national-affairs/policy/abbott-confident-of-closer-defence-ties-with-china/story-e6frg8yo-1226881762444.

partners, and in a series of meetings over the course of 2014 the Abbott and Abe governments worked to raise the relationship to a new level, particularly in security and defense affairs. These included the visit of Prime Minister Abbott to Japan in April, the fifth Japan-Australia 2+2 Foreign and Defense Ministerial Consultations in June, and the return visit of Prime Minister Abe to Australia in July. Of particular note, Australia and Japan reached an agreement on defense equipment cooperation with a focus on submarine-related technologies. Australian foreign minister Julie Bishop signaled the future direction for the bilateral relationship:

> I am pleased at the progress being made in cooperation between Japan and Australia in the area of security and defense, and hope to leverage this opportunity to further elevate such cooperation into a new stage. Japan and Australia have a relationship based on shared values and interests. In particular, Australia believes that it is meaningful for Japan to perform regional and global roles, including an exercise of the right of collective self-defense. It is also important to coordinate with the U.S., not just between Japan and Australia, and I hope that cooperation between Japan, the U.S. and Australia in the area of security and defense also moves forward in a practical manner.[35]

In addition to these key bilateral relationships, Australia will also seek to strengthen the role of regional multilateral organizations to bolster a rules-based order founded on commonly shared interests. Canberra will likely give particular emphasis to the East Asia Summit, the Association of Southeast Asian Nations (ASEAN), and the hoped-for Trans-Pacific Partnership (TPP) trade arrangement. More broadly, the Australian government will look to devote increased resources to building deeper linkages with the region—economic, social, educational, and cultural—including efforts at home to generate greater expertise about the Indo-Pacific region.

Strengthening the Posture of the Australian Defence Force and Improving Core Capabilities

As described earlier, the Australian defense budget will not likely grow dramatically in the near term. Nevertheless, the Australian Defence Force (ADF) is committed to meeting its four principal tasks (in order of priority): deter and defeat armed attacks on Australia; contribute to stability and security in the South Pacific and Timor-Leste; contribute to military contingencies in the Indo-Pacific region, with priority given to Southeast Asia; and contribute to military contingencies in support of global security.[36]

---

[35] Ministry of Foreign Affairs (Japan), "Fifth Japan-Australia Joint Foreign and Defense Ministerial Consultations ('2+2')," June 11, 2014, http://www.mofa.go.jp/a_o/ocn/au/page3e_000188.html.

[36] Department of Defence (Australia), *Defence White Paper 2013*, 28.

To perform these tasks, the ADF faces a number of critical decisions to improve its force posture and core capabilities. This will include steady progress on certain defense procurement programs and continued efforts to gain synergies through cooperation with the United States and other close security partners. In addition, the ADF (similar to the U.S. military) will need to work through the significant drawdown of forces abroad (especially from Afghanistan but also in Timor-Leste and the Solomon Islands) and refocus on missions closer to home. The ADF intends to draw on the lessons it learned from a decade of high-tempo operations in places like Afghanistan to increase its capabilities in activities such as stability operations, humanitarian relief, and peacekeeping, with an emphasis on the South Pacific and broader Indo-Pacific region. Interoperability with the United States' military—which was enhanced through close bilateral cooperation in Afghanistan—is also seen as a key component to strengthening Australia's overall force posture. The ADF will seek to increase interoperability through "regular training, exercising, exchanges, intelligence cooperation, improved ICT [information and communications technology] connectivity, and implementation of the Defense Trade Cooperation Treaty" as well as through acquisition of U.S. defense platforms.[37]

To achieve these goals, Australian authorities envision an ambitious procurement program over the coming two decades emphasizing increased joint amphibious capability, maritime strike, surveillance and antisubmarine assets, advanced air combat fighters, and battlefield airlift capability. Between now and 2020, this includes the delivery of 2 Canberra-class helicopter dock amphibious vessels, 3 Hobart-class air warfare destroyers, EA-18G Growler electronic warfare aircraft, 10 C-27J battlefield airlift aircraft, MH-60R Seahawk antisurface and antisubmarine helicopters, and 72 F-35A Joint Strike Fighters. In addition, procurement plans also propose future frigates and submarines. The precise nature of this future submarine capability remains especially uncertain. It is widely understood, however, that the country will need, as a core defense capability, a modern submarine program to replace the aging Collins-class fleet with up to 12 new boats built in Australia. This process will likely span decades and involve the United States and possibly other partners such as Japan.

In addition to budgetary constraints in the near to medium term, other factors will complicate these plans. Introducing the new Canberra-class amphibious ships—the largest ships ever operated by the Royal Australian Navy—will present new challenges of logistics and interoperability across the services of the ADF. Planning for future submarines and frigates will

---

[37] Department of Defence (Australia), *Defence White Paper 2013*, 41.

also raise difficult questions and choices regarding design, construction, capabilities, and sustainment, as well as involving the complicated but necessary requirement of working with foreign partners to develop and integrate certain systems for these platforms.

Improving the Country's Ability to Address Nontraditional Threats

The three recent government white papers devoted considerable attention to nontraditional security challenges, classifying the following four issues among the seven key national security risks facing the country: "malicious cyber activity, proliferation of weapons of mass destruction, serious and organised crime…[and] terrorism and violent extremism."[38] As part of its strategic outlook, the 2013 white paper on defense devotes lengthy sections to the adverse effects of the global financial crisis as well as climate change and resource security.[39] As noted above, the issues of irregular migration, human trafficking, and refugee flows also have come to the fore in Australian domestic politics in recent years. While there may be a change in the emphasis the new Abbott government places on nontraditional security—for example, it will not give the same weight to the issue of climate change as did its predecessors—nonetheless questions of border security, organized crime, cybersecurity, protection of national infrastructure, and counterterrorism will remain top priorities for Australia. With the upsurge in violence in Syria and northern Iraq in 2014, the Australian government raised the country's terrorism alert level from mediuim to high with concerns about homegrown terrorists as well as citizens returning to Australia from fighting for ISIS.

To address these challenges, Australia will seek to not only bolster its own capabilities but also strengthen partnerships with regional allies and neighbors, including the United States. In its national security white paper the Gillard government put forward plans to improve the country's cybersecurity, including through the creation of the Australian Cyber Security Centre, which aims to "bring together [the Ministry of] Defence's Cyber Security Operations Centre, the Attorney-General's Computer Emergency Response Team (CERT) Australia, [the Australian Security Intelligence Organization's] Cyber Espionage Branch, the [Australian Federal Police's] High-Tech Crime Operations capability and all-source-assessment analysts from the Australian Crime Commission."[40] More broadly, the government recognizes the need for greater cooperation across agencies within Australia and with partner governments and institutions outside of Australia. This will mean greater

[38] Australian Government, *Strong and Secure*, part 2.

[39] Department of Defence (Australia), *Defence White Paper 2013*, 9–11, 18–19.

[40] Australian Government, *Strong and Secure*, 40.

information-sharing, outreach to nontraditional security partners (especially in the business and information-technology communities), investment in new technologies, and the strengthening of Australia's ability to deter and halt disruptive or malign incursions at the country's border. Regarding this latter objective, efforts to stem irregular migration to Australia will likely remain a top political priority for the Abbott government—couched in terms of combating international criminal activity—in spite of both domestic and international outcry that these measures violate Australia's commitments to humanitarian conventions.

Policy Implications

Given the mix of Australian strategic perceptions, domestic constraints, and security priorities, what are the future policy implications for the U.S.-Australia partnership? Answering this question in part involves finding the right balance between U.S. expectations, on the one hand, and Australian willingness and ability to meet those expectations, on the other. Overall, U.S. expectations mesh relatively well with Australian interests and capabilities, which should result in a broadening range of joint policy initiatives, both now and in the future. These initiatives will aim to bolster the alliance and deliver greater security for Australia, the United States, and the region across a spectrum of economic, diplomatic, and defense activities.

U.S. Expectations

The United States will look to its allies to cooperate in implementing a flexible, expanded, multifaceted, and integrated framework for security. It will encourage more action and responsibility among allies, both individually and collaboratively, to address both traditional and nontraditional security challenges at the national, regional, and global levels. This approach has been part of U.S. alliance strategy for many years and has assumed further impetus in light of the U.S. "rebalance" to Asia and tightening defense budgets in the United States and among its allies in the region.

Given these priorities, Washington will look to Australia to broaden the framework for realizing greater security in four important aspects: building economic, diplomatic, and security cooperation with other partners to complement and enhance the bilateral alliance pact; deepening the bilateral security relationship; expanding Australia's security role in the region; and engaging China in constructive ways that both assure and deter.[41] In all of these areas, the two countries have much work to do together.

Economic, Diplomatic, and Security Cooperation with Regional Partners

The United States and Australia share very strong common interests in ensuring and strengthening a stable, open, and rules-based international order achieved through economic, diplomatic, and security initiatives. In the area of economic cooperation, the United States has sought strong bilateral and multilateral trade agreements with Australia, including the Australia-U.S. FTA, which entered into force in January 2005. The TPP trade agreement also involves Australia and the United States, as well as ten other regional partners. Australia has a particularly strong interest to see the TPP move ahead. The two countries are also well-linked through their robust bilateral investment relationship and should work to assure a continued deepening of these ties. The United States accounts for about a quarter of all FDI in Australia and has a stock of over $600 billion in the country. Similarly, some 35% of all Australian FDI goes to the United States, with a stock of over $400 billion.[42]

The two countries work closely together in the diplomatic realm, both multilaterally and bilaterally, and this partnership will likely strengthen. Australia will host the annual group of 20 (G-20) summit in November 2014, and Washington and Canberra have stated their joint commitment to ensure that the group "remains focused on generating sustained growth and jobs, resisting protectionism, and enhancing financial resilience."[43] Australia held a nonpermanent seat on the UN Security Council in 2013 and 2014, where it worked closely with the United States and other council members across a range of international security issues, including the effectiveness of sanctions regimes and the protection of civilians during armed conflict. Australia was especially active in promoting the Arms Trade Treaty within the UN. The two countries also cooperate in a range of other multilateral security forums based in the Asia-Pacific, including the ASEAN Regional Forum, the East Asia Summit, the ASEAN Defence Ministers' Meeting-Plus, and the Expanded ASEAN Maritime Forum, in each case collaborating to strengthen the effectiveness of these organizations. This is an area ripe for

---

[41] On U.S. expectations of its Asia-Pacific alliances, including Australia, see Bates Gill, "Alliances Under Austerity: What Does America Want?" Australian National University, Strategic and Defence Studies Centre, Centre of Gravity Series, no. 10, September 2013.

[42] U.S. Department of State, "2013 Investment Climate—Australia," February 2013, http://www.state. gov/e/eb/rls/othr/ics/2013/204594.htm.

[43] U.S. Department of State, "Australia–United States Ministerial Consultations (AUSMIN)," November 20, 2013, http://www.state.gov/r/pa/prs/ps/2013/11/217794.htm.

greater U.S.-Australia partnership—for example, by assuring that maritime security and the peaceful resolution of disputed territorial claims are among the highest priorities within these institutions.

The United States and Australia are also working to strengthen multilateral cooperation with other U.S. allies and security partners in the Asia-Pacific region. For example, the Trilateral Strategic Dialogue and the Security and Defense Cooperation Forum (SDCF) bring together Australian, Japanese, and U.S. officials and military personnel to discuss common concerns and develop joint activities to address security challenges in the Asia-Pacific. The Trilateral Strategic Dialogue, established in 2002 and upgraded to the foreign-minister level in 2006, held its fifth ministerial meeting in October 2013. The SDCF was launched in 2007 and held its fifth meeting in February 2013.[44] The three countries have also begun to hold an annual trilateral defense ministerial meeting on the sidelines of the Shangri-La Dialogue in Singapore, with the third such meeting occurring in June 2013.[45] In addition, Australia, Japan, and the United States conduct joint military training exercises, such as Southern Jackaroo. This exercise was hosted by Australia for six days in May 2014 and focused on tactical warfighting skills involving troops from the ADF, the U.S. Army, and the Japanese Ground Self-Defense Force.[46] As noted above, Australia has shown particular interest in Japan's Soryu-class submarines, considered among the most advanced non-nuclear submarines in the world.[47] The United States and Australia have also committed to working more closely with the Republic of Korea (ROK). Though not yet establishing a formalized trilateral mechanism with the ROK, as they have with Japan, Washington and Canberra intend to step up trilateral cooperation through "practical defense engagement…counter-proliferation efforts and working together in the UN on maritime cooperation, humanitarian assistance, and disaster relief."[48]

In another significant move demonstrating Australia's commitment to multilateral cooperation, the Royal Australian Navy guided missile frigate

---

[44] U.S. Department of State, "Australian, Japanese, and U.S. Officials Meet for Security and Defense Cooperation Forum," February 13, 2013, http://www.state.gov/r/pa/prs/ps/2013/02/204574.htm; and "Trilateral Strategic Dialogue Joint Statement," October 4, 2013, available at http://www.foreignminister.gov.au/releases/2013/jb_mr_131004.html.

[45] U.S. Department of Defense, "Australia, Japan, United States Defense Leaders Trilateral Meeting Joint Statement," June 1, 2013, http://www.defense.gov/releases/release.aspx?releaseid=16053.

[46] See "Japan, the United States and Australia Conduct Joint Training in Australia," *Japan Defense Focus*, June 2014, 5, http://www.mod.go.jp/e/jdf/pdf/jdf_no53.pdf; and Brian Hartigan, "The Height of Joint Ops," *Army* (Australia), June 19, 2014, 4.

[47] "Australia to Sign New Submarines Deal with Japan as Prime Minister Shinzo Abe Visits Tony Abbott in Canberra," News.com.au, July 7, 2014, http://www.news.com.au/national/australia-to-sign-new-submarines-deal-with-japan-as-prime-minister-shinzo-abe-visits-tony-abbott-in-canberra/story-fncynjr2-1226980720135.

[48] U.S. Department of State, "Australia–United States Ministerial Consultations."

HMAS *Sydney* was embedded with the USS *George Washington* carrier strike group during 2013. Based in Yokosuka, Japan, the deployment was intended to improve Australian capability in protecting high-value naval assets at sea, but it also had the effect of further strengthening operational and military-to-military relations with the United States and Asian partner navies, including Japan and the ROK.[49] Looking beyond U.S. allied relationships, Australia and the United States have also committed to increase defense cooperation with Indonesia and engagement with other Southeast Asian militaries. The force posture agreement reached during Prime Minister Abbott's visit to Washington in June 2014 will facilitate such trilateral cooperation on military training among Australia, the United States, and third parties.[50]

U.S.-Australia Bilateral Security Initiatives

The Australia–United States Ministerial Consultation (AUSMIN) is a 2+2 process that brings the Australian foreign and defense ministers together with their U.S. counterparts. Held regularly since the 1980s and meeting on an annual basis, AUSMIN can provide an important "forcing function" to advance security-related initiatives between the two countries. Recent AUSMIN meetings have seen the two sides move to expand their discussions to encompass new security challenges that fall outside the realm of traditional security and intersect with economic, resource, and society-related concerns: cybersecurity, refugee and population flows, and humanitarian assistance and disaster relief.[51] The 2014 AUSMIN meeting solidified progress on bilateral force posture agreements. That said, given the increasing complexity of Australia-U.S. security ties and the rising expectations each side has for the other, AUSMIN meetings in the future will need to carve out more time for consultations among the principals and do more to explain to the public, especially in the United States, the value of the U.S.-Australia partnership. Given the growing importance of this relationship, an annual bilateral leadership summit between the U.S. president and the Australian prime minister should be established.

---

[49] Sarah West, "HMAS *Sydney* Joins USN Carrier Strike Group," May 7, 2013, http://www.navy.gov. au/news/hmas-sydney-joins-usn-carrier-strike-group.

[50] U.S. Department of State, "Australia–United States Ministerial Consultations"; and James Brown, "Australia-U.S. Defence Deal: What It Means," Lowy Institute, Interpreter, web log, June 13, 2014, http://www.lowyinterpreter.org/post/2014/06/13/Australia-US-defence-deal-What-it-means. aspx?COLLCC=3017056487&.

[51] See, for example, U.S. Department of State, "Australia–United States Ministerial Consultations"; and U.S. Department of State, "AUSMIN 2012 Joint Communique," November 12, 2012, http://www. state.gov/r/pa/prs/ps/2012/11/200497.htm.

More specifically, Washington and Canberra plan to implement a number of concrete steps that will deepen their security relationship, improve their joint capabilities, and provide for an enhanced U.S. force posture in the Asia-Pacific. The rotational deployment of U.S. Marines to Darwin continues to expand: 1,150 Marines will be rotated to Darwin in 2014 with the target of establishing a full Marine Air Ground Task Force of around 2,500 personnel and equipment within the next three to four years. As discussed above, plans are underway for the relocation from the United States of a C-band space surveillance radar in 2014 and the relocation and joint operation of a highly advanced space surveillance telescope, both to Western Australia. The two countries are also aiming to increase the rotation of U.S. Air Force aircraft—including long-range bombers, transport, and air-to-air refueling aircraft—through facilities in northern Australia, and they continue to explore options for increased U.S. access to Australian naval bases such as HMAS Stirling in Western Australia. The two countries are also likely to reach a number of new force posture agreements in the coming years involving greater U.S. access to Australian facilities and increased joint activities between the U.S. military and the ADF.[52]

Another important area for Australian-U.S. defense cooperation that has gained momentum in recent years is ballistic missile defense (BMD). As Australian security analysts Andrew Davies and Rod Lyon have observed, the joint Australian-U.S. defense facility at Nurrungar, South Australia, has provided surveillance and early warning intelligence for missile launches in Eurasia (such as during the 1991 Gulf War). BMD cooperation was prominently noted a decade ago as an area for Australian-U.S. cooperation by then defense minister Robert Hill when he stated that Australia had "agreed in principle to greater participation in the U.S. Missile Defence program."[53] Australia's most recent defense white paper states that while the country will "continue to examine potential Australian [BMD] capability responses— including for the defence of deployed forces and the defence of strategic interests," nevertheless, "Australia does not advocate the development of national ballistic missile defence systems that would potentially diminish the deterrent value of the strategic nuclear forces of major nuclear powers."[54] Under the new government, BMD has gained a renewed profile in Australian-U.S. relations. For example, the 2013 AUSMIN joint communiqué stated:

---

[52] Brown, "Australia-U.S. Defence Deal."

[53] Andrew Davies and Rod Lyon, "Ballistic Missile Defence: How Soon, How Significant, and What Should Australia's Policy Be?" Australian Strategic Policy Institute (ASPI), Strategic Insights, no. 71, May 2014, 12, https://www.aspi.org.au/publications/ballistic-missile-defence-how-soon,-how-significant,-and-what-should-australias-policy-be/SI71_BMD.pdf.

[54] Department of Defence (Australia), Defence White Paper 2013, 82.

> The United States and Australia agreed to examine opportunities to expand their cooperation on ballistic missile defense, including working together to identify potential Australian contributions to ballistic missile defense in the Asia-Pacific region.
>
> They agreed to continue cooperative research on technologies to counter ballistic missile threats, and continue their consultation regarding options that increase capability development in this area.
>
> The two countries will continue to consult as the United States develops its phased adaptive approaches to regional ballistic missile defense, which will allow missile defense to be adapted to the threats unique to the Asia-Pacific region.[55]

This approach was further reinforced in public statements following the June 2014 meeting between Prime Minister Abbott and President Obama in Washington. A White House fact sheet following the meeting states, "We are also working to explore opportunities to expand cooperation on ballistic missile defense, including working together to identify potential Australian contributions to ballistic missile defense in the Asia-Pacific region."[56] The precise nature of Australia's future involvement in U.S. BMD plans is not known publicly but would probably involve enhanced surveillance and early warning intelligence from joint facilities on Australian soil, as well as the deployment of BMD capabilities—such as the Aegis antimissile systems—on future Australian air warfare destroyers. The 2014 AUSMIN meeting called for the establishment of a bilateral working group to further explore opportunities for BMD cooperation.[57]

Defense technology is another area where the two countries should see increased cooperation in the future. This is facilitated by the U.S.-Australia Defense Trade Cooperation Treaty, which provides Australia with greater access to U.S. defense capabilities and technology and allows for more bilateral sharing of defense equipment, expertise, technologies, information, and services. (The United States has only one other such defense trade agreement, which is with the United Kingdom.) According to the 2013 AUSMIN joint communiqué, with an eye toward enhancing the interoperability of U.S. and Australian forces, the two sides will put a particular emphasis on cooperation related to "combat and transport aircraft, helicopters, and submarine systems and weapons, with special focus on future submarine efforts."[58]

The development of Australia's future submarine fleet is of critical importance not only for Australia's defense but for allied operations in

---

[55] U.S. Department of State, "Australia–United States Ministerial Consultations."

[56] White House, "The United States and Australia: An Alliance for the Future."

[57] Department of Foreign Affairs and Trade (Australia), "AUSMIN 2014 Joint Communiqué," August 12, 2014, https://www.dfat.gov.au/geo/us/ausmin/ausmin14-joint-communique.html.

[58] U.S. Department of State, "Australia–United States Ministerial Consultations."

the Asia-Pacific region more broadly. The United States and U.S. defense contractors should be closely involved in this process, particularly in the provision of weapons systems. With the signing of a defense technology cooperation agreement between Canberra and Tokyo in July 2014 and Australia's continuing interest in the Japanese Soryu-class diesel-electric submarine, it appears that Japanese technologies will also be involved in the future submarine program. Such cooperation should include the encouragement and involvement of the United States, both to strengthen trilateral security relations and help assure the highest possible capability for Australia's future force.

In short, Australian defense procurement plans for the next several years will include a range of U.S. equipment and technologies, as shown in **Table 1** below. All of these current and likely future steps in defense procurement serve to further an already robust set of bilateral interactions.

TABLE 1   Current and planned Australian procurement of U.S. defense equipment

Quantity	System
19	M777A2 lightweight towed howitzers
6	Australian Defence Force communications satellites
24	MH-60R Seahawk Romeo helicopters
6	E-7A Wedgetail airborne early warning and control aircraft
10	C-27J battlefield airlift aircraft
12	EA-18G Growler electronic attack aircraft
72	F-35A Joint Strike Fighter

SOURCE: Department of Defence (Australia), "Top 30 Programs," http://www.defence.gov.au/dmo/tap/index.cfm.

NOTE: This is only a selected list of major acquisitions.

Expanding Australia's Security Role

While Australia is justifiably proud of its ability to punch above its weight, its role as a middle power is understandably constrained. With only 50,000 military personnel in the Australian Defence Force, a continent-sized territorial expanse and lengthy coastline, and a high dependence on expeditionary capacity owing to its relatively remote location, Australia has limits to what it can achieve militarily on its own to assure global and regional order. With this in mind, the United States and Australia will need to work together to maintain and expand Australia's capability to assume a greater responsibility not only for Australian security but also for operations in the near abroad and farther afield. Washington should encourage Canberra to maintain its important contributions to global and regional stability—such as participation in antipiracy operations, UN peacekeeping, counterterrorism activities, mine clearance, enforcement of nonproliferation, and the training of the Afghan National Security Forces—as part of Australia's overall strategy. The United States and Australia should also explore options to modestly expand Australian deployments in bilateral and multilateral operations alongside U.S. forces, even if relatively large-scale, long-term, and high-tempo expeditionary operations far from Australian shores seem unlikely in the near term. Australia's decision in September 2014 to commit 400 airmen and 200 Special Forces personnel, along with up to eight Super Hornet fighter bombers, a KC-30 refueling and transport aircraft, and an airborne early warning and control aircraft, to the fight against ISIS is an especially important example of this kind of contribution.

Here again, interoperability and joint operations with U.S. forces will be critical. Washington will look to the Australian navy to continue its important contributions to three combined task forces (CTF-150, CTF-151, and CTF-152) of the Combined Maritime Forces. These forces operate in the Gulf of Aden, Red Sea, Indian Ocean, Gulf of Oman, and Persian Gulf and conduct counterpiracy, counterterrorism, and other maritime security operations. Similarly, Australia's preparedness to embed with U.S. and allied operations—for example, the deployment in 2013 of the HMAS *Sydney* with the U.S. Seventh Fleet in Northeast Asia—is viewed positively by both sides as a model for future cooperation. The United States will also encourage Australia to expand its activities with other U.S. allies and partners in the Indo-Pacific, such as through the ongoing training for Philippine armed forces and the establishment of the Australia-Indonesia 2+2 dialogue in March 2012.

Australian moves to strengthen its role and security-related ties bilaterally with other countries in the Indian Ocean and Asia-Pacific regions are viewed as a plus from Washington's perspective. Of particular importance is Australia's critical role in providing economic, development, diplomatic, and security assistance to neighbors in the South Pacific and to Timor-Leste. Australia is the single-largest donor of development assistance to South Pacific nations and Timor-Leste and also provides a range of defense assistance programs to these countries. This includes the Australia-led stabilization operations in the Solomon Islands—the Regional Assistance Mission to the Solomon Islands (RAMSI)—now transitioning from providing security to a police training and capacity-building mission. Australia also provides advisory teams and professional training for other security forces in the South Pacific and Timor-Leste, as well as donating patrol vessels for use by these countries' maritime security authorities. With Australian leadership, the first annual South Pacific Defence Ministers' Meeting was held in 2013.

Australia's efforts to establish stronger security ties with countries such as Japan, South Korea, and India—including through the issuance of joint security statements and the development of regularized 2+2 meetings of defense and foreign ministers—are likewise positive steps from a U.S. point of view.[59] The Australia-Japan 2+2 meeting in June 2014 built on the countries' leadership summit in Tokyo earlier in the year. The two sides put forward a suite of recommendations aimed at furthering their security and defense relationship, including deeper defense science and technology cooperation (with a special focus on submarine technology), high-level consultations on cybersecurity, and the provision of joint assistance to South Pacific nations.[60]

Relations with China

Washington and Canberra clearly share an interest in pursuing constructive and beneficial relationships with Beijing and in working to assure the emergence of a stable and prosperous China that is at peace with its neighbors and contributes to global and regional security. These goals form the core of both Australian and U.S. policies toward China. For Washington, the deepening of Australia-China relations—including through their strategic partnership, economic ties, and increased, though still modest, military-to-military cooperation—is by and large in the long-term strategic interest of the United States and fits squarely with the U.S. approach to engaging China. Ongoing defense and military-to-military ties, such as the annual Australia-China Defense Strategic Dialogue and joint humanitarian

---

[59] See, for example, "Vision Statement for a Secure, Peaceful and Prosperous Future between the Republic of Korea and Australia," April 8, 2014, https://www.pm.gov.au/media/2014-04-08/vision-statement-secure-peaceful-and-prosperous-future-between-republic-korea-and; "India-Australia Joint Declaration on Security Cooperation," November 12, 2009, http://www.india.embassy.gov.au/ndli/pa5009jsb.html; and "Japan-Australia Joint Declaration on Security Cooperation," March 13, 2007, http://www.mofa.go.jp/region/asia-paci/australia/joint0703.html.

[60] "5th Japan-Australia 2+2 Foreign and Defence Ministerial Consultations," June 12, 2014, http://foreignminister.gov.au/releases/Pages/2014/jb_mr_140612a.aspx. On the submarine technology agreement, see Mari Yamaguchi, "Japan, Australia Agree on Stealth Technology Agreement," Associated Press, June 11, 2014, http://bigstory.ap.org/article/japan-australia-eye-sub-deal-closer-defense-ties; and Paul Kallender-Umezu and Nigel Pittaway, "Japan, Australia Deal Poses Tech Issues," Defense News, June 15, 2014, http://www.defensenews.com/article/20140615/DEFREG03/306160010/Japan-Australia-Deal-Poses-Tech-Issues.

assistance and disaster relief exercises, should also be welcomed as part of the common interests Washington and Canberra share in dealings with Beijing. Consistent with this approach, soldiers from the Australian, Chinese, and U.S. armies will conduct a small joint exercise dubbed Exercise Kowari in October 2014 in northern Australia. Focusing on survival training, the land-based exercise will be the first involving troops from the three countries and the first time Chinese armed forces have exercised on Australian territory.[61] Also in late 2014, China will host Exercise Phoenix Spirit, focusing on disaster relief and bringing together Chinese, Australian, New Zealand, and U.S. participants. This will mark the first time Australian troops have exercised on Chinese soil.[62] The United States and Australia should continue to explore forms of trilateral and other multilateral military diplomacy and joint activities with China.

The United States does not seek a confrontation with China and sees great value in engagement with Beijing. But it also has a larger interest in assuring continued regional prosperity and stability, and in order to do so will seek to reassure its allies and partners in the Asia-Pacific by trying to deter China from taking provocative and destabilizing steps and, more broadly, by seeking to shape the strategic choices a rising China makes. For Washington, this is a difficult balance to strike: one which recognizes and encourages the constructive potential inherent in China's rise but also hedges against possible confrontation with a more powerful China. This balance is all the more difficult to achieve in partnership with regional allies such as Australia, given their varying interests, concerns, and capabilities in the face of a rising China. On the one hand, the past decade has seen a steady intensification of Australia's economic relations with China. On the other hand, China in recent years has become increasingly engaged in troubling regional confrontations as Beijing asserts its interests in the East China Sea, the South China Sea, the western Pacific, and beyond.

Looking ahead, if U.S.-China relations devolve into greater rivalry or even conflict, Australia could face some very difficult trade-offs between its economic partnership with China and its security partnership with the United States.[63] In Australia, this tricky balancing act has generated a lively policy debate among its strategists. Policy prescriptions range across the spectrum.

---

[61] Ministry of Defence (Australia), "Minister for Defence—Defence Minister David Johnston Hails Closer Australia-Chinese Defence Ties," July 18, 2014, http://www.minister.defence.gov.au/2014/07/18/minister-for-defence-defence-minister-david-johnston-hails-closer-australia-chinese-defence-ties.

[62] Brendon Nicholson, "ADF Is All the Way with the PLA," *Australian*, August 1, 2014, http://www.theaustralian.com.au/national-affairs/defence/adf-is-all-the-way-with-the-pla/story-e6frg8yo-1227009348978?nk=9dd39c3c2c604aeb911bfa6cfd8eabfc.

[63] This is the core conundrum posed by Hugh White in *The China Choice*.

Former prime minister Malcolm Fraser advocates abandoning the alliance to avoid being dragged into a conflict with China. Some suggest a less dramatic response by offering greater "strategic space" to China and encouraging "power sharing" between Washington and Beijing. Other analysts urge a basic continuation of current policy by accepting a future of "power balancing and prudent hedging" by Beijing and Washington, while working more closely with the United States to realize Australia's strategic aspirations.[64] Political leaders on the left and right in Australia officially state that it is not necessary to choose between China and the United States, and that the best course for the country is to pursue deeper economic and security-related ties with both. This is precisely the path that leaders in Canberra have taken in the expectation that by doing so Australia can play a modest role in mitigating potential tensions between the two great powers and be in a better position to anticipate and respond to a serious U.S.-China confrontation.

How would Australia respond to a serious crisis and confrontation between Beijing and Washington? It is impossible to tell without knowing the precise circumstances at the time. If China is clearly the aggressor in an action that results in the loss of American and Australian lives or otherwise seriously affects Australian interests, Canberra will condemn Beijing and consult closely alongside Washington to determine an appropriate response. But if the circumstances are not so clear-cut, if another party—such as Japan or the Philippines—is the provocateur, or if the resulting confrontation does not directly affect Australian interests or its ANZUS Treaty obligations, Canberra's response would probably be far less forthright. Speculation on a possible Australian response must take into account a host of uncertainties, shifting trends, and changing strategic circumstances, and can obfuscate more than clarify. But it seems certain that if U.S.-China relations significantly deteriorate in the near term, Australia will face a complex policy challenge making it difficult to be a friend to both sides. Australian leaders will do everything possible to ensure they do not face that conundrum.

---

[64] For a sampling, see Peter Hartcher, "Does Australia Really Need the U.S. Alliance?" *Sydney Morning Herald*, May 12, 2014, http://www.smh.com.au/comment/does-australia-really-need-the-us-alliance-20140512-zraey.html; Fraser and Roberts, *Dangerous Allies*; White, *The China Choice*; White, "Australia's Choice"; Paul Keating, "Why America Cannot Ignore the China Choice," East Asia Forum, August 8, 2012, http://www.eastasiaforum.org/2012/08/08/why-america-cannot-ignore-the-china-choice; Mark Thomson, "Power Sharing and Risk Management in Hugh White's 'China Choice,'" ASPI, Strategist, web log, February 2014, http://www.aspistrategist.org.au/power-sharing-and-risk-management-in-hugh-whites-china-choice; and Paul Dibb, "Why I Disagree with Hugh White on China's Rise," *Australian*, August 13, 2012, http://www.theaustralian.com.au/opinion/why-i-disagree-with-hugh-white-on-chinas-rise/story-e6frg6zo-1226448713852.

Conclusion

Australia and the United States benefit from a robust ongoing and prospective security policy agenda. This reflects a strong alliance that will only grow stronger as both countries increase their attention and resources toward the Asia-Pacific. Increasingly, both sides have come to appreciate that the foundation and future strength of the alliance arise not just from the security pact itself but also from a growing array of common interests and challenges relevant to U.S. and Australian national security. Looking ahead, the two countries are well-positioned to enhance and deepen their cooperation—economically, politically, diplomatically, technologically, and militarily.

But while we can expect a generally positive and constructive future for the U.S.-Australia partnership, a number of challenges lie ahead. To begin, the two sides will need to stay focused on one another's security debates, concerns, and expectations. There remains a persistent concern in some Australian political circles that the country must not be unduly acquiescent to U.S. expectations—a view that can be heard on both sides of the Australian political aisle. Hence, while Australia-U.S. security and defense ties will expand, including on the ground on Australian territory, they will evolve steadily and carefully. Abroad, Australian leaders will be cautious to avoid the perception that closer defense ties with the United States and an enhanced security role in the Asia-Pacific are intended to target any particular country, with Indonesia and China being particularly sensitive cases.

A larger challenge for Australia-U.S. relations in the coming decades will be how the alliance adjusts in the face of an expansive Asia-Pacific security environment characterized by rising powers and geopolitical rivalries as well as by an increasingly complex set of nontraditional security concerns. A critical and difficult part of this challenge will be for Australia and the United States to balance the benefits of their economic relationships with China with their concerns about China as a growing and often more assertive regional military power. In this context, the two allies should seriously explore how they can engage trilaterally with China in the security sphere, including in humanitarian assistance and disaster relief, counterpiracy missions, military-to-military exchanges, and joint exercises. In addition to the many steps outlined above, Washington and Canberra will clearly need to intensify consultations about their bilateral relationship in the context of an emerging Asia and examine what they can do together to assure the continued regional stability and prosperity that both sides recognize to be fundamental to their national security interests.

Among the five major treaty alliances in the Asia-Pacific, the U.S.-Australia alliance is the closest and least problematic. Australia—which is not involved in any of the controversial territorial disputes that afflict Northeast and Southeast Asia—is in a better position than other major U.S. allies in the region to be actively engaged as an objective partner working to increase stability, confidence building, and security in the Asia-Pacific. As part of their respective national security strategies, both countries recognize the need to deepen their engagement across both government and private sectors and are expanding ways they can do so for mutual benefit. Their strategic perceptions, interests, and goals converge in a way that points to the likelihood of further cooperation across the board in spite of—and even because of—defense budget austerity, on the one hand, and the increasing complexity of the regional security environment, on the other.

In sum, given their closely shared interests globally and regionally, the United States and Australia can be expected to deepen their security relationship in the years ahead. This will include a larger U.S. military presence at facilities in Australia, increased joint training and operational activities abroad, and closer cooperation across a range of defense procurement projects. As both countries increasingly engage the Asia-Pacific region, but do so with tighter budgets, they will jointly step up diplomatic and security collaborations with third parties in the region in areas such as humanitarian assistance and disaster relief, antipiracy, counterproliferation, security-force training, military exercises and exchanges, defense procurement, and institution building. With the Australian economy likely to remain heavily reliant on resource exports to Northeast Asia—especially to China but also to Japan and South Korea—Canberra will be highly sensitive to any significant and destabilizing deterioration in relations among the major players in the region, particularly between the United States and China. Australia definitely does not wish to choose between its alliance relations and China, and will push back against efforts to make it do so.

EXECUTIVE SUMMARY

This chapter examines the history, current state, and trajectory of the U.S.-Philippine alliance in light of evolving security perceptions in the Philippines and ongoing changes to Asia's regional security environment.

MAIN ARGUMENT:
The alliance between the U.S. and the Philippines has evolved significantly in recent years. Changes to the external and internal security environment of the Philippines have combined to catalyze a transition in the country's security perceptions and priorities, especially a shift from an inward focus to one that is more externally directed. To meet rising external security demands, the Philippines has pursued a three-part strategy: internal balancing through increased spending, security cooperation with the U.S. and others in the region, and a diplomatic-legal strategy centered on international arbitration. This approach offers new opportunities for U.S.-Philippine cooperation but will also encounter both domestic and international challenges and constraints.

POLICY IMPLICATIONS:
- Given that significant political sensitivity still exists in the Philippines about the U.S. presence, broadening the alliance beyond traditional security concerns to encompass humanitarian, economic, and cultural cooperation will help demonstrate its benefits to ordinary Filipinos and create a stable, long-term foundation for the alliance.

- For the foreseeable future, Washington and Manila will likely operate under domestic political and resource constraints. Each side should be aware of the other's constraints and be prepared to handle divergences constructively.

- Creating a balance between a strong bilateral alliance and security relationships with other regional actors will reduce fears in the Philippines about overdependence on the U.S., achieve complementarity among actors with differing capacities, and foster a balance between reassurance and restraint.

The U.S. Alliance with the Philippines: Opportunities and Challenges

Sheena Chestnut Greitens

The past five years have seen a steadily increasing tempo in the relationship between the United States and the Republic of the Philippines. Not only has the alliance shown some of the greatest development among the United States' Asian alliances, but current initiatives also suggest that this cooperation is likely to increase in both breadth and depth in the years ahead. The Philippines is the twelfth-largest country in the world by population, a former U.S. colony with deep cultural and historical ties to the United States, a country positioned at a strategically and economically critical vantage point in the Pacific Ocean, and a U.S. treaty ally enmeshed in a web of East Asian territorial disputes and maritime claims that also involve the People's Republic of China. For all these reasons, the Philippines will play a key role in efforts to achieve U.S. foreign policy objectives in Asia.

Developments in the U.S.-Philippine relationship are occurring in the context of broader changes to Asia's regional landscape. These include leadership transitions in multiple countries, the emergence of a modernizing and seemingly more assertive China, and shifts in U.S. foreign policy and resource allocation. U.S. policy itself is bifurcated between two potentially contradictory trends. The first is an increasing emphasis on Asia, including Southeast Asia, as part of the Obama administration's "rebalancing" policy. The second trend is that U.S. power projection and diplomacy in Asia are

Sheena Chestnut Greitens is an Assistant Professor of Political Science at the University of Missouri and a Nonresident Senior Fellow at the Brookings Institution's Center for East Asia Policy Studies. She can be reached at <greitenss@missouri.edu>.

increasingly constrained by the more limited defense budgets imposed by sequestration and ongoing crises elsewhere that have distracted attention from the United States' intended focus on the region. The postponement of Obama's trip to the Philippines from October 2013 to April 2014 is one example of how attention to the Philippines, and Asia more generally, is likely to continue to take a backseat to domestic issues, raising concerns among the United States' regional allies and partners.[1] The key challenge for U.S. policymakers in the coming years, then, is how to strengthen the U.S.-Philippine relationship in ways that strike the right balance between reassurance and restraint and that account for likely constraints amid continued regional dynamism.[2]

In contrast with most of the United States' other alliance relationships in Asia, and despite its importance, there exists relatively little academic or policy analysis assessing the state and future development of the U.S.-Philippine alliance.[3] This chapter attempts to fill that gap. The first section reviews the Philippines' perceptions and priorities in security and foreign policy. It traces evolutions in Philippine views of the United States, China, internal security factors, and the role of overseas Filipino workers. The second section outlines current initiatives in Philippine foreign policy and cooperation with the United States, including alliance and security issues, economic and cultural factors, and regional and multilateral frameworks. It also discusses the trajectory of future policies and cooperative efforts, especially in light of potential domestic limitations. Finally, the chapter concludes by identifying the most promising areas for cooperation as well as probable risks and limitations.

---

[1] Alex Wong and Lanhee Chen, "Nonessential: Has Obama Given Up on the Asia Pivot?" *Foreign Policy*, October 2, 2013, http://www.foreignpolicy.com/articles/2013/10/02/nonessential_barack_obama_asia_pivot_shutdown; Kurt Campbell and Ely Ratner, "Far Eastern Promises: Why Washington Should Focus on Asia," *Foreign Affairs*, May/June 2014; and Michael J. Green and Zack Cooper, "Revitalizing the Rebalance: How to Keep U.S. Focus on Asia," *Washington Quarterly* (forthcoming).

[2] On the challenge of alliance management, see Sheena Chestnut Greitens, "U.S.-China Relations and America's Alliances in Asia," Brookings Institution, Brookings Northeast Asia Commentary, no. 65, June 11, 2013, http://www.brookings.edu/research/opinions/2013/06/11-us-china-relations-asia-alliances-greitens.

[3] For short exceptions, see Sheena Chestnut Greitens, "Obama's Visit to Asia and the U.S.-Philippine Alliance," Brookings Institution, Brookings East Asia Commentary, no. 77, April 2014, http://www.brookings.edu/research/opinions/2014/04/07-us-philippine-alliance-greitens; and Sheena Chestnut Greitens, "Drama on the High Seas: The China-Philippines Standoff and the U.S.-Philippine Alliance," *Foreign Policy*, April 12, 2012, http://www.foreignpolicy.com/articles/2012/04/12/drama_on_the_high_seas. See also Jim Thomas and Harry Foster, "The Geostrategic Return of the Philippines," Center for Strategic and Budgetary Assessments, CSBA Highlight, April 2012, http://www.csbaonline.org/publications/2012/04/the-geostrategic-return-of-the-philippines; Renato Cruz de Castro, "Future Challenges in the U.S.-Philippines Alliance," East-West Center, Asia-Pacific Bulletin, no. 168, June 26, 2012; and Felix K. Chang, "GI Come Back: America's Return to the Philippines," Foreign Policy Research Institute (FPRI), FPRI E-Notes, October 2013, http://www.fpri.org/articles/2013/10/gi-come-back-americas-return-philippines.

Philippine Security Perceptions and Priorities

Philippine foreign policy and security perceptions have been profoundly shaped by the evolution of the country's relationship with the United States. The Philippines has evolved from a flagship colony in the first half of the twentieth century, to a Cold War ally almost entirely dependent on U.S. bases and forces for external defense, to a post–Cold War power that, while weak in terms of defense capacity, was fully sovereign and independent in the foreign policy realm.

In recent years, however, the Republic of the Philippines has undergone a dual shift in threat perceptions. First, Chinese expansionism has replaced American neocolonialism as the chief risk to Philippine sovereignty. As the Philippines has shifted from perceiving China as an economic opportunity to perceiving it as a security threat, the United States has come to be viewed as a partner in resisting Chinese encroachment. Second, changing external perceptions have gone hand-in-hand with a shift in emphasis within the Armed Forces of the Philippines (AFP), which has moved away from its traditional focus on internal security to concentrate more on external defense missions and the development of increased maritime and air capabilities.

External maritime defense is likely to be a major priority for the AFP moving forward. Several factors, however, will constrain this transition for the foreseeable future: continued internal challenges, nontraditional security demands such as the need for humanitarian assistance and disaster relief (HADR), and domestic political characteristics that are likely to reinforce institutional and cultural inertia within the armed forces. Beyond these security considerations, contemporary Philippine foreign policy reflects the priority placed by the Aquino administration on economic growth. In particular, the economic importance of millions of overseas Filipino workers (OFW), coupled with a strong domestic perception of this population's vulnerability, has made their protection a foreign policy and diplomatic priority.

Perceptions of the United States

The Philippines has kept a relatively low profile in U.S. foreign policy in the past several decades, but that is atypical. For most of the twentieth century, the Philippine archipelago played a central role not just in U.S. policy toward Asia but in the United States' global foreign policy vision. Correspondingly, involvement with the United States has fundamentally shaped the security perceptions of the Philippine people and their leaders.

For the first half of the twentieth century, the Philippines was a U.S. territory and the United States' flagship effort at overseas democracy-building. The United States annexed the Philippines after the

Spanish-American War (1898) and fought a counterinsurgency conflict there, the Philippine-American War (1899–1902, though fighting lasted until 1913).[4] During the colonial period, American models of governance in areas ranging from education to police organization were imposed on the archipelago.

Plans for Philippine independence were delayed by the outbreak of World War II in the Pacific. Japanese forces launched air raids on the Philippines hours after the attack on Pearl Harbor and landed on Luzon days later. In spring 1942, after the fall of Manila and Corregidor, Filipino and American prisoners of war suffered alongside one another in the infamous Bataan death march. Throughout the war, Philippine soldiers fought together with Americans as auxiliary forces (and as U.S. citizens) under U.S. command. Historians estimate that over 200,000 Filipinos served in the Pacific theater and that over 100,000 died in defense of the United States and its Philippine territory. Following the war, on July 4, 1946, the Republic of the Philippines became independent.[5]

The current U.S.-Philippine security relationship came into being quickly after World War II. With the country devastated and prewar defense plans unaffordable, President Manuel Roxas saw cooperation with the United States as the best and only way to ensure external safety while Manila concentrated on reconstruction.[6] This cooperation had three foundational components. The first was the 1947 Military Bases Agreement, granting the United States the right to keep and use bases in the Philippines.[7] The second was the 1947 Military Assistance Agreement, establishing the Joint U.S. Military Advisory Group, which set the AFP's postwar size and structure. The group recommended, and Roxas and others agreed, that the AFP should concentrate on internal security, while the United States managed external defense.[8] The

---

[4] Debates during this time in Washington—over the need to demilitarize the occupation and declare the U.S. military's efforts a success, as well as over how to sustain public support and spending for a conflict that was officially winding down—bear a close resemblance to discussions in the past decade about Iraq.

[5] At that time, the Rescission Act stripped these veterans of their claim to benefits, a decision that was not corrected until the passage of the Filipino Veterans' Equity Act in February 2009. The Manila Veterans Affairs office is the only one outside U.S. territory. U.S. Embassy (Manila) and U.S. Department of Veterans Affairs, Fact Sheet, April 2013, http://photos.state.gov/libraries/manila/880176/factsheetsforwebapril2013/Fact%20Sheet%20-%20VA%20_Feb%202013_.pdf. See also "Speier Seeks to Extend Military Benefits to Filipino WWII Vets," CBS, http://sanfrancisco.cbslocal.com/2011/01/10/speier-seeks-to-extend-military-benefits-to-filipino-wwii-vets.

[6] Manuel Roxas, *Speeches, Addresses, and Messages as President of the Philippines*, vol. 1 (Manila: Bureau of Printing, 1954), 150, quoted in Ricardo T. Jose, "The Philippines during the Cold War: Searching for Security Guarantees and Appropriate Foreign Policies, 1946–1986," in *Cold War Southeast Asia*, ed. Malcolm H. Murfett (Singapore: Marshall Cavendish, 2012), 52.

[7] There were thirteen bases at the time of signing. The initial period of 99 years was reduced to 25 in 1966, expiring in 1991.

[8] Jose, "The Philippines during the Cold War," 57.

third component was the 1951 Mutual Defense Treaty (MDT), the United States' first in Asia.

Throughout the Cold War, the Philippines tied itself "more closely to the United States than any country in Southeast Asia," establishing a nearly symbiotic security relationship.[9] The AFP concentrated on internal security, confronting the Hukbalahap insurgency, the Communist New People's Army (NPA), and Muslim separatist groups in Mindanao, and administering martial law after its declaration in 1972.[10] These internal duties were the "principal security pre-occupation" of the Philippine government.[11] Meanwhile, U.S. forces used Philippine bases to "secure sea and air lanes, balance the Soviet military presence in Cam Ranh Bay, Vietnam, and provide regional defense for Southeast Asia."[12] Two key facilities were Clark Air Base and Subic Bay Naval Station, the United States' largest overseas naval installation in the Pacific and one of only two deepwater ports in the Pacific capable of hosting an aircraft carrier. Defense officials referred to these installations as "the greatest concentration of U.S. logistics, communication, and training facilities in the world."[13] The Philippines also participated in the Southeast Asia Treaty Organization (SEATO) and contributed forces to the conflicts in Korea and Vietnam. Manila sometimes expressed concern, however, that it was not bound tightly enough to the United States, largely because the MDT promised consultation rather than automatic assistance in the case of armed attack.[14]

The U.S.-Philippine relationship deteriorated after President Ferdinand Marcos fell from power in 1986. Many Filipinos believed that the United States had bought its access to bases by giving Marcos a free hand for domestic repression and corruption in the name of anti-Communism. The current president, Benigno "Noynoy" Aquino III, is the son of Benigno "Ninoy" Aquino Jr., the opposition leader assassinated by Marcos's security forces in 1983 after returning from exile in the United States. Protests after Ninoy's death raised his widow, Corazon Aquino (the current president's mother), to the presidency, while Marcos fled to Hawaii. As the Cold War ended,

---

[9] Ian Storey, *Southeast Asia and the Rise of China: The Search for Security* (Abingdon: Routledge, 2011), 252.

[10] Renato de Castro, "Adjusting to the Post-U.S. Bases Era: The Ordeal of the Philippine Military's Modernization Program," *Armed Forces & Society* 26, no. 1 (1999): 119–38.

[11] Charles Morrison, ed., *Asia Pacific Security Outlook 1997* (Honolulu: East-West Center, 1997), 97.

[12] Andrew Yeo, *Activists, Alliances, and Anti-U.S. Base Protests* (Cambridge: Cambridge University Press, 2011), 38–39.

[13] U.S. House of Representatives Armed Services Committee, Military Installations and Facilities Subcommittee, hearings in March and April 1991, cited in Yeo, *Activists, Alliances, and Anti-U.S. Base Protests*, 40.

[14] Jose, "The Philippines during the Cold War," 57. For the text of the mutual defense treaty (MDT), see http://www.chanrobles.com/mutualdefensetreaty.htm.

nationalist elites and anti-base activists argued that the security rationale for U.S. bases had disappeared. A volcanic eruption at Mount Pinatubo in 1991 also rendered Clark Air Base essentially inoperable. The Corazon Aquino administration emphasized Subic Bay's economic benefits, but the Philippine Senate, newly invested with post-Marcos authority over foreign policy, deemed the benefits too small and unequal. After acrimonious negotiations, the Senate rejected a renewal of the basing agreement in September 1991.[15] The post-democratization constitution explicitly forbids foreign military bases without Senate ratification and possibly a national referendum.[16]

The events of September 11, 2001, partially revitalized cooperation in the security realm, albeit on a narrower basis. Since January 2002, approximately six hundred U.S. special operations personnel have partnered with and trained Philippine forces to fight Islamic extremist groups in the southern Philippines. The two countries have also conducted military exercises such as the Balikatan training exercises, which have focused on HADR. Given constitutional restrictions, U.S. military personnel operate under the 1999 Visiting Forces Agreement, which has been subject to controversy following allegations of crimes committed by American servicemen and the dumping of toxic waste involving a U.S. Navy ship.[17]

Today, Philippine citizens share strong cultural and people-to-people ties with the United States and generally have strong pro-American feelings. Around 4 million U.S. residents consider themselves Filipino. An estimated 630,000 Americans visit the Philippines annually, and 300,000 live there.[18] A 2010 BBC survey found that 82% of Filipinos believe the United States plays a positive role in the world, a reservoir of goodwill that exceeded public sentiments in South Korea (57%) and Canada (44%).[19] That number has held constant over time and across different polls. For example, the Pew Research Center found that 90% of Filipinos had a positive view of the United States in 2002, and 85% retained that favorable view in 2013.[20] Even in 2006, near the height of Sino-Philippine cooperation, approval of the United States was

---

[15] Ratification required a two-thirds majority. The economic negotiations were particularly contentious: Filipinos saw the U.S. offer as insulting, whereas Richard Armitage complained that his counterparts were engaging in "cash register" diplomacy. Yeo, *Activists, Alliances, and Anti-U.S. Base Protests*, 61.

[16] The 1987 Philippine constitution is available online at http://www.lawphil.net/consti/cons1987.html.

[17] Michael Lim Ubac, "Senate Asks Arroyo to Scrap, Renegotiate VFA," *Philippine Daily Inquirer*, September 24, 2009; and Cathy Yamsuan, "Santiago, Bello to File Joint Resolution Seeking End to Visiting Forces Agreement," *Philippine Daily Inquirer*, November 17, 2012.

[18] U.S. Department of State, "U.S. Relations with the Philippines," Fact Sheet, January 31, 2014, http://www.state.gov/r/pa/ei/bgn/2794.htm#relations.

[19] Globescan, "Global Poll: Iran Seen Playing Negative Role," http://www.globescan.com/news_archives/bbc06-3/index.html.

[20] Pew Research Center, "Opinion of the United States," Global Attitudes Project, http://www.pewglobal.org/database/indicator/1/country/173.

around 85%.[21] The Pew survey also showed that 85% of Filipinos held positive views of the American people (as distinct from the government) and believed that the United States considered the interests of countries like the Philippines in formulating its foreign policy. One notable former U.S. resident is the secretary of foreign affairs, Albert del Rosario, who was educated in New York and is considered an advocate for the Philippines' pro-U.S. foreign policy.[22]

However, positive feelings toward the United States or Americans generally do not translate to unequivocal support for specific aspects of U.S. foreign policy or support for a particular security relationship. Anti-colonial nationalism has informed Philippine foreign policy since the country's independence and has usually been the principle at work in the few cases when Philippine foreign policy has significantly diverged from that of the United States.[23] Early in the Cold War, Philippine nationalists described U.S. bases as targets likely to attract an attack rather than deter one; the bases were also seen as an encroachment on Philippine sovereignty by a United States that was not fully reciprocating its ally's loyalty. Opponents of Marcos used this point to criticize him, and during the years of his dictatorship, the Philippine left also argued, with justification, that the bases were complicit in oppressing Filipinos.[24] As a result, nationalists and leftists have a long-standing distrust, and sometimes outright antagonism, toward dependence on the United States, thereby creating the potential for strong domestic opposition to U.S. policy and bases.

Perceptions of China

China's growing presence in the Asia-Pacific, especially since 2005, appears to be a critical factor that has prompted reconsideration of the Philippines' security and foreign policy priorities. During the Cold War, relations between the Philippines and the People's Republic of China (PRC) developed slowly, owing to a combination of Manila's distrust of Communism, its fear that Beijing would openly back the Communist Party of the Philippines, and the influence of the U.S. alliance. However, the U.S.-China rapprochement and Beijing's offer to supply oil at below-market prices after the 1973 oil crisis contributed to the normalization of Sino-Philippine relations in 1975 Nonetheless, relations remained tepid because of Manila's concerns about

---

[21] Globescan, "Global Poll: Iran Seen Playing Negative Role."

[22] Author's interview with a U.S. government official, June 2013.

[23] Jose, "The Philippines During the Cold War," 60; and Benjamin B. Domingo, *The Re-making of Philippine Foreign Policy* (Quezon City: University of the Philippines, 1993), 29.

[24] Yeo, *Activists, Alliances, and Anti-U.S. Base Protests*, 41. On the use of bases for internal repression, see Sheena Chestnut Greitens, "Coercive Institutions and State Violence under Authoritarianism" (PhD dissertation, Harvard University, 2013).

Beijing's support for the Communist Party of the Philippines and Beijing's concerns about Manila's relationship with Taipei. Territorial issues also became increasingly prominent at the end of the Cold War, especially after the 1995 Mischief Reef crisis, in which China built structures on territory in the Spratly Islands that is claimed by both Beijing and Manila.

Under President Gloria Macapagal Arroyo, who was in office from 2001 to 2010, the Philippines appeared to lean toward Beijing. At a 2005 summit with Hu Jintao, for example, she lauded a "golden age" of Sino-Philippine cooperation.[25] This stance was incentivized by booming two-way trade—from $1.77 billion in 2001 to $8.3 billion in 2006, a trade surplus for the Philippines—and by over $2 billion in Chinese overseas development assistance aimed at improving Philippine infrastructure and agriculture.[26] In 2005 the Philippines agreed to the Joint Marine Seismic Undertaking (JMSU), a tripartite project with China and Vietnam to survey contested maritime territory for oil and gas exploration. Arroyo's administration argued that this exploration made sense for the Philippines' energy security: for a country that imports a substantial amount of fossil fuel from the Middle East, Reed Bank offered important alternative (or additional and complementary) energy resources. Arroyo's emphasis on relations with China soured, however, as corruption allegations and subsequent congressional investigations tarnished China's development assistance projects and opponents claimed that the JMSU had conceded too much to Beijing. Broader concerns about corruption, as well as the shifting contours of domestic and electoral politics, ultimately contributed to the cancellation of these projects, and the JMSU lapsed in 2008.[27] Concern has grown since then that trade dependence on China would result in security compromises, and today Philippine politicians who promote the economic benefits of closer ties with China are in the minority.[28]

China's more aggressive behavior in the South China Sea after 2008 has also helped to harden Philippine perceptions. In spring 2011, Manila charged that China had harassed an oil exploration vessel near Reed Bank and opened fire on Philippine fishermen off Jackson Atoll in the Spratly Islands.[29] In April 2012 a standoff began at Scarborough Shoal (called Panatag in the Philippines and Huangyan in China) when a Philippine naval vessel attempted to detain

---

[25] Ian Storey, "Conflict in the South China Sea: China's Relations with Vietnam and the Philippines," *Japan Focus*, April 30, 2008, http://www.japanfocus.org/-ian-storey/2734.

[26] Storey, "Conflict in the South China Sea."

[27] Barry Wain, "*Manila's Bungle* in the South China Sea," *Far Eastern Economic Review*, January/February 2008.

[28] Chico Harlan, "Philippines Pushes Back Against China," *Washington Post*, July 23, 2013.

[29] Tessa Jamandre, "China Fired at Filipino Fishermen in Jackson Atoll," ABS-CBN, June 3, 2011, http://www.abs-cbnnews.com/-depth/06/02/11/china-fired-filipino-fishermen-jackson-atoll.

two Chinese boats that it claimed were fishing illegally. Despite reports that the United States had brokered a deal for both sides to withdraw, the episode resulted in a loss of Philippine control and Chinese occupation of the disputed area.[30] At the time of this chapter's writing, Sino-Philippine tensions centered on the Second Thomas Shoal (known as Ayungin in the Philippines and Ren'ai Reef in China) in the Spratly Islands. In March 2014, Chinese ships blocked efforts to resupply Philippine personnel stationed on the grounded BRP *Sierra Madre* and insisted that the Philippines withdraw its personnel. The Philippines, citing lessons learned from the Scarborough standoff, refused to withdraw and has resupplied the ship by air (and, once, by sea).[31]

As a result, from the Philippine perspective, China has shifted from presenting an economic opportunity to posing a security threat. Public opinion toward the PRC is somewhere between lukewarm and negative. Even at the height of the Sino-Philippine golden age under Arroyo, in 2006, positive views of China hovered around 56% (far below the United States at 85%).[32] After coming to power in 2010, the Aquino administration made overtures toward China—for example, by not attending the Nobel Peace Prize ceremony for Chinese dissident Liu Xiaobo. Yet maritime tensions, along with the execution of several Filipino drug mules despite high-level intervention by Manila, turned both public opinion and Aquino's administration increasingly negative in their views of Beijing.[33] In 2013, 69% believed that China had a fair amount of influence on the Philippines, and 58% believed that China took Philippine interests into consideration. However, only 48% held a favorable view of China, and 39% actually believed that China was an enemy, compared with 22% who saw it as a partner and 35% who saw it as neither.[34]

Philippine officials now see themselves as an Asia-Pacific David standing up to the Chinese Goliath. To this end, the Aquino administration has pursued a three-part strategy, the first part of which consists of efforts at internal balancing, which have occurred since around 2011. In May 2013, in a speech marking the Philippine Navy's 115th anniversary, President Aquino called for the country to stand up to "bullies" and announced a $1.82 billion defense modernization program intended to upgrade maritime capabilities by

---

[30] Greitens, "Drama on the High Seas"; and Jane Perlez and Steven Lee Myers, "In Beijing, Clinton Will Push for Talks over Disputed Islands," *New York Times*, September 3, 2012.

[31] Jim Gomez, "Philippine Supply Ship Evades Chinese Vessel," Associated Press, March 29, 2014; and Jeff Himmelman, "A Game of Shark and Minnow," *New York Times*, October 27, 2013.

[32] Globescan, "Global Poll: Iran Seen Playing Negative Role."

[33] Author's interview with a U.S. government official, June 2013; and "Philippine Nobel No-Show a Bid to Save Drug Mules in China," Agence France-Presse, December 12, 2010.

[34] Pew Research Center, "Opinion of the United States."

2017.[35] The increase is commensurate with an overall increase in investment in defense capabilities under Aquino from an average of $51 million per year before his tenure to approximately $1 billion per year now.[36]

Internal balancing, however, has limits. Despite increased Philippine investment, the military imbalance between China and the Philippines will not be overcome in the foreseeable future. Counting the increases under Aquino, the Philippines' annual defense spending remains a fraction of China's $115 billion annual defense budget. Because of this reality, Philippine academic Renato Cruz de Castro has cautioned that "no amount of material and technical assistance will enable the Philippines to confront an assertive China," and that "Filipino territorial defense is predicated on the U.S. assertion as the dominant naval power in the Pacific."[37] According to de Castro, the best that Manila can hope for is joint operations capabilities that complement, rather than substitute for, the deterrence provided by U.S. military power.

The second component of the strategy, therefore, is external balancing via a stronger alliance with the United States (which will be the focus of the next section). An increasing contingent of U.S. policymakers appears to share the Philippines' view that the archipelago is a strategic bellwether of the trajectory of the Asia-Pacific. One report referred to it as "a natural barrier to check Chinese expansion" and, on those grounds, called for the United States to help the Philippines develop its own anti-access/area-denial capabilities to counter China's growing attempts at power projection.[38]

The primary issue with external balancing, however, is alliance coordination. Thus far, Beijing's strategy seems to have been to escalate to just below the level where U.S. policymakers might feel compelled to intervene. This leaves open the question of how the Philippines, alone or in combination with the United States, can best contest Chinese maritime supremacy in the zones below open conventional combat—whether the Philippines can adopt its own strategy of "posing problems without catching up."[39]

The third component of the Philippines' strategy is the use of international law, together with an active international campaign to win public support for

---

[35] Cecil Morella, "Philippines to Spend 1.8 Billion Dollars on Defense to Resist 'Bullies,'" Agence France-Presse, May 21, 2013; and "China's 'Behavior' Needs Even Larger PHL Defense Spending—NSC," GMA News, http://www.gmanetwork.com/news/story/312799/news/nation/china-s-behavior-needs-even-larger-phl-defense-spending-nsc.

[36] Richard D. Fisher Jr., "Defending the Philippines: Military Modernization and the Challenges Ahead," Center for a New American Security (CNAS), East and South China Sea Bulletin, no. 3, May 3, 2012.

[37] Renato Cruz de Castro, "Future Challenges in the U.S.-Philippines Alliance," East-West Center, Asia-Pacific Bulletin, no. 168, June 26, 2012.

[38] Thomas and Foster, "The Geostrategic Return of the Philippines," 2.

[39] This phrase was originally used to describe China and its ability to pose problems without catching up to the United States. Thomas. J. Christensen, "Posing Problems without Catching Up: China's Rise and Challenges for U.S. Security Policy," International Security 25, no. 4 (2001): 5–40.

its cause. In January 2013 the Philippine government filed a four-part claim for international arbitration under the mandatory dispute-resolution process of the UN Convention on the Law of the Sea (UNCLOS). The filing contests China's assertion of its "nine-dash line," which claims a significant area of the South China Sea, and challenges the legality of several other aspects of PRC behavior.[40] Beijing has thus far rejected Manila's right to file for arbitration, calling it an attempt to "legalize its infringements and provocations" and gain international sympathy by using deception.[41]

Internal Considerations

Internal issues play a larger role in the Philippines' security perceptions than they do for any of the United States' other major security partners in Asia (except perhaps Thailand). These include armed conflict and separatist violence in Mindanao that has persisted for decades and the archipelago's high demand for HADR.

In late March 2014 the Philippine government signed a peace accord (the Comprehensive Agreement on the Bangsamoro) with the Moro Islamic Liberation Front (MILF), the major armed group fighting the government in the southern region of Mindanao.[42] The four-part agreement, reached after seventeen years of intermittent negotiation, provides autonomy to the predominantly Muslim area (to be called Bangsamoro) and outlines a disarmament process that leaders hope will end a 45-year-long conflict thought to have killed more than 120,000 people. The deal diminishes the risk of continued armed conflict but does not eliminate it, especially the risk of conflict involving splinter groups that could reject the terms of the deal and continue to fight. The MILF was itself a splinter group that separated from the Moro National Liberation Front (MNLF) after the latter signed its own peace deal with the government in 1996, and the MNLF has expressed reservations about the terms of the agreement reached by the MILF and the government. The MILF's stipulation that its 12,000 fighters will disarm after other groups have done so increases the probability that various spoilers could delay the implementation of a complex and multi-actor peace process. Various implementation steps—such as drafting and passing legislation to

---

[40] Peter A. Dutton, "The Sino-Philippine Maritime Row: International Arbitration and the South China Sea," CNAS, East and South China Seas Bulletin, no. 10, March 15, 2013.

[41] Louis Bacani, "China: Philippines Getting Int'l Sympathy through Deception," *Philippine Star*, June 16, 2014.

[42] Government of the Philippines, "The Comprehensive Agreement on the Bangsamoro," March 27, 2014, http://www.gov.ph/2014/03/27/document-cab.

replace the existing autonomous region and holding a plebiscite to determine its borders—are also potential triggers for renewed conflict.[43]

Moreover, Mindanao is home to other armed groups, as well as to a host of private armies and less-organized criminal violence. The other most prominent groups are Abu Sayyaf, a Muslim extremist group that the United States has linked to al Qaeda, and the New People's Army, considered Asia's longest-running Communist insurgency (having fought the government since 1969). The AFP stated in early 2014 that the NPA, though not the country's largest armed group (at around 4,000 fighters), is its "most potent" internal security challenge; operating mostly in Mindanao but with some presence elsewhere, the NPA engages in extortion, smuggling, and banditry to fund its activities.[44] It is therefore likely that the Philippines will continue indefinitely to face internal security threats that draw the military's attention and resources away from conventional, external, and maritime-oriented defense.

The other major internal demand on the AFP is HADR, which was highlighted by Super Typhoon Haiyan/Yolanda in November 2013.[45] The typhoon, one of the strongest tropical cyclones ever recorded, caused tsunami-level flooding, wind damage, landslides, and damage to homes, agriculture, infrastructure, and services, including power, communications, and water supply. The International Institute for Strategic Studies estimated that as of late January 2014 the death toll had exceeded 6,201, with 1,785 still missing, nearly 30,000 injured, and over 4 million displaced.[46] Although the AFP was the lead agency responding to the typhoon, the incident demonstrated the military's existing limitations in HADR operations. In particular, the lack of airlift and sea transport—with, for example, only three C-130 cargo planes—particularly hampered relief efforts.[47] Philippine legislators have clear electoral and political incentives to focus on and budget for building HADR capacities that serve their constituents, even if it means spending less on reform and modernization projects aimed at external defense.

---

[43] "Philippines, Muslim Rebels Sign Final Peace Deal to End Conflict," *Reuters*, March 27, 2014; "A Fragile Peace," *Economist*, February 1, 2014; International Crisis Group, "The Philippines: Breakthrough in Mindanao," Asia Report, no. 240, December 5, 2012; and International Crisis Group, "The Philippines: Dismantling Rebel Groups," Asia Report, no. 248, June 19, 2013.

[44] Nikko Dizon, "NPA Still the Most Potent Threat—AFP," *Philippine Daily Inquirer*, January 18, 2014; and Amanda Fernandez, "NPA Guerillas Mostly Concentrated in North-eastern, Southern Mindanao—AFP," GMA News, March 29, 2014.

[45] Greitens, "Obama's Visit to Asia."

[46] International Institute for Strategic Studies, "Asian Disaster Relief: Lessons of Haiyan," *Strategic Comments* 20, no. 2 (2014); and Thomas Lum and Rhoda Margesson, "Typhoon Haiyan (Yolanda): U.S. and International Response to Philippines Disaster," Congressional Research Service, CRS Report for Congress, R43309, February 10, 2014.

[47] Wu Shang-su, "Typhoon Haiyan and the Philippine Military," *Diplomat*, November 25, 2013; and Andrew Jacobs, "Typhoon Response Highlights Weaknesses in Philippine Military," *New York Times*, November 19, 2013.

As a result of its historical orientation and of these relatively high internal demands, the AFP has been an internally focused, land-dominated institution. The army remains the largest of the AFP's services by far, with 70,000 soldiers; by contrast, the navy has 22,000 personnel and the air force has 18,000.[48] Reorienting the AFP toward external defense in a maritime environment will take time, resources, and political capital. Even as Philippine perceptions of external security evolve and demands increase, the presence of internal security demands is likely to keep the focus of the political leadership more diversified than that of most U.S. allies. In combination with domestic political factors (discussed in more detail in the next section), these challenges will likely exert significant countervailing pressure on the military to prioritize internal contingencies—ranging from terrorism and armed conflict to HADR and public works projects.

Overseas Filipino Workers: A Global Community

The final foreign policy priority of the Philippines—declared to be the "third pillar of Philippine foreign policy" under President Aquino—is the protection and safety of overseas Filipino workers.[49] The Commission on Overseas Filipinos estimated in 2010 that approximately 9.5 million Filipinos worked or resided abroad either temporarily or permanently (out of a population of 95 million); in July 2013, the Philippines' National Statistics Office estimated the total number of OFWs at 2.2 million.[50] In addition to the United States, common OFW destinations include Singapore, Saudi Arabia, Qatar, the United Arab Emirates, and other locations in the Middle East. Remittances sent by these workers are the country's second-largest source of foreign reserves, exceeding FDI during the mid-2000s and totaling over $25 billion (8.4% of GDP) in 2013.[51] OFW remittances, while valuable to the Philippines simply from an economic perspective, are also a source of

---

[48] Author's interview with Philippine defense officials, June 2013. Some sources place the army's strength at closer to 85,000.

[49] Alberto G. Romulo, "The 3 Pillars of Philippine Foreign Policy. Economy, Security, and OFWs," *Philippine Star*, January 7, 2011.

[50] Commission on Overseas Filipinos, "Stock Estimate of Overseas Filipinos," December 2010; and National Statistics Office (Philippines), "Total Number of OFWs Is Estimated at 2.2 Million (Results from the 2012 Survey on Overseas Filipinos)," July 11, 2013, http://www.census.gov.ph/content/total-number-ofws-estimated-22-million-results-2012-survey-overseas-filipinos. The Central Intelligence Agency's *World Factbook* estimated the population of the Republic of the Philippines at 105 million in 2013. See Central Intelligence Agency, *World Factbook* (Washington, D.C.: Central Intelligence Agency, 2013).

[51] "Remittances Hit Record High of $25B in 2013," *Philippine Star*, February 17, 2014; and Bangko Sentral ng Pilipinas, "Overseas Filipinos' Cash Remittances," http://www.bsp.gov.ph/statistics/keystat/ofw2.htm.

economic independence from China that distinguishes the Philippines from others in the region.

Domestically, however, these workers are perceived as vulnerable. Stories of women raped or abused by employers have been intensely covered by domestic media.[52] The worldwide dispersion of OFWs is a particularly tricky issue from the standpoint of the Philippines' political leaders, since it creates a global interest in a country that does not have the global military reach and capacity to match. As a result, the Philippine government has taken strong and visible diplomatic steps to advocate for the safety of OFWs, including repatriating them from crises abroad, and has highlighted these activities to its domestic audience.[53]

Philippine Foreign Policy and Cooperation with the United States

The upward trajectory of U.S.-Philippine relations looks likely to continue. Bilateral cooperation has increased in tempo, a new defense agreement has been signed, and the two governments are discussing additional ways to augment the security relationship. The key questions, therefore, are how this increased bilateral activity will fit within the overall context of Philippine foreign policy, and how it can be executed given domestic constraints on both sides. To consider this requires taking into account the multilateral and regional institutional framework within which the Philippines operates, as well as the domestic limitations to security cooperation with the United States and other countries.

Security Cooperation: The U.S.-Philippine Alliance

The bilateral relationship between the United States and the Philippines has become increasingly active. The two countries launched a bilateral strategic dialogue in early 2011, and in November of that year, U.S. secretary of state Hillary Clinton stopped in Manila to celebrate the 60th anniversary of the alliance, speaking at a theatrically staged ceremony held on a U.S. destroyer, the USS *Fitzgerald*, in Manila Bay. She referred to the disputed waters of the South China Sea as the "West Philippine Sea" and referenced

---

[52] Leila B. Salaverria, "Solon Slams Gov't for Failure to Stop Exploitation of OFWs," *Philippine Daily Inquirer*, June 21, 2013.

[53] "Expanded OFW Protection Law to Take Effect August," GMA News, July 30, 2010, http://www.gmanetwork.com/news/story/197367/pinoyabroad/expanded-ofw-protection-law-to-take-effect-august; and Albert del Rosario, "Closing Remarks: Two Years Thereafter: The Best of the Philippine Diaspora," Department of Foreign Affairs (Philippines), February 27, 2013.

boxer and Philippine congressman Manny Pacquiao, promising that "the United States will always be in the corner of the Philippines and we will stand and fight with you."[54] April 2012 marked the first "2+2" summit involving both sides' defense and foreign secretaries, and President Aquino visited the White House in June of that same year.[55] The two countries also hold annual military exercises, including the Balikatan exercises (most recently in May 2014) and the PHIBLEX amphibious landing exercises (most recently in September–October 2014). In April 2014, President Obama visited Manila for a state visit to mark the signing of the new Enhanced Defense Cooperation Agreement (EDCA).[56]

U.S. assistance to the AFP has so far placed primary emphasis on training, consultation, and advising.[57] Arms sales, however, are an increasing component of the defense relationship. After the April 2012 2+2 meeting, the Philippine foreign ministry announced that the United States had increased its foreign military financing to the Philippines from $11.9 million in 2011 to $30 million in 2012 (out of a total assistance package of $158.8 million).[58] Under the Excess Defense Articles and Military Assistance Program, the United States has provided two Hamilton-class coast guard cutters for use in the Philippine Navy—which named the vessels the BRP *Ramon Alcaraz* and the BRP *Gregorio del Pilar*—and is assisting the Philippines in the development and expansion of a national coast watch system established in

[54] Shaun Tandon, "Clinton Uses Warship to Push Philippines Alliance," Agence France-Press, November 16, 2011.

[55] U.S. Department of State, "Joint Statement of the United States–Philippines Bilateral Strategic Dialogue," January 27, 2012, http://www.state.gov/r/pa/prs/ps/2012/01/182688.htm; Hillary Rodham Clinton, "Remarks with Secretary of Defense Leon Panetta, Philippines Foreign Secretary Albert del Rosario, and Philippines Defense Secretary Voltaire Gazmin after Their Meeting," U.S. Department of State, April 30, 2012, http://www.state.gov/secretary/rm/2012/04/188982.htm; Ernest Z. Bower and Gregory B. Poling, "Implications and Results: The United States–Philippines Ministerial Dialogue," CSIS, May 4, 2012, http://csis.org/publication/implications-and-results-united-states-philippines-ministerial-dialogue; and White House, "Statement on the President's Meeting with President Aquino of the Philippines," June 8, 2012, http://www.whitehouse.gov/the-press-office/2012/06/08/statement-president-s-meeting-president-aquino-philippines.

[56] Government of the Philippines, "Enhanced Defense Cooperation Agreement between the Philippines and the United States," April 29, 2014, http://www.gov.ph/2014/04/29/document-enhanced-defense-cooperation-agreement.

[57] Renato Cruz de Castro and Walter Lohman, "U.S.-Philippines Cooperation in the Cause of Maritime Defense," Heritage Foundation, Backgrounder, no. 2593, August 8, 2011.

[58] Embassy of the Philippines (Washington, D.C.), "PH-U.S. Bilateral Relations," http://www.philippineembassy-usa.org/philippines-dc/embassy-dc/ph-us-bilateral-relations-dc.

2011 to improve maritime domain awareness.[59] The Philippine Marine Corps also received six riverine patrol boats from the United States in August 2013.[60]

The EDCA is intended to build on the MDT and facilitate future defense cooperation by expanding U.S. access to Philippine military bases.[61] Negotiators were well aware of the Philippines' constitutional limits on foreign bases, and the new agreement—an executive agreement that does not require ratification by the Philippine Senate—is designed to minimize domestic opposition by explicitly affirming Philippine sovereignty and establishing a framework for an increased rotational presence rather than permanent bases. The United States will have operational control and the ability to preposition equipment in the agreed locations, but the Philippines will have full access to and retain ownership of the facilities. The exact locations of these future rotational forces will be determined under subsequent implementing agreements, though U.S. Air Force personnel have indicated that these may include jets stationed at airfields at Kubi Point (next to Subic Bay) and Puerto Princesa in Palawan, close to the disputed Spratly Islands.[62] Additional forms of cooperation are also under consideration, including bilateral information sharing, joint-use maritime security support facilities, and maritime security activities, including integrated and coordinated initiatives between the AFP and U.S. Pacific Command and U.S. capacity-building assistance to the AFP. In July 2013, Philippine secretary of national defense Voltaire Gazmin confirmed that U.S. surveillance aircraft were providing intelligence on Chinese military activities in areas disputed by the Philippines and China.[63]

Beyond Security: Economic and Cultural Cooperation

To make the alliance stable and sustainable, the United States must look beyond conventional defense cooperation with the Philippines to think more broadly about the relationship. In the long term, the alliance will be most stable if it accomplishes two things: (1) accruing benefits to the Philippine

[59] U.S. Embassy (Manila), "DTRA Hosts National Coast Watch System Tabletop Exercise in Manila," Press Release, May 17, 2013, http://manila.usembassy.gov/dtracoastwatchsystem.html. See also "U.S. to Deliver Battle-Ready 2nd Hamilton-Class Cutter," *Daily Tribune*, October 29, 2012.

[60] Sam LaGrone, "U.S. Gives Philippines Six Riverine Patrol Boats for Counter Terrorism Missions," U.S. Naval Institute (USNI), USNI News, September 26, 2013, http://news.usni.org/2013/09/26/u-s-gives-philippine-marines-six-riverine-boats-counter-terrorism-missions.

[61] Carl Thayer, "Analyzing the U.S.-Philippines Enhanced Defense Cooperation Agreement," *Diplomat*, May 2, 2014, http://thediplomat.com/2014/05/analyzing-the-us-philippines-enhanced-defense-cooperation-agreement.

[62] John Reed, "U.S. Deploying Jets Around Asia to Keep China Surrounded," *Foreign Policy*, July 29, 2013.

[63] Jason Gutierrez, "Philippines Reveals U.S. Spy Planes Monitoring China at Sea," Agence France-Presse, July 31, 2013.

people, rather than only a handful of elites, and (2) clearly demonstrating and communicating those benefits. Broader outreach to Philippine society, especially on the economic and development front, will signal that the United States is not seeking to exploit Philippine territory for geopolitical interests that do not align with Filipinos' own security and prosperity; instead, the United States is interested in building a stable partnership based on the shared interests of the two societies. Especially given the vicissitudes of the relationship between the Philippines and China, a broad base of cooperation will make for a more durable and less tempestuous U.S.-Philippine alliance.

This argument has implications for both security cooperation and nonsecurity measures. Given that U.S. involvement with the AFP contributed to repression and violence against Filipinos in the past, it is important that foreign military assistance and training be perceived as a form of cooperation that protects ordinary citizens rather than harming them. The Philippines is a prime candidate for the kind of humanitarian missions that the U.S. Navy has used to build goodwill toward ordinary citizens in Southeast Asia in the past; its ships can provide services badly needed in a country whose seven thousand islands are prone to typhoons, landslides, and other natural disasters. The EDCA's inclusion of HADR missions in the scope of envisioned cooperation and the importance that Presidents Obama and Aquino placed on this cooperation during Obama's April 2014 visit are therefore welcome. Continued counterterrorism and security assistance to the Philippines must also be conditioned on clear standards of accountability and adherence to human rights in order to avoid repeating the post-Marcos blowback. The human rights–based intelligence policies recently adopted by the Philippine National Police and AFP indicate that such standards are not only sensible but eminently feasible.[64]

Complementing the security relationship with enhanced economic and nonmilitary cooperation will be important to mitigate lingering concerns in the Philippines about sovereignty and U.S. dependency, as well as to move the alliance beyond shared animosities to a foundation of constructive mutual benefit. This cooperation, already underway, can be built on and expanded naturally over time.

On the economic front, the United States remains one of the Philippines' largest trade partners, second only to Japan. The United States has traditionally been the Philippines' largest foreign investor, with two-way goods and services

---

[64] Armed Forces of the Philippines, *Human Rights–Based Intelligence Operations Guidebook* (Quezon City, 2011), http://www.chr.gov.ph/MAIN%20PAGES/writings/Human%20Rights%20Based%20 Intelligence%20Operations%20Guidebook%20ver5.pdf. See also Philippine National Police, *PNP Guidebook on Human Rights–Based Policing* (Quezon City, 2011), http://pnp.gov.ph/portal/images/ stories/publicrelations/PNP_GUIDEBOOK_opt.pdf.

trade totaling approximately $24 billion in 2012.[65] The Trade and Investment Framework Agreement, first signed in 1989, was last revised in 2010, and at the November 2011 Asia-Pacific Economic Cooperation (APEC) summit, the two countries signed an agreement on customs administration and trade facilitation. They have also begun technical consultations on the requirements for the Philippines to join the Trans-Pacific Partnership (TPP). The TPP is consistent with the Philippines' preference for multilateral rather than bilateral trade agreements, and in April 2014 President Aquino expressed the Philippines' interest in eventually joining. Both sides, however, acknowledge that the Philippines would need to further liberalize its economy—including lifting restrictions on foreign ownership of land and some businesses, which would require constitutional amendment—in order to join the second round of negotiations.[66]

Other cooperative efforts focus on aid, development, and economic growth. The United States provides development assistance to the Philippines, including an agreement in 2010 to extend a $434 million grant for poverty reduction efforts from the Millennium Challenge Corporation (MCC).[67] The five-year U.S.-Philippine Partnership for Growth, signed by Secretary Clinton and Secretary del Rosario in November 2011, is intended to build on MCC assistance and improve governance in ways that will prepare the Philippine economy for eventual accession to the TPP. Measures include improving the transparency of the regulatory regime, fighting corruption, strengthening the courts and the rule of law, fostering a more open business environment, and improving fiscal stability.[68] Moreover, as of late January 2014, the United States had provided more than $87 million in post-typhoon humanitarian assistance, as well as $59 million in private donations.[69]

---

[65] U.S. Embassy (Manila), "Why the Philippines," http://manila.usembassy.gov/why-philippines.html.

[66] Amy Remo, "U.S., PH Establish New TIFA Work Program," *Philippine Daily Inquirer*, March 22, 2014; and "Aquino Presses for PH Inclusion in Pacific Trade Deal," *Rappler*, April 28, 2014, http://www.rappler.com/business/economy-watch/56626-aquino-obama-philippines-trans-pacific-partnership.

[67] Kurt M. Campbell, "The U.S.-Philippines Alliance: Deepening the Security and Trade Partnership," testimony before the House Committee on Foreign Affairs, Subcommittee on Terrorism, Nonproliferation, and Trade, February 7, 2012, http://www.state.gov/p/eap/rls/rm/2012/02/183494.htm.

[68] U.S. Department of State, "U.S.-Philippines Partnership for Growth," Fact Sheet, November 16, 2011, http://www.state.gov/r/pa/prs/ps/2011/11/177225.htm. See also "Partnership for Growth: Philippines–United States 2012–2016," Joint Country Action Plan, November 2011, http://photos.state.gov/libraries/manila/19452/pdfs/Philippines_PFG_JCAP_public_final_11-29-11.pdf.

[69] Lum and Margesson, "Typhoon Haiyan (Yolanda)."

Regional and Multilateral Efforts in Philippine Foreign Policy

Alongside increased interaction with the United States, the Philippines has pursued active engagement with other Asia-Pacific powers. Such engagement has involved both bilateral initiatives—especially with Australia, South Korea, Japan, and Vietnam—and the region's various multilateral frameworks.

In July 2012, for example, the Philippines ratified a status of forces agreement signed in May 2007 with Australia, setting the framework for future exercises, exchanges, and security cooperation.[70] Australia also participated in the U.S.-Philippine Balikatan exercises in May 2014, after observing in 2013.[71] South Korea, one of the Philippines' largest providers of overseas development assistance in recent years, supplied two patrol boats in 2006. The country also agreed in 2014 to donate a corvette warship to the Philippine Navy and signed an agreement to sell the Philippines twelve FA-50 fighter aircraft as part of a $421 million contract.[72] Defense cooperation between the Philippines and Vietnam has also increased—particularly naval and coast guard cooperation and high-level visits—since the initial signing of a memorandum of understanding in 2010, but these activities have not yet reached the level of joint exercises.[73]

Outreach to Japan has picked up as well. In late 2012, Secretary del Rosario expressed support for a rearmed Japan, saying that it could provide balance to the region—an attitude that distinguishes the Japan-Philippines relationship from relations between Japan and either South Korea or China, who remain much more sensitive to historical issues in their relations with Tokyo.[74] After the January 2013 visit of Japanese foreign minister Fumio Kishida to Manila, Japan agreed in May to provide communications assistance for coastal patrolling and ten multi-role response vessels to the Philippine Coast Guard (at a cost of $11 million each through a concessional loan from Japan's overseas development assistance agency, the Japan International Cooperation Agency).[75] Japan had also previously said that its coast guard

---

[70] Australian Embassy (Philippines), "Status of Visiting Forces Agreement with Australia Ratified by the Philippines," July 24, 2012, http://www.philippines.embassy.gov.au/mnla/medrel120726.html.

[71] Elena L. Aben, "Balikatan to Become Multilateral Exercise," *Tempo*, April 14, 2013, http://www.tempo.com.ph/2013/04/balikatan-to-become-multilateral-exercise; and Isis Ramirez, "U.S., Philippine Forces Begin Balikatan Exercise," U.S. Department of Defense, Press Release, May 6, 2014, http://www.defense.gov/news/newsarticle.aspx?id=122191.

[72] "S. Korea to Donate Warship to Philippines Amid Sea Tensions," Agence France-Presse, June 7, 2014.

[73] Carl Thayer, "Is a Philippine-Vietnam Alliance in the Making?" *Diplomat*, March 28, 2014.

[74] Ida Torres, "Philippines Welcomes a Re-armed Japan," *Japan Daily Press*, December 10, 2012, http://japandailypress.com/philippines-welcomes-a-re-armed-japan-1019587; and Sheena Chestnut Greitens and Caitlin Talmadge, "The U.S.-Japan Alliance in a Time of Transition," German Marshall Fund of the United States, Policy Brief, July 2013.

[75] Oliver Teves, "Japan Vows Support for Philippines in China Row," Associated Press, July 27, 2013.

would provide training to the Philippines and Vietnam.[76] In July 2013, at a summit in Manila, Prime Minister Shinzo Abe and President Aquino agreed to strengthen maritime cooperation under the two countries' strategic partnership. Japan has also eased visa requirements for Philippine citizens, and the two countries have held talks on economic cooperation.

On the multilateral front, the Philippines has traditionally looked to the Association of Southeast Asian Nations (ASEAN) for security, and the country continues to play an active role in regional multilateral frameworks. Progress among the ten members of ASEAN to transform the 2002 Declaration on the Conduct of Parties in the South China Sea into a legally binding code of conduct, however, has been slow at best. Moreover, policymakers in Manila have been frustrated by ASEAN's failure to offer support during confrontations with Beijing—a frustration that dates back to the perceived lack of support that the Philippines received from ASEAN over China's encroachments into Mischief Reef in 1995. The Philippines has departed from the general ASEAN approach to China at times in the past and appears to be doing so again—perhaps as a result of strong trade relationships with the United States and Japan that render it less dependent on China's economy. Whatever the reason, the Philippines has adopted a bolder stance than most of the other countries who are contesting territory in the South China Sea, including Taiwan, Brunei, Malaysia, and Vietnam.[77]

Thus, one key question is how the Philippines will square its participation in ASEAN with its current David-against-Goliath approach to China. Although the Philippines has previously welcomed China's participation in discussions on a code of conduct,[78] it has mounted a clear legal challenge to China's territorial claims by filing for arbitration under UNCLOS in January 2013, followed by submission of a four-thousand-page memorial on Manila's position in late March 2014.[79] The Philippines has not asked UNCLOS to rule

---

[76] Ida Torres, "Japanese Leaders Reaffirm Ties with the Philippines," *Japan Daily Press*, January 10, 2013, http://japandailypress.com/japanese-leaders-reaffirm-ties-with-the-philippines-1021200; and Ida Torres, "Japan to Donate Coast Guard Patrol Boats to the Philippines," *Japan Daily Press*, February 11, 2013, http://japandailypress.com/japanto-donate-coast-guard-patrol-boats-to-the-philippines-1123093.

[77] Chico Charlan, "Philippines Pushes Back against China," *Washington Post*, July 23, 2013, http://www.washingtonpost.com/world/asia_pacific/philippines-pushes-back-against-china/2013/07/23/4dfa6058-f043-11e2-bed3-b9b6fe264871_story.html; and Michaela Del Callar, "PHL Proceeds with Case vs. China over West Philippine Sea," GMA News, March 30, 2014.

[78] Tarra Quismundo, "U.S. Pushes Code of Conduct," *Philippine Daily Inquirer*, July 2, 2013, http://globalnation.inquirer.net/79351/us-pushes-code-of-conduct; and T.J. Burgonio, "Aquino Hopeful about Talks on West Philippine Sea Code of Conduct," *Philippine Daily Inquirer*, April 23, 2013, http://globalnation.inquirer.net/72861/aquino-hopeful-about-talks-on-west-philippine-sea-code-of-conduct.

[79] Department of Foreign Affairs (Philippines), "Senate Resolution Strongly Supporting the Filing of an Arbitration Case Against China under Article 287 and Annex VII of the United Nations Convention of the Law of the Seas by President Benigno S. Aquino."

specifically on sovereignty over the disputed areas but rather on whether China's nine-dash line is consistent with UNCLOS, to which the PRC is a party; on China's occupation of submerged features and "rocks" rather than "islands"; and on the legality of China's behavior toward Philippine nationals at sea.[80] Although the tribunal has ordered Beijing to respond by December 2014, China has thus far refused to participate in the arbitration process, waiving the right to appoint its own member to the tribunal and arguing that the Philippines' claims fall outside UNCLOS jurisdiction. The Philippines, on the other hand, argues that arbitration is consistent with "peaceful and rules-based resolution of disputes…in accordance with international law."[81] Whether the international tribunal will assert jurisdiction remains to be seen.

It is unclear how the Philippines' decision to seek arbitration, which appeared to surprise many of the country's Southeast Asian neighbors, will affect relations with the rest of ASEAN. Some ASEAN members expressed concern over the Philippines' lack of prior consultation, and their reactions may not be positive if the claim produces a contentious Chinese response that negatively affects their interests or ASEAN's attempts to negotiate a code of conduct. If, on the other hand, the arbitration process convinces Beijing of the benefits of a code of conduct, the move is likely to be received more positively. Perhaps foreseeing this, China appears to be actively trying to split the Philippines from the rest of ASEAN in order to strengthen its bargaining position. The Philippines, on the other hand, appears to be pairing its legal strategy with a concerted effort to win over international public opinion, even reaching out to journalists to make its case.[82]

The United States, though not a member of UNCLOS, has traditionally supported a multilateral framework for dispute resolution in Asia and is likely to continue to do so for three reasons. First, multilateral approaches maximize the leverage of smaller U.S. partners, who are the weaker parties in any bilateral dispute with Beijing. Second, they signal respect for the region's traditional way of doing things and avoid antagonizing other Asian countries by appearing to take only one country's side on sovereignty claims. Third, they minimize the risk that a country like the Philippines could embroil the United States in a conflict with China. Beijing is already prone to seeing its disputes with U.S. allies (such as Japan) as Washington's responsibility, and it

---

[80] Ian Storey, "Manila Ups the Ante in the South China Sea," Jamestown Foundation, China Brief, February 1, 2013.

[81] Albert del Rosario, "Statement by Secretary of Foreign Affairs Albert del Rosario on the UNCLOS Arbitral Proceedings against China to Achieve a Peaceful and Durable Solution to the Disputes in the WPS," *Official Gazette*, January 22, 2013, http://www.gov.ph/2013/01/22/statement-the-secretary-of-foreign-affairs-on-the-unclos-arbitral-proceedings-against-china-january-22-2013.

[82] Carl Thayer, "To Isolate Philippines, China Woos ASEAN," *Diplomat*, October 1, 2013; and Shannon Tiezzi, "The Philippines' UNCLOS Claim and the PR Battle Against China," *Diplomat*, April 1, 2014.

is in the United States' interest to avoid framing these as U.S.-China disputes. U.S. officials characterize their desired approach as one of moderation and confidence, but not emboldenment.[83]

Domestic Limitations on Philippine Foreign Policy

The Philippines' efforts to expand and modernize its armed forces to meet the changing external security environment in Southeast Asia are likely to face domestic political constraints. These limitations are of three types: competition between external security needs and internal security demands that will draw resources and attention, as discussed above; overall resource constraints on the Philippines' defense modernization efforts; and political constraints imposed by Philippine institutions and political culture.

The first issue is finding sufficient resources to support the Philippines' modernization ambitions. As one analyst commented, since 1965 "successive Philippine governments have been unable or unwilling to invest in a credible external defense capability."[84] Even after the U.S. withdrawal in 1992 ended the Cold War's long-standing division of labor between U.S. forces and the AFP, the Philippines did not invest in conventional defense capabilities; the last defense modernization program—also spurred by Chinese maritime encroachments in the mid-1990s—was shelved with the 1997 Asian financial crisis. In 2003 the Bush and Arroyo administrations developed the Philippine Defense Reform Program and a capabilities upgrade program for the AFP. U.S. assistance, however, remained relatively limited, and on the Philippine side, modernization was hampered by a cumbersome bureaucracy, an inefficient procurement process, and a lack of support from the Philippine Congress.[85]

The result was summarized by President Aquino in July 2010, when he noted in his state of the nation address that the Philippines—an archipelago of seven thousand islands and over 36,000 miles of nautical coastline— had only 32 boats, most of them as old as General Douglas MacArthur.[86] Assessments by the Philippine Department of National Defense and the AFP have concluded that the Philippine Navy has insufficient patrol ships (only 15) to protect its maritime waters and exclusive economic zone, and that the Philippine Air Force lacks modern air-defense, surveillance, air-lift, and ground-attack capabilities. Under the Aquino administration's Long-Term

---

[83] Author's interview with a U.S. government official, June 2013.

[84] Fisher Jr., "Defending the Philippines," 1.

[85] De Castro and Lohman, "U.S.-Philippines Cooperation in the Cause of Maritime Defense."

[86] Benigno S. Aquino III, "State of the Nation Address of His Excellency Benigno S. Aquino III, President of the Philippines, to the Congress of the Philippines," *Official Gazette*, July 26, 2010, http://www.gov.ph/2010/07/26/state-of-the-nation-address-2010-en.

Capability Development Plan, Defense Secretary Gazmin has accelerated the modernization program envisioned under Arroyo, with the goal of quickly achieving territorial defense capabilities. Despite its heavy weighting of naval and air capabilities, however, Aquino's modernization program is beginning from a low baseline, and a lack of funding has continued to hamper the program. Even with the announcement of supplemental funding in 2013, the reforms are aimed more at border patrol and defense than advanced naval warfighting.[87]

The changes required for defense reform within the armed forces are not only structural but cultural. As the AFP builds out its new capabilities, it will need to rethink its force structure and base locations, which it is already doing to some extent.[88] The AFP must also consider the role of the Philippine Army and cultivate a military culture that places more emphasis on air and naval capabilities. This will be especially imperative as police forces in Bangsamoro are formed and the Philippine National Police takes a stronger role in domestic policing elsewhere in the country.[89] Yet developing the procedures and training to achieve effective interservice coordination of assets will take time, even after the new capabilities are fully in place.

Other domestic constraints involve the Philippines' broader political climate and institutions. The Philippines does not typically release a document outlining its defense policy or national security strategy; the last defense white paper was issued in 1998. Long-term strategic planning is hampered by a presidential system with a single six-year term, making it difficult to predict Manila's strategic direction and willingness to invest resources to match its articulated goals beyond the next presidential election. This system also contributes to the difficulty of maintaining momentum and continuity in the reform process. Moreover, the Philippine legislature has typically focused more on patronage politics than on the development of strategic expertise and oversight capacity; it has electoral incentives to direct the land-heavy AFP toward domestic public works projects and public goods provision.[90] According to Filipino analysts, significant reforms are still needed to tackle such bureaucratic inertia and corruption.

---

[87] De Castro and Lohman, "U.S.-Philippines Cooperation."

[88] "Philippines May Move Warships to Subic," Agence France-Presse, July 29, 2013.

[89] Author's interview with a U.S. government official, June 2013; and author's interview with two Philippine National Police officials, Manila, November 2011.

[90] For further discussion of the impact of domestic politics on Philippine foreign policy, see David Wurfel, "Philippine Foreign Policy," in *The Political Economy of Foreign Policy in Southeast Asia,* ed. David Wurfel and Bruce Burton (London: Palgrave MacMillan, 1990); Evan Medeiros et al., *Pacific Currents: The Responses of U.S. Allies and Security Partners in East Asia to China's Rise* (Santa Monica: RAND Corporation, 2008); and Aileen S.P. Baviera, "The Influence of Domestic Politics on Philippine Foreign Policy," S. Rajaratnam School of International Studies (RSIS), RSIS Working Paper, no. 241, June 5, 2012, http://www.rsis.edu.sg/publications/WorkingPapers/WP241.pdf.

Conclusions and Challenges

Philippine security perceptions are evolving, and so is the U.S.-Philippine alliance. External and internal changes to the security environment have catalyzed a fundamental strategic reorientation of the Philippine armed forces, from internally focused and land-oriented to externally focused and maritime-oriented. This shift will require significant changes within the AFP and tough political choices as Philippine leaders confront trade-offs imposed by resource constraints.

Alongside these developments, there is increased interest in reformulating the Philippines' security partnership with the United States to fit the Philippines' new environment and thinking. This presents both countries with new opportunities to advance cooperation in areas of mutual interest. A number of domestic political factors on both sides, however, could inhibit cooperation, and policymakers should assess these factors realistically in crafting their efforts.

On the Philippine side, long-standing nationalist and leftist sensitivity to potential violations of sovereignty by foreign military forces remains an issue. Although the EDCA appears to have avoided some potential flashpoints, policymakers in both countries will need to continue to tread cautiously. One way to do so is for the United States to continue to emphasize HADR cooperation.[91] This provides visible, demonstrable benefits to the Filipino people and is easier for politicians to support, since it aligns with their own electoral incentives and lacks the sensitivities that accompany a more traditional U.S. military presence. HADR cooperation also emphasizes the unique capabilities of the United States and its security partners, which provided far more personnel and financing to assist in the relief effort after Super Typhoon Haiyan/Yolanda than either China or ASEAN.[92] The United States can also emphasize capacity-building in areas that are needed for HADR but that might have secondary benefits for maritime defense, such as maritime awareness, communications, and logistics. Finally, Washington can emphasize its interest in the welfare of the Filipino people by supporting the Aquino administration's efforts to protect OFWs, either by highlighting

---

[91] Greitens, "Obama's Visit to Asia."

[92] Japan, for example, sent one thousand personnel and provided a $67 million aid package, whereas China initially offered only $100,000 in aid, though it raised its contribution to $1.6 million and sent a hospital ship after receiving international criticism. Australia and South Korea pledged $10 million and $5 million, respectively. "Phl to Get $67.26 Mil Grant from Japan," *Philippine Star*, March 25, 2014, http://www.philstar.com/headlines/2014/03/25/1305157/phl-get-67.26-m-grant-japan; Daniel Baltrusaitis, "China's Revealing Typhoon Haiyan Response," *Diplomat*, November 14, 2013, http://thediplomat.com/2013/11/chinas-revealing-typhoon-haiyan-response/; and Walter Lohman, "What Typhoon Haiyan Taught Us about China," *National Interest*, November 18, 2013, http://nationalinterest.org/commentary/what-typhoon-haiyan-taught-us-about-china-9417.

the issue in an international forum or by quietly assisting with repatriation efforts where OFWs may be threatened by global instability and conflict.

At the same time, Washington and Manila must acknowledge that they are unlikely to ever perceive the value and ideal focus of the alliance identically and may have different preferences for the scope of cooperation. Even in a realm like maritime security, where the overlap of interests is substantial, it is possible, even probable, that the Philippines will emphasize intra-archipelago concerns while the United States will adopt a much more geographically dispersed outlook. This is not unlike the debate within the U.S.–South Korea alliance over whether U.S. forces in South Korea should be focused on peninsular contingencies or be available on a more flexible basis for regional operations. Some disagreement over the alliance's focus, as well as over the implications for burden sharing, should be interpreted as a normal part of alliance management rather than as an indication of impending disaster.

Both sides must also be aware of and realistic about the resource constraints that shape their own policy choices and those of the other alliance partner. Sequestration, budget cuts, and partisan divisions in Washington may have a long-term impact on the United States' ability to assist in external balancing and provide diplomatic support for Asian allies. Capacity building is seen as a key tool for the United States to help offset these constraints, but it is unclear how close even the strongest push for capacity building in the Philippines will actually get to creating the kind of complementarity the United States is seeking from its allies. The United States must also be aware of the potential for a redirection in Philippine foreign policy depending on the outcome of the next presidential election, scheduled for May 2016.

Washington can also encourage the Philippines' current emphasis on a foreign policy that pursues both bilateral cooperation with the United States and broader security cooperation with a range of countries in the Asia-Pacific. In part because of worries about overdependence on the United States, Philippine foreign policy has oscillated throughout the country's history between emphasizing the bilateral relationship with the United States and seeking to enmesh the Philippines in a web of regional and multilateral security arrangements. Broadening Manila's security ties will lessen concerns about overdependence, as well as allow the alliance to benefit from the comparative advantages of other security partners.

Finally, the United States must strike a balance between supporting a long-standing ally in the face of Chinese encroachment and encouraging restraint and de-escalation in a potential crisis. On the one hand, Washington needs to be realistic about the growing perception in Asia that the rhetoric of the rebalance has not been matched by concrete actions and firm commitments. A combination of factors—including U.S. policies in Syria and Crimea, the stalling of TPP negotiations, budget cuts, a perceived lack of senior officials focused on Asia policy, and administration officials' partial acceptance of China's rhetoric about a "new model of great power relations," which regional powers fear will take the shape of a U.S.-China condominium—has exacerbated uncertainty about the United States' commitments.[93] Although in Manila President Obama stressed Washington's "ironclad" commitment to the defense of the Philippines, analysts were quick to note that the MDT and EDCA provide only for consultation, not automatic assistance, in the case of attack. These analysts unfavorably compared the U.S. commitment to the Philippines with the U.S. commitment to Japan, under which President Obama explicitly included the disputed Senkaku/Diaoyu Islands.[94]

On the other hand, some uncertainty in Manila may be not only expected but desired on the part of the United States. Washington's position toward territorial disputes in East Asia has long been that the United States is neutral on questions of sovereignty but not neutral on the use of force, and that its fundamental interest is in ensuring that these disputes are resolved peacefully rather than in ensuring one specific outcome over another.[95] The United States must therefore address legitimate Philippine concerns about the inequality of commitments within the U.S. alliance structure, while also avoiding overly broad security guarantees that could incentivize allies to behave provocatively based on aggressive interpretations of sovereignty in disputed areas as well as mistaken assumptions about the inevitability of U.S. support.

As the Philippines, the United States, and the regional security environment develop, changes in the U.S.-Philippine alliance will continue as well. What the United States and the Philippines decide to do with respect to arms sales, the nature of the military footprint in the archipelago (and in East Asia more broadly), and the alliance's combination of security and economic policies will set the stage for the success or failure of U.S.-Philippine cooperation. Washington and Manila must be aware of each other's legitimate interests and goals, as well as domestic restraints, and acknowledge that some divergence will occur even in the strongest alliance. They must share

---

[93] Victor Cha et al., "Obama's Trip to Asia," CSIS, April 21, 2014, http://csis.org/publication/president-obamas-trip-asia; and Green and Cooper, "Revitalizing the Rebalance."

[94] Richard Javad Heydarian, "Will the U.S. Help the Philippines against China?" Yahoo News, June 23, 2014, https://ph.news.yahoo.com/blogs/learning-curve/will-the-u-s--help-the-philippines-against-china--095507083.html; and Manuel F. Almario, "U.S.' Unequal Treaties," Philippine Daily Inquirer, April 26, 2014, http://opinion.inquirer.net/73941/us-unequal-treaties.

[95] Alan D. Romberg, "American Interests in the Senkaku/Diaoyu Issue, Policy Considerations" (unpublished paper, 2013).

responsibility for building an alliance partnership to meet each side's evolving needs, while also improving relationships with other regional actors and employing all tools available to create the appropriate balance between reassurance and restraint. Although achieving these goals will not be easy, the U.S.-Philippine alliance can make important contributions to peace, stability, and prosperity in the Asia-Pacific for years to come.

EXECUTIVE SUMMARY

This chapter assesses Thailand's strategic role in Southeast Asia and the broader Asia-Pacific and considers the impact of the country's return to military rule on relations with external powers, particularly the U.S. and China, as well as on regional integration.

MAIN ARGUMENT:

Thailand's geographic position, the size of its economy, and its strong ties to both the U.S. and China have made it the major player on mainland Southeast Asia since the end of the Vietnam War. However, with Vietnam's normalization of relations with the West and the major Asian powers in the 1990s and the re-emergence of Myanmar in the international community, Thailand's dominant position has steadily eroded after a decade of political instability. Although military rule could provide some measure of short-term stability, it will do little to resolve Thailand's fundamental political conflict. As a result, international partners, ranging from military powers to foreign investors, will be reluctant to write Thailand into their long-term plans. In particular, Thailand's relations with the U.S. will be limited while the military remains in power, and the two countries will be unable to develop a joint vision of the future of the alliance during this time.

POLICY IMPLICATIONS:

- Western sanctions on Thailand, although mild, will inhibit the progress of multilateral security cooperation in Southeast Asia.

- The U.S. reaction to the coup and continued military rule is focused on the security relationship. Washington will attempt to salvage key aspects of the U.S.-Thailand alliance, particularly access, while strengthening ties with other Southeast Asian countries.

- Constrained U.S.-Thailand military relations will have an impact on the Pentagon's ability to develop security relations with Myanmar, since third-country dialogue and training options will be blocked.

The U.S.-Thailand Alliance: Continuity and Change in the 21st Century

Catharin Dalpino

When the government of Prime Minister Yingluck Shinawatra ended in tumult in early 2014, it brought to a halt a brief interlude of stability in Thailand's foreign relations, which had previously been disrupted following the 2004 coup against former prime minister Thaksin Shinawatra, Yingluck's older brother, and during protracted episodes of political violence in 2008 and 2010.[1] This "lost decade" for Thailand has eroded U.S.-Thailand relations in general and the U.S.-Thailand alliance in particular.

Thailand is the oldest diplomatic partner of the United States in Asia, dating back to 1833, and its only treaty ally on mainland Southeast Asia. However, the height of the alliance—the Vietnam War era, when the two countries maintained nine joint bases on Thai territory—is rapidly receding into the distant past of U.S.-Thailand relations, although elements of a "special relationship" linger.

Nevertheless, Thailand remains a valuable asset in the U.S. security posture in Southeast Asia for three reasons. First, it offers unparalleled access to facilities for refueling and repair on mainland Southeast Asia, as well as flyover rights. Second, as demonstrated by the annual Cobra Gold exercises, the U.S.-Thailand alliance acts as an entry point for U.S. promotion of multilateral security in Southeast Asia. Last, Thailand's position as the largest and most developed economy on mainland Southeast Asia can at

Catharin Dalpino is a Contract Course Chair at the State Department's Foreign Service Institute and an Adjunct Professor at Seton Hall University. She can be reached at <dalpinoce@earthlink.net>.

[1] For an account of Thailand's foreign relations and the U.S.-Thailand alliance over the past decade of political instability, see Catharin Dalpino, "The United States–Thailand Alliance: Issues for a New Dialogue," National Bureau of Asian Research (NBR), NBR Special Report, no. 33, October 2011.

times make it a natural partner for Washington in expanding relations with neighboring countries such as Myanmar. For example, Thailand is a key player in the U.S.-sponsored Lower Mekong Initiative.

This chapter examines the impact of the 2014 coup in Thailand on the country's external relations, most notably those with the United States. It assesses Thailand's geostrategic position in Southeast Asia and its hub role on the mainland in particular. The chapter then considers the impact of Thailand's decade of political instability on the U.S.-Thailand alliance. Last, it considers whether the coup has presented an opportunity, if only a short-term one, for China to expand its relations with Thailand at the expense of U.S. security interests in the region.

The Coup and the International Response

The events by which Yingluck was brought down—widespread demonstrations, a series of critical judicial decisions, and ultimately a military coup, which are now all common features of Thai political life—indicate that little had changed to resolve Thailand's long-standing internal conflict while the government was attempting to normalize the country's external relations. It is axiomatic that Bangkok will not be able to steer a steady course in its foreign affairs until it has established more durable domestic stability.

It is just that search for stability that army chief General Prayuth Chan-ocha put forward as his primary justification for launching the May 22 coup.[2] Few would disagree that demonstrations by the People's Democratic Reform Council, a street movement opposed to the Shinawatra political clan, had created ongoing and severe gridlock in Bangkok. Equally serious, Yingluck had run her Pheu Thai Party (PTP) as a family firm, using the PTP parliamentary majority to push a broad-based amnesty bill through parliament that would benefit her older brother in exile, former prime minister Thaksin, who was himself overthrown by a military coup in 2006. Although the "yellow shirts" of 2008, who had opposed Thaksin, and the "red shirts" of 2010, who had supported him, were relatively quiet in 2014, the deep-seated cleavage between old-style establishment politics, guided to some degree by nonelected forces, and more recent grassroots and populist politics was clearly intact.

The stated mission of the National Council for Peace and Order (NCPO), the coalition of military coup leaders, was to suspend partisan politics and public demonstrations in order to "reform the political structure, the

---

[2] "Thai General Justifies Coup after 'Royal Endorsement,'" Associated Press, as printed in *China Daily Asia*, May 26, 2014, http://www.chinadailyasia.com/news/2014-05/26/content_15137080.html.

economy and society."[3] This broad and open-ended agenda, General Prayuth's appointment as interim prime minister, the preponderance of military leaders in the interim National Legislative Assembly, and a timetable for a return to an elected government that is already slipping all point to military rule in Thailand for the near term. In its control, the 2014 coup differs from military interventions in 1991 and 2006, which allowed more room for civilians in the interim structure. The 2014 coup and its aftermath more closely resemble the direct military rule of the Cold War era in Thailand (in the 1950s and 1960s). In that period the United States made common cause with Thailand's military leaders and reinforced their rule with large assistance packages. In the 21st century, however, support for leaders who have forcibly gained power runs counter to U.S. paradigms of promoting democracy and human rights, which complicate policymaking even if they do not always dictate it, and to U.S. law.

Under the terms of Section 508 of the Foreign Assistance Act, Washington was required to suspend economic assistance to Thailand after the coup. Roughly $4.7 million of $10.5 million in assistance has been suspended, a modest amount by any measure.[4] However, this assistance is concentrated in the Thai security sector. In response to the coup, the Australian government placed the NCPO leaders on a visa ban list, and the European Union suspended negotiations with Thailand on a free trade agreement. Additionally, Japan joined the West in issuing statements calling for a return to elected government.

Response from other Asian nations has stood in contrast with the West. The Chinese government recognized the coup leaders shortly after the overthrow and received an official visit from them in Beijing.[5] The Association of Southeast Asian Nations (ASEAN) has provided no official response, since the "ASEAN way" proscribes interference in the internal affairs of member states. Although prior to the coup the statements from some ASEAN meetings had expressed concern for Thailand's political situation,[6] ASEAN has made no public post-coup statement.

---

[3] John Brandon, "Having Amassed Power, Thailand's Junta Still Faces Legitimacy Gap," *World Politics Review*, September 11, 2014, http://www.worldpoliticsreview.com/articles/14052/having-amassed-power-thailand-s-junta-still-faces-legitimacy-gap.

[4] "U.S. Cuts More Thailand Aid in Response to Military Coup," Agence France-Presse, as carried in the *South China Morning Post*, June 25, 2014, http://scmp.com/news/world/articl/1540184/us-cuts-more-thailand-aid-in-response-military-coup.

[5] Thitinan Pongsudhirak, "Thai Coup Elicits Mixed Global Reaction," *Bangkok Post*, August 1, 2014, http://www.bangkokpost.com/opinion/opinion/423534/thai-coup-elicits-mixed-global-reaction.

[6] For example, on December 14, 2013, the ASEAN Statement on Current Developments in the Kingdom of Thailand called "on all parties concerned to resolve the current situation through dialogue and consultations in a peaceful and democratic manner." The statement is available at http://www.asean.org/news/asean-statement-communiques/item/statement-on-current-developments-in-the-kingdom-of-thailand.

Although the junta leaders do not agree, most U.S. policymakers consider the United States' response to the coup to be mild. U.S. diplomats express their intention to remain flexible and to "continue to do business with Thailand, although it will not be business as usual."[7] This policy is motivated not only by the law binding U.S. assistance after the overthrow but also by concern over strong limits on freedom of expression and assembly under martial law, which effectively have criminalized opposition to the current military rule. Beyond this, U.S. and Thai officials have a fundamental disagreement over the best path toward genuine stability in Thailand. The NCPO appears to believe that political reform that will stabilize Thai politics while it maintains democracy can be achieved through a top-down process that requires an unspecified period of military rule, whereas U.S. officials and analysts believe that political reform is best forged through an inclusive process, which includes an elected government.

Thailand's Geostrategic Importance

The last quarter of the twentieth century helped elevate Thailand as the most developed state on mainland Southeast Asia. Although the U.S.-Thailand alliance was downsized and reconfigured after the Vietnam War, other factors contributed to Thailand's rise: Indochina's isolation from the West for two decades and Vietnam's self-impoverishment through collectivization of agriculture after 1975, Myanmar's self-isolation, China's normalization of relations with Southeast Asia and an early rapprochement between Beijing and Bangkok, and Thailand's own "peace dividend" (an economic boom in the 1980s after the demise of the Communist Party of Thailand). In the early 1990s, when the Cambodian peace process was in motion and Vietnam had begun to normalize relations with the West and with Asian powers, Thailand's role as a transportation hub and a service center became more pronounced.

Thailand's position on mainland Southeast Asia makes it a critical crossroads for north-south and east-west transportation routes. With China's growing economic role in the region and ASEAN economic integration—including the establishment of the ASEAN Economic Community in 2015—Thailand is essential to the development of expanded trade routes and ASEAN connectivity. Indeed, Thailand's own infrastructure plans could alter these trade routes. A joint plan with Myanmar to develop a deep-sea port in Dawei would provide a new path for east-bound shipments that would allow trade to avoid the Strait of Malacca, reducing the time,

---

[7] Author's interview with a U.S. State Department official, Washington, D.C., September 4, 2014.

cost, and risk of that route to mainland Southeast Asian traders. As the second-largest economy in Southeast Asia and the largest economy on the mainland, Thailand is better prepared to service this new connectivity than its neighbors.

This role as a regional hub is both geostrategic and economic. With its proximity to China, but without the tensions often inherent in sharing a border, Thailand is an obvious and necessary link in China's plans to strengthen its commercial routes in Southeast Asia from north to south. ASEAN economic integration, as well as India's growing interest in trade with the region, places Thailand in the center of the east-west transportation grid for mainland Southeast Asia.

Thailand's tourist trade and its foreign investment sector also enhance its role as a regional hub. The Bangkok international airport can accommodate upward of 45 million passengers a year. Often referred to as the "Detroit of Asia," Thailand is Southeast Asia's largest destination for foreign automobile factories, with approximately seven hundred facilities. High economic and education levels compared with its neighbors on mainland Southeast Asia make Thailand the regional center of information communications and technology, again supported by foreign investment. Thailand is the largest exporter of hard-disk drives, for example.[8]

A more existential element of Thailand's crossroads role is the Thai diplomatic tradition, which favors equilibrium in relations with greater powers. In the mid-nineteenth century, the country was able to sidestep colonization by developing relations with as many European powers as possible. In this regard, the United States had particular appeal for Thailand, and vice-versa. King Mongkut could be reasonably certain that the newly independent United States would not soon join the "great game" of seizing colonies that preoccupied Europe; conversely, Thailand offered the United States access and trade that was more difficult in other Southeast Asian countries under European domination. During the Cold War, Thailand broke with its own tradition to ally itself closely with the United States. However, the end of the Vietnam War and the U.S. strategic realignment in Asia compelled Thailand to return to its historical flexibility on foreign relations, although it has retained its security alliance with the United States. The signal event in this return was Thailand's rapprochement with China in the early 1970s, which accelerated in 1975 with the fall of Saigon and Communist takeovers in Laos and Cambodia. These developments have helped ensure receptivity in Thailand to new rail and road systems that give Chinese traders and tourists greater access to Thai territory.

---

[8] Matthew Simpson, "Logistically—Thailand as a Transport Hub," *Thai-American Business*, September–October 2006.

But the very attributes that make Thailand a strategic hub can also make it a source—or at least a conduit—for transnational threats. Trafficking in persons, narcotics, and small arms and vulnerability to epidemics (such as avian flu) have been long-standing issues for the country. The concept of crop substitution to eradicate opium was pioneered in Thailand and is considered a model for success.[9] The government has had a more difficult time, however, stemming trafficking in persons, and in 2014 the United States placed Thailand (along with Malaysia) on the lowest rung (tier 3) for human trafficking.[10]

The double-edged nature of Thailand's position has also been seen in terrorism. A long-standing, if low-level, Muslim separatist insurgency in the country's three southernmost provinces has created a pocket of potential instability for Southeast Asia, particularly for Malaysia, although there is a consensus that the conflict is localized and not part of a larger jihadist movement in the region. However, other radical groups have at times found easy passage there and been able to establish a berth, if not a beachhead, in Thailand. In 2003, Hambali, an Indonesian leader of Jemaah Islamiyah, Southeast Asia's main al Qaeda franchise, was apprehended north of Bangkok and handed over to U.S. authorities.[11] Hezbollah cells were uncovered in Bangkok in 2012 and 2014 and are believed to have been planning attacks on Israeli tourists.

In general, however, Thailand has not been a major locus for terrorism in the post–September 11 equation in Southeast Asia. The situation in southern Thailand notwithstanding, U.S.-Thailand cooperation on counterterrorism is aided by the fact that groups such as Jemaah Islamiyah and Abu Sayaf did not originate in Thailand. Although Thailand is undeniably a pass-through for radical groups at times, U.S.-Thailand cooperation on addressing terrorism and other strains of international crime tends to be less controversial with the domestic population than is the case in some other Southeast Asian states, such as Indonesia. Moreover, the long history of security cooperation between Thailand and the United States afforded an easier transition into counterterrorism cooperation after September 11, although September 11 presented undeniable opportunities to expand relations with several other states.

---

[9] See, for example, Ronald D. Renard, *Opium Reduction in Thailand 1970–2000: A Thirty-Year Journey* (Chiang Mai: Silkworm Books, 2001).

[10] "U.S. Downgrades Thailand, Malaysia Human Trafficking Status," Voice of America News, June 20, 2014, http://www.voanews.com/content/us-downgrades-thailand-malaysia-human-trafficking-status-/1941428.html.

[11] "Asia's Most Wanted in U.S. Hands," *CNN.com*, August 15, 2003, http://www.cnn.com/2003/WORLD/asiapcf/southeast/08/15/hambali.capture.

Changing Dynamics in the U.S.-Thailand Alliance

Thailand's geographic position, combined with the country's long history of military cooperation with the United States, has made it a strategic linchpin in U.S. security policy in the Asia-Pacific. Although this dynamic is changing slightly given expanding U.S. security relations with nearby countries such as Vietnam, Laos, Cambodia, and Myanmar, there is at present no serious alternative to Thailand as a geostrategic resource on mainland Southeast Asia. U.S. military leaders report that developing alternative flyover routes and refueling arrangements in the region would require a considerable effort.[12] Although U.S. security relations with Singapore have deepened significantly in the past decade, cooperation with the city-state cannot substitute in every event. For example, U.S. forces that deployed to assist in disaster relief after the 2004 Indian Ocean tsunami used Utapao, the Thai naval airbase, as their base of operations because Singapore by that time was overwhelmed.

However, Bangkok's customary acquiescence to U.S. flyovers as well as access to Thai military facilities is not always automatic. In an attempt to remain neutral during the U.S. intervention in Iraq, then prime minister Thaksin attempted to deny flyovers to U.S. planes headed there, though he eventually relented under pressure from Washington.[13] Less recent but still remembered in Thailand was the failure of the United States to consult Thailand before using Utapao as a base from which to launch a rescue mission for the SS *Mayaguez*, a U.S. merchant ship captured by the Khmer Rouge in 1975.

Both incidents point to a degree of inherent uncertainty in the U.S.-Thailand alliance. In contrast with the other U.S. treaty allies in Asia—Japan, South Korea, and the Philippines—the alliance with Thailand is not governed by a written, ongoing treaty that is periodically reviewed and approved by both sides. In lieu of a status of forces agreement (as the United States has with Japan and South Korea) or a visiting forces agreement (as the United States has with the Philippines), U.S.-Thailand security cooperation is largely based on precedent and ongoing dialogue. The two primary documents that refer to the alliance—the 1954 Manila Pact and the 1962 joint communiqué between U.S. secretary of state Dean Rusk and Thai foreign minister Thanat Khoman—were Cold War constructs and are arguably outdated.[14]

---

[12] Author's interview with Bangkok-based U.S. military official in Washington, D.C., August 1, 2014.

[13] See Center for Strategic and International Studies (CSIS) Southeast Asia Initiative, *U.S. Alliances and Emerging Partnerships in Southeast Asia: Out of the Shadows* (Washington, D.C.: CSIS, 2009).

[14] This is probably true more of the joint communiqué—in which the two leaders pledged to defend Thailand against Communism—than the Manila Pact, which is still occasionally invoked in the region. For example, in 2001 Philippine president Gloria Macapagal Arroyo justified support for the U.S. invasion of Afghanistan on the basis of the Manila Pact.

The immediate post–Vietnam War era in U.S.-Thailand security relations was a period of adjustment, with the greater adjustment arguably on Thailand's side. Although the Communist threat to Thailand had not diminished—on the contrary, it could be argued that the threat had increased with the presence of Vietnamese troops and Russian "advisers" on the Thai-Cambodian border after Vietnam's invasion of Cambodia—it was tacitly understood that the United States would not reintroduce ground troops to Southeast Asia.

Instead, the alliance was reconfigured as the U.S. presence in Thailand receded. U.S. troops were withdrawn from the nine joint bases in 1976, and more flexible arrangements were put into place for the use of these facilities. The close, almost fraternal relationship between U.S. and Thai officers forged during the Vietnam War could not be maintained at that level, but contact was maintained through the International Military Education and Training (IMET) program.[15] Although Thailand has gradually diversified its arms purchases in the post-Vietnam and post–Cold War periods, the United States has remained a preferred vendor when possible. Washington's designation of Thailand as a "major non-NATO ally" in 2003 offered some advantages in weapons acquisitions.

But the flagship instrument for U.S.-Thailand security cooperation, and increasingly for multilateral cooperation, has been the Cobra Gold exercises, established in 1982 and held annually in Thailand. The exercises have both bilateral and multilateral windows and conduct training both for conventional warfare and for disaster relief and other forms of humanitarian assistance. The range includes land, air, and sea exercises as well as live-fire drills. Now the largest multinational exercises in the world, Cobra Gold was originally a bilateral effort but has added several formal partners in recent years: Japan, South Korea, Indonesia, Malaysia, and Singapore. The exercises also draw numerous observers on occasion, ranging from China and Vietnam to South Africa and France. In 2003, Myanmar participated as an observer for the first time. Although China originally eschewed the Cobra Gold exercises and viewed them as an unwelcome intrusion by the United States into the region, Beijing is quietly changing its view. China has held observer status since 2002, and People's Liberation Army (PLA) troops participated in Cobra Gold for the first time in 2014 in humanitarian assistance drills in northern Thailand. In press statements, PLA officials hailed the event as a positive

---

[15] Dalpino, "The United States–Thailand Alliance," 7.

step not only in U.S.-China military-to-military relations but also in China's military cooperation with ASEAN.[16]

Cobra Gold may best embody U.S. and Thai visions of a 21st-century alliance. The U.S.-Thailand alliance acts as a base for expanding regional security cooperation and parallels the ASEAN Defence Ministers' Meeting (ADMM) and the ADMM's activities with its external partners. This benefits the United States, which is able to deepen its security relations in the region without an overbearing U.S. imprimatur, and also provides a more acceptable route for new security relations, such as those with Myanmar. Conversely, Cobra Gold puts Thailand jointly at the helm of a major security exercise and underscores its role as a regional convener. The latter is particularly important in the wake of Thailand's weak performance as ASEAN chair in 2009–10, when red shirt violence broke up one ASEAN meeting and continued turbulence persuaded the ASEAN Secretariat to move the annual summit to Jakarta.

Within the U.S.-Thailand alliance, the greater benefit in bilateral cooperation may accrue to the United States. In this regard, the primary U.S. objective is to secure access, whereas Thailand's main objective is more intangible: public recognition as a valued ally.[17] However, some recent attempts to expand the bilateral aspect of the alliance have been problematic. In 2012, talks between U.S. and Thai military leaders on jointly developing a regional response facility for disaster relief and humanitarian assistance at Utapao foundered because of domestic opposition.[18] In addition, high-level U.S. defense diplomacy with Thailand has often lagged in the past decade, in part because of continual political instability in Thailand. For example, one Pacific commander failed to visit Thailand during his tenure at the U.S. Pacific Command. This trend had been in an upswing in more recent years, but fell precipitously with the May 2014 coup.

Beneath these false starts and missteps is a strong sense of drift in the alliance. The dangers in the present security environment notwithstanding, Thailand and the United States no longer face a common vital threat of the magnitude of Cold War Communism. Moreover, the spectrum of security partners has widened for both countries, putting into question the function and value of a treaty alliance in the 21st century. Although

---

[16] Minnie Chan and Darren Wee, "Chinese Troops Join U.S.-Thailand Cobra Gold Military Exercises," *South China Morning Post*, February 12, 2014, http://scmp.com/news/china/article/1425918/chinese-troops-join-asia-us-drills-positive-step-amid-regional-tensions. For a thoughtful analysis of this event, see Nicole Yeo, "China's Participation in Cobra Gold 2014: A Golden Opportunity for the United States?" *China-U.S. Focus*, March 11, 2014, http://www.chinausfocus.com/foreign-policy/chinas-participation-in-cobra-gold-a-golden-opportunity-for-the-united-states.

[17] The author is indebted to Abraham Denmark for this observation.

[18] Newley Purnell, "U.S. Plans for U-Tapao Airfield Cause Stir," *Wall Street Journal*, June 25, 2012.

both countries have demonstrated their inclination to call on the "special relationship" when national interests require, they are increasingly unable to define that relationship.

The Impact of Military Rule on U.S.-Thai Security Relations

U.S. officials report that the United States repeatedly cautioned Thai military leaders against launching a coup in the past year of political instability.[19] In response to the 2006 coup, the U.S. government suspended military assistance, barred Thai officers from IMET, and, although diplomatic relations were not formally downgraded, kept the interim government at arm's length. Presumably the NCPO took this consequence into account when it decided to mount the May coup.

Indeed, General Prayuth has surprised foreign governments with the promulgation of direct military rule and his determination that the May overthrow not be a "soft coup." In contrast with the 1991 coup, when the supreme commander of the Royal Thai Armed Forces, General Suchinda Kraprayoon, designated a highly respected technocrat, Anand Panyarachun, as interim prime minister, Prayuth has taken that role himself. He is also determined not to follow the course of General Sonthi Boonyaratglin, leader of the 2006 coup, by returning the country to civilian rule too quickly. Following the May coup, Prayuth indicated that new elections would be held in October 2015, but he has since said that they would be held in 2016 at the earliest. At the time of writing, Thailand continues to be under martial law, with no date set for lifting it. Partisan politics are banned, as is criticism of the NCPO. An interim constitution that gives extraordinary powers to the military has replaced the 2007 constitution until a reform council, which is expected to be heavily populated by military and other pro-establishment figures, drafts a new charter.

In response to the coup, the Pentagon has withdrawn funds for training Thai officers under IMET and other programs, although those officers currently in training programs will be allowed to finish them. Thailand was barred from participating in the 2014 Rim of the Pacific (RIMPAC) maritime exercises in Hawaii. The Royal Thai Navy had not planned to send ships to the exercises, but it had planned to send a number of officers. A bilateral military exercise, Cooperation Afloat Readiness and Training (CARAT) 2014, was canceled. The U.S. Pacific Command also rescinded an invitation to General Tanasak Patimapragorn, armed forces supreme

---

[19] Author's interview with U.S. State Department officials in Washington, D.C., September 4, 2014.

commander, to visit Hawaii.[20] (Tanasak has since been designated as deputy prime minister and foreign minister in the interim government, a move that has dismayed some U.S. diplomats.) Washington also canceled a small trilateral exercise on disaster response involving the U.S., Thai, and Myanmar militaries. The last measure suggests that U.S. third-country training, which uses Thailand as a base, may suffer during the period of Thai military rule. This would have particular impact on the Pentagon's efforts to engage Myanmar's armed forces while staying within the bounds of U.S. laws that prohibit giving funds to that military.[21]

These restrictions chip away at goodwill between the two countries, but a greater indication of the state of U.S.-Thailand relations following the coup will be the Cobra Gold exercises while Thailand remains under military rule. The exercises typically run nearly a month in length, and critical decisions on their operation must be made months in advance. This decision-making process is increasingly complex, given the larger number of formal partners, the growing list of observers, and the broader menu of activities.

Following the 2006 coup, Cobra Gold was postponed but not canceled. It is unlikely that the 2015 exercises will be canceled, a decision that would probably have to be made with the full set of formal partners as well as U.S. and Thai officials. However, the United States may trim (or even remove) the bilateral aspects of the exercises. Although proposals have been made in Washington to move the exercises to another ally, possibly Australia, U.S. military officials fear that doing so would invite retribution from the Thai military, including possibly a significant restriction or denial of access.[22]

Another key concern is that China may capitalize on this rough patch in U.S.-Thailand relations, particularly in the security sector. Some Thai defense officials have hinted that Bangkok may make a dramatic shift toward Beijing because of Western reaction to the coup.[23] U.S. diplomats are skeptical that Thailand will over-invest in China and disturb the equilibrium that undergirds Thai foreign policy.[24] Nevertheless, China will likely expand its military-to-military relationship with Thailand as a result of U.S. and other Western reactions to the coup. Although China and Thailand have had military relations since the late 1980s, U.S. defense officials have observed

---

[20] William Cole, "Military Coup Gets Thailand Booted from RIMPAC Lineup," *Honolulu Star-Advertiser*, June 25, 2014, http://www.staradvertiser.com/news/breaking/20140625_Military_coup_gets_Thailand_booted_from_RIMPAC_lineup.html?id=264688131.

[21] Author's interview with a Bangkok-based U.S. military official in Washington, D.C., August 1, 2014.

[22] Ibid.

[23] Author's interview with a Thai military official in Washington, D.C., June 23, 2014.

[24] Author's interview with a U.S. State Department official in Washington, D.C., September 4, 2014.

that Beijing has recently aimed to mirror U.S.-Thailand military-to-military relations in its security cooperation with Bangkok and point to high-level military dialogues, officer training, joint exercises, and weapons sales.[25] Bilateral counterterrorism exercises have been held since 2007, and in 2010 Chinese and Thai marines began joint training exercises, codenamed Blue Strike, which were the first joint maritime exercises the PLA Navy had conducted with foreign forces outside China. Beijing is currently pressing Bangkok to establish joint exercises between the two countries' air forces.[26]

Thailand's Security Interests and Regional Relations

The impact of the Thai coup will likely be felt most acutely in Thailand's security relations, but the new government is aware of the broader challenge of restoring international confidence in the country after nearly a decade of political conflict. In the post–Cold War environment, Thailand's security concerns and its regional goals have altered little, even as the domestic political situation has presented a continual challenge to their pursuit. Foremost among these is to maintain an appropriate balance among external partners in order to ensure that Thailand is not too dependent on any one partner. This goal is no different than that of Vietnam, Indonesia, Malaysia, and virtually all Southeast Asian countries at this time. However, Thailand's close relations with both the United States and China are at once an advantage and a disadvantage, since either side can make demands that disturb the equilibrium. Another goal is more recent. As other Southeast Asian economies move up the ladder, Thai policymakers are increasingly aware that Thailand's dominance on mainland Southeast Asia is challenged. Moreover, in recent years domestic political problems have made it difficult for Bangkok to match its logistical and economic advantages with a strong diplomatic role in the region, exacerbating the perception that Thailand is losing influence.

The Thai economy has faltered in the past year, and estimates of the economic growth rate for 2014 have been cut in half to barely 2%. Shortly after the coup, the military moved to make past-due payments to rice farmers under the Yingluck administration's rice mortgage scheme, which gave the government an early boost in the polls. However, the interim government has announced an ambitious economic agenda, which includes jump-starting dormant infrastructure projects that will feed into regional connectivity,

---

[25] Author's interview with a Bangkok-based U.S. military official in Washington, D.C., August 1, 2014.

[26] Phuong Nguyen and Brittany Billingsley, "China's Growing Military-to-Military Engagement with Thailand and Myanmar," CSIS, CogitAsia, September 12, 2013, http://cogitasia.com/chinas-growing-military-to-military-engagement-with-thailand-and-myanmar.

both north-south and east-west. Some policy initiatives have a distinctly nationalist ring, such as the government's promise to expel illegal workers from neighboring countries, a move that has sent 100,000 Cambodians back across the border in a single weekend.[27]

With the West uneasy over what looks to be a protracted period of military rule ahead, Prime Minister Prayuth has turned his geographic focus to Thailand's immediate neighborhood and the broader concentric circle beyond that, which includes China and Japan. Prayuth's first official visit abroad as interim prime minister will be to Myanmar, after which he has said he will visit a number of other ASEAN capitals. Close—and conspicuous—cooperation with Myanmar will be necessary to revive the Dawei port project; one major step in that regard will be to attract foreign capital, which both countries hope will be provided by Japan. Prayuth also hopes to consult with President Thein Sein on repatriation of Myanmar's four million workers in Thailand. In return, Naypyidaw is likely to ask Bangkok to help repatriate ethnic separatist leaders from Myanmar's border states who have taken refuge across the border in Thailand.[28]

Prayuth will also pay early attention to Thailand's neighbor to the south, Malaysia. The Muslim separatist movement in Thailand's deep south has been an ongoing, if often ignored, problem since 2004, and communal violence has continued unabated since the military takeover. As have all of the country's incoming prime ministers, Prayuth has vowed to resolve the conflict, although he is not likely to be sympathetic to calls for autonomy in the region.[29] But he will be unable to have any positive impact on the situation without cooperation from his counterpart in Malaysia, Prime Minister Najib Razak.

A third neighbor that Prayuth must engage is Cambodia, where bilateral tensions have been high for several years. The border conflict over the Preah Vihear temple has diminished with the 2013 ruling by the International Court of Justice, which granted sovereignty over the temple to Cambodia but left open the issue of control of the surrounding land. Prayuth is likely to be more worried over Cambodian prime minister Hun Sen's close relations with former prime minister Thaksin, who has often used Cambodia as a political base since his exile in 2006.

[27] See "Coup Risks Lasting Damage to Thai Economy," Oxford Analytica, Daily Brief, June 17, 2014.

[28] Kavi Chongkittavorn, "The Prayuth Government's Strategic Dilemmas," *Nation* (Bangkok), September 15, 2014, http://www.nationmultimedia.com/opinion/The-Prayuth-governments-strategic-dilemmas-30243270.html.

[29] "Prayuth Rules Out Split in South," *Bangkok Post*, July 29, 2014, http://www.bangkokpost.com/news/security/422939/prayuth-rules-out-split-in-south.

The new government's determination to revive and accelerate infrastructure plans that have been stalled over the past year will have obvious implications for relations with China. Prayuth sent an early and no doubt welcome signal to Beijing when he approved two high-speed rail projects that will link Thailand to Kunming in Yunnan Province by 2021.[30] Both of these lines will bypass Bangkok, an obvious sign that they are intended to serve the movement of Chinese goods in Southeast Asia rather than passenger travel.

Greater closeness between Thailand and China will raise red flags with Japan, which appears to be more alarmed than the United States by this possibility. Bangkok has numerous reasons to reassure Tokyo, however. Apart from attracting Japanese investment in Dawei and other infrastructure projects, Thailand hopes to stem the outward flow of long-established Japanese investment to other Southeast Asian countries with lower labor costs. The "Thailand-plus-one" strategies of Japanese investors, in which facilities in Thailand are gradually phased out as new investment goes to surrounding countries with cheaper labor, could see more automobile production shift to Indonesia and, in time, Myanmar.

Despite an early focus on strengthening relations with Thailand's ASEAN neighbors, the new government will attempt to gain backdoor approval from the West through its foreign policy. Prayuth has announced that working with neighboring states to stem human trafficking is a high priority, a move no doubt intended to assuage U.S. concerns in this area and to build backdoor momentum for the relationship.[31] Another key area is Thailand's role in resolving tensions among the claimant states in the South China Sea. As a non-claimant state, Thailand had attempted to avoid involvement in the issue, despite pressure from Washington and the claimant states to join mediation efforts. However, Thailand currently acts as the ASEAN liaison for relations with China, a role it will perform until the end of 2015. Bangkok and Beijing chair the ASEAN-China dialogue on a code of conduct in the South China Sea, and the new Thai government is anxious to produce a concrete indication of progress. This is more likely to take the form of an agreement to implement some aspect of the Declaration on the Conduct of Parties in the South China Sea rather than a finalized code itself. However, any measurable progress on this score will reflect well on Thai diplomacy.

Bangkok is likely to receive particular support in this effort from Kuala Lumpur, the 2015 ASEAN chair. Although Malaysia is a more distant claimant

---

[30] Jane Perlez, "China Looks to High-Speed Rail to Expand Reach," *New York Times*, August 8, 2014, http://www.nytimes.com/2014/08/09/world/asia/china-looks-to-high-speed-rail-to-expand-reach.html.

[31] "Prayuth Targets Human Traffickers," *Bangkok Post*, June 20, 2014, http://www.bangkokpost.com/lite/topstories/416492/prayuth-goes-after-traffickers.

country in the South China Sea than Vietnam and the Philippines, it has been alarmed by recent Chinese incursions into its exclusive economic zone. Apart from its own national interest in lowering maritime tensions with China, Malaysia takes pride in its authorship of several ASEAN institutions: the ASEAN +3 grouping (ASEAN plus China, Japan, and South Korea); the Eminent Persons Group, which helped draft the ASEAN Charter; and the Working Group for an ASEAN Human Rights Mechanism, which was the first formal human rights activity accorded to ASEAN.[32] Progress toward a code of conduct in 2015 would be a diplomatic victory for Thailand, China, and Malaysia. More important for Bangkok, it could be a significant icebreaker in relations with the Western powers, not least the United States.

Conclusion

The coup and its aftermath will not extinguish the U.S.-Thailand alliance, but it will likely keep the alliance offline for the duration of this episode of military rule. Both sides will attempt to preserve as much informal space for cooperation as possible in the relationship. Assuming there is no violent suppression of dissent, as there was in 1992, and that Thailand eventually finds its way back to elected government, broader U.S. sanctions are unlikely. In the meantime, Bangkok will attempt to rebuild the country's international legitimacy by seeking a more vigorous regional role, strengthening the Thai economy, and addressing transnational threats, all undeniably worthy objectives.

However, this interval of estrangement, although relatively mild, will prevent Thailand and the United States from pursuing meaningful dialogue on the course of the alliance and will force Washington to exclude Bangkok from near-term plans to rebalance the U.S. force structure to Asia. For example, episodic discussions between the United States and Thailand over expanded access to the Thai naval airbase at Utapao are likely to stall completely during the era of military rule in Thailand. During this time, as U.S.-Thailand security relations remain stagnant, the United States will likely increasingly use Philippine naval facilities. Moreover, new dynamics are developing among the United States and its Asian allies, with greater maritime cooperation among the United States, Japan, and the Philippines. Washington is also moving closer to lifting the ban on selling lethal weapons to Vietnam, and the U.S.-Vietnam security relationship will take an important step forward as a result. Joint U.S.-Malaysia maritime exercises

---

[32] The Working Group for an ASEAN Human Rights Mechanism has since become the permanent ASEAN Intergovernmental Commission on Human Rights.

are increasing as Kuala Lumpur's concern over conflict in the South China Sea rises. The maintenance of U.S. security relations with Indonesia likewise will be a key priority for the Pentagon as Joko Widodo assumes the presidency. And although they will heed red lines on funding the Myanmar military, the U.S. State Department and Department of Defense are united in their view that supporting the reform process in Myanmar will require engaging its military.

When Thailand and the United States are able to resume full military-to-military relations, the subtle changes and realignments in the security landscape and in U.S. policy in Southeast Asia will add to the challenge of resuming and reinvigorating the alliance. Both countries will attempt to preserve the long-term strategic advantage of the relationship until then, but the open-ended nature of military rule at this time leaves both sides uncertain of how to navigate that course.

STRATEGIC ASIA 2014–15

STRATEGIC PARTNERS

EXECUTIVE SUMMARY

This chapter assesses the prospects for U.S. collaboration with India on Asian security and considers how Washington and New Delhi can work together more systematically on a range of common strategic challenges.

MAIN ARGUMENT:

As uncontested U.S. primacy in Asia gives way to intensified geopolitical competition with China, Washington has a grand strategic interest in the development of friendly centers of power in the Indo-Pacific capable of sustaining a non-Sinocentric order. Since 2005, the U.S. has pursued a conscious policy to facilitate the rise of India as a strategic actor in order to reinforce a set of core U.S. interests that India also shares. The Indo-U.S. partnership is a strategic stabilizer in a region riven by dynamic power shifts, arms racing, and territorial conflict and could recast the global balance of power and values in ways that make these two countries, rather than China alone, the pacesetters of the 21st century. U.S. leadership in the Indo-Pacific is thus more likely to endure through cooperation with a rising India that broadly supports American regional interests—because they mirror India's own strategic priorities—than if the U.S. and India go their separate ways.

POLICY IMPLICATIONS:

- The U.S. and India share a compelling interest in defeating terrorism, shaping an Asian security environment that is pluralistic rather than Sinocentric, and sustaining a liberal international economic order.

- From a U.S. perspective, India will be a stronger anchor of the Asian balance of power, and a better partner, if its development drive and military modernization are successful.

- Washington and New Delhi should focus their cooperation on the following: (1) defense supply, military training, and joint operations, (2) intelligence sharing and counterterrorism, (3) trilateral partnerships with like-minded countries, particularly Japan, (4) energy partnerships, (5) the deepening of trade and investment ties, and (6) the promotion of good governance abroad.

Building U.S. Partnerships for the 21st Century: The Case of (and for) India

Daniel Twining

As uncontested U.S. primacy in Asia gives way to intensified geopolitical competition with China, Washington has a grand strategic interest in the development of friendly centers of power in the Indo-Pacific that are capable of sustaining a non-Sinocentric order. Looking ahead, India is the major non-Chinese Asian power whose scale and potential aggregate capabilities will most decisively determine the future regional order. To the extent that a core U.S. strategic priority is preventing Chinese domination of mainland and littoral Asia, India's trajectory and orientation assume an overriding importance to American national interests. Even though the two countries are not allies, the future of U.S. leadership in Asia will be affected directly by India's ability to assume the responsibilities of a great power for maintaining regional balance and contributing to regional order.

India's rise has been uneven; many Americans remain skeptical that the country will truly emerge as a world power given its governance challenges and recent lackluster economic growth. But the demographic and economic trends propelling India's geopolitical emergence are powerful. The U.S. National Intelligence Council (NIC) predicts that India will be the world's leading driver of middle-class growth by 2030.[1] According to the World Bank, China's working-age population has already peaked, which, along with China's

Daniel Twining is Senior Fellow for Asia at the German Marshall Fund of the United States and an Associate of the U.S. National Intelligence Council. He can be reached at <dtwining@gmfus.org>.

The author is grateful to several reviewers for their excellent suggestions to improve this chapter and assumes full responsibility for its contents.

[1] U.S. National Intelligence Council, *Global Trends 2030: Alternative Worlds* (Washington, D.C., 2012), http://globaltrends2030.files.wordpress.com/2012/11/global-trends-2030-november2012.pdf.

structural economic and political challenges, correlates with a slowdown of growth in that country.[2] By contrast, half of India's population is under the age of 25 and two-thirds is under 36. This demographic voted overwhelmingly for the new government of Prime Minister Narendra Modi, whose promise to revitalize India's economic growth and governance contributed to the most decisive victory by any Indian political party in decades.

According to the NIC, India's working-age population will continue to expand for decades, creating the same sort of demographic tailwind that boosted East Asian tiger economies during their industrialization. In part for this reason, the Organisation for Economic Co-operation and Development predicts that India could account for nearly 20% of global GDP by 2060.[3] It already possesses one of the world's biggest armed forces and is the world's largest arms importer. Ongoing military modernization, military competition with two of the world's largest armed forces in China and Pakistan, and India's pivotal geographic position—astride Indian Ocean maritime routes vital to the global economy and continentally anchoring the southern Eurasian landmass—suggest that an increasingly dynamic India will be an important swing state in the Asian balance of power. The United States has a compelling interest in close partnership with this key emerging actor.

The United States has never had a security partner on this scale. Following World War II, NATO partners in Europe and new ally Japan were militarily weak, even as economic recovery under the U.S. security umbrella ultimately made them prosperous. Continuing tensions and the uneven development of U.S.-India relations since the strategic opening of the 2000s are partly a function of the novelty for both Washington and New Delhi of building a strategic relationship outside an alliance framework, where neither country consents to be a subordinate partner, as the NATO allies and Japan did after 1945. That said, today's Indian establishment has a comfort level with U.S. power—although Indians would like to see a more multipolar world with India as one of the poles, they certainly do not want to see China replace the United States as the international system's preeminent power. For its part, Washington has sought not to constrain India's power trajectory but instead to help boost it. Since 2005, the United States has pursued a conscious policy to facilitate the rise of India as a strategic actor in order to reinforce a set of core U.S. interests that India also shares.

This chapter assesses the prospects for U.S. collaboration with India on Asian security. It begins with an exploration of how India perceives its

---

[2] World Bank, "China: Data," 2013, http://data.worldbank.org/country/china.

[3] Asa Johansson et al., "Looking to 2060: Long-Term Growth Prospects for the World," Organisation for Economic Co-operation and Development (OECD), OECD Economic Policy Papers, no. 3, November 2012, http://www.oecd.org/eco/outlook/lookingto2060.htm.

regional strategic environment and its place in the international order, as well as what this means for the United States. It then describes the backdrop and logic of the Indo-U.S. strategic partnership, examining India's domestic debates over foreign policy, including the quest for strategic autonomy and how the United States factors into it. The chapter then identifies India's strategic priorities and their convergence with a range of U.S. interests and assesses the implications of more intimate Indo-U.S. strategic cooperation for the United States and the international order. Finally, the chapter maps out an agenda for Washington and New Delhi to collaborate on building Indian capabilities to facilitate greater bilateral cooperation.

India's Strategic Environment

Modern India is the inheritor of a grand strategic tradition developed during the British Empire, when the subcontinent was the center of a vast security system that stretched from Aden in the Persian Gulf to the Strait of Malacca. India was in many ways the centerpiece of Britain's global empire.[4] The early twentieth-century viceroy of India, Lord Curzon, celebrated India's importance in *The Place of India in the Empire*, declaring that "the master of India must, under modern conditions, be the greatest power in the Asiatic Continent, and therefore…in the world."[5] Independent India's leaders inherited this sense of India as the strategic fulcrum of a wider region. As founding prime minister Jawaharlal Nehru put it, "we are of Asia…. [India] is the pivot of Western, Southern and Southeast Asia."[6] This sense of geopolitical centrality collided with newly independent India's extreme poverty and exclusion from the U.S.-Soviet bipolar order of the Cold War. India in many ways was relegated to the sidelines of great-power politics, even as its leaders maintained their sense of national exceptionalism and were at the forefront of developing-world coalitions such as the Non-Aligned Movement.

Despite several decades of rapid economic growth, India remains the poorest of the world's rising powers, and the country's constrained resources compound its regional and domestic security challenges. One-third of all poor people on earth live in India, more than in all of sub-Saharan Africa. The average Indian is over four times as poor as the average Chinese and nearly

---

[4] C. Raja Mohan, "The Return of the Raj," *American Interest*, May 1, 2010, http://www.the-american-interest.com/articles/2010/05/01/the-return-of-the-raj; and Thomas Metcalf, *Imperial Connections: India in the Indian Ocean Arena, 1860–1920* (Berkeley: University of California Press, 2008).

[5] Cited in Robert D. Kaplan, *Monsoon: The Indian Ocean and the Future of American Power* (New York: Random House, 2010), 181.

[6] Cited in Robert M. Hathaway, "India and the U.S. Pivot to Asia," *YaleGlobal Online*, February 24, 2012, http://yaleglobal.yale.edu/content/india-and-us-pivot-asia.

ten times as poor as the average Brazilian.[7] These factors limit the resources available for Indian military modernization and have traditionally focused domestic political attention on social welfare and redistribution rather than national defense.

At the same time, India is lucky to have emerging partners in its quest for security and development, including the United States, Japan, and Europe, all of which have courted it in various ways. India also benefits from its identity as both a continental and maritime power, which provides it strategic room to maneuver and opens up possibilities for trade and commerce. But with respect to the international system, India is an incomplete great power, given its lack of full integration into a liberal international order that for so long excluded it from membership in leading institutions.

Security Challenges at Home and in the Near Abroad

India and China were for many centuries separated by the vast Tibetan plateau, particularly when Tibet enjoyed either true autonomy or independence. However, China's invasions of Tibet in 1950 and 1959 brought the People's Liberation Army to India's Himalayan doorstep, setting the stage for the 1962 war over the countries' contested border.[8] India today has a 2,500-mile border dispute with China—now a rising superpower—and is engaged in an uneven contest in which the logic of terrain and offense favor China. In addition, India possesses a contiguous border with Pakistan, a nuclear-weapons state that is complicit in regular state-sponsored terrorism against India. India also has one of the world's longest coastlines, which creates not only commercial opportunities but serious risks of attack by sea, as occurred in November 2008 in Mumbai.

India's most serious security challenge is its underdevelopment. Prime Minister Modi has described "stagnancy" as the biggest problem facing the country. "I believe a strong economy is the driver of an effective foreign policy…. [W]e have to put our own house in order so that the world is attracted to us," he said during the election campaign.[9] Externally, China, Pakistan, and the rest of the South Asian neighborhood all pose varying dangers to India's integrity and welfare.

The development imperative. To India, security begins with the imperative to sustain and further national development. India is still a country where,

---

[7] World Bank, "GDP Per Capita (Current US$)," http://data.worldbank.org/indicator/NY.GDP.PCAP.CD.

[8] John W. Garver, *Protracted Contest: Sino-Indian Rivalry in the Twentieth Century* (Seattle: University of Washington Press, 2001).

[9] This statement is cited in Dhruva Jaishankar, "Eeny, Meeny, Miney, Modi: Does India's Prime Minister Actually Have a Foreign Policy," *Foreign Policy*, May 19, 2014, http://www.foreignpolicy.com/articles/2014/05/19/does_narendra_modi_have_a_foreign_policy_india_pakistan_china.

to most people, security starts with having enough to eat and a roof for shelter. One out of every two Indian children is malnourished, a quarter of the population lives on less than $2 a day, and over half of Indians do not have access to modern sanitation or regular electricity. Under the Congress Party–led government that held office from 2004 to 2014, the government's spending priorities included massive (and expensive) welfare schemes to employ and feed the rural poor, as well as a bewildering array of affirmative action programs. Combined, these policies aggravated corruption, worsened India's fiscal outlook, and left scarce government resources for investment and infrastructure, much less for the foreign ministry and armed forces. Prime Minister Modi's decisive electoral victory in May 2014 underlines the failure of India's antiquated model of state socialism and the aspiration of the nation's voters for the fruits of dynamic economic growth.

India's poverty and underdevelopment also create insecurities—for instance, the Naxalite insurgency that touches as many as a third of India's states—that detract from the country's will and ability to project power abroad. India's pressing development requirements, such as its dependence on imported energy from countries such as Iran, complicate its foreign relations with more important countries, including the United States. A forward policy of military and diplomatic leadership abroad is not politically sustainable in India's democratic system unless the government can tie foreign policy partnerships to domestic development goals, as the Indian government did in 2005–8 with respect to civilian nuclear cooperation with the United States and more recently in deepening a strategic partnership with Japan.[10] Modi has suggested that he will prioritize relations with Japan, China, the United States, and Germany—all advanced powers whose markets, technology, and capital have much to offer India's modernization drive.

The China challenge. India's national security establishment increasingly identifies China, rather than Pakistan, as the country's primary strategic competitor. As a rising world power, India has pulled away from Pakistan, its troubled and far smaller neighbor. But New Delhi resents China's claims to speak for Asia, which India's civilization-state has historically shaped as much as China's has. On the one hand, Modi hopes to expand Chinese trade

---

[10] As Prime Minister Manmohan Singh told a Japanese audience in Tokyo last May, "India needs Japanese technology and investment. In turn, India offers increasing opportunities for the growth and globalization of Japanese companies for the overall prosperity and growth of Japan.... [We] have increasingly convergent world views and growing stakes in each other's prosperity.... There are strong synergies between our economies, which need an open, rule-based international trading system to prosper." Ministry of External Affairs (India), "Prime Minister's Address to Japan-India Association, Japan-India Parliamentary Friendship League and International Friendship Exchange Council," May 28, 2013, http://www.mea.gov.in/in-focus-article.htm?21754/Prime+Ministers+add ress+to+JapanIndia+Association+JapanIndia+Parliamentary+Friendship+League+and+Internati onal+Friendship+Exchange+Council.

and investment to boost India's modernization drive. On the other hand, he and his advisers are wary of what Modi has called China's "expansionist mindset" that leads to "encroaching on another country."[11]

However, China's economy, like its military budget, is more than four times the size of India's. Three decades ago, China and India had similar levels of per capita income. The gap between the Asian giants will widen until India can generate growth that not only matches but exceeds China's, given the latter's broader base. Strikingly, Chinese GDP expansion produces economic growth on the scale of a "new India" every two years.[12] This mismatch in power has important strategic consequences, including that India cannot rely purely on internal balancing against China but must pursue external alignments to compensate for its relative weakness.

China lays claim to settled Indian territory the size of Switzerland and has demonstrated little interest in resolving the long-running border dispute with India dating to both countries' modern creation in the late 1940s. China controls the high ground of the Tibetan plateau in the dispute. India thus can defend the contested state of Arunachal Pradesh only by moving military forces through a very narrow land corridor between India and Bhutan that provides the only access to India's northeast. It is estimated that China's superior road, rail, and airbase infrastructure on its side of the Line of Actual Control would allow it to move over 30 divisions (comprising some 450,000 soldiers) to the border region in the event of a conflict, outnumbering Indian forces by three to one.[13] For this reason, India is raising a new mountain strike corps with offensive capabilities to complement existing defensive deployments along the northern border.[14] In addition, the northern location of India's capital city means its decision-makers would have little warning of a Chinese first strike from nuclear missiles deployed in nearby Tibet. By contrast, China's center of political gravity in Beijing is thousands of kilometers from Indian land-based launchers.

More broadly, China appears determined to be Asia's dominant power and sees little room for power-sharing with India, as attested by Beijing's policy of blocking any UN Security Council reform that would elevate India to membership. The new Chinese leadership has also called for "a new type

---

[11] These statements are cited in Niharika Mandhana, "China Set to Step Up Investment in India," *Wall Street Journal*, September 15, 2014.

[12] Jim O'Neill, "Why China Will Disappoint the Pessimists Yet Again," Bloomberg, September 25, 2013, http://www.bloomberg.com/news/2013-09-25/why-china-will-disappoint-the-pessimists-yet-again.html.

[13] Rajat Pandit, "Army Kicks Off Raising New Mountain Strike Corps Against China," *Times of India*, January 9, 2014, http://timesofindia.indiatimes.com/india/Army-kicks-off-raising-new-mountain-strike-corps-against-China/articleshow/28571907.cms.

[14] Ibid.

of great-power relationship" between the United States and China that relegates every other nation to a lesser tier. Indians are historically wary of any U.S.-China condominium, or group of two (G-2), which subjugates India's interests to those of China—as witnessed in 2009 when President Barack Obama and Chinese president Hu Jintao issued a joint statement that seemed to suggest a role for China in resolving conflict in South Asia.[15] From New Delhi's perspective, China has seeded conflict in South Asia by helping arm Pakistan with nuclear weapons. Following the 2009 U.S.-China joint statement, Indian prime minister Manmohan Singh urgently "sought assurances from the U.S. president that Washington's partnership with Beijing [would] not be at the expense of Delhi."[16]

Pakistan as spoiler. Rivalry with Pakistan is the most enduring source of India's security dilemmas on the subcontinent. China enjoys an intimate alliance with Pakistan, which it helped arm with nuclear weapons in order to counterbalance India. Pakistan has been the cause of four "hot wars" in South Asia since 1947, and a number of other provocations—such as the bombing of the Indian parliament in 2001 and the siege of Mumbai in 2008 by Pakistan-based terrorists—nearly led to full-blown conflict. Pakistan's nuclear arsenal in many ways neuters India's conventional military advantage against it. Support for terrorism against India by elements of the Pakistani state gives Islamabad an asymmetric card it can play with some impunity, given its nuclear deterrent to Indian retaliation. While India can manage the threat of ongoing low-level conflict with Pakistan, terrorist attacks and the less-than-trivial prospect of nuclear war in South Asia absorb budget resources for India's security forces that could otherwise be put to more productive use elsewhere.

From a military perspective, the prospect of a two-front war against Pakistan to the west and China to the north leads India to divide its forces and deprives it of the strategic luxury of focusing on only one geopolitical competitor. The India-Pakistan conflict also complicates India's diplomatic relations with the United States, China, and the Muslim world. And to the considerable extent that Pakistan is complicit in supporting the Taliban and other militant groups in Afghanistan with a known history of sponsoring terrorism against India, Afghanistan's status as a cockpit of Indo-Pakistani rivalry will only intensify as the U.S. military drawdown proceeds.

Foreign policy begins in the neighborhood. In many respects, India has a neighborhood policy rather than a truly global foreign policy, given tensions

---

[15] "U.S.-China Joint Statement," Office of the Press Secretary, White House, November 17, 2009, http://www.whitehouse.gov/the-press-office/us-china-joint-statement.

[16] C. Raja Mohan, "The G-2 Dilemma," *Indian Express*, June 11, 2013, http://archive.indianexpress.com/news/the-g2-dilemma/1127572/.

in its relations not only with Pakistan but also with Nepal, Sri Lanka, and Bangladesh. The general problem is India's disproportionate power relative to its smaller South Asian neighbors, as well as New Delhi's inheritance of suzerainty over the subcontinent. India's domestic politics unduly complicate its foreign relations: a historic water-sharing agreement with Bangladesh was nixed due to opposition from the ruling Trinamool Congress in West Bengal, and Tamil politics in southern India have limited New Delhi's engagement with the government of President Mahinda Rajapaksa in Sri Lanka.

Domestic politics in neighboring countries are driven in part by political actors' opposition to India. In Nepal, a Maoist insurgency with Chinese support toppled the pro-Indian political order, leading to the abolition of the monarchy in 2008. In Sri Lanka, India's censure of the government over the mistreatment of the Tamil minority reinforced Colombo's drive to deepen its privileged relationship with Beijing, lubricated by arms sales and economic assistance, at the expense of New Delhi. In Bangladesh, domestic politics vis-à-vis India revolve around the legacy of the 1971 war of independence, in which New Delhi decisively intervened to secure the country's secession from Pakistan; the management of border controls and trade relations; and the struggle against violent extremists, who in the past have been responsible for attacks on India.

Modi's invitation of eight South Asian neighbors to his inauguration—an unprecedented move by an incoming Indian prime minister—and early visits by him and key cabinet ministers to Bhutan, Nepal, and Bangladesh signal a new focus in New Delhi on resolving conflicts in the neighborhood in order to economically integrate the region and mitigate security challenges within it. As Ministry of External Affairs spokesman Syed Akbaruddin put it, "the prime minister's inbox relating to foreign policy is very crowded. India's foreign policy priorities are in the neighborhood."[17] Restoring the strategic unity of the subcontinent through economic enmeshment and positive-sum security ties is a compelling requirement for India's emergence as a genuine global power. As Shyam Saran, the former foreign secretary and current chairman of the prime minister's National Security Advisory Board, argues:

> It is India's neighborhood that holds the key to its emergence as a regional and global power. If India's neighborhood is politically unstable and economically deprived, there will be bigger challenges to India's security and its own economic prospects. India's security is inseparable from that of the Indian subcontinent. Its economic destiny is likewise enmeshed with that of its neighbors. Here is an

---

[17] Cited in "India's Modi to Visit U.S. in September, First Trip to Bhutan," Reuters, June 6, 2014, http://www.reuters.com/article/2014/06/06/us-india-modi-idUSKBN0EH1C320140606.

opportunity to clear the decks in our neighborhood, so that India is able to break out of its subcontinental confines and expand its footprint beyond its borders.[18]

From the perspective of the United States, this is an urgent task. Multiple U.S. presidents have defined a strategic stake in India's rise as a democratic great power. India punches below its weight in world affairs in part because of the need to defend itself against the instability of its near neighborhood. In addition to threatening India's security by producing terrorism, refugees, and weak states along its borders, such instability invites penetration by outside powers like China, eroding India's natural leadership of its wider region. To become a world power, India will not only need to transform itself; it will also need to transform its neighborhood from an obstacle to its development and security into an asset.

In sum, India possesses one of the world's most complex security environments. It faces a set of serious military challenges from a strong Chinese state, a different set of threats from a flailing nuclear-armed and terrorist-ridden Pakistan, and the spillover from weak neighbors on the subcontinent arising from civil conflict, deep poverty, and poor governance. India cannot emerge as a fully formed great power until it stabilizes its neighborhood so that it can be a launch pad for global leadership rather than a tar pit.

Engagement Farther Afield

In addition to managing its periphery, India has seized opportunities farther afield to enhance its role and prospects in an evolving international order.[19] In 1991, only 18% of India's GDP was tied to the global economy; now, that figure is approaching 50%, raising the stakes for India to prioritize ties with the world's leading powers. At the same time, India's status aspirations and security considerations (including the fact that it is the world's largest arms importer) have led it to pursue a multidirectional policy of engagement with European powers, Russia, and Japan, as well as with a range of middle powers such as Australia.

European Union and Russia India is negotiating a free trade agreement (FTA) with the EU and has deepened its defense supply relationship with France in particular. But its relationships with EU countries pale in

---

[18] Shyam Saran, "Modi Must Re-establish India's Global Clout," *Hindustan Times*, May 18, 2014, http://www.hindustantimes.com/comment/analysis/modi-must-re-establish-india-s-global-clout/article1-1220638.aspx.

[19] Dhruva Jaishankar, "A Wider View of India's Foreign Policy Reveals Clear Strategy," *New York Times*, India Ink, web log, June 14, 2013, http://india.blogs.nytimes.com/2013/06/14/a-wider-view-of-indias-foreign-policy-reveals-clear-strategy.

comparison with its historic and pragmatic military-supply relationship with Russia. Following the U.S. opening to China in the early 1970s and the imposition of Western technology sanctions on India for its budding nuclear weapons program, New Delhi turned to Moscow as a source of military technologies and advanced weapons platforms. The United States recently replaced Russia as India's top source of defense imports, but India's air force and navy remain replete with Russian weapons platforms, including a large range of MiG fighter-bombers as well as a former Russian aircraft carrier. Indian leaders today cast a wary eye on Moscow's growing geopolitical alignment with Beijing. Although directed against the United States, growing Sino-Russian ties have negative implications for an India that is used to being Russia's privileged partner in Asia and that sees China as its primary peer competitor. India-Russia relations are likely to cool if President Vladimir Putin continues his pivot toward Beijing.

Japan. In Asia, New Delhi has moved from its "look east" policy to one of "acting east," particularly with regard to forging the foundations of a potentially far-reaching economic and strategic partnership with Japan. The obvious economic complementarities between Japan, as East Asia's technology leader, and India, with its vast human capital and developmental requirements, make India-Japan trade and investment ties among the more exciting, if underappreciated, economic relationships in 21st-century Asia.[20] The convergence of concern over managing China's rise and protecting the security of sea lanes further unites Japan and India. So does their joint engagement of Southeast Asia, where both countries are actively supporting Myanmar's political and economic opening while systematically engaging strategically important emerging players like Indonesia and Vietnam. Both Tokyo and New Delhi are also playing a greater role in institutions led by the Association of Southeast Asian Nations (ASEAN) to prevent these forums from tilting in a Sinocentric direction and to boost regional webs of economic connectivity.[21] The current nationalist leaders in Tokyo and New Delhi, similarly focused on revitalizing economic growth and managing the China challenge, look set to push forward their far-ranging economic and security partnership.

---

[20] Ministry of Foreign Affairs (Japan), "Japan-India Relations: Basic Data," 2013, http://www.mofa.go.jp/region/asia-paci/india/data.html.

[21] For more on the India-Japan relationship, see Daniel Twining, "The Indo-Japanese Strategic Partnership: Asia's Response to China's Rise," *Asan Forum*, December 6, 2013, http://www.theasanforum.org/the-indo-japanese-strategic-partnership-asias-response-to-chinas-rise.

India and the International Order

With respect to its place in the international order, India is ambivalent: it cares a great deal about being treated as a great power on par with China and other nations, including through membership in clubs such as the UN Security Council, even as it resents a distribution of power in the international system that favors the West and China. On the one hand, one of India's primary geopolitical grievances during the second half of the twentieth century was its exclusion from that order—its lack of a seat on the UN Security Council, its (self-imposed) sidelining from the U.S.-Soviet bipolar order that structured international politics until 1991, and its exclusion from a global nonproliferation regime that ascribed pride of place to great powers like China (even as Beijing actively proliferated nuclear weapons to Pakistan) but sanctioned India for pursuing nuclear capabilities even though it was not a party to the Nuclear Non-Proliferation Treaty (NPT). To rectify what it views as these historical wrongs, India today therefore strives for membership in clubs such as the UN Security Council and entities like the Nuclear Suppliers Group.

At the same time, India's voting record during its recent two-year term on the Security Council highlighted its discomfort at having to make the choices expected of a great power and revealed the influence of domestic sensitivities—for example, over its large Muslim population and the contested state of Kashmir—on India's foreign policy posture. New Delhi abstained from key resolutions on Libya and Syria and pursued what were criticized as passive or reactive policies. More recently, in 2014 the Indian government found itself in the awkward position of appearing to defend the Russian army's invasion of Ukraine, even though India itself has been a victim of secessionist conflicts supported by hostile external powers (by Pakistan in Kashmir, for instance). This history had led observers to assume that New Delhi might have an enlightened self-interest in strongly opposing uninvited foreign intervention to "defend" minority rights in a neighboring state.

Indians also remain wary of U.S. expectations that India should assume global governance responsibilities with respect to issues such as climate change, questioning why the country should limit its development potential through strict environmental controls that the West itself did not adopt during its own period of industrialization. On governance of the global economy, successive Indian administrations have scuttled World Trade Organization (WTO) deals (in 2008 and 2014) on narrow national-interest grounds, demonstrating a degree of exceptionalism that shows high regard for particular Indian voting constituencies but little regard for international opinion and the multilateral process.[22] Indians are also wary of entrapment in any U.S. design to contain China. An argument of Indians on the left and right fringes of politics during the debate over the U.S.-India civil nuclear deal was that strategic partnership with the United States would require New Delhi to abandon its independent foreign policy, including with respect to China and Iran. No U.S. official made these arguments, however.

Nonetheless, India does not seek to overthrow the existing liberal international order but rather seeks greater status and prestige within it.[23] This is partly a function of India's sense of grievance at its exclusion from international institutions, which has had the side effect of stifling the country's economic development. By contrast, China's elevation to the rank of a world power through its permanent membership on the UN Security Council and recognition as a nuclear weapons state under the NPT rankles many Indians. They wonder why their unprecedented experiment with democracy, panoramic pluralism as an open society, extraordinary civilizational accomplishments, and record of nonproliferation (in contrast with China) earn them less status and prestige globally.

Nehru's foreign policy of universalism and nonalignment was one manifestation of India's attempt to leverage its sense of exceptionalism to shape a different kind of international order from the bipolar one of the early Cold War and to put India in pride of place as the leader of the developing world. Having been relegated to the sidelines of global politics by the hardening of the Cold War and marginalized from the global economy until recently by an outmoded state socialism, Indians today seek a seat at the top table of international politics consistent with Nehru's notion that India is the international system's pivotal power and a natural peer to both the leader of the West, the United States, and Asia's other vast civilization-state, China.

For now, a resurgence of economic growth and activism under its new government bodes well for India's ambition to improve relations with all major powers, maximizing the country's room for maneuver in foreign policy and its ability to attract foreign investment. There remains the question of whether such a multivector foreign policy is sustainable, requiring as it does diplomatic nimbleness as well as the necessity of postponing hard choices. For instance, should China and Japan come into conflict over the disputed Senkaku/Diaoyu Islands, New Delhi would surely come under pressure to support Japan, which Beijing could interpret as a hostile act. For now, Modi's

---

[22] J.P. Singh, "India's Multi-Faceted WTO Refusal," *Washington Post*, Monkey Cage, web log, August 5, 2014, http://www.washingtonpost.com/blogs/monkey-cage/wp/2014/08/05/indias-multi-faceted-wto-refusal.

[23] For an elucidation of the non-revolutionary Indian establishment worldview, see "Patel, India and the World: Lecture by Shivshankar Menon, Indian National Security Advisor," *South Asia Monitor*, October 16, 2013, http://southasiamonitor.org/detail.php?type=emerging&nid=6220.

emphasis is on generating transformational economic growth so that India is taken more seriously by all major powers.

India and the United States: Forging a New Partnership for a New Century

Warming U.S.-Indian Relations

India's dramatic foreign policy turn toward the United States over the past fifteen years is understandable in light of Indian aspirations to assume greater status within the international system, security concerns vis-à-vis China and terrorism, and development objectives. India's most important break from half a century of nonalignment and autarky has been building a strategic partnership with the United States rooted in energy and defense cooperation. As will be discussed further below, successive Indian governments since 1998 have made the determination that India can rise faster and more readily fulfill its development, security, and diplomatic objectives in partnership with the world's predominant power rather than in opposition to it. While breakthroughs in Indo-U.S. ties have slowed since the heady days of the George W. Bush administration, the long view suggests that India's tilt westward after decades of hostility to the U.S.-led global order constitutes no less than a revolution in Indian foreign policy.[24]

What made the development of an Indo-U.S. strategic partnership in the 2000s so striking was the decades of geopolitical alienation that preceded it.[25] In its pursuit of the "third way" of nonalignment, India was excluded from the U.S. alliance network during the Cold War, even though it was not part of the Soviet camp (notwithstanding an entente with the Soviet Union during the 1970s and 1980s that was defensive in nature, given the U.S. opening to China and China's role in arming Pakistan with missile and nuclear technologies). India felt threatened by the development of a close military alliance between the United States and Pakistan from the 1950s, which was designed to bolster the ring of southern allies that could block Soviet approaches to the Persian Gulf but had the unintended effect of allowing Pakistan to achieve near parity in military terms with its much larger neighbor and more forcefully press its claims to the disputed territory of Kashmir. The United States cut off military assistance to India during the 1965 war with Pakistan, demonstrating its unreliability in Indian

---

[24] For a full exposition, see C. Raja Mohan, *Crossing the Rubicon: The Shaping of India's New Foreign Policy* (New York: Palgrave Macmillan, 2004).

[25] For a fine survey, see Dennis Kux, *India and the United States: Estranged Democracies* (Washington, D.C.: National Defense University Press, 1992).

eyes, and fecklessly intervened militarily on Pakistan's side during the war of Bangladeshi independence, suggesting a U.S. hostility to Indian leadership of the region that made a deep mark on India's strategic community.

India was also not part of the East Asian "economic miracle" that grew out of American hegemony in the Pacific and saw key U.S. allies such as Japan, Taiwan, South Korea, and Thailand achieve economic takeoff on the back of Washington's security guarantees. These guarantees allowed national leaders to pursue modernization strategies premised on exporting manufactured products to the developed economies of the West. Following India's "peaceful" nuclear explosion of 1974—a direct response to the perceived threat from a nuclear-armed China—the United States led its European allies to impose multilateral technology sanctions against India, which had the side effect of crippling its economic development. What the Indian strategist K. Subrahmanyam called a "technology apartheid" left a deep scar on the Indian psyche, as became apparent during the debate in the mid-2000s over the civil nuclear deal the U.S. government devised to overcome this legacy and strengthen India's development prospects.[26]

Washington and New Delhi spent the 1990s feuding over the status of Kashmir, India's outspoken support for a multipolar world rather than a U.S.-led unipolar order, and India's internal proliferation leading to its 1998 nuclear tests. The latter led to the imposition of severe and automatic U.S. economic sanctions against India, suggesting that a further downward spiral in the relationship would follow. Yet the nuclear tests also had the effect of revealing to Clinton administration officials that India's national security outlook was not dissimilar to the United States' own.[27] As Prime Minister Atal Bihari Vajpayee privately told President Bill Clinton, India had tested nuclear weapons in response to a "deteriorating security environment" driven by existential threats from China and Pakistan.[28] To the United States, China was emerging as a potential peer competitor, and Pakistani-generated terrorism would soon change American history with the attacks of September 11. Not only were U.S. and Indian interests convergent around these dangers, but the nuclear tests and nearly a decade of rapid Indian economic growth following the economic reforms of 1991 opened American eyes to the potential of India as a powerful partner in the emerging Asian order. President Clinton's unprecedented support for India over Pakistan in 1999, when tensions

[26] K. Subrahmanyam, "Costs of Rejection," *Times of India*, July 25, 2006, http://timesofindia.indiatimes.com/edit-page/Costs-of-rejection/articleshow/1802791.cms.

[27] Strobe Talbott, *Engaging India: Democracy, Diplomacy, and the Bomb* (Washington, D.C.: Brookings Institution, 2006).

[28] "Nuclear Anxiety: Indian's Letter to Clinton on the Nuclear Testing," *New York Times*, May 13, 1998, http://www.nytimes.com/1998/05/13/world/nuclear-anxiety-indian-s-letter-to-clinton-on-the-nuclear-testing.html.

between the two countries nearly erupted into war, followed by his 2000 trip to India, in which he echoed Vajpayee's call for an alliance of interests and values, made possible the breakthroughs that came later.[29]

President George W. Bush assumed office with a view of India as a future world power, a front-line Asian balancer, and a pluralistic democracy with which the United States should naturally cooperate in world affairs.[30] The September 11 attacks and the war in Afghanistan to overthrow the Taliban regime created a new context for what were otherwise radical steps in U.S.-India cooperation. New Delhi offered the United States the use of Indian territory for military logistics and transit, and the Indian Navy provided protective escort to U.S. naval vessels supporting the war in Afghanistan, which was a development unimaginable just months earlier. India was also one of the few countries to welcome the United States' abrogation of the Anti-Ballistic Missile Treaty in late 2001. Closer security and intelligence cooperation ultimately led to a ten-year defense cooperation agreement signed in June 2005.[31] Many countries without a long history of partnership often begin their engagement with trade and diplomatic agreements and only after building trust on these issues move on to military cooperation. The opposite held true for the United States and India because of the compelling security threats—from China, Pakistan, and terrorism—that drew them together. The defense agreement was a particularly radical step for India to take: having allied with the United States' primary competitor during the Cold War and condemned U.S. military primacy in the international system throughout the 1990s, Indian leaders decided by the mid-2000s that the United States was their partner of choice to help in modernizing the Indian military and supplying its needs as the world's biggest arms importer.

For all this progress in the strategic partnership, including on space, defense, and technology trade, India's exclusion from the international nuclear order constructed by the United States and its allies stood in the way of normal relations.[32] Not only did the Indian and U.S. bureaucracies have no tradition of working together, but the nuclear nonproliferation control regime that the United States had put in place following India's 1974 nuclear explosion remained in place. The solution to this problem came in the form of the 2005 U.S.-India Civil Nuclear Agreement, under which India would

---

[29] "Remarks by President Clinton to a Joint Session of the Indian Parliament," Federal News Service, March 22, 2000.

[30] Robert Blackwill, "The India Imperative," *National Interest*, no. 80 (2005): 9–17.

[31] Embassy of India (Washington, D.C.), "New Framework for the U.S.-India Defense Relationship," Press Release, June 28, 2005.

[32] Ashley J. Tellis, "India as a New Global Power: An Action Agenda for the United States," Carnegie Endowment for International Peace, July 2005, http://www.carnegieendowment.org/files/CEIP_India_strategy_2006.FINAL.pdf.

separate its civil and military reactors, submit the former to international monitoring, and make a series of binding commitments not to proliferate nuclear materials or technologies. In return, India secured the support of the U.S.-led international cartel governing trade in civil nuclear components and gained access to these materials on the international market. The judgment of the Bush administration, Congress, the International Atomic Energy Agency, and the Nuclear Suppliers Group ultimately was that the nuclear nonproliferation regime would be stronger if India were a part of it on these terms rather than remaining excluded and untethered as a nuclear weapons state not bound by the NPT.[33]

With support from the U.S. Congress, the Bush administration elevated India to a top U.S. foreign policy priority from 2005 to 2008, upending four decades of Western policy by working systematically to support India's entry into the international nuclear club. Normalization as a nuclear power gave India access to the international trade in civil nuclear components and promised to substantially boost India's energy production in ways that would fuel long-term economic development. It also made possible dramatically expanded high-technology trade and cooperation with the United States in civil space, defense, and other areas.[34]

Although often difficult to work with, Indian leaders took political risks to transform relations with Washington. To overcome parliamentary opposition to the nuclear deal, Prime Minister Singh submitted his government to a high-stakes confidence vote. Singh and his allies argued that India's future prosperity, security, and prestige hinged on this strategic opening to the West. By enacting the nuclear deal, they argued, India would finally assume its seat at the top table of world politics—with U.S. sponsorship.[35]

During 2009–13, the U.S. and Indian bureaucracies engaged each other in an unprecedented depth and breadth of cooperation—on issues ranging from counterterrorism and intelligence sharing to education and agricultural training and exchange—attesting to how Indo-U.S. cooperation had been made routine, even in the absence of visionary leadership from heads of government in both countries. Today, Modi's overwhelming mandate to spark a new decade of vigorous economic growth through bold reform bodes well for efforts to revitalize U.S.-India ties. Such reforms could include opening India's defense sector and other industries to greater foreign investment,

---

[33] See, for instance, R. Nicholas Burns, "America's Strategic Opportunity with India: The New U.S.-India Partnership," *Foreign Affairs* 86, no. 6 (2007): 131–46.

[34] U.S. Department of State, "U.S.-India Civil Nuclear Cooperation Initiative," Fact Sheet, March 9, 2006, http://2001-2009.state.gov/r/pa/scp/2006/62904.htm.

[35] For a useful summary, see C. Raja Mohan, *Impossible Allies: Nuclear India, United States, and the Global Order* (New Delhi: India Research Press, 2006).

streamlining land acquisition laws, ending retroactive taxation of foreign companies operating in India, and privatizing or reforming loss-making state-owned enterprises. From a U.S. foreign policy perspective, it is especially important to create a stronger private-sector anchor for cooperation alongside closer diplomatic and security ties. Indo-U.S. ties are reinforced when the U.S. corporate sector is a cheerleader for the relationship; over the past few years, U.S. business complaints about Indian regulatory hurdles to greater trade and investment have slowed the momentum of the strategic relationship.

Failure to Launch: Explaining the Recent Drift in Indo-U.S. Relations

Despite the exuberance in both Washington and New Delhi over the nuclear deal and the wider shift to strategic cooperation, problems cropped up that have prevented the relationship from reaching the levels predicted or desired by either side in 2008. India and the United States have clearly not fulfilled the potential of their strategic partnership. Several factors explain the drift. A rapid deceleration in Indian economic growth over the past four years has made India a less attractive partner for the United States, which had anticipated levels of economic growth on par with China's. As India's economic dynamism seeped away due to lack of reforms by the Congress Party–led government, both the U.S. strategic and business communities became more skeptical of India's ability to serve as an effective counterweight to China in the Asian balance of power and to emerge as a top-tier global economy. The Indian parliament's failure to enact clean legislation to implement the civil nuclear agreement, preventing its entry into force, raised hard questions in Washington about New Delhi's seriousness and reliability after years of assiduous work by U.S. officials, both within international institutions and with the U.S. Congress, to normalize India's status as a nuclear power in good standing.[36] India's decision in 2011 to buy French fighter aircraft rather than U.S. ones, in the largest combat-aircraft tender in India's history, left a similarly bad taste in the mouths of U.S. defense officials, who had viewed military cooperation as the centerpiece of the strategic partnership.

New Delhi also disappointed Americans who never understood the Bush administration's contention that India would never be a traditional U.S. ally but, despite increased cooperation, would remain an independent partner

---

[36] George Perkovich, "Towards Realistic U.S.-India Relations," Carnegie Endowment for International Peace, October 2010, http://carnegieendowment.org/files/realistic_us_india_relations.pdf.

who would often go its own way without seeking Washington's approval.[37] India's opposition to Western interventions in Libya, Syria, and Ukraine; its continued (although diminished) energy imports from Iran, even as the United States worked concertedly to tighten international sanctions; and New Delhi's role as an implacable opponent of U.S. trade negotiators at the WTO led skeptics in Washington to question India's reliability as an international partner.[38]

In contrast with the mid-to-late 2000s, when India grew nearly as fast as China and even surpassed the latter's economic growth rate in several quarters, China pulled far ahead in economic and military terms in the period 2010–14 as Indian growth slowed and the government's reform energies seemed exhausted.[39] These developments made it much harder in 2014 than in 2004 to support a U.S.-India strategic partnership on the grounds that India is "the next China," albeit one that is democratic and shares a range of national security interests with the United States. During the Obama administration, therefore, U.S. relations with Beijing have attracted far more high-level attention and energy than those with New Delhi.

Indians have had their own set of parallel grievances with Washington during the Obama administration. Although their bureaucracies worked more closely together on day-to-day matters, New Delhi has not enjoyed the same degree of high-level attention from Washington after President Bush, who some joked had served as "the desk officer for India,"[40] left office. President Obama's early outreach to Beijing, which created impressions in both Europe and Asia that he favored a "G-2" U.S.-China condominium of interests at the expense of the United States' traditional allies, led Indians to believe that he might risk a separate peace with China that discriminated against Indian interests.[41] This sense was reinforced by the United States' hasty military withdrawal from Iraq and early drawdown from Afghanistan, creating the clear impression that Washington was pursuing a policy of

---

[37] For more on this point, see Daniel Twining, "Were U.S.-India Relations Oversold?" *Foreign Policy*, Shadow Government, web log, April 26, 2012, http://shadow.foreignpolicy.com/posts/2012/04/26/was_the_us_india_relationship_oversold_part_1; and Daniel Twining, "Were U.S.-India Relations Oversold? Part 2," *Foreign Policy*, Shadow Government, web log, June 12, 2012, http://shadow.foreignpolicy.com/posts/2012/06/12/were_us_india_relations_oversold_part_2.

[38] James C. Clad and Robert A. Manning, "New Beginning: What a Modi Victory Means for India and the U.S.," *Foreign Policy*, May 15, 2014, http://southasia.foreignpolicy.com/posts/2014/05/15/new_beginning_what_a_modi_victory_means_for_india_and_the_us.

[39] Raymond Zhong, "The 13-Year Divide: India's Economy Looks Much Like China's in 2001," *Wall Street Journal*, September 14, 2014.

[40] Senior Indian participants in the Aspen Institute's U.S.-India Strategic Dialogue made this point at meetings of the high-level group in New Delhi and Washington, D.C., in 2009 and 2010, praising President Bush's attention to India in comparison with President Obama's record.

[41] G. Parthasarathy, "The Axis of Grudging Cooperation," *Wall Street Journal*, May 4, 2010, http://online.wsj.com/news/articles/SB10001424052748704608104575221303790430846.

retrenchment that would destabilize India's fragile western neighborhood, including Pakistan. Heightened U.S. cooperation with Islamabad to secure the logistics corridors into Afghanistan to enable the drawdown of U.S. forces there also grated on New Delhi. Indian officials continued to believe that the United States was looking the other way as Pakistan's security establishment sponsored terrorist groups targeting not only NATO forces in Afghanistan but Indian civilians there and in India.

In the economic sphere, India was excluded from the Obama administration's signature trade initiatives, the Trans-Pacific Partnership and the Transatlantic Trade and Investment Partnership, while the bureaucracies in Washington and New Delhi continued to feud over the terms of a basic bilateral investment treaty. U.S. officials, backed by the U.S. Congress and private sector, increasingly pushed India to roll back retroactive taxation policies, foreign investment restrictions, and domestic-content requirements, as well as improve patent protection in certain sectors—even as Indian officials defended these protectionist policies as being necessary to India's different stage of development.[42] The United States, for its part, failed to liberalize the H-1B visa program for highly skilled immigrant workers in the United States, a plurality of which came from India. Much to Indian officials' dismay, Congress instead raised fees on companies employing these workers, generating further friction in bilateral relations.

In short, lackluster growth and leadership in both capitals since 2009 have made India and the United States less attractive partners to each other. Nonetheless, the structural pressures compelling their closer cooperation—in managing the danger of terrorism, shaping a balance of power in Asia that constrains rather than enables China's ability to dominate the region, and spurring economic growth in both countries through trade, investment, immigration, and energy cooperation—have only grown. Americans must accustom themselves to cooperation with a country that will always be, at best, an independent-minded partner rather than a blindly loyal ally. Conversely, Indians must understand that Washington's foreign-policy inbox is crowded with Middle Eastern crises that leave little time and space for the kind of concerted, high-level cultivation India enjoyed during the George W. Bush administration. Greater economic dynamism and stronger leadership in both countries would accentuate the strategic cooperation that is manifestly in both Indian and U.S. interests.

---

[42] See, for instance, Rod Hunter, "India's Attack on Innovation," *Wall Street Journal*, September 25, 2013, http://online.wsj.com/news/articles/SB10001424052702303342104579096772343088810.

India's Quest for Strategic Autonomy
and Its Impact on U.S.-India Relations

If India has a modern foreign policy doctrine, it falls under the framework of strategic autonomy.[43] Of course, all countries seek strategic autonomy, in the sense of being free to make sovereign choices about their external alignments and geopolitical orientation. India, however, has pursued strategic autonomy to such an extent that it is unwilling to enter into "entangling alliances" of the kind George Washington once warned another rising democracy to avoid. It is also acutely sensitive to foreign pressure, particularly from the West. This is in part a function of India's colonial history. But it is also a result of Indian elites' dissatisfaction with their country's place in the international order since independence, and the failure of the great powers to treat India with the deference and respect befitting its status as one of the world's great civilization-states. Indian official prickliness toward the United States in particular—despite the fact that polling shows a solid majority of Indians to be pro-American[44]—is in part a reaction to unwarranted fears that the United States intends to trap India in an anti-China containment plot, sacrifice Indian energy security by compelling it to cut all ties to Iran, or suborn Indian sovereignty by forcing it to cede its claims in the dispute with Pakistan over Kashmir.[45]

In fact, the record (rather than the rhetoric) suggests that Indian prioritization of strategic autonomy is in many ways a myth. Although New Delhi refused to join Washington's early Cold War containment coalition against Communism, the first call Nehru made as Chinese troops pushed across the Indian border in 1962 was to President John F. Kennedy to request U.S. military support. Similarly, in the 1970s, New Delhi formed an alliance with the Soviet Union with an eye on countering Chinese power and securing Soviet weapons for India's defense. In both cases, India pursued external alignment with a superpower to address a security threat.

With regard to the principle of sovereign noninterference that is at the core of strategic autonomy, India intervened massively in Pakistan's internal

---

[43] For a recent expression of this sentiment by some of India's leading strategic thinkers, see Sunil Khilnani et al., "Non-Alignment 2.0: A Foreign and Strategic Policy for India in the Twenty-First Century," Centre for Policy Research, 2012, http://www.cprindia.org/sites/default/files/NonAlignment%20 2.0_1.pdf. For astute critiques, see Ashley J. Tellis, "Non-Alignment Redux: The Perils of Old Wine in New Skins," Carnegie Endowment for International Peace, 2012, http://carnegieendowment.org/files/ nonalignment_redux.pdf; and Sadanand Dhume, "Failure 2.0," *Foreign Policy*, March 16, 2012, http:// www.foreignpolicy.com/articles/2012/03/16/India_nonalignment_2.0_failure.

[44] Pew Research Center, "Opinion of the United States: India," Global Attitudes Project, September 2014, http://www.pewglobal.org/database/indicator/1/country/100.

[45] See, for instance, the Communist Party of India (Marxist)'s "apprehensions that through the [Indo-U.S.] nuclear deal, [the] U.S. will arm-twist India to change its foreign policy to kowtow to U.S. strategic global designs." This statement is cited in "Left Parties Again Object to Indo-U.S. Deal," *Rediff*, June 28, 2006, http://www.rediff.com/news/2006/jun/28ndeal5.htm.

affairs in 1971 to support the secession of Bangladesh with military force, in Sri Lanka in the late 1980s by sending its army into that country's civil war, and in the politics of Nepal and Bhutan, where India has, to varying degrees, played a guiding role in foreign and sometimes domestic affairs. In short, despite the rhetoric of strategic autonomy, India has acted very much as a traditional great power in its neighborhood and beyond.

Just as India has struggled to balance its record of practicing great-power politics with its rhetorical support for high principles like nonalignment and global nuclear disarmament, Indian grand strategy today struggles to balance external threat management with the risks of external dependency. The examples of Indian policies toward China, Pakistan, and arms imports highlight this tension. India alone is not capable of balancing its primary rival China, given the latter's material and geographic advantages. Yet Indians chafe at the notion of a more formal alliance with the United States to balance Chinese power, given the risks of dependency. These risks have been reinforced by an unfortunate history in which the United States, at several critical points in India's history, suspended arms sales during times of national crisis (for instance, during the 1965 war with Pakistan).

With regard to Pakistan, India's conventional military advantages over its smaller neighbor are in many ways neutered by Pakistan's nuclear arsenal, which is at parity with, if not actually larger than, India's. Given Pakistan's inclination to support "jihad under the nuclear umbrella,"[46] New Delhi would benefit from a strategic alliance with Washington to restrain the generals and spymasters in Pakistan from their support for radical extremists. But the ups and downs of the United States' own history with Pakistan, which was for many decades its favored ally in South Asia, mean that Indians are unwilling to outsource their Pakistan policy to Washington. Nor do they feel they can confidently rely on the United States to restrain its wayward ally. With regard to arms sales, India is the world's largest arms importer. But rather than "Americanize" its military through privileged long-term supply and joint-development contracts with the world's most advanced military power, India has consciously sourced its weapons imports from a range of countries, particularly Israel, Russia, and France, in addition to the United States. The result is reduced dependency on any one external power—but at the cost of a mishmash of weapons platforms that may not be fully interoperable, create logistical headaches, and are frequently technologically suboptimal, if not obsolescent.

More broadly, strategic autonomy means different things to different people in India. For some Indians, it reflects the Nehruvian ideal of a country

---

[46] This is the title of chapter 9 of C. Christine Fair's *Fighting to the End: The Pakistan Army's Way of War* (New York: Oxford University Press, 2014).

that stands apart from the power politics and competitive rivalries that dominate the international system, with an emphasis instead on nuclear disarmament and G-77 politics.[47] For other, more hawkish strategists, strategic autonomy implies an India that plays the great-power game vigorously but on its own terms, with an emphasis on internal rather than external balancing through the aggressive development of advanced military and economic capabilities.[48] For yet other Indians on the far left and far right, strategic autonomy is code for resisting partnership with the United States specifically, given their belief in its fickleness, inconstancy, and ambition to corral India into one or more containment coalitions (against China or Iran) that will materially undermine Indian interests.[49]

The reality in the 21st century, with the intensification of global economic competition and the persistence of both great-power and subnational security threats, is that only a strong and successful India can be strategically autonomous. This is particularly true in light of the growing challenges posed by India's dangerous neighborhood, as well as the risk that persistently high economic growth will permanently elevate China into the ranks of world powers—even as India remains bogged down by internal poverty, misgovernance, and a troublesome regional security environment that does not allow India to escape its region to play a role on the world stage befitting its size and interests.

Moreover, India's economy is tied to the world in a way it has not been since the days of the Raj. Nearly half of Indian GDP is constituted by exports and imports, and its heavy dependence on imported energy supplies will only increase as economic growth accelerates. This economic structure is very different from the more autarkic one India had in the past. It demands that New Delhi shape the external environment, including in collaboration with other powers, rather than merely prevent the world from impinging on the nation's choices.

Given India's diversity of constituencies and interests, it is also unclear that strategic autonomy has the same meaning for its globalized business elite that it does for its bureaucratic mandarins. Nor does the concept unite in any way the young, aspirational, urban middle classes with politicians whose policy prescriptions seem more apt for a time when India was poor, weak, and isolated than when it is rising, growing more prosperous, and finding itself in demand from other great powers to play a more leading role in world affairs. Looking ahead, India's developmental and security imperatives in the

---

[47] See, for instance, Khilnani et al., *Non-Alignment 2.0*, which reflected elements of this philosophy.

[48] Among other Indian strategists, Brahma Chellaney and Bharat Kharnad are reflective of this tendency.

[49] This was seen during the Indian debate over the civilian nuclear deal when leaders of the Communist Party of India (Marxist) touted this line.

21st century require a strategy of integration that stabilizes its neighborhood, shapes a balance of power through selective partnerships with like-minded great states, and harnesses India's economy to global flows of trade and investment. The doctrine of strategic autonomy is a better guide to India's past than to the future of a rapidly modernizing society with an expanding array of interests beyond its immediate region.

The Convergence of Indian and U.S. Strategic Interests

India's vital interests lie in securing its territory and autonomy against predatory powers and terrorists and building a prosperous society through economic growth and enhanced productivity that can pull hundreds of millions out of poverty. The United States has defined a compelling interest in helping India meet these objectives through defense collaboration and economic cooperation to steepen the slope of India's development trajectory. Indeed, the U.S. investment in India's ascent is unprecedented: rarely in history has a primary power sought to systematically invest in the rise of a secondary great power without regard for relative gain.

The United States declared its intention to do exactly that, with an eye on shaping the future Asian and global balances of power, when a senior official announced in 2005 a U.S. policy to "help India become a major world power in the 21st century," adding that the United States "understand[s] fully the implications, including military implications, of that statement."[50] That sentiment was not limited to the George W. Bush administration but has been a continuous goal of U.S. policy for nearly a decade. In late 2011, Deputy Secretary of State William Burns cited President Obama's statement to the Indian parliament that "the United States not only supports India as a rising power; we fervently support it, and we have worked to help make it a reality." Burns added: "Indeed, we are counting on India's rise as a global power—one that engages from the Middle East and East Asia to Africa and beyond."[51]

A review of India's core interests as a rising power in the 21st century attests to the convergence with U.S. interests across a full spectrum of issue areas and highlights how collaboration with Washington could help New Delhi achieve its strategic goals. These include securing the country's energy supply: India imports more than 80% of the oil it consumes, mostly from the Persian Gulf, which accounts for more than half of its sizable overall

---

[50] U.S. Department of State, "Background Briefing by Administration Officials on U.S.-South Asia Relations," March 25, 2005, http://2001-2009.state.gov/r/pa/prs/ps/2005/43853.htm.

[51] William J. Burns, "U.S.-India Partnership in an Asia-Pacific Century" (remarks at the University of Pune, Pune, India, December 16, 2011), http://www.state.gov/s/d/2011/178934.htm.

trade deficit.[52] The 2008 civil nuclear agreement and ongoing talks over the U.S. provision of liquefied natural gas (LNG) to India on privileged terms of the kind U.S. allies and FTA partners enjoy reflect U.S. efforts to strengthen India's energy security. India's military modernization is also a fundamental objective that has been strengthened by the United States' emergence as India's top arms supplier, as well as a leading partner in military training and joint exercises. Indian aspirations for a seat at the high table of international politics received boosts from Washington's support for India's inclusion in the Group of Twenty (G-20) in 2008, in the Nuclear Suppliers Group, and in other clubs that play an influential role in the civilian nuclear energy trade, as well as from President Obama's call in 2010 for Indian membership on the UN Security Council.[53]

China's ascension also gives New Delhi a strong stake in managing an Asian balance of power that is not controlled by Beijing, given the ongoing border dispute between the two sides. The United States has a parallel interest in a plurality of power in Asia that prevents hegemonic control of the economic resources of the eastern half of Eurasia. Washington and New Delhi also share an acute concern over the export of terrorism from Pakistan and Afghanistan. Both in the near-term struggle against violent extremism and in addressing the longer-term China challenge, India is a front-line state that benefits substantially from intelligence sharing and defense cooperation with the United States.

Shifting the discussion from land threats to opportunities in the maritime domain, India has a compelling interest in freedom of the seas and the security of the maritime commons, where its equities stretch from the Gulf of Aden and the Strait of Hormuz in the west to the Strait of Malacca and South China Sea in the east. At the global level, New Delhi has a strong interest in sustaining and strengthening a liberal international economic order that will allow India to deepen flows of trade, capital, technology, direct investment, and knowledge workers to dynamic markets abroad as a catalyst for development at home. As with the wider maritime commons in the Indian Ocean, Indian and U.S. interests overlap substantially with regard to the open international economic order, even if more particular Indian and U.S. policies lead to sector-specific clashes in international trade and investment negotiations.

---

[52] Victor Mallet, "India's Reliance on Imported Energy Threatens Long-Term Recovery," *Financial Times*, September 13, 2013, http://www.ft.com/intl/cms/s/0/c20792e2-1b84-11e3-b678-00144feab7de.html#axzz2jeWnBCSx.

[53] Barack Obama (remarks to the Joint Session of the Indian Parliament, New Delhi, November 8, 2010), http://www.whitehouse.gov/the-press-office/2010/11/08/remarks-president-joint-session-indian-parliament-new-delhi-india.

Implications of Indian-U.S. Strategic Cooperation for Asia and the World

The United States has a considerable stake in India's success. Washington anticipates an Indian resurgence that could help drive global growth and tilt Asia's power balance in a democratic direction. A dynamic India would be an example to the emerging world of economic transformation under democratic institutions and could uplift its region, including troubled Pakistan. As sectarian violence engulfs the Middle East, India and its nearly 200 million Muslims are a bastion of tolerance.

Beyond the many affinities that link the American and Indian people, and the many interests that compel their governments to pursue closer cooperation, India and the United States have a vital role to play in ensuring that Asia remains pluralistic and free rather than Sinocentric. China cannot claim to speak for Asia as long as there is an equally populous civilization-state in the region that contests unilateral Chinese leadership. India's rise requires China to be more cautious in supporting Pakistan because Beijing now has more to lose from pursuing policies that undermine Indian interests. Closer Indo-U.S. alignment also gives China a greater stake in stabilizing its own relations with India because Chinese military threats and territorial revanchism risk putting China on a path to conflict not only with India but with the United States.

Japan's resurgence as a great power, its continued relevance as a core U.S. ally, and its ability to maintain its autonomy against the threat of Chinese hegemony may hinge on the development of a pan-Asian axis with India that uses both countries' weight to sustain a regional equilibrium that is not Sinocentric. Japan's position at the mouth of the sea lanes into the western Pacific and India's as the buffer between China and the warm waters of the Indian Ocean raise the possibility of a natural maritime alliance to safeguard the regional commons and give lesser regional powers alliance options they might not otherwise have. There is little question that the development of an Indo-Japanese alliance would reinforce U.S. interests given the role of both countries as leading U.S. security partners. The future of the U.S. leadership role in Asia will be critically affected by India's great-power rise, Japan's evolution into a more active regional security provider, and the partnership between these countries to sustain a non-Chinese axis that maintains a pluralism of power in Asia. Prime Minister Modi's state visit to Japan in September 2014, following Prime Minister Shinzo Abe's state visit to India in January, reinforced a Japan-India strategic entente that could map a very different future for Asia than one centered on Beijing.[54]

Alongside Washington's existing alliance network in the region, the Indo-U.S. partnership is thus a strategic stabilizer in an Asia riven by dynamic power shifts, arms racing, and territorial conflict. India is also now broadly comfortable with U.S. leadership and power in the international system, as a result of both Indian opposition to Chinese primacy and the shift in U.S. policy over the past decade from seeking to contain Indian power to working to promote it. Moreover, a partnership with a rising India that broadly supports the United States' regional interests—because they mirror India's own strategic priorities—is more likely to strengthen U.S. leadership in the Indo-Pacific than is a scenario in which Washington and New Delhi go their separate ways. Looking ahead, the prospects for American renewal and Indian reform could recast the global balance of power and values in ways that make these two countries, rather than China alone, the pacesetters of the 21st century.

An Agenda to Advance U.S.-Indian Strategic and Economic Cooperation

There are at least six discrete areas in which Washington and New Delhi could deepen their nascent strategic partnership with an eye toward building habits of cooperation and materially facilitating India's economic and military rise.

The first is in defense supply, military training, and joint operations. For all the publicity surrounding the 2005 draft agreement on civilian nuclear cooperation, that deal was preceded by the far-reaching defense cooperation agreement under which the United States would help modernize the Indian armed forces. U.S. military sales to India since then have approached $10 billion. Although New Delhi wishes to avoid dependence on any single military supplier, the quality of U.S. defense materiel and scale of the U.S. defense-production establishment suggest that the United States may ultimately emerge as India's most important external military supplier. Indian forces already exercise more with the United States than with any other country, and India's Ministry of Defense should lift unnecessary restrictions on the scope and intimacy of military exchanges and exercises to enable the Indian armed forces to more fully engage their U.S. counterparts. More ambitiously, Washington and New Delhi should develop a joint concept

---

[54] Bruce Einhorn, "Visiting Japan, India's Modi Pokes at China," *Bloomberg Businessweek*, September 2, 2014, http://www.businessweek.com/articles/2014-09-02/visiting-japan-indias-modi-pokes-at-china.

of operations for the Indian Ocean region. This would have the effect of maximizing both countries' ability to patrol and monitor the Indian Ocean air and sea lanes, as well as reassuring India that there will be no unilateral U.S. military moves that deliver a strategic surprise (as did the 1971 deployment of a U.S. aircraft carrier battle group to the Bay of Bengal during the Bangladesh war). Washington and New Delhi should also engage in far more strategic and contingency planning with regard to maritime security and scenarios for potential Chinese aggression in Asia.

The second area for broader and deeper cooperation is in intelligence sharing and counterterrorism. U.S.-Indian intelligence exchange experienced a sea change after the November 2008 terrorist attacks in Mumbai, in part due to the deaths of Americans in the attacks as well as the complicity of U.S. citizen David Headley in planning them. The reality is that India and the United States are among the countries most threatened by external terrorism (as opposed to the internal variety that afflicts societies like Iraq and Pakistan) and share a common set of extremist adversaries, ranging from al Qaeda to Lashkar-e-Taiba. Washington and New Delhi must continue to ensure that their national intelligence establishments, which were until recently unconditioned to serious and sustained cooperation, maintain the post-2008 momentum and expand the set of intelligence targets on which they closely share information. Counterterrorism cooperation should become easier as well as increasingly necessary: the drawdown in Afghanistan will reduce the United States' dependence on Pakistani supply lines but also create regional instabilities that both India and the United States will need to manage through more expansive sharing of information and experience.

The third area for cooperation is in enlarging partnerships with like-minded countries to firm up the architecture of Asian security. While the Indo-U.S. strategic rapprochement after 2000 garnered the most headlines, India has been making important progress in building new security partnerships with U.S. allies Japan, South Korea, and Australia, as well as with Southeast Asian heavyweights Vietnam and Indonesia.[55] These efforts constitute "an unambiguous signal to China...of India's strategic preference"[56] for a non-Sinocentric Asia. India has formalized a robust strategic partnership with Japan in particular and participates in the U.S.-Japan-India trilateral

---

[55] Government of India, "Prime Minister's Address to Japan-India Association," Press Information Bureau, May 28, 2013; and Pranab Dhal Samanta, "In Signal to China, Manmohan Singh Embraces Japan's Idea," *Indian Express*, May 29 2013, http://www.indianexpress.com/news/in-signal-to-china-manmohan-singh-embraces-japans-idea/1121761.

[56] Samanta, "In Signal to China."

strategic dialogue launched in 2011.[57] Modi visited Japan multiple times as chief minister of Gujarat and shares Abe's goals of national resurgence through stronger economic growth and expanded contributions to regional security. India's development of strategic relationships in East Asia—including its deepening partnership with Japan and growing military ties with nations as diverse as South Korea, Australia, and Malaysia—will create further opportunities for New Delhi and Washington to more systematically pursue strategic cooperation with like-minded centers of strength in order to stabilize the regional balance of power.

A fourth area for cooperation lies in promoting India's strategic heft and economic development through new energy partnerships. The civilian nuclear deal consciously sought to do this, but its effects to date have been muted by an anomalous Indian nuclear liability law that prevents the agreement from coming fully into force. Beyond enlarging India's access to nuclear power, the United States and India have been negotiating preferential arrangements for the export of LNG to India. Such a partnership would strengthen Indian energy security through a source of assured supply and diminish the incentives for India to compete with China in the developing world—including Iran—for access to natural gas. India is among the countries most dependent on energy imports and will soon be one of the world's largest energy consumers. Thus, an arrangement to boost India's development in ways that expand its market for U.S. goods and services, while enhancing the country's ability to compete strategically in Asia, would be mutually beneficial for both India and the United States.

U.S. trade with India is only one-seventh of U.S. trade with China, despite the fact that one country is a strategic partner and the other a strategic competitor. A fifth area for cooperation, therefore, lies in deepening economic ties between India and the United States to balance out a relationship that to date has been led by defense and security ties.[58] Conclusion of a bilateral investment treaty should be a way station to the launch of negotiations for an FTA that would further integrate the two economies and ensure that actual or pending Indian economic cooperation agreements with Japan, the EU, and ASEAN do not disadvantage the United States. The United States remains India's top economic partner in terms of trade in goods and services, even as China is now India's top partner in traded goods alone. India and the United States should leverage their deep people-to-people

---

[57] Josh Rogin, "Inside the First Ever U.S.-Japan-India Trilateral Meeting," *Foreign Policy*, December 23, 2011, http://thecable.foreignpolicy.com/posts/2011/12/23/inside_the_first_ever_us_japan_india_trilateral_meeting.

[58] For a more detailed agenda for economic cooperation, see Daniel Twining, prepared remarks before the House Ways and Means Committee's Trade Subcommittee, March 13, 2013, http://waysandmeans.house.gov/uploadedfiles/twining_testimony31313.pdf.

ties, rich and complementary human capital, and status as the world's leading and emerging "knowledge economies" through additional bilateral agreements designed to facilitate high-skilled immigration, joint research and development, and innovation initiatives in the fields of health, energy, and climate. The two countries could also form the core of a global partnership dedicated to promoting Internet openness—on which India's development as a knowledge-and-services superpower will depend—against efforts by China and other powers to nationalize and otherwise build barriers to free exchange and open commerce online.

A final agenda item for the United States and India lies in cooperation to promote the rule of law and good governance abroad. This should be a natural instinct of the world's largest democracies, but defensive Indian views of sovereignty and nonalignment have precluded sustained cooperation on promoting democracy abroad. India and the United States have in fact worked in parallel to support democratic institution-building in Afghanistan since 2001 as well as in fragile states like Nepal, Bangladesh, and Myanmar. They have also cooperated at the global level in institutions like the UN Democracy Fund, of which India was a founding member.[59] Nonetheless, the countries need to leverage their higher comfort level with cooperation in defense and diplomacy to shape an agenda that promotes pluralism in Asia and the Middle East—not as a feel good policy but as a matter of unsentimental strategic interest. Both countries have much to lose from radicalization and chaos in the Arab world following the revolutions of the past few years and much to gain from democratic progress in strategically situated nations such as Myanmar. An agenda for Indo-U.S. cooperation to promote open government and civil society in fragile states on India's western and eastern flanks—less in a proselytizing sense and more in an effort to construct a firewall between the extremist pathologies of the Arab world and the open societies of the Indian subcontinent—is overdue and would benefit both countries' interests in stability, security, and prosperity.[60]

Conclusion

The United States and India share a compelling interest in defeating terrorism, shaping an Asian security environment that is pluralistic rather than Sinocentric, and sustaining a liberal international economic order as a

---

[59] See Government of India, "PM's Remarks at the Launching of UN Democracy Fund," Press Information Bureau, September 14, 2005, http://pib.nic.in/newsite/erelease.aspx?relid=11993.

[60] For further discussion, see Daniel Twining and Richard Fontaine, "The Ties That Bind? U.S.-India Values-Based Cooperation," *Washington Quarterly* 34, no. 2 (2011), http://csis.org/files/publication/twq11springtwiningfontaine.pdf.

driver of prosperity in both countries. From a U.S. perspective, India will be a stronger anchor of the Asian and global balances of power, as well as a better economic and diplomatic partner, if its push for development and military modernization is successful. The risks to the liberal international order come from Indian weakness or disengagement rather than from Indian strength and expanded participation. Similarly, India can only enjoy true strategic autonomy if it is strong, prosperous, and vigorously engaged with both its neighborhood and the wider world—including through partnerships that do not constrain its freedom of maneuver but in fact strengthen it by providing India with geopolitical options of the kind it never enjoyed under autarky and nonalignment.

A 21st-century world order anchored by strong democracies would look very different from one in which revisionist, authoritarian powers dominate, much less one in which weak and failed states proliferate. India and the United States have a compelling convergence of interests. These include sustaining an Asian balance of power; defeating terrorism; maintaining the freedom of the global air, sea, cyber, and space commons on which their prosperity and security as open societies is predicated; promoting good governance abroad as a source of security at home; and developing the human capital and technologies to manage cross-cutting challenges from climate change to aging. In an increasingly non-Western world, the United States would benefit from an Asian partner whose people share its values and outlook. As India pursues domestic economic transformation, the world's presiding economic, technological, and military superpower is a useful ally. Although there will certainly be frictions, the benefits of cooperating unquestionably outweigh the costs to both countries.

EXECUTIVE SUMMARY

This chapter examines both Indonesia's perception of its strategic environment and the increasing influence of domestic political factors on Indonesian foreign policy and assesses their implications for the U.S.-Indonesia partnership.

MAIN ARGUMENT:
Indonesia's perception of its external security environment has traditionally been fairly benign, enabling Jakarta to promote its interests in a peaceful, autonomous Southeast Asia through diplomatic means, particularly in regional institutions like ASEAN. Recently, Indonesian threat perceptions have been rising as a result of the changing balance of power in the Asia-Pacific and China's actions in the South China Sea, which threaten Indonesia's maritime security, its leadership in ASEAN, and its commitment to the peaceful settlement of disputes. A growing convergence of strategic interests dictate strengthening the U.S.-Indonesian partnership. At the same time, the rising influence of nationalism, Islam, and public opinion on Indonesian foreign policy creates obstacles to closer ties with the U.S. With incoming president Joko Widodo likely to adopt a more domestically focused foreign policy, the prospects for strengthening the partnership are unclear.

POLICY IMPLICATIONS:
- Although the U.S.-Indonesian partnership has improved dramatically in recent years, whether the partnership continues to strengthen will likely depend on whether strategic or domestic considerations drive Indonesian foreign policy.

- Given domestic pressures on Indonesia's leadership, if the U.S. takes a more assertive, independent role in regional institutions, it will trigger tensions with Indonesia.

- As a status quo middle power, Indonesia is acutely aware that its interests lie in a stable balance between the U.S. and China. Indonesia's commitment to an independent policy stance means it will resent any overt attempt by the U.S. to push it into a balancing coalition against China.

Indonesia's Partnership with the United States: Strategic Imperatives Versus Domestic Obstacles

Ann Marie Murphy

Indonesia is an increasingly pivotal international actor across a range of issues critical to U.S. interests. At a time when changes in the balance of power in the Asia-Pacific are producing tensions, Indonesia has emerged as a swing state in the region.[1] At a time when China's assertiveness in the South and East China Seas is threatening freedom of navigation, Indonesia's strategic location astride some of the world's most vital sea lines of communication (SLOC) makes it a critical maritime partner. At a time when the threat of terrorism is increasing as a result of political upheavals in the Middle East, Indonesia's status as the only Muslim-majority country to navigate a democratic transition while instituting a successful counterterrorism program makes it an important partner on political and security issues. And at a time when democracy is in retreat in Southeast Asia and around the globe, Indonesia's 2014 parliamentary and presidential elections buck this trend. Indeed, that the election of Joko Widodo (Jokowi) as president was challenged by the losing candidate, Prabowo Subianto, but upheld by the Constitutional Court, whose ruling was accepted by the public, illustrates the continued consolidation of Indonesia's democratic institutions.

U.S.-Indonesian relations have improved dramatically in recent years as the two sides have forged a comprehensive partnership to enhance cooperation

Ann Marie Murphy is an Associate Professor in the School of Diplomacy and International Relations and founding Director of the Center for Emerging Powers and Transnational Trends at Seton Hall University. She can be reached at <annmarie.murphy@shu.edu>.

[1] Ted Osius, "Global Swing States: Deepening Partnerships with India and Indonesia," *Asia Policy*, no. 17 (2014): 67–92.

across a wide range of security, economic, and social issues. Only a decade ago, the relationship was fraught with tensions over the U.S. insistence on making aid from the International Monetary Fund (IMF) conditional on structural adjustments, the U.S. suspension of military-to-military ties in response to human rights abuses, differences regarding how to approach the threat of terrorism, and the universal Indonesian opposition to the U.S. wars in Afghanistan and Iraq.[2] Bilateral ties have improved dramatically since the 2004 election of President Susilo Bambang Yudhoyono. Under Yudhoyono, Indonesia has consolidated democracy, adopted one of the world's most successful counterterrorism programs, and sustained strong economic growth. The country has also reinvigorated its leadership of the Association of Southeast Asian Nations (ASEAN) and the ASEAN Regional Forum (ARF) and played a pivotal role in creating new regional institutions such as the East Asia Summit (EAS) and ASEAN Defence Ministers' Meeting, all of which seek to promote regional peace and stability. As Yudhoyono sought to raise Indonesia's international profile to a level consistent with its status as the fourth most populous state, third-largest democracy, and country with the world's largest community of Muslims, he adopted a cosmopolitan policy of democracy promotion, became a leader on climate change issues, and made key contributions to UN peacekeeping operations. Across a broad spectrum of issues, Indonesia has demonstrated a willingness to invest its diplomatic energies to support the current international order in a manner consistent with U.S. interests.

Indonesian foreign policy under President Jokowi is likely to become more domestically focused for a number of reasons. First, Jokowi lacks international experience and has none of the credentials that helped transform Yudhoyono into an international statesman, such as English-language fluency, a master's degree from an American university, and years of high-level government service. Jokowi rose from the lower classes and was a small-scale furniture maker before becoming mayor of Solo and later Jakarta, earning a reputation as an honest, effective manager. Second, Jokowi won the election by pledging to tackle long-standing domestic problems such as weak infrastructure, bureaucratic inefficiency, and education and will want to devote his energy to fulfilling campaign pledges. Third, the election campaign witnessed an extraordinary amount of nationalist rhetoric, both political and economic. For the first time ever, one of Indonesia's presidential debates was devoted to foreign policy, and the public learned that neither candidate had a well-developed foreign policy agenda. Instead, the candidates pledged support for popular policies that were sure to win votes, such as

[2] Ann Marie Murphy, "U.S. Rapprochement with Indonesia: From Problem State to Partner," *Contemporary Southeast Asia* 31, no. 3 (2010): 362–87.

preserving Indonesian economic independence and protecting Indonesian migrant workers and Muslim minorities abroad. Fourth, Jokowi's Indonesia Democratic Party–Struggle (PDI-P) only won 18.9% of the parliamentary vote, meaning it will have a weak parliamentary position to support its foreign policy. Given his lack of international experience and desire to focus on domestic reform, Jokowi is likely to leave foreign policy to the professionals in the Ministry of Foreign Affairs, in contrast with Yudhoyono, whose keen interest in promoting Indonesia abroad meant foreign policy initiatives often came from the palace. At the time of writing, it is unclear who will become foreign minister, although Jokowi's pledge to appoint cabinet members on the basis of professional credentials rather than political calculation makes the appointment of a career diplomat likely.

Whether the U.S.-Indonesian partnership continues to strengthen will depend on whether strategic or domestic factors drive Indonesian foreign policy. The United States and Indonesia share a growing convergence of strategic interests that dictate a deepening of cooperative efforts. However, the rising nationalism and anti-foreign sentiment so prevalent in the divisive election campaign could thwart efforts to deepen the relationship. Managing the U.S.-Indonesian partnership will likely become more difficult in the near term.

This chapter proceeds as follows. First, it provides an assessment of Indonesia's external environment, arguing that the country's perceptions of external threats have risen recently. The second section then examines how three domestic factors—democracy, Islam, and nationalism—are influencing foreign policy, often in ways detrimental to U.S.-Indonesian relations. Third, the chapter reviews Indonesia's key foreign policies and examines how Indonesia has used its position in ASEAN to promote regional peace and a rule-based order in the Asia-Pacific. Fourth, it examines the South China Sea disputes to illustrate how recent Chinese actions threaten Indonesian maritime security, ASEAN cohesion, Indonesia's leadership in regional organizations, and the status quo that Jakarta has worked to promote. The chapter concludes with recommendations to strengthen the U.S.-Indonesian partnership.

Indonesia's Assessment of Its External Environment: Rising Threat Perceptions

Indonesia has traditionally viewed its external security environment in a fairly benign manner. Indonesia's geographic status as a nation of seventeen thousand islands makes it relatively immune to external attack. Indeed, the country's last defense white paper, published in 2008, foresaw no external military threat in the next fifteen years.[3] In 2010 the Ministry of Defense issued its Minimum Essential Force document, which outlined the country's defense requirements to 2029 based on an assessment of actual and potential threats.[4] The ministry identified terrorism, separatism, border disputes, outer island management, natural disasters, communal conflicts, and energy security as actual threats, while climate change, violations of Indonesia's waterways, environmental degradation, pandemics, foreign aggression, financial crises, cybercrime, and water and food crises were identified as potential threats.[5] Since then, China's assertive pursuit of its maritime claims and the escalation in Sino-U.S. tensions have raised Indonesian threat perceptions.

Indonesia's key security interests are maintaining the social cohesion of its heterogeneous population and the sovereign integrity of its far-flung archipelago, which stretches over three thousand miles across some of the world's most strategic SLOCs. Acutely aware of their country's social and territorial fragility, Indonesian leaders have historically viewed their primary security threats as internal ones. As a result, they have perceived external threats not in terms of traditional military invasion but as foreign actions that breach Indonesian sovereignty—whether to intervene directly in separatist conflicts, secure passage through Indonesian SLOCs, secure access to energy resources, or support terrorism.[6] Dutch attempts to divide the Indonesian state, U.S. support for anti-Jakarta rebels in the 1950 outer islands disputes, a widespread belief of Chinese complicity in the 1965 coup, and foreign intervention in East Timor have reinforced these fears, producing what prominent scholar Dewi Fortuna Anwar calls an "ambivalent" worldview. In this worldview, "the outside world was a hostile place, replete with forces constantly threatening Indonesian independence and integrity and seeking to exploit its natural wealth and strategic location; but at the same time the outside world represented a source of aid and support."[7]

---

[3] Rizal Sukma, "Indonesia's Security Outlook, Defense Policy and Regional Cooperation," in *Asia Pacific Countries' Security Outlook and Its Implications for the Defense Sector* (Tokyo: National Institute of Defense Studies, 2010). Indonesia was scheduled to produce a white paper in 2012 but has yet to publish one.

[4] Iis Gindarsah, "Politics, Security and Defence in Indonesia: Interactions and Interdependencies," Australian National University, National Security College Issues Brief, no. 3, May 2014, http://nsc. anu.edu.au/documents/Indonesia-Article4.pdf.

[5] Evan A. Laksmana, "Indonesia's Rising Regional and Global Profile: Does Size Really Matter?" *Contemporary Southeast Asia* 33, no. 2 (2011): 166.

[6] Evan A. Laksmana, "The TNI: Strategic Changes and Implications," *Jakarta Post*, September 1, 2010. Regarding external support for terrorism in Indonesia, a major fear today is that the Islamic State of Iraq and Syria (ISIS) will develop ties to local terrorist groups.

[7] Dewi Fortuna Anwar, "Indonesia: Domestic Priorities Define National Security," *Asian Security Practice: Material and Ideational Influences*, ed. Mutiah Alagappa (Stanford: Stanford University Press, 1998), 481.

Indonesian security officials traditionally describe their grand strategy in terms of concentric circles aimed at creating a *cordon sanitaire* around the country. The first circle focuses on internal security threats arising from the social cleavages of the country's heterogeneous population and on nontraditional security threats such as terrorism and natural disasters. Regional security in Southeast Asia occupies the second circle, and maintaining Southeast Asia's stability and autonomy from great-power hegemony is Indonesia's key interest here. The third circle encompasses the entire Asia-Pacific and the great powers such as the United States and China. Indonesia's key interest in this realm is to promote a flexible balance of power in which rising powers such as China and India can be accommodated with existing powers such as the United States without resorting to conflict. The emergence of conflict or hegemony in the broader Asia-Pacific region would directly threaten Indonesia's critical interest in a peaceful and autonomous Southeast Asia.

Today, China's claims to large swaths of the South China Sea, including Indonesia's Natuna Island exclusive economic zone (EEZ), and its use of military force in the area pose a direct threat to Indonesian national interests, regional stability, and the rule-based order Jakarta has long promoted through ASEAN. Rising Sino-U.S. competition also raises the prospect that Indonesia will need to choose between the two sides, something it and other ASEAN states have long sought to avoid. Indonesia, therefore, is beginning to view its external environment as more threatening than it has in the past.

Domestic Politics and Foreign Policy: Nationalism, Islam, and Democracy

Indonesia's foreign policy has always been guided by the *bebas dan aktif* or "free and active" doctrine promulgated by Prime Minister Mohammad Hatta in 1948.[8] The free component holds that Indonesia should chart its own course in international affairs rather than follow the diktats of any great power. The active component holds that Indonesia should play a role in shaping the international order. Hatta titled his seminal speech "Mendajung antara dua karang," or "Rowing between Two Reefs," in reference to the challenges Indonesia faced in its quest for an independent foreign policy amid the Cold War competition between the United States and Soviet Union. Today, Indonesian analysts have invoked the phrase to refer to the challenges of

---

[8] Michael Leifer, *Indonesia's Foreign Policy* (London: George Allen and Unwin, 1983).

navigating Sino-U.S. competition.[9] Indonesia's commitment to a free foreign policy means that it foreswears alliances and would never permit foreign bases on its soil, thereby setting outer limits to U.S.-Indonesian security cooperation. The staunch Indonesian opposition to the rotational deployment of U.S. troops to Darwin, Australia, makes it unlikely that Indonesia would consider a similar arrangement absent a direct security threat to the country.[10]

Indonesian foreign policy has long been influenced by a strident nationalism and anticolonial sentiment that can hamper ties not only with Western countries but also with Southeast Asian neighbors. Indonesia's nationalist leader Sukarno, who was president from 1945 to 1967, nationalized foreign economic assets, declared that the United States could "go to hell with its aid," launched a low-level war against Malaysia, joined a Jakarta-Peking-Hanoi-Pyongyang axis, and became the only country ever to quit the United Nations. The lesson drawn by President Suharto (1967–98) and many foreign policy elites was that stoking nationalism could lead to dangerous foreign policy adventures that were detrimental to Indonesian security and economic interests.[11] During the Suharto era, therefore, societal influences in policymaking were suppressed as foreign policy became the purview of an insulated elite group of military officials, professional diplomats, and economic technocrats. With pragmatism overriding nationalism, the United States became Indonesia's key military patron and Indonesian economic technocrats forged close ties with the United States and liberal institutions such as the World Bank and IMF.

The Impact of Democracy on Indonesia's Foreign Policy

Democracy has opened up Indonesia's traditionally insulated policymaking process. In the post-Suharto era, Indonesia's traditionally strong executive has been weakened, the military has lost its formal political role, and parliament has unprecedented oversight over foreign policy decisions. Groups traditionally absent from foreign policy debates, such as political parties, Muslim groups, human rights organizations, and businesses, now actively participate in them. A vibrant press covers all government policies, and the political competition inherent in democracies gives opponents of the

---

[9] Daniel Novotny, *Torn between America and China: Elite Perceptions and Indonesian Foreign Policy* (Singapore: Institute of Southeast Asian Studies, 2010).

[10] Dewi Fortuna Anwar, "An Indonesian Perspective on the U.S. Rebalancing Effort toward Asia," National Bureau of Asian Research, Commentary, February 26, 2013, http://www.nbr.org/research/activity.aspx?id=320.

[11] The classic work comparing foreign policy under Sukarno and Suharto is Franklin B. Weinstein, *Indonesian Foreign Policy and the Dilemma of Dependence: From Sukarno to Suharto* (Ithaca: Cornell University Press, 1976).

government an incentive to score domestic political points through a critique of its foreign policies.[12]

Balancing the responsibilities of international leadership with the imperatives of domestic politics thus can be difficult in Indonesia's new democracy. Serving on the UN Security Council (UNSC) for the 2007–8 term forced Indonesia to take positions on issues it would have preferred to avoid. In March 2007, for example, Indonesia voted to sanction Iran for its nuclear activities, which triggered a domestic uproar. Islamic groups decried the government's breach of Muslim solidarity, while nationalist politicians, citing a phone call from President George W. Bush to President Yudhoyono ahead of the vote, accused Yudhoyono of caving in to U.S. pressure.[13] Parliament used its powers of interpellation to compel the administration to explain the decision. Prior to a subsequent UNSC vote to tighten Iranian sanctions in March 2008, Yudhoyono refused to take a phone call from Bush. Indonesia abstained from voting and was the only UNSC member not to vote for sanctions.

Yudhoyono's refusal to take Bush's phone call illustrates that the United States must be extremely sensitive to how its actions are perceived in Indonesia, lest Washington inadvertently weaken Indonesian leaders amenable to U.S. interests. The rising influence of societal actors on Indonesian foreign policy has generated new demands that the government speak out for the rights of Indonesian migrant workers and Muslim minorities abroad, which complicates relations with neighboring countries. Over 6.5 million Indonesians work abroad, including over 2 million in Malaysia and 180,000 in Singapore.[14] Disagreements over working conditions, wages, and recruiting methods and allegations of abuse led to a 2009 ban on sending workers to these two countries, which was only lifted in 2011 when new agreements with greater protections were implemented. Many Indonesians contend that the protection of migrant workers should be Indonesia's number one foreign policy priority, illustrating a much more domestically focused conception of national interest than that espoused by Yudhoyono. Likewise, persecution of Muslim minorities abroad, particularly the Rohingyas in Myanmar, has generated strong public demands on Jakarta to pressure foreign governments to halt the violence. In both cases, societal pressure for Indonesia to influence the internal policies of neighboring

---

[12] Ann Marie Murphy, "Democratization and Indonesian Foreign Policy: Implications for the United States," *Asia Policy*, no. 13 (2012): 83–111.

[13] Bill Guerin, "Yudhoyono Paints Himself into the West's Corner," *Asia Sentinel*, April 7, 2007.

[14] Bassina Farbenblum, Eleanor Taylor-Nicholson, and Sarah Paoletti, *Migrant Workers' Access to Justice at Home: Indonesia* (New York: Open Society Foundations, 2013), http://www.opensocietyfoundations.org/publications/migrant-workers-access-justice-home-indonesia.

countries runs headlong into ASEAN's cardinal rule of noninterference in the domestic affairs of member states. Adherence to ASEAN norms has played a key role in maintaining regional stability in Southeast Asia, and Indonesia is finding it increasingly difficult to balance the demands of its citizenry with ASEAN conventions.

Islam in Indonesian Foreign Policy: A New and Powerful Factor

With 88% of the country's 250 million people adhering to Islam, the Middle East is the most important region outside of Asia for Indonesia. Events in the Middle East can reverberate domestically in Indonesia, often in ways that complicate U.S.-Indonesian relations. The United States justified its wars against Afghanistan and Iraq in part on the basis of the terrorist threat, but from the Indonesian perspective these wars provided an opportunity for Indonesian radicals to mobilize support for their cause, thereby intensifying the terrorist threat at home. Regarding the Arab-Israeli conflict, Indonesia has never recognized the state of Israel, and Indonesians of all political persuasions support the cause of Palestinian independence—secular nationalist groups on the basis of anticolonialism and Islamic groups on the basis of religious solidarity. Israeli violence against Palestinians generates anti-American sentiment, and the absence of an Israeli embassy in Jakarta means that the U.S. embassy becomes the target of anti-Israeli demonstrations.

Indonesia's Muslim community, however, is not monolithic. Its two large Muslim social organizations, Nahdlatul Ulama and Muhammadiya, support Fatah, whereas some Islamic political parties and transnational groups such as Hizbut Tharir support Hamas. Moderate Indonesians who believe that violence in the Middle East creates opportunities for radical Islamic groups to rally support in Indonesia often cannot understand why the United States continues to support Israel, or at least fails to restrain its smaller ally. The very different domestic constituencies in the United States and Indonesia mean that managing differences on the Israeli-Palestinian issue will be a long-term project.

Terrorism is a common security challenge that initially created significant tension between the United States and Indonesia but has become a successful example of managing differences to forge effective cooperation. Coming amid the anti-American sentiment generated by controversies over the IMF, East Timor, and Afghanistan, loud U.S. demands in the wake of September 11 for Indonesia to crack down on terrorism generated a backlash and public denials that local radical groups like Jemaah Islamiya (JI) were linked to al Qaeda. The U.S. designation of Southeast Asia as the second front in the war on terrorism raised fears that the United States or its Australian ally would preemptively attack Indonesia.

Indonesia's position began to change after the bombings in Bali on October 12, 2002, killed 202 people. Prior to Bali, terrorism was perceived as an American issue and the adoption of counterterrorism policies was viewed as submission to external pressure. After the attacks, terrorism was viewed as a threat to Indonesia, and counterterrorism policies could be justified as serving Indonesia's national interests. Since then, Indonesia has adopted what many observers consider one of the world's most successful counterterrorism programs while making a successful transition to democracy.[15] U.S.-Indonesian cooperation on counterterrorism is strong, with the United States providing funding, equipment, and training for Detachment 88, Indonesia's elite police counterterrorism unit.[16]

The process through which the United States and Indonesia forged a cooperative partnership on counterterrorism holds important lessons. First, the fact that two countries objectively share common interests is no guarantee of cooperation. Second, the United States recognized that its public "megaphone" diplomacy of demanding Indonesian action was counterproductive because it made cooperation with Washington politically costly for the Indonesian leadership. U.S. officials instead began relying on private, quiet diplomacy that produced more effective results. Third, despite the strong cooperation between the two sides, differences will persist. Indonesia's unwillingness to clamp down on press freedom to censure radical Islamic publications, close radical schools, or ban groups like JI due to a belief that doing so would generate support for the radicals often frustrated Washington. The contrasting worldviews and domestic operating environments of the United States and Indonesia mean that the two countries will often take different approaches to an issue even when they share the same basic interests.

Economic Nationalism:
A Source of Conflict with the United States and China

Indonesian suspicion of external influence extends to the economic arena. Indonesia is a country rich in resources that endured over three hundred years of Dutch colonialism, and its constitution vests ownership

---

[15] Zachary Abuza, "Indonesian Counter-Terrorism: The Great Leap Forward," Jamestown Foundation, Terrorism Monitor, January 14, 2010.

[16] Bruce Vaughan, "Indonesia: Domestic Politics, Strategic Dynamics, and U.S. Interests," Congressional Research Service, CRS Report for Congress, RL32394, January 31, 2011, 36, http://www.fas.org/sgp/crs/row/RL32394.pdf.

of resources with the state.[17] Despite the country's strong economic growth according to market-oriented development plans, Indonesians view capitalism as exploitative: there is little support for liberal economics in the country, and the word "liberal" is often used as an epithet. Indonesians view some of the rules of the global liberal economic order, particularly intellectual property rights, as means to keep developing countries down. Indonesian import restrictions on horticultural and animal products led the United States in 2013 to file a complaint with the WTO dispute panel. Indonesia is currently witnessing a rise in resource nationalism, which is causing frictions because the bulk of U.S. investment in Indonesia is in the resource sector. Jakarta is seeking to renegotiate revenue-sharing agreements, and effective January 1, 2014, banned the exportation of unprocessed ore, calling instead for foreign investment in downstream industries.[18] Indonesia views its actions as fully consistent with the logic of infant industry protection, but the United States sees them as threats to the liberal economic order. Given Jokowi's campaign pledge to make Indonesia more self-reliant economically, economic tensions are likely to rise in the near term.

China has also become a target of Indonesian economic nationalism. In the wake of the implementation of the ASEAN-China Free Trade Area in 2010, the widespread availability of low-cost Chinese consumer goods has led to the hollowing out of some domestic industries. Indonesia is the world's largest producer of rattan, and when China's rattan furniture makers were decimating the local rattan furniture industry a few years ago, Indonesia banned the export of rattan. At the same time, China's demand for natural resources to fuel its economic growth has created a surge in raw material exports. Five raw materials—coal, palm oil, gas, crude petroleum, and rubber—constituted approximately 60% of Indonesian exports to China in 2011. The pattern of trade that has emerged is one in which Indonesia imports manufactures and exports raw materials. This neocolonial pattern has stoked Indonesian economic nationalism, creating perceptions of China as an exploitative economic power and contributing to the adoption of protectionist measures.[19]

---

[17] "Preamble to the 1945 Constitution," in *Indonesian Political Thinking 1945–1965*, ed. Herbert Feith and Lance Castles (Jakarta: Equinox Classics Reprints, 2007).

[18] The *Jakarta Globe* has an archive of excellent articles on the ore ban that can be accessed at http://www.thejakartaglobe.com/tag/indonesia-ore-ban.

[19] Anne Booth, "China's Economic Relations with Indonesia: Threats and Opportunities," School of Oriental and African Studies, University of London, Working Paper, October 2011, 5.

Indonesian Foreign Policy Priorities

Indonesia's key foreign policy priorities are to ensure that Southeast Asia remains peaceful and autonomous from outside hegemony and to promote a stable balance of power in the broader Asia-Pacific in which disputes are resolved in accordance with international law. Indonesia seeks to achieve these goals largely through a soft-power approach of engaging outside powers in organizations such as the ARF and EAS and promoting ASEAN norms of noninterference and peaceful settlement of disputes.

Indonesia has long mediated disputes between its Southeast Asian neighbors. Following Vietnam's invasion of Cambodia, Indonesia played a pivotal role in helping end the Vietnamese occupation and was a co-convener of the Paris Peace Accords. In the Philippines, it has helped mediate the conflict between the central government and the Muslim area of Mindanao. During the recent Thai-Cambodian border dispute over the Preah Vihear temple, Foreign Minister Marty Natalegawa helped negotiate a ceasefire agreement, and Indonesia offered to provide soldiers to monitor it. In the case of Myanmar, Indonesian leaders were instrumental in convincing the country's military rulers that it was in their interests to embark on a program of political reform, something that clearly supports the U.S. interest in a liberal international order.

In the broader Asia-Pacific, Indonesia seeks what Natalegawa calls a "dynamic equilibrium" or "state of affairs where there is not one preponderant country."[20] Ensuring that regional architecture is built on ASEAN, which gives its members agenda-setting influence and helps prevent their domination by larger powers, is a key Indonesian interest. Indonesia's purported ability to lead ASEAN is an important source of its international influence.

Under President Yudhoyono, Indonesia made a concerted effort to raise its international profile on the global stage. Like many middle powers, Indonesia strongly supports multilateral institutions and actively participates in the Group of Twenty (G-20), the Non-Aligned Movement, and the Organisation of Islamic Cooperation. Indonesia also plays an active role in the UN system. In recent years, it has been elected as a nonpermanent member of the UNSC and to a third consecutive term on the UN Human Rights Council, and it is a key contributor to UN peacekeeping operations. Indonesia, therefore, is clearly willing to play its part in sustaining the international order. Nonetheless, its interests at times diverge with those of the United States. Indonesia, for example, strongly believes that only the

---

[20] See "A Conversation with Marty Natalegawa, Minister of Foreign Affairs, Republic of Indonesia," Council on Foreign Relations, Transcript, September 20, 2010, http://www.cfr.org/indonesia/conversation-marty-natalegawa-minister-foreign-affairs-republic-indonesia/p22984.

UNSC possesses the power to legitimize the use of force against member states. As a result, Indonesians of all political persuasions condemned the U.S. invasion of Iraq as a violation of international law.

Facing Sino-U.S. Competition: Rowing between Two Reefs

Indonesia long viewed China as its key international threat. During the Suharto era, the belief that China had played a role in the October 1965 coup through its support of the Indonesian Communist Party led Jakarta to freeze diplomatic relations in 1967 and not restore them until 1990.[21] The United States developed a strong relationship with the Suharto regime based on shared opposition to Communism and became Indonesia's key provider of military aid, equipment, and training. In the early 1990s, the United States began conditioning military ties on Indonesian policy toward East Timor. In response to the violence unleashed by pro-Indonesia militias and Indonesian soldiers following East Timor's 1999 vote for independence, Washington cut military ties completely. This decision came in the wake of U.S. insistence that Indonesia follow an IMF program during the Asian financial crisis that even disinterested observers contend deepened and prolonged the crisis, causing widespread resentment of the United States across the Indonesian political spectrum and creating an opening for China.[22]

The period between the Asian financial crisis and China's 2009 publication of its "nine-dash line" map laying claim to a large area of the South China Sea was marked by a Sino-Indonesian rapprochement as Beijing adopted policies to underscore its commitment to a peaceful rise strategy.[23] Economic ties expanded, and today China is Indonesia's largest trading partner. China's support for ASEAN-based multilateral institutions and commitment to the principle of noninterference stood in sharp contrast with the United States' decision to skip ASEAN meetings under the Bush administration, whose concern over terrorism led it to advocate for the right to preemptively attack other countries. In 2005, Indonesia and China signed a strategic partnership that was part of a concerted effort by Jakarta to expand its strategic options at the height of the unilateralism of the Bush era.

Over the past five years, however, China's statements and actions have threatened all of Indonesia's key foreign policy priorities. First, China's claims to the South China Sea threaten Indonesian territorial waters and the right to

---

[21] Rizal Sukma, *Indonesia and China: The Politics of a Troubled Relationship* (New York: Routledge, 1999).

[22] Joseph E. Stiglitz, *Globalization and Its Discontents* (New York: W.W. Norton, 2002). This argument is made forcefully in chapter 4, pp. 89–132.

[23] Michael A. Glosny, "Heading toward a Win-Win Future? Recent Developments in China's Policy Toward Southeast Asia," *Asian Security* 2, no. 1 (2006): 24–57.

exploit the resources beneath them. If China achieves its goals in the South China Sea, it will be in a position to exert hegemony in Southeast Asia, something antithetical to Indonesia's interests. Second, China's willingness to resort to violence undermines ASEAN's fundamental norm of the peaceful settlement of disputes, which Indonesia has assiduously promoted. Third, China's unilateral actions and unwillingness to abide by the UN Convention on the Law of the Sea (UNCLOS) threatens both the rule-based regional order and multilateral approaches favored by Jakarta. Fourth, China's willingness to use its leverage over some of Southeast Asia's smaller states to intervene directly in ASEAN negotiations undermines the organization's unity and compromises Indonesia's ability to lead ASEAN. In all of these areas, Indonesia views Chinese actions as upsetting the status quo it has long sought to promote. Since the territorial disputes in the South China Sea engage all of these interests and illustrate how Jakarta is reassessing its priorities and relationship to the United States, this issue is discussed in depth below.

Chinese Assertiveness in the South China Sea

Given the South China Sea's strategic SLOCs, rich fishing grounds, and significant oil and gas deposits, disputes are not new. Overlapping territorial claims to the Paracel (China and Vietnam) and the Spratly island chains (China, Taiwan, Malaysia, Brunei, the Philippines, and Vietnam) date back decades, as does competition to occupy and control them. The use of force by China to assert its claims is not new either: China forcibly took the Paracels from Vietnamese control in 1974 and occupied Mischief Reef, located 130 miles off the coast of the Philippines' Palawan island, in 1994.[24] Jakarta had always viewed Beijing's interests in the South China Sea with suspicion, but it was China's occupation of Mischief Reef and concurrent clashes with Vietnam that made the South China Sea a critical foreign policy issue for Indonesia. Viewing these actions as a test for the organization, ASEAN responded collectively by telling China directly at a 1994 meeting in Hangzhou that ASEAN would not tolerate the use of force to resolve regional disputes.[25]

As a non-claimant, Indonesia believed that it had the independence to serve as mediator, and in the 1990s it began holding workshops to reduce tensions between rival claimants. Ultimately, ASEAN and China signed the

---

[24] Since 1994, China has transformed Mischief Reef into a heavily fortified multistory naval facility, complete with helipads, piers, and radar powered with electricity generated by windmills. Mischief Reef provides China with a forward-operating base from which it can project power in the South China Sea.

[25] This statement draws on the author's interview in Bangkok in May 2008 with an ASEAN official present at the Hangzhou meeting. The official acknowledged that it is difficult to imagine the blunt language used then by ASEAN being used now—in part due to China's rising power and in part due to the admission of Laos, Cambodia, and Myanmar into ASEAN.

Declaration on the Conduct of Parties in the South China Sea in 2002, which committed the signatories to the peaceful settlement of disputes, the non-use of force, and the exercise of restraint.[26] Importantly, it called for all claimants to refrain from occupying uninhabited islands, reefs, and shoals in the South China Sea. The declaration, however, lacked an enforcement mechanism to ensure compliance with its principles. To remedy this problem, Indonesia has taken the lead in negotiating a legally binding code of conduct (COC) that would include measures to prevent military escalation at sea. These efforts clearly indicate Indonesia's willingness to play a role in promoting a rule-based regional order.

Indonesia's fears of China's irredentist claims to the South China Sea were realized by China's 2009 submission to the UN Commission on the Limits of the Continental Shelf in which it claimed that it had "indisputable sovereignty over the islands in the South China Sea and their adjacent waters and enjoy[s] sovereign rights and jurisdiction over the relevant waters as well as the seabed and subsoil thereof."[27] The submission was accompanied by a nine-dash line map that includes virtually the entire South China Sea. The claims are expansive and China's justification for them is ambiguous, relying mostly on its version of historical rights, not UNCLOS. China did not claim any Indonesian islands, but the nine-dash line includes parts of the Natuna Island EEZ, home to one of the world's largest recoverable gas fields. Indonesia protested China's submission in 2010, contending that it "clearly lacks any international legal basis."[28]

At stake for Indonesia is not only the Natuna Island waters but also the sanctity of UNCLOS. Indonesia is the world's largest archipelagic state, but it lacks the naval capacity to defend itself. Its conception of its national territory encompasses not only the seventeen thousand islands that make up the archipelago but also the waters that connect them. Indeed, the Indonesian word for country is *tanah air*, literally land and water. When UNCLOS came into force in 1994, it included the archipelagic principle, which grants island nations sovereignty over their internal waters. Ensuring that larger powers adhere to UNCLOS, therefore, is a key Indonesian security interest.

Since 2009, Indonesia has repeatedly requested that China clarify its claims—drawn freehand in 1947—by providing precise coordinates. It has also sought assurances that Chinese claims do not extend to the Natuna

---

[26] The Declaration on the Conduct of Parties in the South China Sea is available at http://www.asean.org/asean/external-relations/china/item/declaration-on-the-conduct-of-parties-in-the-south-china-sea.

[27] Donald E. Weatherbee, *Indonesia in ASEAN: Vision and Reality* (Singapore: Institute of Southeast Asian Studies, 2013), 70.

[28] Ann Marie Murphy, "Indonesia Responds to China's Rise," in *Middle Powers and the Rise of China*, ed. Bruce Gilley and Andrew O'Neill (Washington, D.C.: Georgetown University Press, 2014).

Island EEZ. According to UNCLOS, rights to waters can only be derived from rights to land or islands. Because China claims no islands near Natuna, it cannot justify claims to surrounding waters through UNCLOS. As a result, Indonesian officials maintain that their country is not a party to the South China Sea disputes, and Indonesia has continued its traditional mediatory efforts through ASEAN to forge a COC, an initiative that the United States supports.

Meanwhile, China has taken a number of aggressive actions against Indonesian interests in the Natuna Island waters. In 2010, for example, after an Indonesian patrol boat captured a Chinese vessel illegally fishing within its EEZ, China dispatched the Yuzheng 311, a maritime enforcement vessel equipped with machine guns, light cannons, and electronic sensors. The Yuzheng 311 allegedly pointed a machine gun at the Indonesian patrol boat, compelling it to release the Chinese vessel. Similarly, in March 2013, Indonesian officials boarded a Chinese vessel illegally fishing in the Natuna Island waters and transferred the Chinese crew to an Indonesian boat to be taken ashore for legal proceedings. Before reaching land, Chinese armed vessels confronted the Indonesian boat and demanded the release of the Chinese fishermen. Outgunned and concerned with the safety of their crew, the Indonesian officials complied.[29]

Indonesia had preferred to address such incidents through quiet diplomacy from a belief that China values Jakarta's regional leadership role and mediation efforts and would therefore accommodate its interest in the Natunas. Recently, however, China has taken a series of assertive unilateral actions that have reduced Indonesian hopes for Chinese reassurance. In November 2013, China imposed an air defense identification zone (ADIZ) over the East China Sea and stated its intention to impose one in the South China Sea after appropriate preparations have been made. Beijing declared a unilateral fishing ban effective January 1, 2014, around Hainan Island that encompasses almost 57% of the South China Sea. The Chinese aircraft carrier *Liaoning* was sent on a mission in the South China Sea, where it stormed Mischief Reef and declared indisputable sovereignty over James Shoal, only 50 miles off the coast of Malaysia.

Indonesia has responded both diplomatically and militarily to these actions. Foreign Minister Natalegawa has informed China that Indonesia will

---

[29] Scott Bentley, "Mapping the Nine-Dash Line: Recent Incidents Involving Indonesia in the South China Sea," Australian Strategic Policy Institute, Strategist, web log, October 29, 2013, http://www.aspistrategist.org.au/mapping-the-nine-dash-line-recent-incidents-involving-indonesia-in-the-south-china-sea.

not accept an ADIZ in the South China Sea.[30] In March 2014, Air Commodore Fahru Zaini stated that China had included parts of the Natuna island chain in its nine-dash line.[31] The public declaration that China does claim waters in Indonesia's EEZ has been accompanied by statements of Indonesia's intention to bolster its military capacity in the Natuna Islands. General Moeldoko, commander-in-chief of the Indonesian National Armed Forces (TNI), stated that Indonesia would beef up its military presence in the area, adding one army battalion and additional fighter jets while also enhancing its naval presence. These measures come as Jakarta has increased the defense budget by double digits in recent years.

China has also taken a series of actions that threaten the interests of other key ASEAN states as well as maritime security more broadly. In April 2012, Philippine naval forces found Chinese paramilitary ships 140 miles off the coast of Luzon in the Scarborough Shoal, protecting Chinese fishermen in the reef collecting live coral, endangered sharks, and other marine life in violation of international conventions on endangered species. As the two sides faced off, fears grew that the conflict might escalate. To avoid that outcome, the United States brokered a deal for both countries to withdraw from the shoal, but in the end only the Philippines withdrew.[32] In the period since, China has reinforced its presence around the shoal and laid an underground cable to keep Philippine fishermen and government authorities out. In early 2014, China attempted to interfere with attempts by the Philippines to resupply the *Sierra Madre*, a naval ship deliberately run aground in Second Thomas Shoal to demonstrate physical control, one of the criteria that UNCLOS uses to assess ownership. Manila has responded by requesting a ruling from the UNCLOS arbitral tribunal and seeking external support.

With respect to Vietnam, China has sought to deter foreign exploration for oil in disputed waters by threatening to punish companies that do so, even in waters well within Vietnam's two-hundred-mile EEZ. Chinese paramilitary boats have deliberately cut the sonar cables of Vietnamese survey ships. China has also imposed a unilateral fishing ban in disputed waters within Vietnam's EEZ. Imposed at the height of the fishing season, China claimed the ban's purpose was to protect the waters from overfishing, but Vietnamese officials note that the fish were only protected from Vietnamese fishermen, while Chinese fishermen exploited the catch. Most ominously, in May 2014 China

---

[30] Zakir Hussain, "Indonesia Tells China It Will Not Accept an Air Defence Zone Over South China Sea: Marty," *Straits Times*, February 18, 2014, http://www.straitstimes.com/breaking-news/se-asia/story/indonesia-will-not-accept-china-air-defence-zone-over-south-china-sea-ma.

[31] "Indonesia Flexes Muscle as S. China Sea Dispute Looms," *Jakarta Globe*, March 13, 2014, http://www.thejakartaglobe.com/news/indonesia-military-flexes-muscle-s-china-sea-dispute-looms.

[32] Ely Ratner, "Learning the Lessons of Scarborough Shoal," *National Interest*, November 21, 2013, http://nationalinterest.org/commentary/learning-the-lessons-scarborough-reef-9442.

placed an oil-drilling rig in disputed waters and sent a flotilla of paramilitary ships to defend it that sank a Vietnamese ship.[33] Vietnam and the Philippines have both requested ASEAN support, thereby putting Indonesia in the position of trying to reconcile its interests in ASEAN cohesion, regional stability, and cordial relations with external powers.

China's Threat to Indonesian and ASEAN Leadership in Asia's Regional Architecture.

China poses a threat to ASEAN centrality and hence Indonesia's leadership in regional organizations. Normally, institutions are created and run by powerful states. In the Asia-Pacific, long-standing tensions between larger countries such as China and Japan created an opening for ASEAN. To date, Indonesia and its ASEAN partners have rebuffed Chinese attempts to usurp ASEAN's formal agenda-setting role. ASEAN members rejected China's proposal to host the second EAS because they feared the country would use the organization as a vehicle for Chinese leadership. Instead, all EAS meetings continue to be hosted by the ASEAN chair. China has also long pushed for regional institution building to take place on a "pan-Asian" basis that would exclude the United States, Australia, and New Zealand, whereas Indonesia advocates institution building along pan-Pacific lines that included those countries. Likewise, China objected behind the scenes to the expansion of the EAS to include the United States and Russia, but under Indonesia's ASEAN chairmanship both became members in 2011.[34]

Unable to secure its leadership ambitions outright, China has resorted to using proxies in ASEAN to pursue its goals, a tactic that directly threatens Indonesia's leadership. At the July 2012 ASEAN meeting, for example, China's used its influence over Cambodia, that year's chair, to ensure that the final communiqué contained no reference to Scarborough Shoal. China's intervention caused ASEAN to fail to issue a chairman's statement for the first time in its 45-year history, an outcome that Natalegawa called "utterly irresponsible."[35] Recognizing the threat to ASEAN cohesion and its own leadership, Natalegawa embarked on a round of shuttle diplomacy to ASEAN capitals to secure agreement on six points related to the South China Sea that were issued in lieu of a chairman's statement.[36]

---

[33] Jane Perlez, "Vietnamese Vessel Sinks in Clash Near Oil Rig," *New York Times*, May 26, 2014.

[34] Ann Marie Murphy, "ASEAN Caught between the U.S. and China," in *China, the United States, and the Future of Southeast Asia*, ed. David Denoon (New York: New York University Press, forthcoming).

[35] Sebastian Strangio, "Cambodia as Divide and Rule Pawn," *Asia Times Online*, July 18, 2012, http://www.atimes.com/atimes/Southeast_Asia/NG18Ae03.html.

[36] Donald K. Emmerson, "Indonesia Saves ASEAN's Face," *Asia Times Online*, July 24, 2012, http://www.atimes.com/atimes/Southeast_Asia/NG24Ae01.html.

China's actions, therefore, have made it increasingly difficult for Indonesia to maintain both its leadership in ASEAN and the association's centrality in broader regional institutions. China's direct intervention in ASEAN affairs and the willingness of countries like Cambodia to privilege its interests with China above those of ASEAN make forging ASEAN unity difficult. Similarly, China's maritime assertiveness has triggered splits in ASEAN, with countries such as Vietnam and the Philippines calling for unified opposition while other members do not want to bear the costs of confronting China. ASEAN centrality in broader regional institutions is predicated on the association speaking in one voice, but forging a common position is becoming increasingly difficult. If Indonesia is unable to overcome such divisions, then its influence in Asia's regional architecture may decline.

Common U.S. and Indonesian Foreign Policy Interests

On the South China Sea issue, the United States and Indonesia share common positions. Both advocate peaceful resolution of the disputes according to international law, particularly UNCLOS. The United States has long maintained that it takes no position on the merits of sovereignty claims in the South China Sea. In a February 2014 statement, however, Assistant Secretary of State Daniel Russel left no doubt whose side Washington favors:

> We do take a strong position with regard to behavior in connection with any claims: we firmly oppose the use of intimidation, coercion or force to assert a territorial claim. Second, we do take a strong position that maritime claims must accord with customary international law. This means that all maritime claims must be derived from land features and otherwise comport with the international law of the sea. So while we are not siding with one claimant against another, we certainly believe that claims in the South China Sea that are not derived from land features are fundamentally flawed.[37]

By stating that South China Sea claims must be based on claims to land features, the United States has made abundantly clear that it rejects China's position. For Indonesia, this is welcome support for its interests in defending the Natunas and the integrity of UNCLOS. With respect to maritime security more broadly, however, the two countries have distinct interests. As the world's predominant naval power, the key U.S. interest in maritime Southeast Asia is freedom of navigation through the region's waters, including some Indonesian archipelagic waterways. In contrast, Indonesia has an interest in the sovereignty of those waters. In the 1980s, policy disagreements led

---

[37] Daniel R. Russel, "Maritime Disputes in East Asia," testimony before the House Committee on Foreign Affairs Subcommittee on Asia and the Pacific, February 5, 2014, http://www.state.gov/p/eap/rls/rm/2014/02/221293.htm.

Indonesia to close the Ombai and Wetar straits to U.S. submarines and such eventualities could occur again.[38]

Indonesian concern over China's maritime actions does not translate into automatic support for the United States as zero-sum balancing theory would predict. Indonesia values the offshore balancing role that the United States plays and helps facilitate this by permitting U.S. access to naval bases and ship repair facilities. It does not, however, necessarily share an interest in maintaining U.S. primacy in the broader Asia-Pacific, and some aspects of Washington's "pivot" to Asia have generated concern. The announcement that the United States would deploy up to 2,500 marines through Australia's Darwin base led Foreign Minister Natalegawa to state his fears that the marine deployment would "provoke a reaction and counter-reaction precisely to create that vicious circle of tensions and mistrust."[39] China responded as Natalegawa predicted, calling the U.S. pivot a "conspiracy to hold down or actually disrupt China's rise."[40]

Although Indonesia may be beefing up its military capacity in the Natuna Islands, Indonesian officials have long viewed diplomacy as the country's first line of defense, and TNI commander General Moeldoko has called for a "zero war" policy in the Asia-Pacific that would create "an Asian order based on the rejection of the threat or use of force."[41] Indonesia is acutely aware that only within an Asian order characterized by a rough balance of power can it maintain its autonomy and pursue its long-standing goal of a free foreign policy. Natalegawa's dynamic equilibrium and Moeldoko's zero-war policy are both efforts to pursue it.

Indonesia realizes, as Moeldoko has stated, that "major powers must find it in their interests to keep the peace, and only then can peace prevail."[42] By playing a prominent leadership role in Asia's regional architecture, Indonesia is attempting to convince China and the United States that their interests lie in forging a stable regional order. The dilemma for Indonesia is that as a middle power distinctly lacking in military resources, its ability to influence how China and the United States perceive and pursue their interests is limited. As a status quo power, Indonesia has demonstrated its willingness to play a role in sustaining a stable regional order. However, if China's use of force to

---

[38] Bronson Percival, *Indonesia and the United States: Shared Interests in Maritime Security* (Washington, D.C.: United States-Indonesia Society, 2005).

[39] Stephen McDonald and Helen Brown, "China, Indonesia Wary of U.S. Troops in Darwin," ABC News, November 17, 2011, http://www.abc.net.au/news/2011-11-17/china-indonesia-wary-of-us-troops-in-darwin/3675866.

[40] Kenneth Lieberthal, "The American Pivot to Asia," December 21, 2011, *Foreign Policy*, http://www.foreignpolicy.com/articles/2011/12/21/the_american_pivot_to_asia.

[41] Moeldoko, "China's Dismaying New Claims in the South China Sea," *Wall Street Journal*, April 24, 2014.

[42] Ibid.

change the status quo continues, Indonesia may be forced to recognize that some major powers place a higher value on pursuing narrow national interests than on ensuring that peace prevails.

How Indonesia would respond in such a scenario is unclear and would likely depend on how closely China's use of force impinged on Indonesia's national interests. When asked about his position on the South China Sea in the third presidential debate, Jokowi stated that Indonesia did not have a direct interest in the area nor did it have problems with China. Indonesia, according to Jokowi, should only intervene if it were able to provide a solution to help settle a dispute.[43] Jokowi's statement—like those of Natalegawa and Moeldoko—illustrates the extent to which faith in soft-power diplomacy has become ingrained in Indonesian strategic thinking. This can be difficult for U.S. officials to grasp, accustomed as they are to thinking in terms of hard-power balancing. A potential danger for the U.S.-Indonesian partnership is that Washington will make too strong a push for Indonesia to adopt a confrontational stance toward China before Indonesian officials have concluded independently that such a shift is in their national interests. As in the case of terrorism, such pressure will simply trigger a backlash and generate a belief that this is an American rather than an Indonesian issue. And given that adopting a confrontational approach runs headlong into both Indonesia's free and active doctrine and Yudhoyono's "thousand friends, no enemies" policy, U.S. officials should be under no illusions about the difficulty of convincing Indonesia to adopt such a stance.

While the United States shares Indonesia's goal of promoting regional stability, Washington has not always been an enthusiastic supporter of ASEAN-centric institutions. Contending that ASEAN's consensus decision-making privileges process over substance, the U.S. secretary of state skipped a number of ASEAN meetings during the Bush administration. Indonesia therefore welcomed the Obama administration's attention to Southeast Asia and its enhanced engagement of ASEAN-led regionalism. Hillary Clinton became the first secretary of state to visit the ASEAN Secretariat, attended all ASEAN meetings, and called ASEAN "a fulcrum of the region's emerging regional architecture."[44] Likewise, until the 2013 government shutdown forced him to cancel his trip to Asia, President Obama had attended all the ASEAN meetings, which had reassured Indonesia and signaled to Southeast Asia Washington's commitment to the region. Given

---

[43] Yohanes Sulaiman and Brad Nelson, "Commentary: Time for Jokowi to Think about Foreign Policy," *Wall Street Journal*, Southeast Asia Real Time, web log, August 1, 2014, http://blogs.wsj. com/searealtime/2014/08/01/commentary-time-for-jokowi-to-think-about-foreign-policy.

[44] Hillary Rodham Clinton, "America's Engagement in the Asia-Pacific" (remarks at Kahala Hotel, Honolulu, October 28, 2010), http://m.state.gov/md150141.htm.

its interests in the region's security and stability, the United States should continue its engagement of regional institutions.

Recommendations for Enhancing Indonesian Capabilities and Bilateral Cooperation

U.S.-Indonesia relations today are arguably the best they have ever been. The presidencies of Yudhoyono and Obama, two leaders with deep connections in the other country, opened a window of opportunity to strengthen the partnership. Officials from both sides should be applauded for using this opportunity to institutionalize the relationship through the Comprehensive Partnership and thereby help inoculate it against political changes in either country detrimental to the relationship. The annual joint commission meetings held at the secretary of state level provide opportunities to review bilateral and third-party cooperation and set the strategic direction for cooperative efforts under the Comprehensive Partnership.[45] The United States and Indonesia also consult prior to meetings of the region's multilateral institutions, and these consultations should be continued. Given these efforts to search for common ground and the significant expansion in the relationship over the past five years, it is critical that both countries work to deepen and broaden the relationship. The following discussion considers several options for doing so.

Security Cooperation

Security cooperation has expanded dramatically since the military-to-military relationship was fully restored in 2010, with the exception of some restrictions on Kopassus (the Indonesian Army's special forces). Nevertheless, there is significant scope to expand security ties—in part because they were circumscribed for so long, in part because Indonesia is in the midst of modernizing its military, and in part because of rising security challenges in the Asia-Pacific. Enhancing Indonesian military, intelligence, and surveillance capacity and fostering interoperability through joint exercises are important. Maritime threats have focused attention on the need to upgrade Indonesia's naval capacity, but recent events in Iraq and Syria have raised the salience of counterterrorism cooperation.

Indonesian officials have been united in their condemnation of the Islamic State of Iraq and Syria (ISIS), which has been banned in Indonesia,

---

[45] U.S. Department of State, "U.S.-Indonesia Fourth Joint Commission Meeting," Fact Sheet, February 17, 2014, http://www.state.gov/r/pa/prs/ps/2014/02/221714.htm.

and mainstream Muslim leaders have called ISIS an un-Islamic common enemy.[46] The reaction from radical groups, however, has been mixed.[47] Abu Bakar Bashir, the head of JI, has pledged allegiance to ISIS from jail, but his two sons, also radical leaders, have refused to do so.[48] Since the late 2000s, Indonesian terrorist groups have distanced themselves from the global jihadi struggle to focus on creating an Islamic state in Indonesia. As a result, the majority of terrorist attacks in recent years have targeted Indonesian government buildings and officials, particularly the police who lead the counterterrorism effort.

In 2014, however, police found ISIS materials during terrorist raids, and members of a radical group allegedly linked to ISIS beheaded a man they claimed gave intelligence to police and threatened to kill others who cooperate with authorities.[49] Indonesia has beefed up security due to concerns that Indonesian terrorist groups will heed calls from ISIS to destroy non-Islamic monuments and strike Western targets. At least 50 Indonesian extremists are known to be fighting in Syria and Iraq, raising fears that returning jihadists will spur a terrorist revival, just as Indonesian extremists returning from Afghanistan formed the core of JI decades ago. According to leading authority Sidney Jones, however, returning jihadis cannot build a movement without social support, and many of the local grievances that helped an earlier generation of terrorists mobilize supporters have been mitigated by Indonesia's political reforms.[50] Yet even if Jones's analysis is correct, the actions of only a few terrorists could cause widespread damage, ensuring that counterterrorism will be an area requiring sustained U.S.-Indonesian collaboration.

Enhancing Indonesia's military modernization. The Indonesian military has been called underfunded, undertrained, and underequipped.[51] Military spending was slashed during the 1998 financial crisis, and although it

---

[46] Aditya Surya and Yenny Herawati, "ISIS: Our Common Enemy," Khabar Southeast Asia, September 13, 2014, http://khabarsoutheastasia.com/en_GB/articles/apwi/articles/features/2014/09/13/feature-01.

[47] Aditya Surya, "Indonesian Extremists at Odds over ISIS," Khabar Southeast Asia, August 23, 2014, http://khabarsoutheastasia.com/en_GB/articles/apwi/articles/features/2014/08/23/feature-02.

[48] Kennial Caroline Laia and Dyah Ayu Pitaloka, "Jailed Terrorist Convict Ba'asyir Pledges Oath with ISIS on the Rise," *Jakarta Globe*, August 4, 2014, http://www.thejakartaglobe.com/news/jailed-terrorist-convict-baasyir-pledges-oath-isis-rise.

[49] "Islamic State–Linked Militants Claim Responsibility for Murder," Kyodo News, September 22, 2014, http://english.kyodonews.jp/news/2014/09/313080.html

[50] Institute for Policy Analysis of Conflict (IPAC), "Indonesians and the Syrian Conflict," IPAC Report, no. 6, January 30, 2014, http://www.understandingconflict.org/conflict/read/22/Indonesians-and-the-Syrian-Conflict.

[51] Sheldon W. Simon, "Southeast Asia Defense Needs: Change or Continuity?" in *Strategic Asia 2005–06: Military Modernization in an Era of Uncertainty*, ed. Ashley J. Tellis and Michael Wills (Seattle: National Bureau of Asian Research, 2005), 281.

rose from 23 trillion rupiah ($2.4 billion) in 2005 to 40.6 trillion rupiah ($4.2 billion) in 2010, it accounted for a paltry 0.78% of GDP.[52] This decrease in military spending, combined with suspension of military sales by the United States, severely degraded Indonesia's military capacity. According to one estimate, only half of the military's aircraft are operational at any time.[53] The increasing focus on maritime security, disaster relief, and transnational threats in Indonesia's 2008 defense white paper means that the air force, navy, and coast guard, which lost turf battles to the army during the Suharto era, are critical to enhancing Indonesia's military effectiveness. Ironically, although the United States' blanket embargo on the sale of military equipment to Indonesia was a response to abuses committed by the army, the sanctions had their greatest impact on the air force and navy, which were extremely dependent on U.S. military equipment.[54]

Indonesia increased its defense budget by 35% in 2012 and has embarked on a military modernization plan.[55] Jokowi has called for Indonesia's defense budget to grow to 1.5% of GDP, which would significantly increase the funds available for military modernization. For political reasons, however, the blueprint for the Minimum Essential Force calls for procurement spending to be divided almost evenly between the army, navy, and air force until 2024, despite their differing operational readiness and capability requirements as well as Indonesia's maritime geostrategic position.[56] Moreover, much of the defense budget goes toward personnel spending, which is estimated at $4.79 billion annually, whereas procurement and R&D are projected to average only $1.45 billion and $150 million annually during 2010–17.[57]

The United States has already taken numerous steps to assist in Indonesia's military modernization. Indonesia has ten F-16 fighter jets and had been considering purchasing six new F-16s. Instead, Congress approved a U.S. grant of 24 older F-16A/B Falcons. A former TNI commander stated that if outfitted with new avionics and weapons systems, the planes would have an operational life of 25 years, making it more efficient for Indonesia to accept a greater number of the older planes.[58] The United States has also agreed to sell

---

[52] Rizal Sukma, "Indonesia's Security Outlook, Defence Policy and Regional Cooperation," in *Asia Pacific Countries' Security Outlook and Its Implications for the Defense Sector* (Tokyo: National Institute of Defense Studies, 2010), 20.

[53] Ibid., 13.

[54] Charles "Ken" Comer, "Leahy in Indonesia: Damned if You Do (and Even if You Don't)," *Asian Affairs: An American Review* 37, no. 2 (2010): 53–70.

[55] Arientha Primanita, "Indonesia Pledges to Raise Defense Spending," *Jakarta Globe*, October 6, 2011.

[56] Evan A. Laksmana, "Beyond Defense Modernization," *Jakarta Post*, June 11, 2014.

[57] Ibid.

[58] "Indonesia Accepts U.S. Offer of 24 F-16 Fighter Jets," *Jakarta Globe*, February 15, 2011.

Indonesia eight new Apache AH-64 attack helicopters and Longbow radar systems in a deal worth approximately $500 million that will significantly enhance Indonesia's capacity to respond to natural disasters and maritime contingencies.[59] The United States has also supplied fast naval patrol boats and installed radar stations along the coastlines of the Sulawesi Sea to give Indonesia the ability to track ships passing through what some have called the "terrorist triangle."[60]

The two main obstacles to greater sales of U.S. military equipment to Indonesia are money and Indonesian wariness of becoming dependent on the United States as a result of the arms embargo. U.S. military equipment is expensive for Indonesia, and Washington's budget difficulties mean it is unlikely to provide significant assistance. Second, the lesson learned by Indonesian defense officials following the suspension of military ties was to diversify sources of military equipment and revitalize its strategic industries sector so that Indonesia will never find its military readiness hostage to a foreign power again. Indonesia currently has approximately 173 weapons systems supplied by 17 different countries, with Russia, South Korea, and Great Britain emerging as important arms suppliers.[61] Indonesia would like to strengthen its defense industrial base, which produces only 5% of Indonesian military goods. Parliament passed a Defense Industry Law in 2012 to move toward this goal, and Jokowi made the pursuit of defense independence a campaign plank.[62] Given Washington's stake in enhancing Indonesia's military capacity and the potential opportunities for U.S. firms to participate in the upgrading of its defense industry, helping Indonesia strengthen its technological base is in the interest of the United States. However, the 2012 Defense Industry Law's technological offset, countertrade, and joint-venture policies relating to foreign arms deals have been criticized for vague benchmarks and the failure to account for a lack of transparency in procurement procedures, which makes them susceptible to the corruption that has plagued Indonesian military purchases in the past.[63] Finding ways to overcome these challenges would strengthen Indonesian military capacity without generating the nationalist sensitivities that led Defense Minister Purnomo Yusgiantoro to stress that defense cooperation "must be equal and

---

[59] Cheryl Pellerin, "Hagel Announces U.S. Deal to Sell Helicopters to Indonesia," U.S. Department of Defense, August 13, 2013, http://www.defense.gov/news/newsarticle.aspx?id=120674.

[60] "U.S. Envoy Dedicates Maritime Radar Equipment for Indonesia," *Antara*, July 1, 2010, http://www.antaranews.com/en/news/1277984307/us-envoy-dedicates-maritime-radar-equipment-for-indonesia.

[61] Leonard C. Sebastian and Iisgindarsah, "Assessing 12-Year Military Reform in Indonesia: Major Strategic Gaps for the Next Stage of Reform," S. Rajaratnam School of International Studies (RSIS), RSIS Working Paper, no. 227, April 6, 2011, 22.

[62] Laksmana, "Beyond Defense Modernization."

[63] Ibid.

balanced, without certain requirements for a party. It is important because we are a sovereign country."[64]

Joint military exercises and cooperative efforts. U.S. joint exercises with Indonesia have expanded dramatically since 2005, and today the two countries conduct over two hundred joint exercises annually. Indonesia now participates in the U.S.-led Cobra Gold exercises, the largest multilateral exercises in Asia. The largest bilateral naval exercises between the United States and Indonesia are the annual Cooperation Afloat Readiness and Training (CARAT) exercises, which focus on maritime security, disaster relief, and counterterrorism. In 2013, approximately 1,200 U.S. navy and marine personnel participated in the exercises alongside 800 Indonesians. These exercises provide opportunities for training Indonesian soldiers and developing the interoperability of weapons systems. The numerous small, humanitarian, and medical visits provide the United States with an opportunity to overcome Indonesians' suspicions of U.S. motives. Bilateral military relations continue to be negatively affected by the "lost generation" of now high-ranking Indonesian military officers who lacked access to U.S. training when military ties were cut. Expanding opportunities for younger officers and finding ways to engage more senior ones should be a U.S. priority.

Strengthening Asia's Multilateral Institutions

The United States' decision to join the EAS during Indonesia's ASEAN chairmanship rather than support another vehicle for maintaining the regional architecture was consistent with Indonesia's interests and enhanced its status.[65] In addition, high-level U.S. participation in the ASEAN Defence Ministers' Meeting-Plus gives ASEAN's newest spin-off clout and provides opportunities for consultations. Such opportunities were also provided by Defense Secretary Chuck Hagel's invitation to his ASEAN counterparts to discuss regional security issues with him in Hawaii.[66] The United States and Indonesia now consult widely prior to key meetings to identify issues of common interest, and these newfound habits of consultation should continue and expand.

As discussed above, however, in 2013 President Obama missed the ASEAN summit and EAS in Brunei, as well as the APEC Summit in Indonesia, because of the government shutdown in Washington. Coming on top of canceled trips to Indonesia in 2010, Obama's absence raised questions

---

[64] Erwida Maulia, "RI Vows to Remain Neutral Amid Global Power Shift," *Jakarta Post*, March 18, 2010.

[65] Australia and Japan have both proposed the creation of new institutions to manage regional order.

[66] Carl Thayer, "U.S.-ASEAN Defense Ministers Meet in Hawaii," *Diplomat*, April 11, 2014, http://thediplomat.com/2014/04/us-asean-defense-ministers-meet-in-hawaii.

about the sustainability of the U.S. commitment to Southeast Asia. As a result, regional countries are assessing their options vis-à-vis the United States and China, and U.S. credibility is on the line. Attending ASEAN meetings matters in Southeast Asia, particularly to Indonesia given the time and resources Jakarta invests in the organization. Yet in some quarters in the United States, participation in ASEAN-based organizations is criticized as merely symbolic rather than substantive, since deliverables are not always clearly articulated. Despite such criticism, the United States should continue to participate actively in regional organizations like ASEAN because it enhances U.S. credibility, provides opportunities for consultations on the sidelines, and prevents Chinese officials from emerging as the key players at meetings, as happened in 2013.

U.S. leaders must recognize, however, that Indonesia's credibility as an honest broker means that in order to demonstrate its objectivity Indonesia may find it necessary at times to take positions that Washington does not like. When this occurs, leaders in Washington would do well to remember that it is precisely Indonesia's reputation for independent action that makes the country such a valuable regional player. Given the interests Washington and Jakarta share in a peaceful, stable, and rule-based order, Indonesia—acting in its own national interests—is unlikely to deviate widely from U.S. interests.

Economics, Trade, and Investment

Managing tensions over FDI, particularly in the resource sector, can be extremely difficult because both Washington and Jakarta are under pressure from domestic constituencies who perceive issues through radically different worldviews and often have divergent interests. The challenge for U.S. policymakers is to find common ground and frame issues so that Indonesian officials can portray a solution domestically as one that accords with Indonesian interests, thereby dampening allegations that they are selling out Indonesian economic interests to Americans. For example, the comprehensive ban on mineral ore has negatively affected the profits of U.S. companies and cost Indonesia jobs and export earnings. Yet this ban is unlikely to achieve Indonesia's goal of building up its domestic processing industries because much of the ore is already highly processed, making smelters unprofitable to U.S. companies.[67] Finding creative solutions that reconcile Indonesia's desire to move up the production curve and U.S. interests in profitability will serve the long-term goals of both parties.

---

[67] Confidential interview with an American executive of a major U.S. mining company with significant investments in Indonesia, conducted in New York on April 27, 2014.

Enhancing Legislative Exchanges

The Indonesian parliament and U.S. Congress both play increasingly large roles in the bilateral relationship, but the level of understanding of the other side is very low in both legislatures. Given that there is no "natural" American constituency in Indonesia or Indonesian constituency in the United States to buttress ties, this lack of expertise is problematic because it allows interest groups or nationalist politicians to hijack policymaking. Encouraging congressional delegations and parliamentary exchanges is one way to enhance mutual understanding of common interests. Providing support to strengthen the capacity of Indonesia's small, parliamentary research unit, which lacks access to online databases, could enhance the quality of parliamentary debate.

Implications for Indonesian Domestic Politics and Foreign Policy

These recommendations will not generate domestic opposition in Indonesia if Washington continues to engage Jakarta respectfully. Tone matters in the United States' dealings with Indonesia. As Washington learned with respect to counterterrorism, loud unilateral demands will trigger a backlash in Indonesia's open democratic system, even when the two sides share common interests. The challenge for the United States is to ensure that efforts to advance its interests do not inadvertently weaken those Indonesian leaders most amenable to cooperation. Strong Indonesian suspicions of external interference in domestic affairs means that statements such as the one made by Ambassador Robert Blake that Indonesia should probe allegations that Prabowo Subianto was involved in human rights abuses can backfire, even though he maintained that the United States does "not take a position on Indonesia's presidential candidates."[68]

The bilateral relationship will be influenced by Indonesia's domestic trajectory. The United States has embraced the vision of Indonesia that Yudhoyono projected: an Indonesia that is consolidating democracy, promoting socio-religious harmony, pursuing mostly market-driven economic policies, and following an internationalist foreign policy. A democratic retreat, a major outbreak of social conflict, a rise in economic nationalism, or the adoption of a more nativist foreign policy would complicate relations.

Forging a strong partnership requires both sides to overcome legacies of the past. At the height of the security relationship under Suharto, the United

---

[68] Richard C. Paddock, "U.S. Envoy Calls for Probe of Indonesian Candidate Subianto's Record," *Wall Street Journal*, June 22, 2014, http://online.wsj.com/articles/u-s-envoy-calls-for-probe-of-indonesian-candidates-human-rights-record-1403433632.

States and Indonesia had a patron-client relationship. Those days are gone forever, but overcoming the attitudes associated with them remains a potential obstacle to enhancing the relationship. What Indonesia really wants from the United States, according to one top Indonesian official, is to be treated as an equal partner.[69] From the Indonesian perspective, being the target of U.S. pressure on issues ranging from human rights to counterterrorism, economic reform, and military accountability has bred resentment. One astute Indonesian analyst has remarked that Indonesians "have always been ambivalent toward the United States…. [I]n the eyes of our elite and public, the United States is a unilateralist power."[70] On the U.S. side, Americans often find dealing with Indonesia difficult given the country's ardent nationalism.[71] The future of the relationship will be dictated in part by the ability of both sides to move beyond these attitudes. As Yudhoyono argued, the U.S.-Indonesia relationship is "too important to be driven by sentiments. We are not in the business of entertaining emotions and stereotypes. We are in the business of promoting national interests. And those national interests dictate us to work closely with one another."[72]

China's attempts to revise the status quo in the Asia-Pacific have highlighted the common interests of status quo states like the United States and Indonesia and underscored the importance of cooperation between them. At the same time, domestic political factors may be making cooperation more difficult. With strategic factors and domestic politics pushing the U.S.-Indonesian relationship in opposite directions, strengthening the partnership may be difficult.

---

[69] "Indonesia Seeks 'Balance' from Obama Visit," Agence France-Presse, February 1, 2010.

[70] Jusuf Wanandi, "Obama and Indonesia-U.S. Relations," *Jakarta Post*, January 22, 2009.

[71] Josh Rogin, "Indonesia Trip Complicates State Department Asia Agenda," *Foreign Policy*, March 17, 2010.

[72] Susilo Bambang Yudhoyono, "Indonesia and America: A Twenty-First Century Partnership" (speech at the USINDO luncheon, Washington, D.C., November 14, 2008), http://www.presidenri.go.id/index.php/eng/pidato/2008/11/15/1032.html.

EXECUTIVE SUMMARY

This chapter assesses Singapore's international strategy; examines the country's relationship with the U.S., China, and other regional states; and makes recommendations for the U.S. and Singapore to deepen their cooperation in the 21st century.

MAIN ARGUMENT:

Although Singapore and the U.S. have never been formal treaty allies, they have developed a strong partnership, one that stretches the definition of the term. Singapore seeks to maintain this relationship with the U.S. because it assesses that Washington will continue to provide global leadership as the country resiliently bounces back from the Great Recession. But Singapore still resists an alliance—both as a matter of principle and because its economic and security requirements for positive relations with both the U.S. and China lead it to urge the two powers to accommodate one another. The history of U.S.-Singapore relations demonstrates that U.S. credibility in Asia grows not only as the U.S. establishes defense agreements but also as it develops economic ties that advance shared prosperity, facilitates travel across the Pacific, enforces norms and practices developed in response to global challenges, drives innovation, and develops with its partners a common vision for the future.

POLICY IMPLICATIONS:

- The U.S. can improve defense cooperation by giving special recognition and benefits to countries like Singapore that do not pursue alliances but meet other criteria of deep partnership with the United States.

- The U.S. should work to expand free trade by continuing close cooperation with Singapore on the Trans-Pacific Partnership.

- The U.S. can support Singapore's growing diplomatic footprint by encouraging its leadership in enhancing Asian roles in international organizations.

The Singapore-U.S. Strategic Partnership: The Global City and the Global Superpower

Matthew Shannon Stumpf

In October 1967, then prime minister Lee Kuan Yew made his first official visit to the United States. "Not within living memory has a visiting head of government made so bluntly evident the purpose of his mission to Washington as Singapore's Prime Minister," observed one columnist. "From President to [Meet the] Press, Mr. Lee let Washington know he had come to find out whether the United States has the will to stick it out in Vietnam. He left the impression on departure that he has considerable doubts."[1]

For Singapore, positive relations with the United States were then a matter of "survival," as Lee put it to Vice President Hubert Humphrey.[2] Fears of communist expansion were rising in Southeast Asia, but U.S. credibility as a partner was suspect and Lee judged U.S.-Singapore relations to be "superficial."[3]

Today, relations are anything but superficial. The United States and Singapore have achieved a "comprehensive relationship" that has "grown in deep cooperation," according to current prime minister Lee Hsien Loong.[4]

Matthew Shannon Stumpf is Director of the Washington, D.C., Office of the Asia Society Policy Institute. He can be reached at <mattstumpf77@gmail.com>.

[1] Chalmers M. Roberts, "Washington Probe by Lee Kuan Yew," *Washington Post*, October 22, 1967.

[2] "Memorandum from Vice President Humphrey to President Johnson," *Foreign Relations of the United States 1964–1968, Volume XXVI, Indonesia; Malaysia-Singapore; Philippines,* document no. 287 (Washington, D.C., October 19, 1967).

[3] Lee Kuan Yew, *From Third World to First: The Singapore Story: 1965–2000* (Singapore: Marshall Cavendish editions, Straits Times Press, 2012), 511.

[4] "Remarks by President Obama and Prime Minister Lee of Singapore Before Bilateral Meeting," White House, April 2, 2013, http://www.whitehouse.gov/the-press-office/2013/04/02/remarks-president-obama-and-prime-minister-lee-singapore-bilateral-meeti.

Across defense, diplomacy, and trade, the two countries have achieved a series of agreements that fix Singapore as a critical contributor to the United States' Asia strategy. Although they have never become treaty allies, they have stretched the definition of "partnership." U.S. policymakers recognize and rely on Singapore's unique commitment as a non-ally. In the public statement following their 2013 Oval Office meeting, President Barack Obama thanked Prime Minister Lee for "extremely close military cooperation…and [the facilities] that allow us to maintain our effective Pacific presence," an economic partnership that helps create U.S. jobs, and "the advice and good counsel of Singapore" as the United States advances the rebalance of its foreign policy toward Asia.[5]

This growing partnership, at its foundation, relies on two premises. First, Singapore has invested in the U.S.-Singapore relationship because it assessed—and continues to assess—that the United States will be "preeminent in setting the rules of the game" for decades.[6] Prime Minister Lee has publicly resisted the declinist argument, often concluding that the United States is a "very resilient country and it has tremendous energy and creativity and drive, and it's going to bounce back" from recession and political gridlock.[7] Second, despite this strong commitment to and optimistic outlook on U.S. power, Singapore's relationship with Washington is not its only foreign policy imperative. Singapore's economic and security requirements for positive relations with both the United States and China lead it to urge the two powers to "accommodate each other."[8]

Singapore is not the only Asian nation with this basic position, but many others have not moved as far on the continuum of partnership with the United States as Singapore has. The U.S.-Singapore relationship, then, can serve as a particularly instructive model in the post–hub-and-spoke era, as the United States negotiates a world in which alliances are more difficult to form. In a world that better accommodates the metaphor of a network than a wheel, the long, hard work of deepening partnerships across all the many elements of a relationship is the only sustainable way for a country to maintain its place at the center of the web. Indeed, engagement across the defense, diplomatic, and trade dimensions differentiates the U.S.-Singapore

[5] "Remarks by President Obama and Prime Minister Lee of Singapore Before Bilateral Meeting."

[6] Graham Allison, Robert D. Blackwill, and Ali Wyne, *Lee Kuan Yew: The Grand Master's Insights on China, the United States, and the World* (Cambridge: MIT Press, 2012), 20.

[7] Susan B. Glasser, "China's Wrong about American Decline," *Politico*, June 30, 2014.

[8] Lee Hsien Loong (speech at gala dinner hosted by U.S. Chamber of Commerce and U.S.-ASEAN Business Council, April 2, 2013, Washington, D.C.), http://www.pmo.gov.sg/content/pmosite/mediacentre/speechesinterviews/primeminister/2013/April/speech_by_prime_ministerleehsienloongatgaladinnerhostedbyuschamb.html.

partnership from Singapore's significant but less robust partnerships with other Asia-Pacific powers.

The history of U.S.-Singapore relations is also instructive because, in the current era of budget austerity, the United States seeks cost-effective ways to advance its interests and fulfill its security commitments in Asia. Its relationship with Singapore shows that demonstrating U.S. commitment to Asia is likely to be more complex substantively and more demanding politically, but less expensive to the U.S. Treasury, than a defense-focused analysis might imply. Today, U.S. credibility in Asia grows as the United States establishes defense agreements for joint training, new deployments, and cost-sharing with partners like Singapore, but also as it develops economic ties that advance shared prosperity, facilitates easy travel between the United States and Asia, enforces norms and practices developed in response to global challenges like illicit trafficking, drives innovation, and develops with its partners shared values and common visions for the future. Focusing on these issues serves to reaffirm the U.S. commitment to the region.

This chapter assesses Singapore's relationship with the United States since Singaporean independence. The first section explores the formation of Singapore's worldview and the country's resulting international strategy. Second, the chapter studies how this strategy has been applied to Singapore's relations with the United States, China, other members of the Association of Southeast Asian Nations (ASEAN), and other regional powers. Third, it considers potential futures for the U.S.-Singapore relationship. Finally, the chapter concludes by making recommendations for U.S.-Singapore cooperation to maximize the opportunities and overcome the obstacles in the relationship in the 21st century.

Vulnerability Amid Prosperity: Singapore's Worldview

The framers of Singapore's foreign policy—in the first generation, Lee Kuan Yew, foreign minister S. Rajaratnam, and defense minister Goh Keng Swee—possessed an affinity for the realist worldview but also a tactical ease in using all the various tools at their disposal to advance Singapore's interests. As Lee Kuan Yew put it, "I do not work on a theory. Instead, I ask: what will make this work?"[9]

Indeed, these leaders found that a nuanced approach allowed Singapore, as a small state, to have disproportionate influence. Rajaratnam encapsulated this view when he told Asia Society in 1973 that "like the sun the great powers will, by their very existence, radiate gravitational power. But if

---

[9] Allison, Blackwill, and Wyne, *Lee Kuan Yew*, 135.

there are many suns then the smaller planets can, by judicious balancing of pulls and counter-pulls, enjoy a greater freedom of movement."[10] The distinguished Southeast Asia expert Michael Leifer identified the origins of Singapore's worldview as historically based in a sense of vulnerability, arguing that "despite its economic and diplomatic accomplishments as well as its defense capability, Singapore is a state whose foreign policy is rooted in a culture of siege and insecurity which dates from the traumatic experience of an unanticipated separation from Malaysia in August 1965." The city-state's small size and vulnerable location in relation to Malaysia and Indonesia further shaped this sense of insecurity.[11]

Singapore's commitment to its defense has remained a top priority as a result. Since the end of the Cold War, Singapore has consistently led defense spending in Southeast Asia, spending $3.8 billion in 1990, $7.5 billion in 2001, and almost $10 billion in 2014. This is the most in Asia on a per capita basis.[12] Moreover, the Singaporean defense commitment has deep roots. Military-to-military cooperation began with Israel and expanded to other countries—including the United States—continuing through Singapore's 1984–85 recession, the end of the Cold War, and the 1997 Asian financial crisis.[13]

But peril is not all Singapore saw abroad. Rajaratnam encapsulated the Singaporean aspiration for the benefits of international engagement in his "global city" speech of 1972, in which he described Singapore as an emerging hub in a global network:

> The Global Cities, unlike earlier cities, are linked intimately with one another.... Linked together, they form a chain of cities which today shape and direct, in varying degrees of importance, a worldwide system of economics. It is my contention that Singapore is becoming a component of that system—not a major component, but a growingly important one.[14]

This speech has also become an enduring element of Singapore's worldview. In 2006, Prime Minister Lee Hsien Loong noted the link between Singapore's

---

[10] S. Rajaratnam (speech to Asia Society, New York, 1973), quoted in S.R. Nathan (remarks at the Ministry of Foreign Affairs Diplomatic Academy's inaugural S. Rajaratnam Lecture, March 10, 2008, Singapore), http://www.mfa.gov.sg/content/mfa/overseasmission/manila/press_statements_speeches/speeches_by_sg_leader/2008/200803/press_200803.html.

[11] Michael Leifer, *Singapore's Foreign Policy: Coping with Vulnerability* (London: Routledge, 2001), 3.

[12] Amounts are in constant 2011 dollars. Stockholm International Peace Research Institute (SIPRI), SIPRI Military Expenditure Database, available at http://milexdata.sipri.org; and International Institute for Strategic Studies, *The Military Balance 2014* (London: Routledge, 2014), 275, 487–88.

[13] Lee, *From Third World to First*, 30–31; and Andrew T.H. Tan, "Singapore's Defence: Capabilities, Trends, and Implications," *Contemporary Southeast Asia* 21, no. 3 (1999): 451–74.

[14] Amitav Acharya, *Singapore's Foreign Policy: The Search for Regional Order* (Singapore: World Scientific, 2008), 129–30.

vision of global interconnectivity and international security. "The more we restrict the flow of trade and investments," he said, "the more likely that we will have rivalry and tensions, rather than shared interests in one another."[15]

As it perceived shared interests, Singapore embraced many aspects of what scholar John Ikenberry describes as the liberal internationalist order.[16] Its policies favor open markets, economic security and the social bargain, multilateral institutional cooperation, security binding, and U.S. hegemonic leadership, though its commitment excludes the elements of Western democratic solidarity and to some extent human rights and progressive change. To this day, Singapore and U.S. leaders hold different views on whether and how the United States and international organizations should be involved in countries' internal affairs.[17]

There is, then, a flexibility in Singaporean foreign-policy practice that defies neat categorization in international relations theory. Scholar Amitav Acharya concludes that "the conventional view of Singapore's foreign policy—that it practices an uncompromising approach to regional order in which national defense capabilities and balance of power considerations reign supreme—obscures a more complex picture in which regional interdependence and interactions have held a prominent place."[18] Indeed, Singapore judges that its interests are best served if the United States maintains a preeminent position in the world for decades, though in a manner that accepts and accommodates China's rise.[19] This is not a hedge, under which Singapore is making offsetting investments or undertaking offsetting engagements with all powers to achieve a positive outcome in any realistically imaginable future. Like U.S. allies Japan and South Korea, in the eventuality of a vast decrease in American influence, Singapore would likely find itself in a precarious position with a relatively strong, U.S.-equipped military and a legacy of deep ties to the United States.

Elements of balancing, where Singapore would ally with the United States to prevent its domination by a rising China, are visible in Singapore's strategy. Yet Singapore resists pursuing balancing so heavily that it would endanger its

---

[15] Lee Hsien Loong (speech at gala dinner hosted by U.S. Chamber of Commerce and U.S.-ASEAN Business Council, April 2, 2013, Washington, D.C.).

[16] G. John Ikenberry, *Liberal Leviathan: The Origins, Crisis, and Transformation of the American World Order* (Princeton: Princeton University Press, 2011), 169–93. He does not apply them in this book to Singapore.

[17] See Bates Gill, Michael Green, Kiyoto Tsuji, and William Watts, "Strategic Views on Asian Regionalism: Survey Results and Analysis," Center for Strategic and International Studies (CSIS), February 2009.

[18] Acharya, *Singapore's Foreign Policy*, 9.

[19] "The best possible outcome," according to Lee Kuan Yew, "is a new understanding that when [the United States and China] cannot cooperate, they will coexist and allow all countries in the Pacific to grow and thrive." Quoted in Allison, Blackwill, and Wyne, *Lee Kuan Yew*, 38.

cooperation with countries other than the United States. As the International Institute for Strategic Studies concluded, "while the depth of their defense links may give the impression that Singapore is a U.S. ally, the city-state has pointedly eschewed this, preferring the strategic autonomy deriving from a less formal—if still close—connection."[20] The limits of balancing are cast in stone for Singapore in its commitment to autonomy and refusal to formalize the relationship with the United States in an alliance.

Where theory fails, practice clarifies. A review of Singaporean practice since independence shows a clear strategy and allows conclusions about the country's future behavior.

A Partner with Purpose:
Singapore's Foreign Policy in Practice

In relations with its most important partners—the United States, China, its ASEAN neighbors, and other major Asian powers—Singapore has built different relationships for different purposes. The comprehensive partnership with the United States and the economic and other cooperation with China are not offsetting strategies covering different possible futures. Rather, they are seen in Singapore as constituting a unified, consistent strategy. Prime Minister Lee Hsien Loong stated to the Chinese Central Party School in 2012:

> Our whole region, including Singapore, will be affected by how China-U.S. relations develop. We hope China-U.S. relations flourish, because we are friends of both countries. We do not wish to see their relations deteriorate, or be forced to choose one or the other. Singapore's influence is modest, but we will do what we can to foster good relations, through our statements and actions.[21]

This section analyzes the development of Singapore's relations with the United States, China, and ASEAN, as well as with other important partners.

Relations with the United States

By hosting rotational deployments of U.S. ships, maintaining robust defense spending, expanding bilateral trade, partnering with U.S. universities, and providing public support for an enduring U.S. role in the region, Singapore

---

[20] "Singapore and the U.S.: Security Partners, Not Allies," International Institute for Strategic Studies, *Strategic Comments*, August 27, 2013.

[21] Lee Hsien Loong, "China and the World—Prospering and Progressing Together" (speech at Central Party School, September 6, 2012, Beijing), available from Prime Minister's Office (Singapore), http://www.pmo.gov.sg/content/pmosite/mediacentre/speechesninterviews/primeminister/2012/September/speech_by_prime_ministerleehsienloongatcentralpartyschoolenglish.html#.UidkDRYQ7lI.

has made notable contributions and done much to embed the United States in Asia. Since 1967, it has invested in a relationship with the United States that has grown steadily across the economic, defense, and diplomatic fronts. At moments when U.S. attention to Asia might wane, Singapore has sought consistently to remind the United States of its enduring interests in the region. Yet despite this robust relationship, Singapore is unwilling to pursue a formal alliance with the United States.

Before 1967, Singapore's strategy abroad was to secure its independence by aligning with other countries emerging from colonization. Initial signs were not positive for the United States, with Prime Minister Lee Kuan Yew hostile to any U.S. role in independent Singapore and offering equivocal statements on Vietnam.[22] But once independence was achieved and recognized, the Singaporean government shifted toward partnership with the United States. Through visits in 1966 and 1967 by the U.S. special adviser to the president on Southeast Asian social and economic development, Eugene Black, and the U.S. assistant secretary of state, William Bundy, the Lee government began to seek economic assistance (with a priority on U.S. purchases of local goods for U.S. military use in Vietnam) and to explore defense cooperation.[23] By March 1967, Lee was communicating publicly his government's support for U.S. efforts in Vietnam.

Over the following years, U.S.-Singapore economic engagement elevated further the explosion of growth in the city-state, as Singapore's economy transitioned quickly from its role as a port for trade in natural resources to its new position as an exporter of Singaporean manufacturing.[24] A critical element of this transition was a massive increase in exports to the United States. Between 1957 and 1959, the United States was the destination for less than 8% ($253 million) of Singaporean exports; between 1988 and 1990, this figure rose to almost 23% ($19.8 billion).[25]

Political cooperation deepened as well. Through inflection points in U.S. policy toward Asia, Lee regularly communicated with U.S. leaders, urging

---

[22] See Chan Heng Chee, "Singapore's Foreign Policy, 1965–1968," *Journal of Southeast Asian History* 10, no. 1 (1969): 183. Interesting accounts of this period are in Lee, *From Third World to First*, 500–505; and Leifer, *Singapore's Foreign Policy*, 101. Some argue that this negative view of the United States was inflamed by Lee's perception that he was not getting adequate support from Washington as he sought medical attention for his wife. This motivation is acknowledged in contemporary U.S. government accounts. See "Intelligence Note From the Director of the Bureau of Intelligence and Research (Hughes) to Secretary of State Rusk," *Foreign Relations of the United States 1964–1968, Volume XXVI, Indonesia; Malaysia-Singapore; Philippines*, document no. 279 (Washington, D.C., August 9, 1967).

[23] Chan, "Singapore's Foreign Policy, 1965–1968," 183.

[24] W.G. Huff, *The Economic Growth of Singapore: Trade and Development in the Twentieth Century* (Cambridge: Cambridge University Press, 1997), 301–7.

[25] Huff, *The Economic Growth of Singapore*, 282–3.

continued engagement. At the end of the Vietnam War, he visited Washington repeatedly, providing advice to the United States on how it might maintain its efforts in Southeast Asia amid questions about its commitment.[26] Ties built through the training of Singapore's next generation of elites in the United States helped build the mutual understanding that commitments are made of. At the time of writing, eleven of Singapore's eighteen cabinet members have studied or worked in the United States.

By the Reagan administration, the patterns of a strong relationship were established. As the Cold War waned, strategists questioned the U.S. role in Asia, but Singapore did not waver: "the American presence, in my view," said Lee Kuan Yew, "is essential for the continuation of international law and order in East Asia."[27] During the George H.W. Bush administration, Singapore used its geographic centrality to make real its hope for an enduring U.S. presence in Southeast Asia. Singapore offered transit to U.S. aircraft and naval vessels en route to the Middle East during the Gulf War and in 1990 provided the United States with access to Singaporean military facilities after the U.S. withdrawal from bases in the Philippines.[28]

Soon after, though, came a rare downturn in relations. In October 1993, American teenager Michael Fay was arrested for vandalism and in 1994 was sentenced to, among other penalties, six strokes of a rattan cane. U.S. public concern was met in Singapore by widespread incomprehension of the criticism.[29] This was the second contretemps in U.S.-Singapore relations related to U.S. involvement in Singaporean society. In 1988, diplomat E. Mason Hendrickson was expelled after Singapore charged that he was using his post to provide assistance to the political opposition, contacts the U.S. embassy saw as normal diplomatic activity.[30]

Once relations were back on track, after the 1997 Asian financial crisis required the two countries to put aside any lingering bad feelings in the interests of stemming economic disaster, the earlier momentum returned. In 1998, the United States and Singapore amended the 1990 agreement on Singaporean military facilities to allow the U.S. military to use the new Changi

---

[26] See "Memorandum of Conversation," *Foreign Relations of the United States, 1969–1976, Volume E–12, Documents on East and Southeast Asia, 1973–1976*, doc. 299 (Washington, D.C., May 9, 1975).

[27] Charles P. Wallace, "Singapore Proves a Welcome Friend for U.S. Military," *Los Angeles Times*, January 3, 1992.

[28] Lee, *From Third World to First*, 535–40.

[29] Joel Hodson, "A Case for American Studies: The Michael Fay Affair, Singapore-U.S. Relations, and American Studies in Singapore," *American Studies International* 41, no. 3 (2003): 4–31. According to Lee Kuan Yew, "Singapore suddenly became *persona non grata* because we were not following the American liberal prescription for how to become a democratic and developed country." See Lee, *From Third World to First*, 552.

[30] Nathaniel Sheppard Jr., "Expulsions Underline U.S.-Singapore Dispute," *Chicago Tribune*, May 11, 1988.

Naval Base as a logistics hub and port of call. This agreement occurred in the context of aggressive Chinese assertion of maritime territorial claims in the South China Sea. In Singapore, notes Leifer, "it is believed that China would not have had the temerity to seize Mischief Reef in the Spratly Islands had the USA not withdrawn previously from its military bases in the Philippines."[31] Once again, Singapore righted a balance it saw as faltering and helped ensure a constant U.S. role in Asia.

In the twilight of the Clinton administration, perhaps the most consequential project in U.S.-Singapore relations was launched. In negotiations toward a free trade agreement (FTA), the two countries sought a comprehensive agreement that achieved substantial openings. The U.S.-Singapore FTA was signed in May 2003 and entered into force in 2004. Its benefits have been extensive on both sides—for example, in its first eight years, the FTA has resulted in a 76% increase in U.S. exports to Singapore and an increase from $61 billion to $106 billion in cumulative U.S. FDI in Singapore.[32]

In the interim, the U.S. reaction to the events of September 11, 2001, created new momentum for cooperation, and Singapore was one of the first nations to participate in both the Proliferation Security Initiative (PSI) and Container Security Initiative in the post–September 11 era. The capstone of this period was the 2005 Strategic Framework Agreement for a Closer Cooperation Partnership in Defense and Security, which expanded cooperation on "counterterrorism, counterproliferation, joint military exercises and training, policy dialogues, and defense technology" and further facilitated the U.S. military's access to Singaporean bases. The agreement recognized Singapore as a "major security cooperation partner" of the United States, a term that summarizes the situation well but does not have a defined meaning in U.S. law or policy beyond the unique relationship with Singapore.[33]

By the Obama administration, the relationship "did not need to be reinvented, only nurtured."[34] Indeed, the breadth of the relationship was illustrated in 2012 by the first bilateral Strategic Partnership Dialogue. The dialogue covered "security, defense, education, trade and environment" and discussed "recent developments in Southeast Asia, Northeast Asia and regional institutions," as well as the Trans-Pacific Partnership (TPP),

---

[31] Leifer, *Singapore's Foreign Policy*, 160.

[32] Sameer Mohindru, "Singapore-U.S. Trade Deal Pays Off," *Wall Street Journal*, December 13, 2011.

[33] Ministry of Defence (Singapore), "Factsheet—The Strategic Framework Agreement," July 12, 2005, http://www.mindef.gov.sg/imindef/press_room/official_releases/nr/2005/jul/12jul05_nr/12jul05_fs.html#.UkBUlRYQ7lI.

[34] Jeffrey A. Bader, *Obama and China's Rise: An Insider's Account of America's Asia Strategy* (Washington, D.C.: Brookings Institution Press, 2012), 102.

development programs, Afghanistan, and Iraq.[35] In 2013 a visit by Prime Minister Lee Hsien Loong to Washington and a return visit to Singapore by Vice President Joe Biden allowed for further senior-level dialogue across this agenda, as did six other minister-level exchanges that year.[36] A second Strategic Dialogue in January 2014 continued the trend.[37]

During this period, analysts observed a concentrated effort by Singapore to deepen defense ties with the United States at a time of perceived aggression by China in asserting its maritime claims in the South China Sea and a contentious set of meetings around the November 2012 ASEAN Summit in Cambodia.[38] This is arguably a rebalancing on Singapore's part toward the United States, evidenced by the consequential arrival in April 2013 of the first rotational deployment of U.S. littoral combat ships to Singapore's Changi Naval Base. The second rotation is scheduled for late 2014, and a third for late 2015.[39]

Singapore and the United States also have consulted closely in their efforts to conclude the TPP agreement, which would reduce barriers to trade among twelve Asia-Pacific nations. The level of comfort established from the countries' experience in negotiating an FTA made the United States and Singapore experienced partners in the negotiations. Recently, Prime Minister Lee sought to build U.S. support for the TPP on his June 2014 visit to Washington. He concluded during his trip that "Singapore and many Asia-Pacific countries welcome [the rebalance to Asia], because America's presence in Asia has enabled regional countries to prosper and underpinned peace and stability throughout the region. But the rebalance is not just a matter of military presence. It must span a broad front—cultural exchanges, tourism links, people-to-people ties, and also economic cooperation."[40]

Lee's remarks underscore the importance for Singapore of the economic and cultural dimensions of the partnership. This broad map of engagement has been fruitful ground for both, and cooperation should only deepen over time. The chief limits to cooperation are external to the immediate bilateral

---

[35] "Joint Statement of the U.S.-Singapore Strategic Partners Dialogue," U.S. Department of State, January 18, 2012, http://www.state.gov/r/pa/prs/ps/2012/01/181488.htm.

[36] These included visits of the Singaporean foreign and defense ministers to the United States and the U.S. defense, commerce, and treasury secretaries, as well as the U.S. trade representative, to Singapore.

[37] "Joint Statement of 2nd United States–Singapore Strategic Partnership Dialogue," Ministry of Foreign Affairs (Singapore), January 27, 2014, http://www.mfa.gov.sg/content/mfa/media_centre/press_room/pr/2014/201401/press_20140127.html.

[38] "Singapore and the U.S.: Security Partners, Not Allies"; and Jane Perlez, "China Stalls Move to Quell Asia Disputes over Territory," New York Times, November 20, 2012.

[39] "Hagel, Singapore Minister Reaffirm Defense Relationship," American Forces Press Service, December 12, 2013.

[40] Lee Hsien Loong (speech at a reception hosted by the U.S. Chamber of Commerce and U.S.-ASEAN Business Council, Washington, D.C., June 24, 2014).

relationship—the United States' ability to renew its politics and economy at home, and its success in striking a workable balance with China.

The results of U.S.-Singapore partnership are clear and consequential for both. Relying on Singapore as a partner, though not a treaty ally, has strengthened, not diminished U.S. influence. Singapore has engaged with the United States across nearly all the threats to Asian security identified by Washington.[41] Singapore has been a venue for official and Track 2 U.S.–North Korea talks; participated robustly in the PSI; urged the peaceful resolution of maritime disputes (though with perhaps a more neutralist approach than Washington would like); engaged in the ASEAN Defence Ministers' Meeting-Plus Expert Working Groups on humanitarian assistance, military medicine, maritime security, peacekeeping, and counterterrorism; was the first Asian nation to join the Container Security Initiative; and has worked with the U.S. Department of Homeland Security to respond to cybersecurity challenges.

Singapore undertakes this work because it sees its interests as well aligned with those of the United States and impossible to achieve in isolation. First, close U.S.-Singapore cooperation helps Singapore, as a small city-state, to maintain a favorable place in the Asian strategic balance and global diplomatic and economic system, a place that offers it substantial security and economic benefits. Second, in order to further its goals as a global city, commercial center, and hub for learning, Singapore needs to engage deeply with the world's largest economy and one of its major engines of innovation and scholarship. Third, even though existential traditional security threats to the country are now limited, U.S. leadership can help Singapore manage its emerging nontraditional security threats, including climate change and water challenges.

At the same time, core U.S. interests in Asia and the rest of the world would be harder for Washington to achieve absent the deep partnership with Singapore. First, U.S.-Singapore engagement embeds the United States in Asia, providing a defense hub, a diplomatic partner, and, at times, a guide. During his time in the Obama administration as senior director for Asian affairs on the National Security Council, Jeffrey Bader, for example, found that "Washington relied heavily on Singapore for advice on issues like the East Asia Summit, trade, the South China Sea, and a host of other regional security and economic issues."[42] Second, Singapore offers the United States a security partner in a strategic location. The city-state is located at the

---

[41] See Chuck Hagel, "The U.S. Approach to Regional Security" (remarks at the 2013 Shangri-La Dialogue, Singapore, June 1, 2013), http://www.iiss.org/en/events/shangri%20la%20dialogue/archive/shangri-la-dialogue-2013-c890/first-plenary-session-ee9e/chuck-hagel-862d.

[42] Bader, *Obama and China's Rise*, 102.

center of Southeast Asia and on the Malacca Straits, one of the world's most important routes for trade in energy and many other goods. Third, the U.S.-Singapore FTA supports American prosperity by expanding trade at a level of commitment only achieved elsewhere in Asia by steadfast U.S. allies Australia and South Korea. Fourth, Singapore is a relatively aligned partner in Asian regional organizations and in establishing a more integrated ASEAN. Although the efficacy of ASEAN-centered regionalism is often questioned, it is also hard to imagine that U.S. engagement in Southeast Asia would be quite so deep and take place at as high a level in the absence of these organizations and partners like Singapore to help advance agendas of common interest.

Relations with China

Since independence, China has presented both a great opportunity and a challenge to Singapore, resulting in a policy that at least one scholar has termed "ambivalent."[43] Singapore sought to avoid the perception that China somehow dominated the country, which is three-quarters ethnic Chinese. Yet, at the same time, Singapore's growing economic might in the post-independence era intersected with cultural and historical ties to create opportunities for Singaporean influence in China, as well as favorable business interactions.

Relations were initially limited by Singapore's anti-Communist stance and China's refusal to recognize Singapore as an independent country because of the city-state's continued recognition of the Republic of China on Taiwan as China's legitimate government. It was not until 1976 that Lee Kuan Yew undertook his first unofficial visit to mainland China. Diplomatic relations would not begin for another fourteen years. On the 1976 trip Lee staked out an independent line: "If China concluded that an independent Singapore was not against China's interest, then many of the differences between our two countries would diminish," he said. "On the other hand, if it believed that an independent Singapore was against its interests or if China therefore wanted to help install a communist government, then disagreements were bound to increase."[44]

Thus began a long era of leadership diplomacy. Singapore's approach to its security remained unchanged, and the most profound impact of this visit was on the Chinese side, where "Singapore helped strengthen Deng's conviction of the need for fundamental reforms," according to Deng biographer Ezra

---

[43] See Seng Tan, "Faced with the Dragon: Perils and Prospects in Singapore's Ambivalent Relationship with China," *Chinese Journal of International Politics* 5, no. 3 (2012): 245–65.

[44] Lee, *From Third World to First*, 643.

Vogel.[45] The growing momentum of these reforms helped align Singapore and Chinese interests in the 1990s. Here were two trade-dependent economies, increasingly pragmatic in their approach to world affairs, finding some common cause as China undertook its "charm offensive" to improve its relations with Southeast Asian countries. In November 1990, the two countries began diplomatic relations after China had re-established relations with Indonesia earlier that same year. A dramatic expansion in trade followed, from $5 billion in 1993 to $80 billion in 2012.[46] A cornerstone of the budding economic relationship was Suzhou Industrial Park, created in 1994 in eastern China to model Singapore's approach to growth. The $30 billion investment did not reach expectations as a business venture but nonetheless provided a mechanism for the governments to work together, share technology, and build economic cooperation.[47]

Political relations were on the rise as well. Throughout the era of China's charm offensive, the intersection of Singapore's regional efforts and its negotiation of a measured but deeper relationship with China facilitated the latter's engagement in Asia. As See Seng Tan observes, at the regional level Singapore "relied on ASEAN-based regionalisms to strategically engage China."[48] The 2003 meeting of the Singapore-China Joint Council for Bilateral Cooperation, an organization that seeks an "upgraded version" of bilateral relations, launched annual senior-level dialogues between China and Singapore. These intensified over time, and by 2010 amounted to a robust set of exchanges, including visits that year by the prime minister, president, deputy prime minister, minister for defense, minister mentor, senior minister, and foreign minister.[49] These official ties were supplemented by growing cultural, tourist, and educational exchanges.

Yet there are limits to this engagement. As China's behavior in Southeast Asia grew more aggressive, some Singaporeans became skeptical of the charm offensive as a "facade."[50] By the beginning of this decade, through its assertion of Chinese interests in maritime boundary disputes, Beijing pursued what was considered in Southeast Asia to be a more confrontational approach. This culminated at the 2012 ASEAN Summit in Cambodia, when

[45] Vogel, *Deng Xiaoping and the Transformation of China,* 291.

[46] Department of Statistics (Singapore), "Trade with Major Trading Partners," available at http://www.singstat.gov.sg.

[47] Martin Richardson, "Singapore Industrial Park Flounders: A Deal Sours in China," *New York Times,* October 1, 1999.

[48] Tan, "Faced with the Dragon," 256.

[49] John Wong and Lye Liang Fook, "20 Years of China-Singapore Diplomatic Relations: An Assessment," *Global Review,* September 2011, 72–83.

[50] Joshua Kurlantzick, *Charm Offensive: How China's Soft Power Is Transforming the World* (New Haven: Yale University Press, 2008), 142.

China implicitly threatened to split ASEAN if Southeast Asian states sought a strong unified front on the resolution of the South China Sea disputes.[51] Singapore has sought neutrality in these disputes, but it was also in this period of greater Chinese assertiveness that Singapore expanded its relationship with the United States.

In this context, recent Singapore-China cooperation focuses primarily on the trade relationship. At the October 2013 meeting of the Joint Council for Bilateral Cooperation, the two countries came to seven agreements, all economic—four types of deeper renminbi-denominated cooperation and three regulatory improvements (for example, enhanced cooperation in banking rules).[52] In 2013, China also passed Malaysia to become Singapore's biggest trading partner.[53] In addition, Singapore is now the largest trade center for the renminbi outside China and Hong Kong.

Meanwhile, political cooperation has continued but with limits. Foreign Minister K. Shanmugam reported during his June 2014 trip to Beijing that "bilaterally, in economical terms, political terms and people-to-people terms, [the relationship] is very positive, and we believe that a lot more can be done."[54] If more can be done, the areas of current focus are circumscribed. In a 2013 speech to China's Central Party School, Prime Minister Lee Hsien Loong mentioned high-tech innovation, international use of the renminbi, food security, the balancing of economic growth and social development through "social management," and management of social media as potential areas for improved cooperation.[55]

In sum, Sino-Singaporean relations demonstrate a strong and deepening economic partnership, but their political and security relationship is qualitatively different from Singapore's cooperation with the United States. Singapore is pursuing different partnerships for different purposes.

Relations with ASEAN

Singapore, a wealthy city-state among much larger neighbors of varying prosperity, is often seen as a case apart in Southeast Asia. Yet the country has

---

[51] Senior U.S. expert and former official, National Bureau of Asian Research (NBR) Roundtable, September 2013.

[52] Ministry of Foreign Affairs (People's Republic of China), "Wang Yi Holds Talks with Foreign Minister K. Shanmugam of Singapore," Press Release, June 12, 2014, http://www.fmprc.gov.cn/mfa_eng/zxxx_662805/t1166103.shtml; and Monetary Authority of Singapore, "New Initiatives to Strengthen China-Singapore Financial Cooperation," Press Release, October 22, 2013, http://www.mas.gov.sg/news-and-publications/media-releases/2013/new-initiatives-to-strengthen-china-singapore-financial-cooperation.aspx.

[53] "China No. 1 Trade Partner of Singapore in 2013," Xinhua, February 20, 2014.

[54] "China, Singapore Vow to Further Deepen Cooperation," Xinhua, June 12, 2014.

[55] Lee, "China and the World."

played a leadership role in promoting ASEAN and in building ties between ASEAN and the United States.

Fearing the gravity of its larger neighbors, Singapore initially focused on defending itself. Having split from Malaysia and responding to the vast size but fragility of Indonesia, Singapore was born into challenging relationships with its immediate neighbors. Singapore had been expelled from Malaysia in 1965 amid political, ethnic, and economic policy differences. The resulting mistrust persisted as the issues around implementation of separation— defense, trade, currency, and other issues—all provided fuel for disagreement. Difficult bilateral relations with Indonesia stemmed from Singapore's hanging of two Indonesian marines in 1968 for the bombing of a Singaporean building in 1965. Relations only improved slowly from this nadir, and Lee Kuan Yew did not visit Jakarta until 1973.[56] Economic and political cooperation began to develop from there.

At the end of the Cold War, the end of the conflict between the Soviet bloc and the U.S.-centered set of alliances led leaders to seek new mechanisms to respond to the new era's challenges. Growing global appreciation of the prospects for regional cooperation encouraged the development of ASEAN forums as regional mechanisms for Asia. Economic growth also built wider interest in cooperation; in 1998, for example, Malaysia was Singapore's second-largest trading partner and Singapore was Malaysia's third-largest.[57] Through the 1990s and 2000s, it was the common agenda of Singapore, Malaysia, and Indonesia to gradually create new patterns of integration, both in ASEAN and bilaterally. A significant improvement in tone between Singapore and Indonesia in recent years has further advanced cooperation.[58]

Many of the most important initiatives for real regional integration show at least some Singaporean fingerprints: ASEAN diplomacy on Cambodia in 1979, in which Singapore presented an ASEAN-drafted UN Security Council Resolution (vetoed by the Soviet Union) to deplore Vietnam's invasion;[59] the 1993 launch of discussions on an ASEAN Free Trade Area originally proposed by Lee Kuan Yew in the 1970s; and the drive (with Thailand) to create the security-focused ASEAN Regional Forum.[60] As Acharya notes, Singapore "proposed the idea of an ASEAN economic community that will create a nearly borderless regional economy and pushed for an ASEAN charter that would make ASEAN's hitherto informal regionalism considerably

---

[56] Leifer, *Singapore's Foreign Policy,* 76.

[57] Ibid., 140.

[58] Acharya, *Singapore's Foreign Policy,* 109.

[59] Leifer, *Singapore's Foreign Policy,* 131.

[60] N. Ganesan, *Realism and Interdependence in Singapore's Foreign Policy* (London: Routledge, 2005).

more institutionalized and legalized,"[61] reforms that serve both Singaporean and U.S. interests. After September 11, 2001, a series of agreements among the Malacca Strait littoral states led to in-depth engagement to secure this strategic sea lane.[62] Singapore has even used ASEAN as a mechanism to encourage peaceful resolution of internal conflicts within Southeast Asia, as it did by criticizing the Myanmar junta in 2007.[63]

Today, Singapore's priority in ASEAN is to continue the economic liberalization process as ASEAN seeks to launch an economic community in 2015, while minimizing the dislocations from divergent ASEAN views on how to address the most divisive issue for the grouping: the competing maritime delimitation claims in the South China Sea. Through its ASEAN engagement, Singapore has sought to continue progress toward eliminating non-tariff barriers across ASEAN, while also seeking to prioritize the maintenance of one ASEAN voice over any particular solution in the South China Sea.[64]

In its bilateral relationships, Singapore fares relatively well with its neighbors. Ties to Indonesia have been mostly positive, though the Indonesian decision this year to name two navy vessels after military personnel involved in the 1965 bombing described above created concern in Singapore. Continued progress seems likely, however, with new Indonesian president Joko Widodo promising an improved Indonesian response to fires that generate haze over Singapore and welcoming additional Singaporean investment to contribute to his economic agenda.[65] The opening of Burma has created new commercial opportunities for Singapore, for example as reforms open the Burmese banking sector to ten international banks.[66]

Other Major Powers in Asia: India, Japan, and South Korea

Although Singapore's hard-nosed perceptions of power have led it to focus first on the United States, China, and its neighbors, it is also developing

---

[61] Amitav Acharya, "Southeast Asia in Asia's Regional Architecture," in *Asia's New Multilateralism: Cooperation, Competition, and the Search for Community,* ed. Michael J. Green and Bates Gill (New York: Columbia University Press, 2009), 178.

[62] Sam Bateman, Catherine Zara Raymond, and Joshua Ho, "Safety and Security in the Malacca and Singapore Straits: An Agenda for Action," Institute of Defence and Strategic Studies, Policy Paper, May 2006.

[63] Donald K. Emmerson, *Hard Choices: Security, Democracy, and Regionalism in Southeast Asia* (Stanford: Shorenstein Asia-Pacific Research Center, 2008), 26–35.

[64] Robin Chan, "PM Lee Calls for Redoubling of Efforts to Integrate Asean's Economies," *Straits Times,* May 11, 2014.

[65] Zuraidah Ibrahim and Zakir Hussain, "Jokowi Vows to Get Tough with Culprits behind Haze," *Jakarta Post,* August 22, 2014.

[66] Robin Chan, "Singapore Banks Have 'Good Propositions' for Myanmar: Lee Hsien Loong," *Straits Times,* May 12, 2014.

partnerships with other major Asian countries. These partnerships vary in content and receive differing levels of attention based on Singapore's perceptions of the potential gains from each.

Lee Kuan Yew's statement in 2011 that India should be "part of the Southeast Asia balance of forces" and "a counterweight [to China] in the Indian Ocean" reflects a long-held view in Singapore.[67] The country has sought from its inception to engage India as a core element of its international strategy. However, India rebuffed Singapore's request for military assistance at the time of independence,[68] and the relationship continued to lag as a result of India's commitment to nonalignment and Singapore's relatively close relationship with the United States. By 1975, trade was only $236 million.[69]

But over time, Indo-Singaporean relations—long sought by Singapore—found a place in India's strategy as well. As India began to "look east" for engagement in rapidly growing East Asia, the two countries found increasingly aligned interests. Through the 1990s, India expanded ties to ASEAN with Singapore's close cooperation. Bilaterally, Singapore and India reached $25 billion in trade by 2011, and from 2000 to 2010, Singapore contributed 9% of India's inward FDI.[70] A comprehensive economic cooperation agreement was signed in June 2005. Security cooperation has also deepened. In 2013, India renewed permission for Singapore to use Indian facilities for military training and exercises, the only country to have this privilege. Joint naval and army training is extensive; for example, in the March 2014 exercise Bold Kurukshetra, 690 Indian and Singaporean soldiers undertook integrated maneuvers.[71] With the new Narendra Modi government promising to revitalize the Indian economy, Singapore sees significant potential for improved relations.[72]

Japan too is seen as a partner of major importance to Singapore, particularly in the economic sphere. As Prime Minister Lee Hsien Loong told a conference in Tokyo in May 2014:

---

[67] Quoted in Harsh V. Pant, "Looking East: India's Growing Role in Asian Security," NBR, Commentary, September 12, 2013, 2.

[68] Sunanda K. Datta-Ray, *Looking East to Look West: Lee Kuan Yew's Mission India* (New Delhi: Penguin Books India, 2009), 1.

[69] Datta-Ray, *Looking East to Look West*, 255.

[70] Amitendu Palit, "India's 'Look East' Policy: Reflecting the Future," Institute of South Asian Studies (ISAS), National University of Singapore, ISAS Insights, no. 96, April 5, 2010, 2.

[71] "India, Singapore Sign Agreement on Training Facilities for Army," Zee News, June 4, 2013; Satinder K. Lambah and Tommy Koh, "A Bright Future Together," *Hindustan Times*, June 27, 2012; and Ministry of Defence (Singapore), "Singapore and Indian Armies Conduct Tenth Bilateral Armour Exercise," Press Release, March 28, 2014, http://www.mindef.gov.sg/imindef/press_room/official_releases/nr/2014/mar/28mar14_nr.html.

[72] Nirmala Ganapathy, "India, Singapore Seek New Areas of Cooperation," *Straits Times,* July 3, 2014.

> I am confident that in 20 years' time, Japan will remain a major power. It will still be one of the world's largest economies, with great strengths in science and technology. It will continue to contribute to regional peace and stability within the framework of the U.S.-Japan Security Alliance.[73]

In 2002, Singapore and Japan concluded Japan's first-ever FTA, which was amended in 2007.[74] By 2013, Japan was Singapore's sixth-largest trading partner, and additional integration was made possible through both countries' participation in TPP negotiations. Defense ties, however, are limited to their common participation in ASEAN working groups such as the Military Medicine Expert Working Group.

Despite burgeoning ties, Singapore's assumptions about Japan's future may limit the relationship. Lee Kuan Yew saw Japan's postwar and post-disaster recoveries as a model for resilience, but today some Singaporean strategists are more pessimistic, pointing to Japan's aging population as a significant drag on its economic potential—and, by extension, its potential as a partner.[75]

Singapore has also engaged South Korea, though Singaporean strategists have often viewed South Korea as a middle power that is too small to play a major role in shaping the Asian balance.[76] As such, the focus of the relationship is economic—5% of Singaporean trade is with South Korea.[77] The two countries' 2006 FTA was South Korea's second trade agreement and first in Asia, and it has led to higher levels of investment in both countries—in 2012, Koreans invested almost $6 billion in Singapore and Singaporeans invested over $9 billion in South Korean real estate, pharmaceuticals, and more.[78] A 2009 memorandum of understanding launched limited defense ties, though the bulk of the countries' engagement is through their common participation in U.S.-driven multilateral exercises such as Cobra Gold. The two governments are not close partners on a bilateral basis but tend to channel dialogue through various ASEAN processes, including ASEAN–South Korea dialogues.[79] This is a different approach for Singapore than with other major powers—for the others, Singapore is sure to maintain robust direct bilateral engagement.

---

[73] Lee Hsien Loong, "Scenarios for Asia in the Next 20 Years" (speech at the Nikkei Conference 2014, Tokyo, May 22, 2014), http://www.pmo.gov.sg/content/pmosite/mediacentre/speechesninterviews/primeminister/2014/May/speech-by-prime-minister-lee-hsien-loong-at-the-nikkei-conferenc.html.

[74] Kwan Weng Kin, "S'pore, Japan Agree to Review Economic Pact," *Straits Times*, June 7, 2012.

[75] Lee, "Scenarios for Asia in the Next 20 Years."

[76] Allison, Blackwill, and Wyne, *Lee Kuan Yew*, 64.

[77] International Enterprise Singapore, "Singapore's External Trade—July 2013," August 16, 2013.

[78] Lee U-Wen, "S'pore Remains Pro-Business, Welcomes Investments: PM," *Business Times*, December 12, 2013.

[79] Sarah Teo, Bhubhindar Singh, and See Seng Tan, "South Korea's Middle-Power Engagement Initiatives: Perspectives from Southeast Asia," S. Rajaratnam School of International Studies (RSIS), RSIS Working Paper, no. 265, November 2013.

Together, Singapore's relations with India, Japan, and South Korea demonstrate a rounded approach that seeks engagement across defense, diplomacy, and trade. Yet these relationships lack the depth of the relationship with the United States and do not receive the same attention from Singaporean leaders. In the end, Singapore has concluded that, as Lee Kuan Yew put it, "the size of China makes it impossible for the rest of Asia, including Japan and India, to match it in weight and capacity in 20 to 30 years. So we need America to strike a balance."[80]

Connect Singapore: A Network Solution to Vulnerability

The historical record reinforces the conclusion that Singaporean ties abroad are deepest with the United States. The critical difference between Singapore's relationship with the United States and its ties with other countries is that the U.S.-Singapore relationship has developed across a broader range of issues and with a sustained depth not seen elsewhere. Other countries, though, do affect core Singaporean interests, and Singapore has also fostered relations in these directions as well.

These tactics add up to a clear Singaporean practice—a strategy this chapter calls "connect Singapore." It has three tenets:

- Cooperation on defense, trade, and diplomacy as a small state seeking partnerships with the most influential actors in each sphere

- Convergent but not unequivocal support for the liberal internationalist order

- Commitment to partnership with the West, while reserving strategic flexibility in the event of a radical change in the international system

In each of the spheres of its international engagement, Singapore seeks to build a productive relationship with the most influential players in that sphere, connecting Singapore to the most advantageous relationships in each area. In its economic relationships, prosperity requires partnership with the world's leading economic powers—including China but also the European Union and the United States. Singapore's security requires defense partnership with the world's most powerful military, the United States. In its diplomacy, savvy politics require close partnership with the world's most powerful nation, a careful but positive relationship with a rising China, and ever stronger ties in Southeast Asia as Singapore's neighbors grow in influence.

---

[80] Allison, Blackwill, and Wyne, *Lee Kuan Yew*, 40.

While pursuing these varying partnerships, Singapore also places a high value on autonomy. Its brand of autonomy seeks strategic flexibility while accepting the structure and most of the practices of the liberal internationalist order. Singapore has built a strategic relationship with the United States that stops short of treaty commitments and so preserves Singapore's ability to change course. Most importantly, these activities are not seen as conflicting but complementary. There is no choice for Singapore between China and the West, as a rupture with either would be deeply challenging to Singapore's interests. Indeed, each of the three pillars of the connect Singapore strategy is equally important in managing the country's place in the world. As a central node in the Asian network, Singapore continually seeks to build more and deeper links to all the other influential nodes.

Given the extent of Singapore's transformation, one could expect more change than continuity in Singaporean foreign policy since 1965, but the reverse is true for three reasons. First, a well-aligned leadership, committed to a precisely articulated model for Singapore's role in the world, has remained in power throughout the period. Second, politics are most contested in Singapore around domestic social issues and the benefits and shortcomings of one-party government, while foreign policy issues are largely left aside, either regarded as matters of consensus or at least delegated to national leaders.[81] For example, in his 2013 National Day speech, Prime Minister Lee Hsien Loong described a strategic shift Singapore faces in reshaping its social safety net for a new era and, by extension, how this shift will alter the well-defined roles of the individual, community, and state in Singaporean life since independence. The international concerns he described were not the rise of China or the future of U.S.-Singaporean relations but competition from emerging economies and the uncertainties and inequalities driven by new technologies and globalization.[82] As a result, domestic politics seem to have little effect on Singapore's foreign policy, though growing political

---

[81] A review of the 2011 Singapore political party manifestos reveals debate on economic development strategies and quality of life in Singapore but shows little discussion on foreign relations or defense. The ruling People's Action Party referred to the need to navigate international economic competition only. Chapter 12 of the Workers Party manifesto covered defense and foreign affairs, but at a level of general principles, all of which accorded with the current government's strategy. The Singapore Democratic Party's manifesto is no longer posted by the party, but its current platform focuses on domestic political reform and Singapore's economic future. The National Solidarity Party had a defense plank in its platform—to emphasize defense against terrorism instead of conventional regional conflict, to expand the air force and navy, and to reduce national military service—but none of these was a criticism of the core Singaporean strategy. The Singapore People's Party called in its constitution for economic union with Malaysia and then the other ASEAN countries. The Reform Party and Singapore Democratic Alliance did not have foreign-policy planks.

[82] Lee Hsien Loong (remarks at the National Day Rally, Singapore, August 18, 2013), Prime Minister's Office (Singapore), August 21, 2013, http://www.pmo.gov.sg/content/pmosite/mediacentre/speechesninterviews/primeminister/2013/August/prime-minister-lee-hsien-loong-s-national-day-rally-2013--speech.html.

competition would seem to advantage those who deliver economic growth, implying a further need for Singapore to manage positive relations with both the United States and China.

Third, and most importantly, Singapore's leaders continue to advance the country's established international strategy simply because they assess that it works. Singapore's foreign policy has supported astounding growth and delivered enduring security. In a changing world, the continuity of the effort to connect Singapore has delivered. It is of course not abnormal for political cultures to persist despite the passing of their original contexts. For example, India's nonaligned foreign policy is a core national value, rooted in its independence movement; China engages in a historically informed drive to regain the influence it believes it lost in the late 19th and 20th centuries; and the United States maintains many of the aspects of its Cold War–derived national security politics despite a widely different set of threats and opportunities. In Singapore, the vision of the first-generation leaders of an insecure Singapore rising, despite its precarious situation, to become a prosperous global city still guides the country.

For these same reasons, we can expect the connect Singapore strategy to persist into the future. Singapore will seek to maintain its centrality in the Asia-Pacific economic and security system by fostering the most consequential partnerships it can find in each area of activity. This strategy allows Singapore to benefit from the international system, defend itself through a partnership with the world's leading military power, and generate new prosperity through its relationships with other Asian states as the region grows economically. Meanwhile, the country's commitment to autonomy allows it flexibility as the international environment changes.

Sustaining the Partnership:
The Limits of U.S.-Singapore Relations

If U.S. and Singaporean interests are aligned and cooperation is enduring, under what circumstances could Singapore shift its strategy? In particular, some international relations theorists predict growing tensions between the United States and a rising China, leading to skepticism that Singapore's strategy is sustainable.[83] Yet to ask what Singapore will do if it must choose is to pose the wrong question. At the core of Singapore's strategy is a commitment not to choose, as a break with either the United States or China would cost

---

[83] For a summary of the contending positions, see Aaron L. Friedberg, "The Future of U.S.-China Relations: Is Conflict Inevitable?" *International Security* 30, no. 2 (2005): 7–45.

it clearly. Based on that premise, there are five scenarios in which Singapore might conclude that its strategy will no longer be effective.

Scenario 1: China or the United States unilaterally subverts the Asian peace. Maintaining trade with China is a core interest and domestic political imperative, but Singapore also identifies with many aspects of the U.S.-led liberal internationalist world order and the country's defense relies on cooperation with Washington. As a result, Singapore considers Sino-U.S. cooperation to be a core interest and could reasonably rethink its relationship with either country if it perceived that one unnecessarily or precipitously provoked conflict.

Scenario 2: The U.S. economy stagnates. Singapore's strategy is premised on its calculation that the United States will maintain its global leadership role for decades to come. Singapore's demographic challenges also inform its view that a core U.S. strength is the United States' ability to attract and welcome immigrants who contribute energy and new ideas to the U.S. economy. Singapore could change its assessment—and perhaps its strategy—if the U.S. economic recovery is not fully realized or the United States chooses a more closed society.

Scenario 3: The U.S. pivot to Asia withers. The Obama administration has won praise in Asia for articulating a new foreign policy recognizing that U.S. peace and prosperity is most affected in the 21st century by events in the Asia-Pacific. Effective implementation of this strategy across all the dimensions of U.S. engagement will be critical to convincing Asian observers that the United States, already perceived as regularly shifting in its strategy and attention, will remain in Asia.[84] It is important not to overdraw this point: Asian governments understand that there will be crises outside East Asia, such as the conflicts in Syria and Ukraine, that will require U.S. attention. But the effects of sequestration on the U.S. federal budget and public skepticism domestically of the benefits to the United States of international engagement after a decade at war raise legitimate questions about the U.S. commitment to Asia.

Scenario 4: The United States is active in Singapore's domestic politics. The nadirs of U.S.-Singapore relations have centered on concerns about U.S. interference in domestic Singaporean affairs. The countries have tacitly agreed to take these issues off the table, and U.S.-Singapore cooperation continues without reference to the dominance of Singapore's government by one party, a practice the United States has at times criticized in other countries. Any dramatic change in this approach would likely have consequences.

---

[84] This finding is based on comments by an Asian diplomat at an NBR roundtable in September 2013.

Scenario 5: Generational shifts and growing prosperity change Singapore's priorities. Anecdotally, there seems to be some concern among the founding generation of Singaporeans that, with distance from the struggle of Singapore's formation, the younger generation is not as committed to maintaining the country's strength in a competitive world. Whether or not that is a fair assessment, it is clear that the primary concerns of Singaporeans are not the outside world or Singapore's vulnerability but their own quality of life; job security, healthcare, and housing rate as much higher concerns than international relations.[85] In this context, politics could dictate less attention to relations with the United States.

Each of these five scenarios is unlikely but possible. As stated above, these alternative futures underscore that the dangers to the U.S.-Singapore relationship mostly exist outside the relationship itself.

Five Recommendations for U.S.-Singapore Cooperation

In most imaginable futures, the United States and Singapore can expect to continue their highly successful partnership. To advance their common interests, the United States should advance five areas of further cooperation.

Widen the network. The opening of Myanmar and efforts to build greater connectivity within South Asia together create the opportunity for geographically uninterrupted and new political, trade, and infrastructure ties from India across all South, Southeast, and Northeast Asia. The inability of China and India to resolve border disputes bilaterally raises the potential for conflict among Asia's emerging powers and creates a further interest in embedding these two critical countries in processes of regional integration that bridge East and South Asia. In addition, the most challenging potential drivers of conflict—water scarcity, territorial disputes, maritime security challenges, terrorism, proliferation, climate change, migration, and human and other illicit trafficking—all cross the boundary between East Asia and South Asia and require a coordinated response. Singapore and the United States, each with unique ties across this boundary, can work together to lead the decades-long effort necessary to connect East Asia and South Asia. Specific cooperation could include helping build infrastructure across this geography; providing technical assistance to officials building new trade connections among India, Bangladesh, Myanmar, and other ASEAN nations; and facilitating the entry and deepening engagement of India in Asian multilateral institutions.

---

[85] Government of Singapore, "Our Singapore Conversation Survey," http://www.reach.gov.sg/Portals/0/Microsite/osc/OSC-Survey.pdf.

Expand free trade through the TPP. Singapore can act as a guide to the United States in managing relations with Asia during TPP negotiations. As of this writing, given the number of countries engaged in the process and the challenging nature of the most difficult issues (for example, compromises between the United States and Japan on the agricultural and auto sectors), the end game will be complicated. As free-trade negotiations tend to conclude with a flood of compromises on the most difficult issues, close cooperation with Singapore—which has experience in negotiating a wide range of FTAs—could help identify the optimal moment for the final compromises to be made. Moreover, as the adoption by signatory countries of the agreement requires challenging political work in each capital, Singapore can also draw from its experience in adeptly helping build U.S. political support for the bilateral FTA and might play a similarly important role if the U.S. Congress eventually considers a TPP agreement.

Enlarge Singapore's diplomatic footprint. Singaporean intellectual and former diplomat Kishore Mahbubani has written that the West has "little appetite for true leadership from Asia" in global institutions.[86] U.S. support for a greater role for Singaporeans in international organizations could demonstrate U.S. commitment to creating a role for Asia in these institutions that accords with the region's growing political and economic power. The United States could propose leading Singaporean diplomats for posts in UN organizations, for example.

Deepen U.S.-Singapore philanthropic engagement. Singapore seeks to be a hub for global learning and the idea economy, and it has sought to attract foreign philanthropies and NGOs to establish offices in Singapore. U.S.-Singapore relations can be deepened if Singapore serves as a platform for U.S. philanthropic and development activities in Asia. Yet, despite the doubling of Singaporean charitable giving over the past decade, there are significant barriers. For example, Singaporean charities must by law expend 80% of their funds in Singapore, limiting their cross-border impact. Even though this rule is suspended for disaster relief and has been reportedly relaxed for international initiatives, it still acts as an impediment. The vast majority of Singaporean philanthropy is directed at education, social development, and healthcare in Singapore.[87] These are certainly critical contributions to the improvement of social welfare. However, as Singaporeans give more each year, the bilateral relationship would also gain from an effort

---

[86] Kishore Mahbubani and Simon Chesterman, "Asia's Role in Global Governance," Lee Kuan Yew School of Public Policy, National University of Singapore, December 2009, 2, http://www.weforum.org/pdf/GRI/GRI-Singapore-Country-Hearing.pdf.

[87] Prapti Upadhyay Anand and Crystal Hayling, *Levers for Change—Philanthropy in Select South East Asian Countries* (Singapore: Lien Center for Social Innovation, 2014), 50–63.

by the two governments and their respective civil societies to collaborate on new projects where Singaporeans and Americans do good together across Asia and around the world.

Redefine defense cooperation. The United States should seek to define a new concept of partnership that is short of alliance. The appellation "major security cooperation partner" does not come with the benefits under U.S. law of the "major non-NATO ally" designation. In an era when new alliances may be rarer, the United States could use the Singapore model to give special recognition and defense cooperation benefits to countries that have engaged with the United States across a wide range of topics. This would include, for example, countries that have implemented an FTA with the United States, joined specified diplomatic partnerships with the United States (such as the PSI and Container Security Initiative), and engaged in defense cooperation of critical value to U.S. national security.

Conclusions

The history of U.S.-Singapore engagement encourages three broad conclusions. First, the U.S.-Singapore relationship succeeds because of well-aligned but not identical interests; a commitment to collaborate across the complex Asia-wide network of economic, political, cultural, and security relations; and decades of investment by both sides in building personal ties and minimizing differences. These ties help both countries play a stronger role in Asia across the broad dimensions of their interests, from trade to politics and security.

Second, the achievements of the U.S.-Singapore partnership can be instructive elsewhere. From antagonism at Singapore's independence to a relationship that some have termed a "quasi-alliance,"[88] this broad and gradually deepening partnership has paid great dividends for both countries and has been sustained despite some U.S. discomfort with Singapore's domestic political system.[89]

---

[88] For example, see William H. Overholt, *Asia, America, and the Transformation of Geopolitics* (New York: Cambridge University Press, 2008), 181–82.

[89] The U.S. State Department's Singapore country report on human rights practices for 2012 finds that "throughout the year legal restrictions on the activities of political opposition groups and parties benefitted the ruling PAP; caning is an allowable punishment for some crimes; restrictions existed on free speech and assembly; there was government intimidation that led to self-censorship by journalists; some limited restriction of freedom of religion; and some restrictions on labor rights." See U.S. Department of State, "Singapore 2013 Human Rights Report," http://www.state.gov/j/drl/rls/hrrpt/humanrightsreport/index.htm?year=2013&dlid=220229#wrapper.

China aspires in part to draw from the Singapore model in its domestic political development.[90] As the United States and China seek a "new type of great-power relationship," Beijing could draw from the model of U.S.-Singapore cooperation in four ways. First, though there are certainly fundamental differences between China's and Singapore's governments, the origins of the U.S.-Singapore partnership show that common purposes—even if limited at first—can be an adequate base from which to deepen cooperation and that a deep partnership does not require universally aligned values. Second, U.S. cooperation with Singapore underscores that prosperity arising from freer trade can help partnerships leap beyond trade issues, but only if international negotiations are supported by domestic efforts to communicate the gains and manage the politics of the proposed cooperation. To date, leaders in Beijing and Washington have been more eager to talk about the challenges in their relationship than to share news of the mutual benefits. Both certainly exist. Third, welcoming future leaders into the U.S. higher-education system creates new ties and builds lasting appreciation of American values and ways of life. Finally, like Singapore, many Asian governments require positive relations with both China and the United States. This means that few are likely to support either side in veering too far from accepted norms of responsible leadership that advance Asian peace and prosperity. As the rising power, China may be at greater risk in this area than the United States.

There are certainly limits to the comparison; Singapore cannot be a peer competitor to the United States as China can, and China's rise reverberates across the international system with an impact that Singapore could not have. Still, there was nothing inevitable about the partnership between the United States and Singapore; indeed, at the latter's independence, it seemed unlikely. The history of U.S.-Singapore relations should remind Washington that the "with us or against us" habits of Cold War alliances could lead to missed opportunities and that shared domestic political values are not the only basis for partnership. The same history should remind Beijing that no matter its views of U.S. policy, there are elements of the liberal internationalist order that it would do well to work with Washington to preserve.

Singapore's example is perhaps even more compelling in the case of U.S.-India relations, given that India, too, is committed to an independent foreign policy but desirous of positive ties with all. The U.S.-Singapore strategic partnership demonstrates in particular that deep relationships can be built on a platform of strategic flexibility if both countries commit to driving greater cooperation over decades to generate long-term results. The 2005 nuclear deal between the United States and India swept away long-

---

[90] David Shambaugh, *China's Communist Party: Atrophy and Adaptation* (Washington, D.C.: Woodrow Wilson Center Press, 2008), 92–95.

held barriers to cooperation and launched a new, more cooperative era in relations. Nearly a decade later, through ebbs and flows of bilateral comity, the two countries have created a new momentum with vast possibilities but no sea change. Still, there are opportunities for trade and defense cooperation, but these are best approached, as in the U.S.-Singapore case, with an eye to partnership and a commitment to invest in and measure progress over the long term.

This longer-term lens is critical because, though Chinese and Indian commitments to foreign-policy autonomy may be more deeply ingrained than Singapore's, recent decades have seen increasing identification of both powers with the U.S.-led order. For example, China's increasing attention to global nonproliferation norms through the 1980s, 1990s, and 2000s and its membership in the World Trade Organization show that China sees benefits to alignment with the liberal internationalist order, though there are certainly limits.[91] In New Delhi, while political rhetoric focuses on India's commitment to autonomy, successive governments have sought greater influence in an international system that is seen as substantially benefiting India. As strategist C. Raja Mohan argues, a "rising India—with its robust democracy, thriving entrepreneurial capitalism, and expanding global interests—is bound to acquire a new identity as a champion of liberal international order."[92]

Third, as Singapore's leaders recognize, in the post–Cold War and post–hub-and-spoke world of U.S. "power, but not authority,"[93] U.S. success depends on the United States' economic vitality and attractiveness as a society. Thus, a strategy that builds as many and as varied connections to Asia as possible, using all the tools of American international engagement, is the strategy most likely to advantage the United States over time. A broader network conception of U.S. engagement in Asia that prioritizes the depth and breadth of a multiplicity of relationships rather than attending to a small number of unbreakable spokes implies that Washington should not define the solution too narrowly. In assessing U.S. intentions, Asia will look as much at the TPP as at the Seventh Fleet. Managing this reality is no easy task. U.S. politics and U.S. government bureaucratics incentivize defense-focused solutions to challenges abroad, given the strong implementation and strategy-development capacity of, political support for, and resource

---

[91] Interesting discussion of the alignment and limits can be found in David M. Lampton, ed., *The Making of Chinese Foreign and Security Policy in the Era of Reform, 1978–2000* (Stanford: Stanford University Press, 2001).

[92] C. Raja Mohan, "India's Strategic Future," *Foreign Policy,* November 4, 2010, http://www.foreignpolicy.com/articles/2010/11/04/indias_strategic_future.

[93] Ikenberry, *Liberal Leviathan,* 277.

allocations to the U.S. military. Support for trade and diplomatic initiatives is more limited and politically fraught.

The United States and Singapore are two of the most influential nodes in an increasingly complex web of Asian economic, political, cultural, and security relations. As Prime Minister Lee Hsien Loong said with some understatement in 2013, "Singapore, in the middle of this dynamic region, can play a useful role connecting the U.S. and Asia."[94] Singapore is committed to this role, and the outstanding question is whether Washington can rise to the opportunity.

---

[94] Lee Hsien Loong (speech at gala dinner hosted by the U.S. Chamber of Commerce and U.S.-ASEAN Business Council, April 2, 2013, Washington, D.C.).

EXECUTIVE SUMMARY

This chapter examines the contemporary history and current trajectory of U.S.-Taiwan relations in the context of trends in cross-strait relations and assesses the choices facing leaders in Taipei and Washington and their impact on the future of the bilateral relationship.

MAIN ARGUMENT:
The current trajectory of U.S.-Taiwan relations requires recalibration. The status quo as it has stood for the past 35 years is unsustainable. An increasing imbalance between Taipei and Beijing in terms of military capabilities, China's economic leverage over Taiwan, and a widening sovereignty gap are subjecting Taiwan ever more to Beijing's coercive pressures. The current U.S. approach to Taiwan is being misguided by a fallacy of false choices due in part to excessive policy deference to Beijing's one-China policy. Despite the thaw in cross-strait tensions, without a corresponding shift in U.S.-Taiwan relations, Taipei will move further toward a situation where it faces a Hobson's choice—and Washington, if it fails to act, a real dilemma.

POLICY IMPLICATIONS:
- With the straightforward agreements in cross-strait negotiations out of the way, Chinese leaders are stepping up pressure on the Ma administration to engage in sensitive political dialogue. The 2016 election in Taiwan will be viewed by Beijing as a test of its policy approaches toward Taiwan.

- The economic relationship between Taiwan and China is characterized by growing interdependency and political separation. However, the trend line for the medium to long term is less clear if China's economic leverage over Taiwan continues to increase.

- China is likely to increasingly rely on military and economic coercion to compel political concessions from Taiwan on sovereignty. Therefore, U.S. military, political, and economic support will be critical for maintaining Taipei's confidence in engaging with Beijing in cross-strait negotiations.

U.S.-Taiwan Relations: Hobson's Choice and the False Dilemma

Russell Hsiao

Although the U.S.-Taiwan relationship has been unofficial since 1979, it remains dynamic, robust, and enduring. In the 35 years since the passage of the Taiwan Relations Act (TRA), the island has emerged as a vibrant democracy with a robust free-market economy, a responsible regional and global actor that respects legal norms and universal values, and a steadfast partner of the United States.

The Republic of China (ROC, also referred to as Taiwan) regards the United States as its most important international partner.[1] The United States has long been an economic and diplomatic friend to Taiwan and has been central to its remarkable economic development and political liberalization. Most importantly, the United States serves as Taiwan's principal security partner, providing the small island nation with the means to defend itself against external threats while also providing it with an implicit security guarantee.

Russell Hsiao is a Nonresident Senior Fellow at the Project 2049 Institute and a National Security Fellow at the Foundation for Defense of Democracies. He can be reached at <hsiao@project2049.net>.

This chapter draws on the author's previously published work. See "Balancing Power across the Strait," *Taipei Times*, February 28, 2013, http://www.taipeitimes.com/News/editorials/archives/2013/02/28/2003555880; "Asymmetry and Coercion across the Strait," *Defense Dossier*, November 2012, 16–18; and "Why U.S. Military Needs Taiwan," *Diplomat*, April 13, 2012, http://thediplomat.com/2012/04/why-u-s-military-needs-taiwan.

The author expresses his gratitude to Lt. Col. (ret.) Mark Stokes, executive director of the Project 2049 Institute, and would also like to thank NBR for its research assistance. Any errors are the author's own. The opinions expressed in this chapter represent the author's personal views and do not necessarily represent the affiliated organizations.

[1] This chapter uses the terms "ROC" and "Taiwan" interchangeably with no intended connotation.

The United States, meanwhile, views the ROC as an important economic partner and as central to its geopolitical interests in Asia. Taiwan's geography and status as a long-time (if unofficial) partner of the United States imbues it with tremendous geopolitical significance. The island's strategic location in the western Pacific makes it a linchpin of regional security. Further, long-standing U.S. efforts to ensure Taiwan's ability to defend itself make the island an important symbol of U.S. access, presence, and power in East Asia.

Relations between Taiwan and mainland China appear to be moving—albeit slowly— toward a more normal relationship. Yet beneath this veneer of normalization, cross-strait relations have been deeply affected by an intensifying strategic imbalance. The imbalance is a function of China's growing economic and military power, coupled with a widening sovereignty gap in the Taiwan Strait. The latter element underscores the challenges implicit in Beijing's continued effort to subjugate Taiwan under the PRC, and how recognition of Taiwan's legal status and the basic requisite functions that a sovereign government performs could result in greater instability in the Taiwan Strait.

Despite these significant changes, Washington's policy toward Taiwan has been slow to keep pace. Indeed, the political evolution of cross-strait relations has contradicted the assessments of many within the U.S. government. Against the backdrop of this new reality, U.S. interests in maintaining future stability and thus balance in the Taiwan Strait will require a strategic readjustment in which U.S. support for Taiwan's hard- and soft-balancing tactics will be integral elements in an overall strategy for managing cross-strait relations. Such measures are necessary to ensure that Taiwan has the capacity and means to resist China's military and economic coercion while the two sides engage in historic diplomatic dialogue. For their part, stewards of the U.S.-Taiwan relationship should guard against a scenario in which the alternate choices presented to Taipei and Washington offer a Hobson's choice for the former and a false dilemma for the latter.[2]

The first section of this chapter provides an overview of U.S.-Taiwan relations and discusses the current status quo, the effects of the widening sovereignty gap, and positive and negative trends in cross-strait relations. The next section discusses growing economic and political ties between Taiwan and China and analyzes Taiwan's security strategy. The chapter then considers the future of the U.S.-Taiwan partnership and concludes by offering recommendations.

---

[2] See John Stuart Mill, *Considerations on Representative Government*, 1st ed. (London: Parker, Son, & Bourn, 1861), 145. Mill makes the following observation: "when the individuals composing the majority would no longer be reduced to Hobson's choice, of either voting for the person brought forward by their local leaders, or not voting at all." In other words, Hobson's choice is a choice in which no real alternatives are offered.

Taiwan's Status and the
Unofficial U.S.-Taiwan Relationship

An Overview of U.S.-Taiwan Relations

Heated contentions over Taiwan's status are rooted in the incomplete conclusion of the Chinese Civil War in 1949. The victorious Communists, led by Mao Zedong, took control of mainland China, while the defeated Nationalists, led by Chiang Kai-shek, took refuge in Taiwan. Both sides claimed to be the sole, legitimate government of all of China, including both the mainland and Taiwan, and engaged in a decades-long struggle for power and international recognition. The island nation's capital, Taipei, has been the seat of the central government for the ROC since 1949. The government on Taiwan also administers the territories of Kinmen, Wuqiu, and Matsu Islands near the coast of Fujian across the Taiwan Strait and the Pratas Islands and Taiping Island in the South China Sea.[3] Taipei also lays claim over the Senkaku Islands (referred to as Diaoyutai by Taipei and as Diaoyu by Beijing).[4]

While the United States initially pursued a hands-off approach to Taiwan following the Chinese Civil War, the outbreak of the Korean War convinced President Harry Truman to commit economic and military aid to Taiwan and to send the U.S. Seventh Fleet into the Taiwan Strait to prevent a Communist invasion. The United States granted the ROC diplomatic recognition and supported its seat in the United Nations. The two sides signed a mutual defense treaty in 1954, which committed the United States to the defense of Taiwan and implicitly defined U.S.-Taiwan relations as fundamentally oriented as a check against the spread of Communism in Asia. Taipei later supported U.S. military efforts during the Vietnam War and sustained close political relations with Washington.

Washington's approach to Taiwan began to change in the 1970s, when the Nixon administration sought to exploit the Sino-Soviet split by engaging Beijing as a counterweight to the Soviet Union and to help end the Vietnam War. A series of exchanges, meetings, and high-level visits between the governments of the United States and mainland China culminated in Washington shifting diplomatic recognition from Taipei to Beijing in 1979.

Taiwan's current status was in part shaped during this period in three joint communiqués between the United States and People's Republic of China (PRC). In the 1972 Shanghai Communiqué, the United States

---

[3] An English translation of the ROC Constitution is available from the Office of the President of the Republic of China (Taiwan) website, http://english.president.gov.tw/Default.aspx?tabid=1107.

[4] Ministry of Foreign Affairs Republic of China (Taiwan), "The Republic of China's Sovereignty Claims over the Diaoyutai Islands and the East China Sea Peace Initiative," http://www.mofa.gov.tw/en/cp.aspx?n=38CD1D3C91067AEC.

acknowledged "that all Chinese on either side of the Taiwan Strait maintain there is but one China and that Taiwan is a part of China,"[5] which provided the diplomatic opening for Washington and Beijing to chart a path ahead in bilateral relations. In the communiqué, the PRC identified the Taiwan question as the primary obstruction to the normalization of U.S.-China relations and declared itself to be the sole legal government over all of China. In response, the United States simply stated that it does not "challenge" Beijing's position. The deliberate ambiguity in the communiqué's language signaled U.S. refrainment from endorsing the PRC's irredentist claim to Taiwan.

In the 1979 Joint Communiqué, in which Washington and Beijing agreed to establish diplomatic relations, the two sides reaffirmed the previous communiqué, and the United States acknowledged (but crucially did not explicitly affirm or challenge) the Chinese position that there is one China and that Taiwan is part of China. Notably, the communiqué said nothing about U.S. arms sales to Taiwan, as the United States and the PRC could not come to a joint position and Beijing agreed to raise the issue again after relations with Washington had normalized.

The U.S. Congress reacted swiftly and negatively to the Carter administration's decision to shift diplomatic recognition from Taipei to Beijing. While efforts fell short of successfully intervening to prevent derecognition, Congress enacted the Taiwan Relations Act (TRA) on April 10, 1979, which set into domestic law the guiding principles of U.S. policy toward Taiwan that continue to this day. As defined by the TRA, U.S. policy toward Taiwan is:

1. to preserve and promote extensive, close, and friendly commercial, cultural, and other relations between the people of the United States and the people on Taiwan, as well as the people on the China mainland and all other peoples of the western Pacific area;

2. to declare that peace and stability in the area are in the political, security, and economic interests of the United States, and are matters of international concern;

3. to make clear that the United States' decision to establish diplomatic relations with the People's Republic of China rests upon the expectation that the future of Taiwan will be determined by peaceful means;

---

[5] "Joint Statement Following Discussions with Leaders of the People's Republic of China," *Foreign Relations of the United States, 1969–1976 Volume XVII*, document no. 203 (Shanghai, February 27, 1972), https://history.state.gov/historicaldocuments/frus1969-76v17/d203#fnref1.

4. to consider any effort to determine the future of Taiwan by other than peaceful means, including by boycotts or embargoes, a threat to the peace and security of the western Pacific area and of grave concern to the United States;

5. to provide Taiwan with arms of a defensive character; and to maintain the capacity of the United States to resist any resort to force or other forms of coercion that would jeopardize the security, or the social or economic system, of the people on Taiwan.[6]

As President Ronald Reagan entered into office in 1981, his Asia team faced a conundrum. Diplomatic recognition had shifted to Beijing and the relationship with mainland China held promise in the ongoing Cold War against the Soviet Union; yet the unresolved nature of the Taiwan arms sales issue and the TRA posed major challenges to the fledgling U.S.-PRC relationship. Beijing had even begun to threaten Washington with the "Soviet card," which would undermine a decade of diplomatic engagement. Secretary of State Alexander Haig was particularly concerned about this development and pushed for a complete suspension of arms sales to Taiwan. While this proposal was not accepted by President Reagan, his administration did agree to a third joint communiqué (the August 17 Communiqué) in 1982 after eight months of painstaking negotiations. The United States declared its intention to

> not seek to carry out a long-term policy of arms sales to Taiwan, that its arms sales to Taiwan will not exceed, either in qualitative or in quantitative terms, the level of those supplied in recent years since the establishment of diplomatic relations between the United States and China, and that it intends gradually to reduce its sale of arms to Taiwan, leading, over a period of time, to a final resolution.[7]

President Reagan was reportedly disturbed by the implications of the third communiqué for Taiwan's security and took two decisive actions. First, he developed a secret National Security Council memorandum, which declared that reductions in arms sales should be conditioned on China's commitment to the peaceful resolution of Taiwan-PRC differences, and that "the quantity and quality of arms provided Taiwan be conditioned entirely on the threat posed by the PRC. Both in quantitative and qualitative terms,

---

[6] United States Congress, *Taiwan Relations Act*, 96th Congress, 1st sess. (Washington, D.C., 1979) sec. 2, item 2, http://photos.state.gov/libraries/ait-taiwan/171414/ait-pages/tra_e.pdf.

[7] United States and the People's Republic of China (PRC), "Joint Communiqué of the United States of America and the People's Republic of China," August 17, 1982, http://photos.state.gov/libraries/ait-taiwan/171414/ait-pages/817_e.pdf.

Taiwan's defense capability relative to that of the PRC will be maintained."[8] Second, he sought to reassure Taipei by directing James Lilley, then the head of the American Institute in Taiwan (the United States' unofficial embassy in Taipei), to orally deliver "six assurances" to ROC president Chiang Ching-kuo. These assurances articulated that:

1. The United States would not set a date for termination of arms sales to Taiwan.

2. The United States would not alter the terms of the Taiwan Relations Act.

3. The United States would not consult with China in advance before making decisions about U.S. arms sales to Taiwan.

4. The United States would not mediate between Taiwan and China.

5. The United States would not alter its position about the sovereignty of Taiwan—which was, that the question was one to be decided peacefully by the Chinese themselves—and would not pressure Taiwan to enter into negotiations with China.

6. The United States would not formally recognize Chinese sovereignty over Taiwan.[9]

These actions—the three joint communiqués, the Taiwan Relations Act, and the six assurances—represent the foundation of today's unofficial, yet robust, U.S.-Taiwan relationship. Consequently, the ROC exists in a political gray zone, whereby it is not officially recognized as a country by the United States, or by most of the world, and is not a member of most international institutions in which statehood is a requirement. Nevertheless, Taiwan is a *de facto* independent state and represented by a sovereign government with a robust economy, a pluralistic democracy, and a vibrant culture. Yet this status quo, which has been tremendously beneficial to Taiwan and its people

---

[8] See, for example, James R. Lilley and Jeffrey Lilley, *China Hands: Nine Decades of Adventure, Espionage, and Diplomacy in Asia* (New York: PublicAffairs, 2004), 248. Indeed, according to then assistant secretary of state John Holdridge in his August 1982 congressional testimony, the U.S. commitment in the 1982 communiqué to reduce arms sales to Taiwan was contingent on the PRC's peaceful approach to resolving the Taiwan issue, which may be generally characterized by its military posture directed against Taiwan. For more on this posture, see "Assistant Secretary of State John Holdridge and Six Assurances," August 18, 1982, http://csis.org/files/media/csis/programs/taiwan/timeline/sums/timeline_docs/CSI_19820818.htm.

[9] Kerry Dunbaugh, "Taiwan: Texts of the Taiwan Relations Act, the U.S.-China Communiques, and the 'Six Assurances,'" Congressional Research Service (CRS), CRS Report for Congress, 96246, May 21, 1998, http://digital.library.unt.edu/ark:/67531/metacrs695/m1/1/high_res_d/96-246f_1998May21.pdf. For more on the history of the six assurances, see Harvey Feldman, "President Reagan's Six Assurances to Taiwan and Their Meaning Today," Heritage Foundation, October 2, 2007, http://www.heritage.org/research/reports/2007/10/president-reagans-six-assurances-to-taiwan-and-their-meaning-today.

economically, remains structurally tenuous, and the country and its people are in a state of political limbo.

Perceptions in Taiwan of the Status Quo

Political leaders and scholars often talk about the need to preserve the "status quo." Yet what precisely that status quo is depends on the individual's point of view as the governments on both sides of the strait define the status quo differently. Beijing defines it as meaning that Taiwan is a renegade province belonging to the PRC that must be eventually "reunified," either peaceably or through the use of force, with mainland China under the "one country, two systems" rubric that it has applied to Hong Kong.[10] For its part, Taipei defines the status quo as meaning that the ROC is a sovereign and independent state and that both Taipei and Beijing are legitimate governments representing areas on each side of the Taiwan Strait.[11] There are many nuances within these two interpretations, and a tacit agreement between Beijing and Taipei to not deny each other's claims has hitherto permitted both governments to engage in substantive dialogue around the margins. However, real progress has been nixed by sensitivities on all sides, and a political resolution has proved to be unattainable, at least in the near term.[12]

Objectively, the status quo today is that Taiwan enjoys de facto but not *de jure* independence, meaning that Taipei has sovereign control over the territories that it currently administers but without the formal recognition of the majority of states in the international community. While not officially renouncing its claim to sovereignty over all of China, the ROC exists as a separate political entity outside the administrative purview of the PRC.

The cross-strait status quo has undergone multiple shifts since 1949, often driven by changes in the political leadership in Taipei and, to a much lesser extent, in Beijing. The deaths of Chiang Ching-kuo in 1988 and Deng Xiaoping in 1997 marked the end of periods of strongmen rule in both Taiwan and China.[13] Their deaths also symbolized a broader shift in the institutions that guided cross-strait relations. Political democratization in

---

[10] Beijing's implementation of the "one country, two systems" formula in Hong Kong, which had been initially designed for Taiwan, is being closely watched by Taipei. Recent decisions by Beijing to further delay suffrage to Hong Kong people flies in the face of the PRC's claim that it will respect the democratic rights of Hong Kong and has sparked a pro-democracy movement there.

[11] Mo Yan-chih, "Ma Defends 'One ROC, Two Areas,'" *Taipei Times*, June 1, 2012, http://www.taipeitimes.com/News/taiwan/archives/2012/06/01/2003534243.

[12] Susan L. Shirk, "China: Fragile Superpower: How China's Internal Politics Could Derail Its Peaceful Rise," *Foreign Affairs*, November–December 2007, http://www.foreignaffairs.com/articles/62976/lucian-w-pye/china-fragile-superpower-how-chinas-internal-politics-could-dera.

[13] Didi Kirsten Tatlow, "In China, Party Trumps a Strongman," *New York Times*, April 3, 2013, http://www.nytimes.com/2013/04/04/world/asia/04iht-letter04.html?_r=0.

Taiwan, which took hold in the 1980s and led to the establishment of the Democratic Progressive Party (DPP) in 1986, created great uncertainty in the delicate political balance, as new stakeholders entered into the equation of the cross-strait détente, and public perceptions in Taiwan increasingly factored into cross-strait politics.

Taiwan's polity is currently represented by two major political parties representing two coalitions: the ruling Kuomintang (KMT), which fought the Chinese Civil War against the Chinese Communist Party, and the "homegrown" opposition, the DPP. While "independence" and "unification" were hot-button campaign issues in the early days of Taiwan's democracy, which were simplistically held to be championed by the DPP and the KMT, respectively, the central theme has been gradually shifting. Current president Ma Ying-jeou's KMT party is generally associated with a more conciliatory political approach and economic policies toward China. Ma has overseen a remarkable rapprochement with the mainland that has inaugurated a historically unprecedented period of relatively warm relations across the Taiwan Strait and significantly expanded cross-strait economic and social interaction. Nevertheless, Ma has so far been unwilling or lacks the political clout to move ahead with political initiatives, primarily those that would clarify Taiwan's status and the nature of the cross-strait relationship, pushed by some members of his ruling coalition that could substantially change the current status quo.[14]

Yet despite the polarizing campaign rhetoric commonplace in democratic politics, there appears to be an emerging societal consensus in Taiwan over the status quo on the island.[15] The Ma administration's stagnant approval ratings, the prospect of the DPP returning to power in 2016, and the student-led Sunflower Movement in 2014 that occupied the parliament in protest against the Ma government's handling of cross-strait economic agreements, demonstrate that unilateral attempts to change the status quo—toward either de jure unification or independence—will not have popular support in Taiwan.[16] This trend is underscored by the two previous presidential elections in Taiwan in 2008 and 2012, which demonstrated that the overwhelming majority of people in Taiwan prefer the status quo. A December 2013 survey found that a majority of respondents (31.8%) want to "retain the status

---

[14] Hsiao-Chi Hsu, "Domestic Vulnerability and Nationalist Propaganda: Taiwan's National Unification Council Campaign in 2006," *Issues & Studies* 46, no. 4 (2010): 37–72, http://iiro.nccu.edu.tw/attachments/journal/add/4/46-4-2.pdf.

[15] Russell Hsiao, "DPP's Cross-Strait Policy Consistent with 'Status Quo,'" Jamestown Foundation, China Brief, December 20, 2011, http://www.jamestown.org/programs/chinabrief/single/?tx_ttnews%5Btt_news%5D=38810&cHash=0363e0375a440746ccdeb5f8c3c5bad7#.U-2UAfmg2So.

[16] William Pesek, "Cozying Up to China? Not Much," *Bloomberg View*, April 10, 2014, http://www.bloombergview.com/articles/2014-04-10/what-has-taiwan-gotten-for-cozying-up-to-china-not-much.

quo now and decide either unification or independence later," while 28.2% preferred maintaining the status quo permanently and 20.1% supported continuing the status quo now and announcing independence in the future. In all, polling shows that 86.7% of Taiwan's population supports maintaining the status quo for some period of time and that 93.3% of the people of Taiwan currently desire either the status quo or independence.[17]

Ma's approval ratings, which according to an independent local survey conducted in May 2014 fell below 18%, continue to lag during the second half of his presidency.[18] The administration's low popularity reflects the public's dissatisfaction more with the Ma administration's lackluster handling of domestic issues such as the economy and food scandals and less with its efforts to improve U.S.-Taiwan relations or manage cross-strait relations.[19] However, Ma's intense efforts to memorialize the economic agreements and, perhaps more symbolically, solidify plans to establish "offices" of the PRC's Association for Relations Across the Taiwan Straits in the ROC's Taiwan and Straits Exchange Foundation in China, which will be charged with handling technical and business matters between China and Taiwan, will likely cause a conflation of these issues. At the same time, with the prospect of a return to power by the DPP in 2016, China is seeking ways to institutionalize the agreements made between Taipei and Beijing over the last six years. These variables will bring the Ma administration's domestic policies, U.S. policies, and cross-strait policies into tension.

U.S. Perceptions of the Status Quo: Based on an Outdated Premise?

Taking note of the significant changes in cross-strait relations since 1979, the United States in 1994 concluded a substantive interagency policy review known as the Taiwan Policy Review (TPR). The TPR is the first and only

---

[17] See Su Yung-yao and Stacy Hsu, "Concern Grows on China Policy: Poll," *Taipei Times*, January 2, 2014, http://www.taipeitimes.com/News/taiwan/archives/2014/01/02/2003580335; and Mainland Affairs Council, Republic of China (Taiwan), "Unification or Independence?" http://www.mac.gov.tw/public/Attachment/472810554844.gif. These polling results are significant because they show that despite the rapid expansion of cross-strait ties under the KMT government with 21 bilateral agreements, the people still overwhelmingly prefer the status quo to any alternatives. Furthermore, this trend suggests that fears that increasing economic integration between Taiwan and China would lead to political integration have not materialized in the past six years. The short- and medium-term trends indicate that there is at best a weak correlation between increasing economic ties with the PRC and a change in people's preference for independence or unification.

[18] Stacy Hsu and Rich Chang, "Separate Polls Put Ma's Approval Rate under 18 Percent," *Taipei Times*, May 15, 2014, http://www.taipeitimes.com/News/front/archives/2014/05/14/2003590295.

[19] Paul Wolfowitz, "U.S. Taiwan Policy Threatens a Face-Off with China," *Wall Street Journal*, October 9, 2014, http://online.wsj.com/articles/paul-wolfowitz-u-s-taiwan-policy-threatens-a-face-off-with-china-1412901193; and Williams Wan, "Taiwan's President, Ma Ying-jeou, Plans to Expand Relations with China," *Washington Post*, October 24, 2013, http://www.washingtonpost.com/world/taiwans-president-ma-ying-jeou-plans-to-expand-relations-with-china/2013/10/24/0e38bb7e-3cbd-11e3-b6a9-da62c264f40e_story.html.

such initiative launched by the U.S. government since it shifted recognition to Beijing. The review and readjustment opened the pathway for the United States to send high-level officials from U.S. economic and technical agencies to visit Taiwan and for a subcabinet-level economic dialogue with Taiwan. According to Winston Lord, who was then assistant secretary for East Asian and Pacific affairs, the policy review was designed "to strengthen [the United States'] unofficial relations with Taiwan, permit the expansion of ties with the PRC, promote regional peace and development, and serve American national interests."[20] The action taken by the United States through the TPR shows that the status quo is malleable and that readjustments may be necessary from time to time to respond to the objective reality in the Taiwan Strait.[21]

Washington and Beijing also interpret the status quo in the Taiwan Strait differently from one another. In response to a question about the United States' policies toward Taiwan at a 2004 congressional hearing—a decade after the TPR, and in the clearest articulation of this difference to date—former assistant secretary of state for East Asian and Pacific affairs James Kelly stated:

> There certainly is a degree of contrast. The definition of one China is something that we could go on [about] for much too long for this event. In my testimony, I made the point of our one China [principle], and I did not really define it. I am not sure I very easily could define it.
>
> I can tell you what it is not. It is not the one China policy or the one China principle that Beijing suggests, and it may not be the definition that some would have in Taiwan, but it does convey a meaning of solidarity of a kind among the people on both sides of the Strait that has been our policy for a very long time.[22]

U.S. policy on Taiwan has not changed much in terms of substance over the intervening decade, and a confluence from the effects of a militarily rising China and partial neglect by official caretakers has prompted long-time stewards of the bilateral relationship to raise concerns about the waning U.S.-Taiwan relationship. For instance, in 2007 former deputy assistant secretary of state Randall Schriver called on the United States to issue "six new assurances":

> The issue of the sovereignty of Taiwan is for the people of the PRC and the people of Taiwan to decide peacefully themselves; the U.S. will not formally recognize the PRC's sovereignty over Taiwan; the U.S. will not support any

---

[20] Winston Lord, statement before the Senate Foreign Relations Committee, September 27, 1994, http://www.ait.org.tw/en/19940927-taiwan-policy-review-by-winston-lord.html.

[21] Indeed, some U.S. lawmakers have called on the Obama administration to initiate a new TPR. See William Lowther, "U.S. Legislators Urge New Taiwan Policy Review," *Taipei Times*, September 27, 2014, http://www.taipeitimes.com/News/taiwan/archives/2014/09/27/2003600691.

[22] "The Taiwan Relations Act: The Next Twenty-Five Years," hearing before the Committee on International Relations, U.S. House of Representatives, April 21, 2004, 40, http://commdocs.house.gov/committees/intlrel/hfa93229.000/hfa93229_0f.htm.

outcome achieved through the use of force, nor any outcome that does not enjoy the support among the majority of the free people of Taiwan.[23]

According to the Obama administration's senior director for Asian affairs at the National Security Council, Evan Medeiros, the United States hopes progress between China and Taiwan will continue "in ways acceptable to both sides." He added that a peaceful resolution to the Taiwan question is an "abiding interest" to the United States.[24]

Yet there is law and policy, and then there is implementation of policy. The latter is based on the administration's calculus of how its interests and values fit within the parameters set by the legal framework. Successive U.S. administrations' guiding principle for navigating the waters of the Taiwan Strait has been "strategic ambiguity," which has afforded stewards of the trilateral U.S.-ROC-PRC relationship maximum flexibility in maintaining a status quo. Indeed, this policy has served U.S. interests well, particularly in the early stages of Taiwan's democratization and while the United States attempted to build a constructive relationship with the PRC. The policy both passively and actively prevented Taipei from taking destabilizing actions, such as continuing its covert nuclear weapons program, and later curbed the enthusiasm of ROC leaders for asserting de jure independence during a highly volatile and transformational period in cross-strait relations.[25] Most importantly, the policy deterred Beijing's political leaders from taking military actions because of concerns of possible U.S. intervention.

Despite the approach's obvious utility for the past 35 years, strategic ambiguity is nonetheless increasingly based on an outdated premise. If this framework continues to dictate Washington's course of action for managing cross-strait relations, without a corresponding adjustment in U.S. policy toward Taiwan, it would likely lead to greater imbalance in the bargaining positions of Taipei and Beijing. Indeed, as the two sides of the Taiwan Strait engage in unprecedented dialogue, the scope of this approach to policymaking has barred U.S. policymakers from actively shaping conditions in the Taiwan Strait that will be more conducive to long-term peace and stability. The outdated and partly flawed premise of the approach is based on a Washington tendency to construct events in the Taiwan Strait in binary terms: independence or unification. This is a false dilemma that Beijing has defined as a choice between peace and war. The assumption is that if the two sides of

---

[23] Randall Schriver, "Randall Schriver on Taiwan: Taiwan Needs 'Six New Assurances,'" *Taipei Times*, August 22, 2007, http://www.taipeitimes.com/News/editorials/archives/2007/08/22/2003375330/1.

[24] "Official Rebukes China Statement, Reaffirms U.S. Position on Taiwan," Central News Agency, March 29, 2007, http://focustaiwan.tw/news/aipl/201403290007.aspx.

[25] "U.S. Opposed Taiwanese Bomb during 1970s," George Washington University, Nuclear Vault, June 15, 2007, http://www2.gwu.edu/~nsarchiv/nukevault/ebb221.

the Taiwan Strait were to unify under the terms set by the PRC's "one country, two systems" policy, then there would be peace. Alternatively, if Taiwan asserts its independence, then China would invade Taiwan or otherwise use military force to coerce its capitulation. This fallacy of a false choice—between peace and war—is the external manifestation of the PRC's one-China policy. The United States' passive approach and excessive deference to the PRC's irredentist claim over Taiwan, which has led to a widening sovereignty gap in the strait, will lead to greater instability in cross-strait relations by potentially undermining Taiwan's confidence during cross-strait negotiations and leaving the island vulnerable to coercion and possibly attack.

The Sovereignty Gap in the Taiwan Strait Is Widening

The sovereignty gap between the PRC and Taiwan has widened since 1979 when the United States switched its diplomatic recognition to the PRC.[26] Taipei is not a member of the United Nations and only 22 out of the 193 UN member states maintain diplomatic relations with the ROC.[27] Despite Taipei's efforts to expand diplomatic outreach, foreign recognition of Taiwan continues to erode and restrains Taiwan's meaningful participation in international institutions. Gambia, for example, severed diplomatic ties with Taiwan on November 14, 2013, and announced its intent to establish diplomatic relations with the PRC.[28] Unfortunately, Gambia's actions are not isolated, signaling a continuing challenge to Taiwan's international space.

Beijing's strategy to officially unify Taiwan as part of the PRC under its one-China policy is guided in part by its political warfare strategy.[29] This framework of analysis suggests that its behavior in dealing with Taiwan's diplomatic space, particularly by not reciprocating offers by third parties to establish formal diplomatic relations, may be motivated by using these diplomatic cards of international recognition to hold over the next ROC

---

[26] Ashraf Ghani, Clare Lockhart, and Michael Carnahan, "Closing the Sovereignty Gap: An Approach to State-Building," Overseas Development Institute, Working Paper, no. 253, August 2005, http://www.odi.org/publications/1819-closing-sovereignty-gap-approach-state-building.

[27] Matthias von Hein, "Taiwan's Diplomatic Charm Offensive," *Deutsche Welle*, January 22, 2014, http://www.dw.de/taiwans-diplomatic-charm-offensive/a-17380254.

[28] From a purely hypothetical perspective, since Gambia does not have diplomatic relations with the ROC or with the PRC, in effect neither government would be the sole representative of China. This could be seen as one external manifestation of the so-called 1992 consensus. If the two sides accept the premise that there currently exists two sovereign and legitimate governments across the Taiwan Strait, then whether a third country has diplomatic relations with both governments is functionally equivalent to it having no diplomatic relations with either—just as long as the other is not considered the sole representative of China.

[29] Mark Stokes and Russell Hsiao, "The People's Liberation Army General Political Department: Political Warfare with Chinese Characteristics," Project 2049 Institute, October 14, 2013, http://www.project2049.net/documents/PLA_General_Political_Department_Liaison_Stokes_Hsiao.pdf.

administration—particularly if the DPP returns to power. In one hypothetical scenario, Beijing may leverage pending and future offers to establish diplomatic relations with China as a tool to demand political concessions from Taipei, threatening to further delegitimize it in the international community and undermine its domestic support. Beijing could achieve the latter by contributing to the perception of the administration as a failure in managing cross-strait relations and safeguarding Taiwan's international space.

In the context of the widening sovereignty gap, a recalibration of how Washington assures Taipei's expectations is pivotal. Beijing's strategy is clear, and there appears to be an emerging societal consensus in Taiwan about the cross-strait status quo. In the absence of any meaningful pressure by the international community on Beijing to change its Taiwan policy, there needs to be a more accurate corresponding representation of the status quo in Washington. Refusal to address the widening sovereignty gap in the Taiwan Strait will become a real source of instability in the medium to long term. Creeping deterioration of U.S. support for Taiwan's sovereignty has the potential to create growing mistrust on both sides of the political spectrum in Taiwan and lead to greater uncertainty for the United States in the Taiwan Strait.[30]

U.S.-Taiwan relations and cross-strait relations are not mutually exclusive; rather they are reinforcing. The bilateral relationship between the United States and Taiwan is shaped by cross-strait relations, just as cross-strait relations are shaped by U.S. relations with Taiwan. Cross-strait relations have a significant impact for U.S. policy toward Taiwan because they affect U.S. perceptions of peace and stability in the strait. The strength or weakness of U.S.-Taiwan relations likewise affects Taipei's confidence in engaging with Beijing.[31]

Although the United States remains committed to Taiwan across a wide range of areas, the chorus of opinion leaders and pundits in the United States calling for Washington's abandonment of Taiwan has been growing louder.[32] This line of argument is based on an assumption held by some in the United States that China is the key to several significant international problems, and that if the United States were to "give up" Taiwan, Beijing would accommodate Washington's interests in other areas of supposedly greater

---

[30] Russell Hsiao and Michael Hsiao, "America Needs a Taiwan Strategy," *Diplomat*, October 5, 2012, http://thediplomat.com/2012/10/u-s-needs-a-taiwan-strategy.

[31] "Chinese Reactions to Taiwan Arms Sales," U.S. Taiwan Business Council and Project 2049 Institute, March 2012, http://project2049.net/documents/2012_chinese_reactions_to_taiwan_arms_sales.pdf.

[32] See, for example, Charles Glaser, "Will China's Rise Lead to War?" *Foreign Affairs*, March/April 2011; and Paul V. Kane, "To Save Our Economy, Ditch Taiwan," *New York Times*, November 10, 2011, http://www.nytimes.com/2011/11/11/opinion/to-save-our-economy-ditch-taiwan.html.

geopolitical significance. This argument is founded on the assumption that Taiwan's absorption by the PRC is inevitable.[33]

However, arguments against the viability and importance of U.S. relations with Taiwan overlook significant elements of the relationship, such as how the abandonment of Taiwan would severely weaken the credibility of the United States' commitment to other partners and allies, the attenuating effect on U.S. influence in the international order, and the significant erosion of democratic solidarity. In addition, such a policy shift would face opposition from a generally supportive Congress that has stood as a bulwark against China's military ambitions against Taiwan. Moreover, the premise behind a strategy of abandoning Taiwan—that the United States could give away Taiwan in the first place and that doing so would lead Beijing to change its policy—is decidedly uncertain. Many of these issues (such as North Korea, maritime disputes in the South China Sea, and human rights) are highly problematic for China.

For these reasons, Washington's policies toward Taiwan require additional recalibration. Taiwan remains important to U.S. interests throughout the Asia-Pacific, and adjusting to the emerging economic, political, and security realities will be essential to sustaining Taiwan's security and its political and economic systems. Still, the future course of Taiwan's relations with mainland China will remain the most significant variable in determining Taiwan's long-term role in the Asia-Pacific.

Developments in Cross-Strait Relations and Taiwan's Multifaceted Economic and Security Strategy

Cross-strait relations have gradually improved over the past two decades, yet the challenges to a peaceful solution continue to accumulate. Although growing cultural, economic, and political ties between Taiwan and mainland China have tempered the more tense security dimensions of the special relationship, the PRC continues to enhance its military capabilities directed at Taiwan. Likewise, as Taiwan's cultural and political identity continues to evolve, it is becoming increasingly unlikely that Taipei will accept reunification on Beijing's terms. These trends are leading Beijing to reconsider its long-term strategy vis-à-vis Taiwan. Consequently, the mainland may seek to apply greater pressure on Taiwan, potentially even through a third party, to engage in more substantive and extensive political dialogue.

---

[33] Russell Hsiao, "Avoid the China Trap, Recognize Taiwan," *Taipei Times*, November 26, 2011, http://www.taipeitimes.com/News/editorials/archives/2011/11/26/2003519231/1.

Expanding Economic Ties and Political Challenges

The expansion of economic ties between Taiwan and mainland China since the 1995–96 Taiwan Strait missile crises is altering the trajectory of cross-strait relations. From 2000 to 2008, relations between Taiwan and mainland China experienced a period of hot economics and cool politics. Indeed, after Taiwan lifted its ban on direct trade and transport links with the PRC in 2000, the total volume of trade increased from $31 billion in 2000 to $105 billion in 2008.[34] To put matters further into perspective, trade between China and Taiwan in 2013 totaled $167 billion, constituting approximately 40% of Taiwan's trade.[35]

This increasingly close economic relationship is drawing the island nation deeper into a dependent relationship with the PRC that some observers argue will make it more vulnerable to Beijing's political demands. Taiwan has long enjoyed a large trade surplus with the PRC, but the trend line is moving downward as the Chinese economy grows and more players are entering the mainland market, challenging Taiwan's access and providing the mainland with additional bargaining leverage. This changing dynamic in theory gives China more leverage and leaves Taipei more exposed to Beijing's coercive strategies. For example, in the future, Beijing may threaten the revocation of Taiwan's preferential trading status with the mainland as a source of leverage at the bargaining table or as a means of disciplining Taipei. Indeed, in recent years China has demonstrated its willingness to use economic leverage to attain political objectives—for example, by halting rare earth exports to Japan in 2010 following an incident involving the detention of the captain of a Chinese fishing vessel that had rammed two Japanese coast guard vessels in the East China Sea. Given the special relationship between Taiwan and China, the former's diminishing economic leverage in cross-strait relations may leave its leaders with less capacity to resist coercion and intimidation over a final political settlement to the long-standing cross-strait dispute.[36]

Even despite Ma's policy of rapprochement with the mainland since his election in 2008 fundamental challenges remain in the relationship. Although Ma's tenure has seen a period of unprecedented economic cooperation, it has been punctured frequently by wrangling between political leaders in Beijing and Taipei, fueling concerns in Washington over the possibility of military action by China. Although conditions for peace between the two countries

---

[34] Hsiao, "Avoid the China Trap."

[35] Guy Taylor and Patrice Hill, "Taiwan's Top Diplomat Seeks U.S. Help in Emerging from China's Shadow," *Washington Times*, August 11, 2014, http://www.washingtontimes.com/news/2014/aug/11/taiwans-top-diplomat-seeks-us-help-in-emerging-fro.

[36] Russell Hsiao, "Balancing Power across the Strait," *Taipei Times*, February 28, 2013, http://www.taipeitimes.com/News/editorials/archives/2013/02/28/2003555880.

appear to be gaining traction in the near term as speculation persists about a potential watershed meeting between Ma and Xi Jinping,[37] the mid-to-long-term challenges are growing. China's People's Liberation Army (PLA) continues to enhance its military advantage over Taiwan, while the process of democratic consolidation in Taiwan deepens its sense of a distinct national identity and moves Taiwan further from the PRC.

To be sure, Beijing is stepping up pressure on the Ma administration to engage in sensitive political dialogue. On the side of the Asia-Pacific Economic Cooperation (APEC) meeting in 2013, Xi stated that "the issue of the political divide that exists between the two sides must step by step reach a final resolution and it cannot be passed on from generation to generation."[38] In this regard, Beijing increasingly views Washington as the channel through which it can pressure Taipei to engage in more extensive dialogue with mainland China. The incentive for the United States to intervene may be concerns that an opposition victory in Taiwan in 2016 would invite Chinese action. Such a scenario is premised on Beijing's contention that cross-strait stability is unsustainable unless the two sides engage in political dialogue under the terms established by the so-called 1992 consensus or the one-China framework with the PRC's "one country, two systems" formula. Despite changes in the DPP's approach to the China issue—as reflected in internal policy reviews, increased engagements with the mainland, and personnel changes—due to substantive developments in cross-strait relations, a DPP return to power in 2016 would likely require a period of readjustment and could heighten tension.[39]

Window for Negotiations?

Whether improved relations during 2008–13 will have any tangible effects on the PRC's approach to Taiwan remains to be seen. Although the Chinese Communist Party's Taiwan policymaking apparatus experienced a change due to the leadership succession from the Hu-Wen administration to the Xi-Li administration, the policy implications for Beijing's approach to

---

[37] "Beijing Open to Ma-Xi Meeting in a 'Third Location,'" *Taipei Times*, March 5, 2014, http://www.taipeitimes.com/News/front/archives/2014/03/05/2003584896.

[38] Teddy Ng, "Xi Jinping Says Efforts Must Be Made to Close the China-Taiwan Political Divide," October 6, 2013, *South China Morning Post*, http://www.scmp.com/news/china/article/1325761/xi-jinping-says-political-solution-taiwan-cant-wait-forever.

[39] For further discussion, see the video from the Center for Strategic and International Studies event "Building a Comprehensive DPP Mainland Strategy," January 14, 2014, http://csis.org/multimedia/video-building-comprehensive-dpp-mainland-strategy. For a KMT view of the 1992 consensus, see "'1992 Consensus' Means 'Different Interpretations,'" *China Times*, November 28, 2012, http://www.kmt.org.tw/english/page.aspx?type=article&mnum=113&anum=12234. See also Shih Hsiu-chuan, "Su Chi Admits the '1992 Consensus' Was Made Up," *Taipei Times*, February 22, 2006, http://www.taipeitimes.com/News/taiwan/archives/2006/02/22/2003294106.

Taiwan set forth by Hu Jintao's "six points" proposition appear at the time of this writing to be minimal.[40] However, personnel changes within the Taiwan Work Leading Small Group (TWLSG) have often intersected with shifts in the PRC's policy toward Taiwan, and the handover of power ushered in by the 18th Party Congress reflects an evolutionary change in the PRC's leadership and approach to Taiwan.[41]

Since Ma's re-election in 2012, Beijing has been stepping up pressure on Taipei to negotiate a cross-strait peace agreement.[42] However, the window for political negotiations with terms favorable to Beijing is narrowing. In 2016, Taiwan will have a presidential election, and the United States and China are facing a potential change in power in Taipei. Beijing will want to aggressively engage in negotiations with Taipei while the KMT is in power in order to lock in favorable terms for a potential peace treaty.[43] This is, however, a nonstarter for the Ma administration, which has repeatedly indicated that the time is not ripe for Taiwan to engage mainland China in substantive political dialogue. Under the "three no's" policy of "no unification, no independence, and no use of force," the current political leadership has emphasized the "one Republic of China, two areas" concept as the foundation for cross-strait relations as defined by the ROC constitution. This, Ma said, has enabled the government to promote cross-strait interaction on the basis of "mutual non-recognition of sovereignty and mutual non-denial of governing authority."[44]

Nonetheless, the administration has indicated that it does not rule out a meeting between the heads of state in the appropriate setting. Indeed, Ma stated in May 2014 "that the 'stage' for a potential meeting with Chinese President Xi Jinping is 'all set.'"[45] However, Beijing has shied away from directly responding to the groundbreaking opportunity. The PRC State Council's Taiwan Affairs Office spokesperson has claimed that a meeting between cross-strait leaders is for the two sides of the strait to decide, adding that such a meeting need not

---

[40] Peng Hsien-chun, Chen Hui-ping, and Stacy Hsu, "PRC's Xi Declares 'Four Noes' on Taiwan," *Taipei Times*, May 8, 2014, http://www.taipeitimes.com/News/front/archives/2014/05/08/2003589822. See also Russell Hsiao, "Hu Jintao's 'Six-Points' Proposition to Taiwan," Jamestown Foundation, China Brief, January 12, 2009, http://www.jamestown.org/single/?no_cache=1&tx_ttnews%5Btt_news%5D=34333.

[41] Russell Hsiao, "Taiwan Work Leading Small Group under Xi Jinping," Jamestown Foundation, China Brief, June 7, 2013.

[42] "Beijing to Step Up Pressure for Political Talks: Taiwan Official," *Want China Times*, December 6, 2012, http://www.wantchinatimes.com/news-subclass-cnt.aspx?id=20121206000108&cid=1101.

[43] Ben Blanchard, "China, Taiwan Agree to Open Offices after Historic Talks," Reuters, February 11, 2014, http://www.reuters.com/article/2014/02/11/us-china-taiwan-idUSBREA1A0EP20140211.

[44] Mainland Affairs Council (Republic of China), "Mainland Policy and Work," January 1, 2013, http://www.mac.gov.tw/ct.asp?xItem=104886&ctNode=6607&mp=3.

[45] Lauly Li, "Ma Eyes APEC as Xi Meeting Venue," *China Post*, May 26, 2014, http://www.chinapost.com.tw/taiwan/china-taiwan-relations/2014/05/26/408646/Ma-eyes.htm.

take place at an international occasion.[46] This posture is consistent with the PRC's desire to not internationalize cross-strait relations.

Yet possible changes in Taiwan's political leadership in 2016 have the potential to catalyze a shift in Beijing's approach to Taiwan. Warming relations with Taiwan were presented in Beijing as a means to build political, economic, and social ties across the Taiwan Strait and thus, theoretically, bring unification closer to reality. Yet President Ma's inability or unwillingness to pursue substantial political talks and the prospect of the DPP returning to power in 2016 have the potential to convince leaders in Beijing that their strategy has not been successful in bringing cross-strait relations closer to unification. If such a determination is made, it is unclear what alternative strategies the PRC may employ, although its behavior vis-à-vis maritime disputes with its neighbors suggests a greater willingness to make quasi or outright military threats to advance its agenda. On the other hand, an example of how events in Taiwan could affect China's approach to the island may be observed in the impact of the Sunflower Movement in postponing the head of the Taiwan Affairs Office's visit and the delegation's subsequent bypassing of the government to get in touch with the grassroots of Taiwanese society.[47]

Taiwan's Pursuit of a Hard Hedge

China-Taiwan relations therefore appear likely to move into uncharted waters. As contention over unification looms, Taiwan is pursuing a hard hedge to deter and blunt Beijing's military advances. The recent thaw in cross-strait relations has not dulled the PRC's military ambitions with regard to Taiwan; the PLA has continued to extend its military advantage over the ROC military, leaving Taiwan in an increasingly exposed and untenable long-term defensive position. A 2013 report by Taiwan's Ministry of National Defense concluded that "China plans to enhance its combat capabilities to a level sufficient to mount a full attack against Taiwan by 2020."[48] Furthermore, according to Kin Moy, the former U.S. deputy assistant secretary of state for East Asian and Pacific Affairs,

as China's economy and military spending grow, and China continues its military deployments and exercises aimed at Taiwan, it is more important than ever for

---

[46] Lauly Li, "President Still Hopes to Schedule Talk with Xi for APEC Summit in Beijing," *China Post*, June 26, 2014, http://www.chinapost.com.tw/taiwan/china-taiwan-relations/2014/06/26/411010/President-still.htm.

[47] Lawrence Chung, "Beijing's Top Taiwan Man Zhang Zhijun Visits Island for First Time," *South China Morning Post*, June 24, 2014, http://www.scmp.com/news/china/article/1539812/beijings-top-taiwan-man-zhang-zhijun-visits-island-first-time.

[48] "China Military Preparing Capability to Control Taiwan by 2020: MND," Central News Agency, October 7, 2010, http://focustaiwan.tw/news/acs/201310070035.aspx.

Taiwan to spend sufficient money on a professional military force that uses asymmetry, innovation, independent thinking, and every defensive advantage Taiwan can muster to deter potential attempts at coercion or aggression.[49]

Yet despite the growing military imbalance in the Taiwan Strait, the ROC's defense budget continues to decline.

In fact, there was a gradual decline in Taiwan's defense budget from 2008 to 2013 during the period of political rapprochement. In 2013, the official defense budget was NT$312.7 billion (US$10.8 billion), which represents a decrease from about 20.2% to 16.2% of total government spending.[50] Taiwan's current defense spending represents 2.1% of its GDP—less than the 3% of GDP level that Ma pledged to maintain and a substantial decrease from the pinnacle of Taiwan's defense spending of 3.8% of GDP in 1994.[51] Taiwan's stagnate defense budget, however, should be seen in the context of a complex balancing of budgetary interests within a fledgling democracy and military in transition.[52]

Despite facing budgetary constraints in recent years, Taiwan's military leaders have been taking active measures to shore up Taiwan's defensive and interdiction capabilities to counter PLA military coercion. In large part to maintain its sovereignty, Taiwan has been strengthening its asymmetric and defensive capabilities to deter, defend, and repel Beijing's advances.[53] The ROC military has also been improving its doctrine. Taiwan's 2013 Quadrennial Defense Review laid out five pillars for Taiwan's national defense strategy: war prevention, homeland defense, contingency response, conflict avoidance, and regional stability. To those ends, the Ministry of National Defense aims to "develop defense technologies, continue to procure defensive weapons, establish 'innovative and asymmetric' capabilities, and strengthen force preservation and infrastructure protection capabilities."[54]

Perhaps most significantly, Taiwan's defense planners are beefing up the island nation's indigenously developed military capabilities. As early as

---

[49] Kin Moy, "The Promise of the Taiwan Relations Act," written statement before the House Foreign Affairs Committee, March 14, 2014, http://www.state.gov/p/eap/rls/rm/2014/03/223461.htm.

[50] Office of the Secretary of Defense, *Military and Security Developments Involving the People's Republic of China 2014*, Annual Report to Congress (Washington, D.C., 2014), http://www.defense.gov/pubs/2014_DoD_China_Report.pdf.

[51] Craig Murray, "Taiwan's Declining Defense Spending Could Jeopardize Military Preparedness," U.S.-China Economic and Security Review Commission, Backgrounder, June 11, 2013.

[52] Mark Stokes, "Taiwan's Security: Beyond the Special Budget," American Enterprise Institute (AEI), March 26, 2006, http://www.aei.org/article/foreign-and-defense-policy/regional/asia/taiwans-security.

[53] Dan Blumenthal et al., "Deter, Defend, Repel, and Partner: A Defense Strategy for Taiwan," AEI and Project 2049 Institute, July 2009, http://project2049.net/documents/deter_defend_repel_partner_taiwan_defense_working_group.pdf.

[54] Ministry of National Defense (ROC), *2013 ROC National Defense Report* (Taipei, 2013), 78, http://report.mnd.gov.tw/en/m/minister.html.

2007, under the former DPP administration, the ROC military deployed the Hsiung Feng (HF)-IIE surface-to-surface cruise missile system developed by the island's leading institution for R&D and design of defense technology, the Chung-Shan Institute of Science and Technology (CSIST). Taiwan also successfully test-fired an advanced HF missile with a range of eight hundred kilometers in January 2008, which is believed to have been another variant of HF-IIE that at the time had not reached mass production stage. In 2008, Ma reportedly authorized the production of 300 HF-IIEs.[55] Following reports in 2010 about new Chinese missile installations in Shandong Province in northeastern China, the ROC military revealed that it was planning to test its indigenously designed HF-IIE surface-to-surface cruise missile in June 2010 and produce 80 units by the end of that year.

More recently, the Wan Chien ("ten thousand swords") cluster bomb was officially unveiled in January 2014, and mass production and deployment of the air-to-surface missile will reportedly begin in 2015.[56] The Wan Chien is the military's first joint standoff weapon, which, according to *Jane's Defence Weekly*, is designed to strike airports and will help enhance the ROC Air Force's long-range strike capabilities while allowing attacking personnel to evade defensive fire from the target area. The Wan Chien missile reportedly "carries more than 100 individual warheads and has a claimed maximum range of around 200 km."[57]

Perhaps most significant for Taiwan's comprehensive defense is that there appears to be forward movement in Taipei's long-standing program to indigenously build diesel submarines. The program—which had been shelved under former president Chen Shui-bian's administration—has been resuscitated in Ma's second term. Public interest resurfaced in late January 2012 after local reports revealed that officials from the ROC Navy reportedly briefed a group of members of the Legislative Yuan's Foreign Affairs and Defense Committee about the program during a classified meeting. In remarks clearly aimed at Washington, Ma stated: "There seems to be a consensus in Taiwan that we should seek foreign technology to help us build [submarines] ourselves."[58] Diesel-electric submarines would contribute to the defense of the island, particularly as they could play a critical role in

---

[55] J. Michael Cole, "Ministry Mum on HF-2Es on Penghu," *Taipei Times*, September 14, 2011, http://www.taipeitimes.com/News/taiwan/archives/2011/09/14/2003513241/1.

[56] Shih Hsiu-chuan, "Wan Chien Cluster Missile Production Date Moved," *Taipei Times*, October 2, 2013, http://www.taipeitimes.com/News/taiwan/archives/2013/10/02/2003573509.

[57] Gavin Phipps, "Taiwan Unveils Upgraded IDF, Wan Chien Stand-off Missile," *IHS Jane's Defence Weekly*, January 15, 2014, http://www.janes.com/article/32443/taiwan-unveils-upgraded-idf-wan-chien-stand-off-missile.

[58] "President Calls for U.S. Assistance to Build Submarines," Central News Agency, April 9, 2014, http://focustaiwan.tw/news/aipl/201404090031.aspx.

interdicting amphibious ships transiting from mainland China to Taiwan and in conducting counter-blockade and maritime surveillance operations. The decision to pursue the indigenous program may be seen as representing a realignment in the domestic political environment amid heightened concerns over China's growing military advantages.[59]

Finally, Taiwan's defense strategy has emphasized collaborative approaches to security: promoting enhanced security dialogues and exchanges, working with others to establish regional security mechanisms, and establishing programs to "jointly safeguard regional sea and air security."[60] According to the Ministry of National Defense, this last objective may be achieved by

> enhancing cooperation with Asia Pacific countries to protect the security of sea and air lines of communication in the East and South China Seas and surrounding waters, establish[ing] institutionalized cooperation channels for strategic dialogues, jointly ensur[ing] freedom of navigation and overflight as well as the security of sea and air lines of communication, and play[ing] a key role in facilitating regional stability.[61]

A hard balancing strategy is indeed a necessary component in a comprehensive strategy for Taiwan in dealing with mainland China. To this end, Taiwan's political and military leaders appear increasingly in agreement that developing the country's indigenous military capabilities, while seeking key technological assistance from the United States and friendly nations, is the way forward to resolve the island's arms-procurement conundrum and ensure comprehensive defense through a collaborative approach to the island's national security.

Improving Taiwan's Regional and International Position

Taiwan's efforts to diversify its foreign engagement extend beyond defense cooperation, but in ways that also have direct and important implications for the island nation's national security. Internationally, Ma has negotiated a diplomatic truce with Beijing that has ostensibly halted the competition for official recognition by foreign governments, which was the highlight of the former DPP administration's foreign policy agenda. Somewhat paradoxically, during Ma's tenure Taiwan gained membership in international institutions such as the World Health Assembly, the International Civil Aviation

---

[59] Russell Hsiao and Jyh-Perng Wang, "Taiwan Navy Sailing Ahead with Indigenous Submarine Program," Jamestown Foundation, China Brief, March 30, 2012, http://www.jamestown.org/programs/chinabrief/single/?tx_ttnews%5Btt_news%5D=39209&cHash=d69131e481442db1b658798c4805282f#.U_EV1_mg2So.

[60] Ministry of National Defense (ROC), 2013 ROC National Defense Report, 83.

[61] Ibid.

Organization, and the United Nations Framework Convention on Climate Change, all of which do not require statehood for membership.

Under the Ma administration, Taiwan has also forged several economic agreements with a more diverse array of regional partners. In addition to signing the 2010 Economic Cooperation Framework Agreement with the mainland, Taipei and Washington restarted negotiations over a trade and investment agreement and signed free trade agreements with New Zealand and Singapore. The Singapore deal quickly followed five smaller economic agreements with Japan. These agreements are significant steps toward greater regional economic integration and sources of confidence for Taiwan to pursue greater economic cooperation with China. Indeed, as the current government continues to economically integrate Taiwan into the greater Chinese market, these free trade agreements are essential to balance this intensifying economic relationship with mainland China. Taipei is also currently seeking membership in the U.S.-led Trans-Pacific Partnership (TPP) as well as trade agreements with Southeast Asian countries to further reduce its reliance on China.[62] With respect to the TPP, Ma has declared his intention for Taiwan to join the agreement by 2020, though the roadmap to achieve that goal has not been detailed.[63]

Taiwan has been active in participating in international humanitarian assistance and disaster relief efforts, most notably following the devastating 2010 earthquake in Haiti, which has been a firm ally of Taiwan since 1956. For Taipei, contributing to the response effort in Haiti was of crucial importance to ensure the safety of Taiwan nationals, engage as a contributing member of the international community, and assume the humanitarian responsibilities toward a steadfast political ally that is the target of Beijing's embrace. Equally important was the desire to improve Taiwan's role in the eyes of the international community. In the end, Taiwan surpassed China by sending $5 million in aid to Haiti while China committed $4.4 million.[64]

Finally, a growing number of disputes between China and its neighbors in Northeast and Southeast Asia around Taiwan's periphery, particularly in the East China and South China Seas, have presented both challenges and opportunities for Taipei. On the one hand, China's aggressive behavior in

[62] David Cohen, "Taiwan Trade Agreements with Singapore, Japan, Should Calm Fears of PRC Economic Domination," Jamestown Foundation, China Brief, November 22, 2013, http://www.jamestown.org/single/?tx_ttnews%5Btt_news%5D=41666&no_cache=1#.U-2PkPmg2So.

[63] Richard C. Bush and Joshua Meltzer, "Taiwan and the Trans-Pacific Partnership: Preparing the Way," Brookings Institution, East Asia Policy Paper, no. 3, January 2014, http://www.brookings.edu/~/media/research/files/papers/2013/10/taiwan%20transpacific%20partnership%20bush%20meltzer/taiwan%20transpacific%20partnership%20bush%20meltzer%20final.pdf.

[64] "Taiwan Leads Rival China in Quake Aid to Haiti," Reuters, January 18, 2010, http://in.reuters.com/article/2010/01/18/idINIndia-45477020100118.

asserting its claims over territorial disputes presents a stark contrast with Taipei's more constructive diplomatic initiatives and spotlights the potential role that Taiwan could play in resolving the disputes. Indeed, Ma's proposal for an East China Sea Peace Initiative very closely resembles U.S. calls for the peaceful resolution of disputes and the support of international law. Taiwan's negotiations with Japan and the Philippines to jointly access fisheries in disputed waters is another example of Taiwan's positive diplomatic approach to these contentious issues. At the same time, Taipei's increased visibility and potential role have also highlighted its politically tenuous position on ROC sovereignty over disputed territories in the region,[65] since its claims mostly overlap with those of Beijing.

Pursuant to Washington's interest in maintaining peace and stability in the Taiwan Strait, the United States encourages Taipei to engage in dialogue with Beijing. At the same time, Washington warns that Taiwan should spend more on its defense and also clarify its claims in regional territorial disputes with mainland China. The latter proposal was conveyed in an opinion piece from February 2014 by Jeffrey Bader, the former senior director for East Asia on the Obama administration's National Security Council staff. Bader proposed that the United States push Taiwan to clarify its position on claims in the South China Sea.[66] This push and pull tactic exerted on Taiwan by Washington creates a quandary particularly for the current ruling party in Taiwan, which has staked its electoral success on improved relations with Beijing. Improved relations, however, will not come without a cost. Indeed, the terms for improving relations, whether they are measured in increased dialogues or economic and trade agreements, are currently defined by Beijing.

If the Ma government were to distinguish Taipei's territorial claims from Beijing's, it may be viewed by the PRC as an act toward independence—not just de facto separation but de jure. Increasing concerns over Taiwan's permanent de facto separation, which Chinese commentators refer to as "type B" independence, have caused Beijing to step up calls for more open economic and cultural exchange to bridge these fault lines. The common thread in Taipei's and Beijing's appearance of a united front is an emphasis on the common legal claim based on their shared territorial claims. Actions taken by Taipei that either reinforces de facto separation or promote de jure separation of Taiwan from mainland China are stringently opposed by Beijing—this opposition underscores Beijing's irredentist claim over Taiwan

---

[65] Russell Hsiao, "Taiwan Pivots in the South China Sea," Jamestown Foundation, China Brief, June 17, 2011, http://www.jamestown.org/single/?tx_ttnews%5Btt_news%5D=38067&no_cache=1#.VDtCEvmg2So.

[66] Jeffrey A. Bader, "The U.S. and China's Nine-Dash Line: Ending the Ambiguity," Brookings Institution, February 6, 2014, http://www.brookings.edu/research/opinions/2014/02/06-us-china-nine-dash-line-bader.

and why it reacted coolly to a proposal by several Taiwanese politicians calling for a "broad one-China framework."[67] Indeed, should Washington push Taiwan to clarify its territorial claims or move to de-emphasize its common claims with Beijing, however, it should be ready to face some trade-offs in terms of temporary instability in cross-strait relations, given that such a move by Taipei may cause Beijing to take political retaliatory actions against Taiwan.

Future U.S.-Taiwan Cooperation

The United States and Taiwan enjoy a vibrant relationship. At the time of writing in 2014, approximately 2,500 U.S. defense officers had visited Taiwan—an increase of 25% from 2013—while Taiwan military officers had visited the United States more than 1,500 times during the same period.[68] In 2012, Taiwan purchased $4.73 billion of U.S. defense hardware and services, making it the largest customer of U.S. defense articles in Asia and the second-largest worldwide.[69] The two sides also enjoy strong economic relations. The United States is Taiwan's third-largest trading partner and its largest source of FDI (totaling $22.8 billion in 2013).[70] Taiwan, meanwhile, is the United States' twelfth-largest trading partner, with two-way trade in 2013 reaching $63.6 billion.[71]

However, these robust and multifaceted ties belie the fact that the United States does not formally recognize Taiwan as a full member of the community of nations and the cross-strait imbalance with mainland China continues to widen. Growing imbalance in the Taiwan Strait will lead to less predictability in the actions taken by leaders in Taipei and Beijing. For one, it could embolden Chinese leaders to take destabilizing action when they see a clear advantage, while increasing coercive pressures may force Taipei to take actions inimical to regional stability. The recalibration of U.S.-Taiwan relations will require significant adjustments across all elements of national power. Many of the policy adjustments that could be made are straightforward. Yet

---

[67] Shih Ming-te et al., "Our Appeal: Five Principles on Cross-Strait Relations," May 27, 2014, http://140.119.184.164/taipeiforum/%E8%98%87%E8%B5%B7%E8%A7%80%E9%BB%9E/Our_Appeal.pdf.

[68] "Taiwan, U.S. Discuss Submarine Issue at Defense Conference: AIT," Radio Taiwan International, October 9, 2014, http://english.rti.org.tw/news/?recordId=12860.

[69] See U.S. Department of State, "Payment to the American Institute in Taiwan," 469, http://www.state.gov/documents/organization/208999.pdf.

[70] Office of the U.S. Trade Representative, "U.S.-Taiwan Trade Facts," http://www.ustr.gov/countries-regions/china/taiwan.

[71] Shirley A. Kan and Wayne M. Morrison, "U.S.-Taiwan Relationship: Overview of Policy Issues," CRS, CRS Report for Congress, R41952, April 22, 2014, http://fas.org/sgp/crs/row/R41952.pdf.

some aspects, especially in the security sphere, will be quite complex and will require additional analysis.

Economic Cooperation

One of the most significant geopolitical accomplishments that Washington and Taipei could take to more strongly tie the two sides together and more firmly embed Taiwan in the broader regional architecture is on the economic side. The quick passage of a bilateral investment framework agreement, and Taiwan's subsequent participation in the TPP, would be of tremendous economic and geopolitical consequence. These actions would greatly diversify Taiwan's economic relationships and militate against Beijing's growing ability to coerce Taipei. They would also catalyze much-needed economic reforms within Taiwan, reforms that are necessary for the ROC to remain competitive in an increasingly interconnected Asian market.

Taiwan's participation in the TPP would be fraught with domestic and international hurdles. Domestically, Taipei would need to overcome several significant interest groups that have a stake in limiting competition with the outside world. Internationally, China would likely seek to block Taiwan's participation in the TPP. Even though membership in the TPP is based on membership in APEC, and Taiwan would thus legally be able to join the TPP, Beijing would only need to convince one TPP member to block Taiwan's participation. Yet that would not necessarily mean that Beijing holds a veto. Washington could use its considerable economic and political influence to encourage TPP members to sign bilateral agreements with Taiwan that, taken as a whole, would make Taiwan a de facto member.

Security Cooperation

According to Schriver, "U.S. support for Taiwan's defense has served as a visible symbol of U.S. commitment to peace and security in the Asia-Pacific region."[72] That representative democracy in Taiwan continues to consolidate requires that the United States maintain Taiwan's capacity to resist the PRC's political and military coercion. For peace and stability, this is a core interest of the United States.

To hedge against PLA military challenges, Taiwan is building a robust air and missile defense network with help from the United States. According to analyst Ian Easton, "this includes significant investments into early-warning radars, other intelligence, surveillance, and reconnaissance (ISR) assets, fighter

---

[72] Randall G. Schriver, testimony before the Senate Foreign Relations Committee, April 3, 2014, http://www.foreign.senate.gov/imo/media/doc/Schriver_Testimony.pdf.

upgrades, missile defense systems, and airbase hardening and resiliency."[73] The future trajectory of U.S.-Taiwan security cooperation will depend in large part on decisions made by official caretakers today and be invariably tied to U.S. arms sales to Taiwan, military integration, Taiwan's increased participation in the existing regional security architecture, and its potential role in air-sea battle. Indeed, one underlying goal of air-sea battle is doing more with less in an era of budgetary constraints—an objective that should be at the center of Taiwan's national security strategy.

In the absence of formal diplomatic relations, the defense partnership between the United States and Taiwan serves not only military but also political purposes. Arms sales to Taiwan are the most visible manifestation of U.S. support for Taiwan's status. Although the United States abrogated its mutual defense treaty with Taiwan in 1980, U.S. arms transfers have been significant despite the absence of a diplomatic relationship. Indeed, Taiwan has ranked among the top recipients of U.S. arms sales. In recent terms, the value of deliveries of arms and services to Taiwan totaled $4.3 billion in 2004–7 and $2.9 billion in 2008–11.[74] To be sure, in 2001, President George W. Bush authorized the sale of a tranche of advanced military platforms to strengthen the island's ability to defend and deter Chinese military provocation and possible invasion.[75] Yet the long-delayed $11 billion arms package has been held up for various reasons since its announcement, continuing to chip away at Taipei's confidence in deterring Chinese provocations. According to the latest ROC assessment, China will be capable of mounting a full-scale military attack on Taiwan by 2020.[76]

The U.S. Defense Department could also consider expanding cooperative R&D with Taiwan's Industrial Technology Research Institute, CSIST, and private industry. Taiwan is a world leader in technology innovation, particularly in applied information and communications technology that should be leveraged for mutual benefit.

In addition, the Defense Department and the ROC Ministry of Defense should consider the formation of a working group on innovative capabilities that could incorporate representatives from both countries' think tanks and defense industries as well as key legislators. Possible focus areas might include

---

[73] Ian Easton, "Able Archers Taiwan Defense Strategy in an Age of Precision Strike," Project 2049 Institute, September 2014, http://www.project2049.net/documents/Easton_Able_Archers_Taiwan_Defense_Strategy.pdf.

[74] Shirley A. Kan, "Taiwan: Major U.S. Arms Sales Since 1990," CRS, CRS Report for Congress, RL30957, August 29, 2014, http://fas.org/sgp/crs/weapons/RL30957.pdf.

[75] See Kelly Wallace, "Bush Pledges Whatever It Takes to Defend Taiwan," CNN, April 25, 2011, http://edition.cnn.com/2001/ALLPOLITICS/04/24/bush.taiwan.abc.

[76] Rich Chang and Jason Pan, "Chinese Could Be Ready to Invade in 2020: MND," *Taipei Times*, March 5, 2014, http://www.taipeitimes.com/News/front/archives/2014/03/06/2003584974.

cruise missile defense, antisubmarine warfare, multi-domain awareness, and Taiwan's central role in the U.S. rebalancing toward Asia.

The fact is that no free and open society understands China as well as Taiwan does, which means that increasing collaboration and studying in Taiwan gives outsiders a unique opportunity to better understand the mainland. Unfortunately, few U.S. military officers conduct in-country training in Taiwan, and there are no known students attending Taiwan's National Defense University or other intermediate and senior service schools. More educational exchanges between the two defense establishments are warranted, particularly for junior and noncommissioned officers.[77]

Integrating Taiwan into the Regional Security Architecture

Taipei is actively seeking to contribute to Asian stability under the current U.S.-led regional security framework. Ma has stressed that "only a strong U.S. commitment, backed by its credibility in East Asia, can guarantee the peace and stability of this region."[78] Taiwan could make a number of contributions to a U.S.-led regional security framework. Taiwan is a principal security partner for the United States in the region that is willing and able to develop the kind of force needed for networked, integrated deep-interdiction operations in an anti-access/area-denial (A2/AD) environment. Taiwan's knowledge of single points of failure in the PLA's air and missile defense system could someday save many lives. By maintaining a capacity to interdict single points of failure in the PLA's A2/AD system, the ROC could relieve the United States of part of its heavy operational burden and reduce risks of escalation. For Taiwan, sufficient self-defense requires an ability to interdict and neutralize critical nodes in the PLA Second Artillery and other increasingly integrated operational systems opposite the island.

Taiwan is also uniquely positioned to contribute to regional situational awareness of the air, space, sea, and cyber domains. Peacetime air surveillance data can be fused with other sources of information to better understand PLA Air Force tactics and doctrine. Long-range UHF early-warning radar data could fill a gap in regional space surveillance. The ROC Navy has a firm grasp of the unique undersea geography and hydrological environment of the western Pacific. In the cyber domain, the U.S. Defense Department and broader cybersecurity establishment could benefit from the expertise possessed by Taiwan as the earliest and most

---

[77] Mark Stokes and Russell Hsiao, "Why U.S. Military Needs Taiwan," *Diplomat*, April 13, 2012, http://thediplomat.com/2012/04/why-u-s-military-needs-taiwan.

[78] "The ROC in Maritime Security Cooperation," National Policy Foundation, NPF Research Report, October 2012, http://www.npf.org.tw/post/2/11465.

intense target of Chinese computer network attacks. In addition, Taiwan's geographic position and willingness to contribute to a regional common operational picture, including maritime domain awareness, air surveillance, and space surveillance and tracking, could be of significant value for both disaster-response and military purposes.

Despite Taiwan's many potential positive contributions to regional security, an exacerbation of political and territorial disputes could constrain Taiwan in its attempts to further integrate itself into the regional security architecture. This dilemma was made evident during the first Ma administration in 2010 when Taipei protested a request from Tokyo that would allow Japan to expand its air defense identification zone (ADIZ) to include airspace above areas west of Yonaguni Island, which are under the jurisdiction of Taiwan's ADIZ.[79] The Ma administration protested the proposal on the grounds that the plan would limit Taiwan's airspace and infringe on the integrity of its national sovereignty.[80] However, the Ma administration's actions on this issue present an interesting contrast with its reaction to China's announcement of an ADIZ in late 2013. Indeed, even though China's ADIZ overlaps with Taiwan's own ADIZ, Ma asserted that it does not involve "airspace" or "territorial sovereignty."[81]

Furthermore, against the backdrop of increasing tensions in the maritime domain, in particular the South China Sea, there have been growing calls for the United States to "discuss with Taiwan whether it can clarify its position on the nine-dash line, to make clear that its claims are consistent with UNCLOS [the UN Convention on the Law of the Sea]."[82] As mentioned earlier, this proposal would likely create a trade-off for the United States—one that would be harder for the Ma administration than the opposition DPP to manage, as the KMT has more vested in the current configuration of cross-strait relations.

Nonetheless, among regional states, Taiwan has perhaps the greatest interest in the success of the U.S.-led regional security architecture. U.S. defense policy is designed to counter China's strategy of raising the cost of U.S. power-projection operations in the western Pacific to prohibitive levels,

---

[79] Yonaguni Island is Japan's westernmost island in the Ryukyu chain, situated 108 kilometers from the coast of the eastern Taiwan county of Hualien.

[80] Shih Hsiu-chuan, "Japan Extends ADIZ into Taiwan Space," *Taipei Times*, June 26, 2010, http://www.taipeitimes.com/News/front/archives/2010/06/26/2003476438.

[81] Chris Wang and Shih Hsiu-chuan, "China's ADIZ Not Connected to Sovereignty: Ma," *Taipei Times*, November 27, 2013, http://www.taipeitimes.com/News/front/archives/2013/11/27/2003577755. For an in-depth discussion on the impact of China's ADIZs on Taiwan, see Mark Stokes, "China's Air Defense Identification System: The Role of PLA Air Surveillance," Project 2049 Institute, May 5, 2014, http://www.project2049.net/documents/Stokes_China_Air_Defense_Identification_System_PLA_Air_Surveillance.pdf.

[82] Bader, "The U.S. and China's Nine-Dash Line."

thereby deterring any U.S. effort to meet its defense obligations to regional allies and partners, including Taiwan. Enhancing the resiliency of Taiwan's defense would not only deter Chinese aggression but enhance peace and stability by providing Taipei with the confidence necessary to more fully engage Beijing.[83]

Conclusions

The United States faces a number of challenges in meeting its security commitments in the Asia-Pacific. Beyond uncertainty, complexity, and rapid change, challenges include growing resource constraints and an increasingly assertive and capable PLA. At least one driver for rethinking U.S. defense strategy is the growing ability of the PLA to complicate U.S. ability to project joint power and operate in the region. China's emerging A2/AD capabilities could not only complicate the United States' ability to operate but also the ability of defense establishments in the region to deny the PLA air superiority and command of the seas. Anti-access threats, designed to prevent an opposing force from entering an operational area, include long-range precision-strike systems that could be employed against bases and moving targets at sea, such as aircraft carrier battle groups.

With the straightforward agreements in cross-strait negotiations concluded, Chinese leaders are stepping up pressure on the Ma administration to engage in more sensitive political dialogue. In the current context, there is a weak correlation between the growing economic interdependency between Taiwan and China and political integration between the two sides. While the U.S.-Taiwan relationship remains resilient, Taiwan and China are moving toward uncharted waters. In order to promote stability and restore balance, the United States should emphasize the benefits of soft balancing. The key is a more accurate representation in Washington of the status quo based on the objective reality.

China's refusal to renounce the use of force to compel unification is a source of instability in cross-strait relations. China is likely to increasingly rely on military and economic coercion to compel political concessions from Taiwan. Therefore, U.S. support in terms of Taiwan's defense, economic, and political interests is critical to maintaining balance and providing Taipei with the confidence to engage Beijing in cross-strait negotiations.

In light of the sovereignty gap that exists in the Taiwan Strait, which on the current trajectory will continue to widen in the future, Washington must carefully recalibrate how it assures the expectations of Taipei. The core U.S. interests should be that the representative democracy in Taiwan continues to

---

[83] Stokes and Hsiao, "Why U.S. Military Needs Taiwan."

consolidate and that the United States maintains the ROC's capacity to resist PRC political and military coercion. In the final analysis, refusal to address the widening sovereignty gap between Taiwan and China will become a serious source of instability in the medium to long term.

How, then, should the United States approach this problem? The status quo, as it has stood for the past 35 years, is unsustainable. The increasing imbalance between Taipei and Beijing in terms of the latter's growing military capabilities, China's economic leverage over Taiwan, and a widening sovereignty gap are subjugating Taiwan ever more to the PRC's coercive pressures. Despite the thaw in cross-strait tensions, Taipei is slipping further into a situation where it is faced with a Hobson's choice, and Washington, if it neglects to act, may be faced with a real dilemma. In the former case, although Beijing suggested that anything under the one-China framework is possible, the current general secretary continues to insist that the "one country, two systems" formula, which governs China's relations with Hong Kong, is the only model for China-Taiwan relations.[84] In a similar context, if the current trajectory continues and assuming that pressures on Beijing to change its policy toward Taiwan persist, the United States will face a dilemma in which the absence of real choice in Taiwan may force leaders in Washington between two absolutes, each with its own complex consequences.

In the final analysis, the current U.S. approach to Taiwan is being misguided by a false dilemma due in part to excessive policy deference to Beijing's one-China policy. If this trend persists, then Washington will more likely face a situation in which a real dilemma will ensue in the medium to long term. Washington should work to actively shore up Taiwan's de facto sovereignty not only by providing it with more military support through strengthening defense cooperation and arms sales but also by deploying soft-balancing means through economic agreements and expanding Taiwan's international space. Furthermore, by integrating Taiwan into the regional architecture, more stakeholders will help provide a balancing effect on the growing imbalance in the Taiwan Strait. As demonstrated by U.S. measures toward Taiwan, a more confident Taiwan is conducive to regional stability. Although Washington has expressed its preference for a particular outcome in Taiwan's presidential election in the past,[85] Washington should remain neutral in the island's upcoming election and not intervene in the

---

[84] "KMT Agrees on 'One China Framework,'" China Central Television, June 14, 2013, http://english. cntv.cn/program/china24/20130614/106261.shtml; and Lawrence Chung, "'One Country, Two Systems' Right Formula for Taiwan, Xi Jinping Reiterates," *South China Morning Post*, September 27, 2014, http://www.scmp.com/news/china/article/1601307/one-country-two-systems-right-formula-taiwan-xi-jinping-reiterates.

[85] Tony Liao and Lilian Wu, "U.S. to Have Voice in Taiwan's 2016 Presidential Election," Central News Agency, September 13, 2014, http://focustaiwan.tw/news/aipl/201409130014.aspx.

democratic process. Taiwan is a vibrant democracy, and its citizens are capable of making their own decisions on the issues. In sum, the United States should move toward a more normal and objective representation of the status quo in the Taiwan Strait.

EXECUTIVE SUMMARY

This chapter examines the development of U.S.-Vietnam relations and discusses how changes in the regional balance of power, as well as changes within Vietnam's domestic political system, since the end of the Vietnam War have driven both Washington and Hanoi to pursue a closer and more strategically significant relationship.

MAIN ARGUMENT:

U.S.-Vietnam relations have come a long way, from enmity to partnership, thanks to two major geopolitical shifts that have created a convergence of strategic interests between both sides: Vietnam beginning to overcome its mistrust of U.S. intentions and commitment, and the rise of China and assertive Chinese behavior in the South China Sea driving worries in both Washington and Hanoi. It is in the interest of the U.S. to seek a strong, stable, and independent Vietnam that is capable and willing to stand up to Chinese pressure. Measures must be taken to improve Vietnam's military and reduce mistrust between the two countries without losing sight of the need to promote the further democratization of Vietnam.

POLICY IMPLICATIONS:

- As the U.S. seeks to hedge against the rise of China as the dominating power in Asia, Vietnam can be an important partner in the construction of a multipolar security structure to maintain peace and preserve U.S. influence in the region.

- Increased security cooperation depends on building mutual trust and convincing Vietnam that the U.S. has no strategic interest in undermining the current regime. At the same time, Vietnam must understand that the lack of progress in human rights is a major impediment to closer bilateral relations.

- The U.S. should find ways to include Vietnam in the Trans-Pacific Partnership and provide technical advice to help Vietnam undertake the economic, legal, and political reforms necessary to create an environment conducive to increased U.S. investment.

U.S.-Vietnam Relations:
Evolving Perceptions and Interests

Nguyen Manh Hung

Relations between the United States and the Socialist Republic of Vietnam have come a long way since the end of the Vietnam War, moving from enmity to partnership. This process has proceeded in stages. Normalization of diplomatic relations came first in 1995, followed by normalization of trade relations in 2006. The improvement of military relations came last. Because the years of war against the United States created in the minds of Vietnamese Communist leaders deep distrust of U.S. intentions, progress in bilateral relations has mostly taken place after Vietnam worked to overcome its own reluctance and distrust of the United States. In addition, the China factor looms large because both the United States and Vietnam have to pay attention to the sensitivity and concern of China over the appearance of a potential alliance between them against China.

This chapter first discusses the evolution of U.S.-Vietnam relations in the diplomatic, economic, and military spheres. The second section examines the major factors affecting the dynamics of U.S.-Vietnam relations. The chapter concludes with a discussion of policy options for the United States to strengthen and deepen bilateral relations in order to make Vietnam an effective partner in the emerging regional security structure that could serve the strategic interests of both countries.

Nguyen Manh Hung is Professor Emeritus of Government and International Relations at George Mason University and Nonresident Senior Associate at the Center for Strategic and International Studies. He can be reached at <hnguyen@gmu.edu>.

The Long Road to the Normalization of U.S.-Vietnam Relations

Diplomatic Relations

During the first years after the Vietnam War, bilateral U.S.-Vietnam relations were characterized by miscalculations and lost opportunities. Fresh from its historic victory over the U.S. superpower, Vietnam believed itself to be the dominant power not only in Indochina but across Southeast Asia, and its foreign policy reflected this newfound position. Instead of accepting an invitation to join the Association of Southeast Asian Nations (ASEAN), Vietnam accused the organization of being an instrument of American imperialism and demanded its replacement by a new regional group. Hanoi also attempted to set preconditions for the normalization of diplomatic relations with the United States, demanding that Washington fulfill its pledge to provide postwar aid of $3.25 billion.[1] The Ford administration was in no mood to be accommodating, rejecting Hanoi's demand on the grounds that Vietnam had massively violated the Paris Peace Agreement. In addition, the United States maintained that there could be no normalization of diplomatic relations without a full accounting of Americans missing in action (MIA) during the war.

In 1977 the new Carter administration began to ease travel and mail restrictions to Vietnam, and stopped vetoing Vietnam's application for United Nations membership. In March of that year, Carter appointed Leonard Woodcock, former president of the United Auto Workers, to head the first official U.S. delegation to visit Vietnam since the war and clear the way for the normalization of relations. As a gesture of goodwill, Vietnam returned eleven sets of MIA remains. Negotiations to normalize relations began in May 1977, but Vietnam repeated its demands for war reparations or reconstruction aid. To prevent the administration from acceding to these demands, Congress voted to forbid the use of funds to provide assistance to Vietnam. Vietnam's misjudgment of its own importance and standing in U.S. politics, therefore, spoiled an opportunity to normalize relations with the United States under the Carter administration.[2]

---

[1] Hanoi's request was based on a message from President Richard Nixon to Prime Minister Pham Van Dong on February 1, 1973, in which the president described the "principles which will govern United States participation in the reconstruction of North Vietnam," including the promise to contribute to "postwar reconstruction in North Vietnam in the range of $3.25 billion of grant aid over five years." This estimate, however, was "subject to revision and to detailed discussion between the Government of the United States and the Government of the Democratic Republic of Vietnam." The letter was released by the U.S. Department of State on May 19, 1977. See Richard M. Nixon to Pham Van Dong, Letter, February 1, 1973, published in the *New York Times*, May 20, 1977.

[2] For a detailed analysis of this period, see Frederick Z. Brown, *Second Chance: The United States and Indochina in the 1990s* (New York: Council on Foreign Relations, 1989), 21–32.

In 1978, Vietnam and the United States parted ways. Failing to normalize relations on its terms, Vietnam turned to the Soviet bloc for support, joining the Council for Mutual Economic Assistance in July and signing a 25-year friendship treaty with the Soviet Union in November. At the same time, the United States moved rapidly to restore formal diplomatic relations with China in an effort to counter the rising Soviet influence in Asia. Vietnam's invasion of Cambodia in December 1978, the Sino-Vietnamese border war in February 1979, and the Soviet invasion of Afghanistan in December 1979 saw Vietnam and the United States on opposite sides of the U.S.-Soviet rivalry and ushered in a period of intense hostility. In Cambodia, the United States joined forces with China and ASEAN to contain Vietnam, perceived as a proxy for Soviet expansion in Southeast Asia.[3] It announced a "three no's" policy (no trade, no aid, and no normalization of diplomatic relations) and led a campaign to isolate Vietnam diplomatically and economically, making the country increasingly dependent on the Soviet bloc.

By 1982 the Soviet Union—Vietnam's main source of international support—had entered exploratory talks on the normalization of relations with China and begun to cooperate with China and the United States to end the war in Cambodia. Meanwhile, China sought to further isolate Vietnam by moving closer to Laos, Vietnam's smaller neighbor and protégé, and by seeking improved relations with the Soviet Union and Eastern European countries. Under these circumstances, Vietnam had to accommodate the changing relationships between the great powers and extricate itself from diplomatic and economic isolation.

When President Ronald Reagan came to power, he declared the Vietnam War to have been a "noble cause" and pledged to search for Americans held as prisoners of war (POW) or who were still officially listed as MIA. In February 1982, Vietnam welcomed the first official U.S. delegation on the POW/MIA issue. Whereas before it was Vietnam that set the preconditions for normalization (war reparations), now it was the United States that set the preconditions. The Reagan administration insisted that the "fullest possible" accounting of American servicemen be viewed as a humanitarian issue to be resolved apart from political issues. Washington also demanded that Vietnam withdraw its troops from Cambodia and contribute to a political solution to the Cambodian conflict before talks on normalization of diplomatic relations could take place.

---

[3] Deng Xiaoping at the time claimed, "China is NATO in the East, and Vietnam is Cuba in the East." See Tran Quang Co, "Reminiscence and Reflection" [Hoi Uc va Suy Nghi] (unpublished manuscript), 5. Vietnam's former deputy foreign minister Tran Quang Co's unpublished memoirs were circulated on January 23, 2001, and revised on May 22, 2003. They were circulated on the Internet at http://khotailieu.com/luan-van-do-an-bao-cao/van-hoa-nghe-thuat/lich-su/hoi-ky-tran-quang-co.html.

Two additional factors forced a basic change in Vietnam's foreign policy and accelerated the process of rapprochement between Vietnam and the United States. First, faced with a severe economic crisis as a result of mismanagement and the cost of the Cambodian war, as well as pressure from the Soviet Union for economic reforms, in December 1986 Vietnam launched the *doi moi* (renovation) process, gradually moving the country away from a command economy toward a market system. The need for trade, foreign aid, and investment, especially from the West, had become critical. Second, Vietnamese leaders were increasingly concerned by antigovernment demonstrations in Hungary, East Germany, and Poland in the spring and summer of 1988. The subsequent collapse of Communist regimes in Eastern Europe in 1989 and the disintegration of the Soviet Union in 1991 forced Vietnam to reorient its foreign relations away from the defunct Soviet bloc toward ASEAN and the West.

The Seventh National Congress of the Communist Party of Vietnam (CPV) in 1991 officially endorsed the new line of "multidirectional foreign policy" within the framework of "independence, self-reliance, multilateralization, and diversification." Vietnam wanted to be a "friend with all countries, regardless of their sociopolitical systems."[4] The political report to the party congress emphasized that "moving toward normalization of relations with the United States is one of the important goals of our foreign policy."[5] That same year, the United States agreed to open a technical office in Hanoi to search for MIAs and gave Vietnam a roadmap listing steps to be taken to establish full diplomatic relations. By 1993, Vietnam had fulfilled the major conditions for talks on normalization with the United States: complete withdrawal of troops from Cambodia, conclusion of the agreements ending the Cambodian conflict, and the establishment of a coalition government in Cambodia following a UN-supervised election. The United States reciprocated by relaxing travel restrictions to Vietnam, authorizing certain educational exchange programs, and declaring its readiness to take steps toward normalizing relations.

By that time, the United States had a new administration. President Bill Clinton was sympathetic to the idea of normalizing relations with Vietnam, but he needed political support at home. Normalization was also supported by the U.S. business community, which saw investment opportunities in a new market, and some members of Congress who had fought during the Vietnam

---

[4] Communist Party of Vietnam, *Van kien dai hoi dang thoi ky doi moi—Dai hoi VI, VII, VIII, IX* [Documents of the Party National Congresses in the Renovation Era: The Sixth, Seventh, Eighth, Ninth Congresses] (Hanoi: Nha xuat ban chinh tri quoc gia, 2005), 294.

[5] Nguyen Dinh Bin, ed., *Ngoai giao Viet Nam, 1945–2000* [Vietnam's Foreign Policy, 1945–2000] (Hanoi: Nha xuat ban chinh tri quoc gia, 2005), 352.

War.[6] In February 1994, after the Senate passed a nonbinding resolution urging the president to lift the embargo on trade, Clinton did so. Admiral Charles Larson, commander of U.S. forces in the Pacific, became the first active duty U.S. military officer to visit Vietnam since the war. In May 1995, Vietnam gave a visiting U.S. presidential delegation a trove of documents on MIAs hailed by the Pentagon as the most detailed and informative of their kind. In June, Senators John Kerry and John McCain, two decorated veterans of the Vietnam War, wrote a letter urging the president to normalize relations and introduced a supporting resolution in Congress. With this support, Clinton announced normalization of diplomatic relations with Vietnam in June 1995, and the first U.S. embassy in a unified Vietnam was opened in Hanoi.

Economic Relations

The collapse of the Soviet Union left the United States the sole reigning superpower in a post–Cold War world in which market economics and globalization became the prevailing trends. After the collapse of Communism in Europe, Vietnamese leaders realized that regime legitimacy depended more on performance than ideology, and Vietnam needed a stable international environment to develop its economy and improve its people's standard of living. Consequently, it was in the interests of both the United States and Vietnam—but especially Vietnam—to strengthen their economic ties.

In 1996 the United States gave Vietnam a blueprint for a trade agreement. Between April 1996 and October 1997, Vietnam cooperated with the United States to speed up the resettlement of eligible Vietnamese who were still in camps of first asylum in Hong Kong and Southeast Asia or who had recently returned to Vietnam. In response to this cooperation, in March 1998 Clinton announced a waiver that excluded Vietnam from the Jackson-Vanik Amendment, paving the way for the Overseas Private Investment Corporation, the Export-Import Bank, and the U.S. Department of Agriculture to deal with the country.

In 1999 a bilateral trade agreement (BTA) was supposed to be signed by Prime Minister Phan Van Khai and President Clinton on the sidelines of the Asia-Pacific Economic Cooperation (APEC) summit in Auckland, New Zealand. Opposition within the CPV leadership criticized the BTA as "an American plot to change Vietnam's political regime and to promote a market economy to undermine our socialist-oriented market economy" and succeeded in derailing the anticipated signing ceremony. Former minister

---

[6] A good discussion of congressional involvement in the process of normalizing relations between the United States and Vietnam is provided in Kelly S. Nelson, "U.S.-Vietnamese Normalization," *Asian Affairs: An American Review* 19, no. 1 (1992).

of trade Truong Dinh Tuyen revealed that he had to persuade those who opposed the BTA that "no country...including 'our good friend in the north'... could develop economically if it cannot export goods to the American market."[7] The signing of a BTA between China and the United States only one month after the Auckland summit effectively removed opposition within the CPV leadership. In July 2000, Vietnam and the United States finally signed a comprehensive BTA, ushering in an era of economic cooperation between the two countries and laying the groundwork for further negotiation to facilitate Vietnam's entry into the World Trade Organization (WTO). This period was crowned by the first visit of a sitting U.S. president, Bill Clinton, to a unified Vietnam in November 2000, followed in July 2005 by Prime Minister Phan Van Khai becoming the first top leader of Communist Vietnam to visit the United States and to be received by the U.S. president.

U.S.-Vietnam economic relations continued to improve during the George W. Bush administration. In 2006 a flurry of visits to Vietnam by high-level executives of large U.S. companies and trade officials was followed by the arrival of President Bush to attend the APEC summit in November of that year. Vietnam elected a new group of leaders committed to global integration, was removed from the list of "countries of particular concern" by the U.S. State Department, concluded trade negotiations with the United States to join the WTO, and was accorded "permanent normal trade relations." This final event completed the process of normalizing economic relations between the United States and Vietnam and helped ensure Vietnam's integration into the global economy.

Trade relations have proved beneficial to both countries. Two-way trade jumped from $1.5 billion in 2001, when the BTA went into effect, to $2.9 billion in 2002 and $5.7 billion in 2003 when the United States replaced Japan as Vietnam's largest export market. Altogether, bilateral trade between 2001 and 2009 increased tenfold, from $1.5 billion to over $15 billion. Four years later, in 2013, that number increased to $29.6 billion.[8] In contrast with its mounting trade deficit with China, Vietnam enjoys a trade surplus with the United States. In 2013, Vietnam ran a $23.7 billion trade deficit with China while accumulating a $19.6 billion trade surplus with the United States. In 2000, before the signing of the BTA and Vietnam's entry into the WTO, U.S.

---

[7] Huynh Phan, "Chuyen chua bao gio ke cua truong doan dam phan BTA" [Untold Story of the Head of Vietnamese BTA Negotiation Team], *Tuan Vietnam*, December 27, 2011, http://tuanvietnam. vietnamnet.vn/2011-12-26-chuyen-chua-bao-gio-ke-cua-truong-doan-dam-phan-bta.

[8] See U.S. Census Bureau, "Trade in Goods with Vietnam," http://www.census.gov/foreign-trade/ balance/c5520.html.

direct investment in Vietnam ranked ninth at $126 million. In 2011, it rose to seventh place at $747 million and then reached $1.1 billion in 2012.[9]

In March 2010 the United States and Vietnam completed the first round of talks on the Trans-Pacific Partnership (TPP). From Vietnam's perspective, joining the TPP will force the country to open its market faster and wider to foreign goods, but at the same time Vietnam will have access to other members' markets, especially that of the United States, which is important for export-oriented businesses. Competition will also force necessary reforms in the Vietnamese economy.[10] The Peterson Institute for International Economics forecasts that by 2025 Vietnam would be 14% richer if it were to join the TPP.[11] Beyond the potential economic benefits, joining the group would enhance the country's status in the region politically and diplomatically for two reasons: First, Vietnam would share membership with the United States in the only multilateral organization in the Asia-Pacific region that does not include China. Second, it would be part of a group where most of the members are non-Communist democracies or quasi-democracies. This would give Vietnam a chance to learn from these countries' economic and political experiences.

Military Relations

The first contact between the U.S. and Vietnamese militaries under the Reagan administration was driven by the United States' desire to account for Americans MIA during the Vietnam War and by Vietnam's desire to find a way to open talks with the United States. However, in 1999 and 2000, Vietnam was pressured into signing two treaties on land and sea borders that ceded some of its territory and territorial waters to China. Vietnamese leaders were aware of the unpopularity of the treaties with their people but were also concerned about China's "peaceful rise" and the increased cooperation between China and the United States in the aftermath of the September 11 terrorist attacks. (China was among the first countries that called and offered support for the U.S. war against terrorism.) They were also worried about China's intentions with regard to the disputed Paracel and Spratly Islands

---

[9] See Nguyen Phi Lan, "Foreign Direct Investment and Its Linkages to Economic Growth in Vietnam," University of South Australia, Center for Regulation and Market Analysis, November 2006; U.S. Trade Representative (USTR), "Vietnam," http://www.ustr.gov/sites/default/files/2013%20NTE%20 Vietnam%20Final.pdf; and USTR, "Vietnam," http://www.ustr.gov/countries-regions/southeast-asia-pacific/vietnam.

[10] Advisory Committee on CSTMQT, "Viet Nam va TPP: Nhung suy tinh thiet hon" [Vietnam and TPP: Calculation of Benefits and Losses], WTO Center–VCCI, http://www.trungtamwto.vn/tpp/ viet-nam-va-tpp-nhung-suy-tinh-thiet-hon.

[11] See David Brown, "Vietnam's Need for TPP," *Asia Sentinel*, September 2, 2013, http://www.asiasentinel.com/index.php?option=com_content&task=view&id=5680&Itemid=238.

and certainly realized their disadvantaged position as a small nation in a U.S.-China-Vietnam triangle. These concerns provided the justification for Vietnam to move closer to the United States militarily.

The first breakthrough in U.S.-Vietnam military relations came with the visit to the United States by Vietnam's defense minister Pham Van Tra in November 2003 and the friendship visit of the USS *Vandegrift* to Ho Chi Minh port. General Tra was the first top Vietnamese military leader to visit the United States since the end of the Vietnam War, while the USS *Vandegrift* was the first U.S. warship to visit Vietnam for peaceful purposes, clearing the way for future port visits by U.S. military vessels.

Vietnamese authorities stress two important achievements of Prime Minister Khai's 2005 visit to the United States to honor the tenth anniversary of U.S.-Vietnam relations. First, the visit marked a new phase in bilateral relations when the concept of "partnership" was mentioned for the first time in the joint communiqué. Second, President Bush reaffirmed "the support of the United States government for Vietnam's security and territorial integrity."[12] The fact that this U.S. support was only mentioned in the Vietnamese-language version of the communiqué but omitted in the official U.S. release indicates that Vietnam seriously wanted public support that the United States was unwilling to provide at that time.[13] Khai also agreed to send Vietnamese military officers to the United States for language and medical services training.

One year after Khai's visit, U.S. secretary of defense Donald Rumsfeld visited Hanoi and agreed to expand military relations on "all levels."[14] Admiral William Fallon, commander of U.S. forces in the Pacific, visited Vietnam a month later.[15] In 2007 the United States invited Vietnam to send military observers to a regional naval exercise and amended State Department regulations to allow the sale of nonlethal defense equipment to Vietnam, including helicopter parts and coastal patrol crafts.[16] Meanwhile, Vietnam agreed to conduct a joint naval search for MIAs off its coast.

When Prime Minister Nguyen Tan Dung visited the United States in June 2008, he made an unprecedented trip to the Pentagon. In the joint

---

[12] Nguyen Vu Tung, ed., *Khuon kho quan he doi tac cua Viet Nam* [Framework of Vietnam's Partnership Relations] (Hanoi: Hoc vien quan he quoc te, 2007), 117, 127.

[13] See "Tuyen bo chung Viet-My" [Vietnam-U.S. Joint Statement], Vietnam News Agency, June 22, 2005, http://vietbao.vn/The-gioi/Tuyen-bo-chung-Viet-My/10914978/159; and "Joint Statement between the United States of America and the Socialist Republic of Vietnam," U.S. Department of State, June 21, 2005, http://2001-2009.state.gov/p/eap/rls/rm/2005/48443.htm.

[14] Michael R. Gordon, "Rumsfeld, Visiting Vietnam, Seals Accord to Deepen Military Cooperation," *New York Times*, June 6, 2006.

[15] See Vietnamese news accounts in *Tuoi Tre*, July 17, 2006; and *Ha Noi Moi*, July 17, 2006.

[16] "U.S. Seeks Closer Defence Ties with Vietnam: Pentagon Official," Agence France-Presse, March 23, 2007.

statement between Dung and Bush, the two leaders endorsed the creation of "new political-military and policy planning talks, which allow for more frequent and in-depth discussions on security and strategic issues." In particular, Bush reiterated the U.S. government's "support for Vietnam's national sovereignty, security, and territorial integrity."[17] Five months after Dung's visit, in October 2008, the first U.S.-Vietnam political, security, and defense dialogue took place in Hanoi, followed by a December 2008 visit to the United States by Vietnam's defense minister, General Phung Quang Thanh. The first U.S.-Vietnam Defense Policy Dialogue took place in August 2010, with discussions focused on enhancing bilateral cooperation in the areas of regional security, peacekeeping, humanitarian assistance and disaster relief, maritime security, search and rescue, nonproliferation, counternarcotics, transnational crime, U.S. naval ship visits to Vietnam, demining, and other areas of mutual interest.

Just a few months prior to this 2010 dialogue, both Vietnam and the United States raised the South China Sea issue at the ASEAN Regional Forum in Hanoi. Secretary of State Hillary Clinton angered China by stating that "the United States has a national interest in freedom of navigation, open access to Asia's maritime commons, and respect for international law in the South China Sea." Aiming at China, she added: "We oppose the use of force or threat of force by any claimant," and "legitimate claims to maritime space in the South China Sea should be derived solely from legitimate claims to land features." This position was clearly in favor of ASEAN and particularly Vietnam. Clinton also praised Vietnam as a "dynamic and great nation" and reported that "the partnership and cooperation with Vietnam is increasing day by day."[18]

In September 2011 a memorandum of understanding was signed between the two militaries to promote defense cooperation in five priority fields, which included "the establishment of a high-ranking dialogue mechanism...sea security, search and rescue, studying and exchanging experience in the United Nations peace keeping activities, and humanitarian aid and disaster relief."[19] During President Truong Tan Sang's visit to the United States in July 2013, the leaders of both countries issued a joint statement committing to open a new phase of bilateral relations and "form a U.S.-Vietnam Comprehensive Partnership to provide an overarching framework for advancing the

---

[17] "Joint Statement between the United States of America and the Socialist Republic of Vietnam," U.S. Embassy Hanoi, June 25, 2008, http://vietnam.usembassy.gov/jointstatement_.html.

[18] See Hillary Rodham Clinton (remarks following the ASEAN Regional Forum, Hanoi, Vietnam, July 23, 2010), http://m.state.gov/md145095.htm; and Greg Torode, "Clinton Stand on a Chinese 'Core Interest' Causes Tension at Forum," *South China Morning Post*, July 24, 2010.

[19] See "Vietnam, U.S. Ink Deal to Boost Defense Ties," *Thanh Nien News*, September 22, 2011, http://www.thanhniennews.com/politics/vietnam-us-ink-deal-to-boost-defense-ties-10500.html.

relationship."[20] Immediately after Sang's trip, the U.S. ambassador to Vietnam, David Shear, indicated that Vietnam had expressed an interest in the lifting of U.S. restrictions on lethal weapon sales. But while pledging to give serious consideration to the request, Ambassador Shear cautioned that "we will need to see some progress in human rights on Vietnam's side."[21]

In U.S.-Vietnam military relations, Vietnam has tended to be the initiator. Chinese pressures in 1999 and 2000, forcing Vietnam to sign two unequal border treaties, prompted the country to improve its bargaining position by seeking closer military relations with the United States, beginning with the first U.S. visit by Defense Minister Pham Van Tra in 2003. In 2009, China's public announcement claiming 80% of the South China Sea and subsequent aggressive behavior to impose this claim, which threatened freedom of navigation, led to a convergence of strategic interests between the United States and Vietnam and served as a driver for closer and deeper U.S.-Vietnam military cooperation. But disagreements over human rights have prevented this cooperation from reaching its full potential, as will be discussed in the next section.

Influencing Factors in U.S.-Vietnam Relations

Vietnam's Perceptions of U.S. Intentions

As a result of past hostilities from two wars—the Vietnam War and the war with Cambodia—and perceptions of the causes of the collapse of European Communism, some Vietnamese leaders suspect that the United States wants to overthrow the world's remaining Communist regimes, including that of Vietnam. Party resolutions, media analyses, and official statements repeatedly refer to the danger of "peaceful evolution" (that is, regime change by subversion) and plots of "hostile forces" to overthrow the regime. In particular, the Vietnamese government views U.S. promotion of democracy and pressure to improve human rights as a means to this end.

This concern, however, does not accurately reflect U.S. strategic interests. While the United States would like to see Vietnam become more liberal and democratic, it has no plans to overthrow the current government. Instead, the United States wants a strong, stable, and independent Vietnam. A violent change of government does not serve U.S. interests, for it would

---

[20] See "Joint Statement by President Barack Obama of the United States of America and President Truong Tan Sang of the Socialist Republic of Vietnam," White House, Office of the Press Secretary, July 25, 2013. When General Do Ba Ty, Vietnam's chief of the general staff, visited the U.S. Defense Department a month earlier on June 20, he expressed his country's desire to develop a comprehensive relationship with the United States, including in defense ties.

[21] James Hookway, "Vietnam Rights Record Cools U.S. Ties," *Wall Street Journal*, August 8, 2013.

create a vacuum that would likely be filled wholly or partly by forces hostile to the United States.

Although Vietnamese leaders see the United States as a destabilizing factor in domestic politics, the United States can also be seen as a stabilizing factor in Vietnam's foreign policy. Despite ongoing concerns about the seriousness and resoluteness of U.S. intentions in Southeast Asia, some Vietnamese strategists view the United States as a potential counterweight to China. In recent years, the U.S. policy of pivoting or rebalancing to Asia, which has included several visits to Vietnam by high-level U.S. officials, has emboldened Vietnam to move closer to the United States. Having bitterly complained that the "neutral" U.S. stance in the South China Sea disputes was tantamount to acquiescing to creeping Chinese expansion, Vietnamese leaders, especially the liberationists (those who want to extricate Vietnam from China's orbit), were encouraged by President Barack Obama's pledge to honor U.S. treaty commitments to defend Japan and the Philippines during his April 2014 trip to Asia, the United States warning China against unilaterally declaring a new air defense identification zone (ADIZ) in the South China Sea, U.S. criticism of China's "provocative" and "aggressive" actions, and the provision of much needed support for Vietnam's position in its conflict with China over the HD-981 oil rig. These developments occurred at a time when Vietnam felt isolated and deprived of the traditional support of Russia, which was busy building ties with China to counter the power and influence of the United States and the West.[22]

In this context of improving relations, Vietnam has expressed the desire to form a strategic partnership with the United States.[23] In a speech at the Shangri-La Dialogue, Prime Minister Dung announced Vietnam's decision to participate in UN peacekeeping missions, and the United States promptly organized a trip for a Vietnamese delegation to observe a mission in South Sudan. In December 2013, in a joint press conference with his Vietnamese

---

[22] For years, Vietnam has been complaining about U.S. neutrality and the lack of U.S. support for its position. See "Tuong Huong than phien ve Bien Dong" [General Huong Complained about the South China Sea], BBC (Vietnamese version), August 31, 2011, http://www.bbc.co.uk/vietnamese/vietnam/2011/08/110831_us_vn_general_nguyenvanhuong.shtml. Regarding Russia's reaction, the newspaper *Giao Duc Viet Nam* published an article criticizing RIA Novosti for "distorting history and slandering Vietnam by calling it a 'China's Ukraine' where anti-China protests in some industrial parks turned to violence against Chinese workers, prompting China to take action to rescue its citizens from violence in Vietnam." Binh An, "Tại sao hang tin uy tin Nga xuyen tạc lịch su, vu khong Viet Nam?" [Why Is a Prestigious Russian News Agency Distorting History, Slandering Vietnam?] *Giao Duc Viet Nam*, May 24, 2014, http://giaoduc.net.vn/Van-hoa/Tai-sao-hang-tin-uy-tin-Nga-xuyen-tac-lich-su-vu-khong-Viet-Nam-post144967.gd (translation by the author).

[23] The desire to modernize the military, "bringing the People's Army into the 21st century," was a key driver of Vietnam's interest in enhanced defense cooperation with the United States. See William Jordan, Lewis M. Stern, and Walter Lohman, "U.S.-Vietnam Defense Relations: Investing in Strategic Alignment," Heritage Foundation, Backgrounder, no. 2707, July 18, 2012, http://www.heritage.org/research/reports/2012/07/us-vietnam-defense-relations-investing-in-strategic-alignment.

counterpart in Hanoi, Secretary of State Kerry announced an aid package of $32.5 million to Southeast Asian nations, more than half of which ($18 million) was allocated to Vietnam in order to strengthen the country's coastal patrols and help its coast guard react more quickly in search and rescue missions.

But as Vietnam moves closer to the United States, it remains wary of the possibility of becoming a pawn to be sacrificed on the altar of great-power politics, as was the case for North Vietnam in 1954 and South Vietnam in 1973. This concern is reinforced by a general perception of the United States as a declining power seeking accommodation with a rising China through the so-called new type of great-power relationship. So long as this mistrust of and uncertainty about U.S. capabilities and commitment remain, U.S.-Vietnam relations will not reach the same state as those between the United States and many of its other Asian partners.[24]

Vietnam is particularly unhappy with the fact that the United States still refuses to sell it lethal weapons. General Do Ba Ty, chief of the general staff of the Vietnam People's Army, argued that normalization of military relations will not be complete as long as the U.S. government does not trust Vietnam sufficiently to sell arms to the country. While the U.S. president could decide to sell arms, Congress is not willing to support such a move until Vietnam improves its human rights performance. Consequently, human rights, along with the China threat, constitute the two chief factors affecting the level of cooperation between the United States and Vietnam. The next two sections will discuss each factor, followed by a brief discussion of the strategic importance of Vietnam for the United States.

The China Factor

Vietnam and China enjoy a special—that is to say, not entirely positive—kind of relationship based on history, geography, and ideology. China provided generous support to the Vietnamese Communists during both the war against France and the Vietnam War. At that time, relations between the two countries were hailed by both sides as being as "close as lips and teeth." But bilateral relations soured during the Cambodian War and the Sino-Vietnamese border wars. Recently, China has emerged as a threat to Vietnam's territorial integrity. China continues to occupy the Paracel

---

[24] During the author's several trips to Vietnam, he was repeatedly asked two questions: (1) Is the promotion of human rights a U.S. scheme to undermine the Vietnamese regime? (2) If Vietnam becomes a partner of the United States, could it become a pawn in a deal between the big powers? As for the capability and intention of the United States helping Vietnam, the author was reminded of the old Vietnamese saying that "distant water can't stop fire in the neighborhood" (*nuoc xa khong cuu duoc lua gan*).

Islands, which belonged to Vietnam before 1974, and in August 2007, against Hanoi's protest, announced plans to develop tourist facilities on the islands. The latest incident occurred in May 2014 when China placed its HD-981 oil rig for exploratory work near the Paracels in violation of Vietnam's exclusive economic zone and continental shelf rights under the United Nations Convention on the Law of the Sea (UNCLOS).

Previously, in 1979, China sent troops across the border to punish Vietnam for invading Cambodia. Chinese troops never completely withdrew from some key strategic and symbolic positions taken during this border war. Secret or unreported wars and skirmishes continued between the two countries between 1984 and 1987. In 1988, China engaged Vietnam in a battle over the Johnson South Reef and occupied a number of islets. In 1997 and 1998, China set up a platform near territory in the Spratly Islands claimed by Vietnam and granted ARCO oil and gas exploration rights in disputed waters. China, for its part, protested vehemently in 2007 when Vietnam and a BP-led consortium prepared to develop an offshore gas and oil field in an area near the Spratlys about 370 kilometers from Vietnam's coast, forcing BP to temporarily suspend the project. In 2008, China also pressured ExxonMobil to withdraw from an exploration contract with Vietnam, and Chinese naval vessels began to arrest Vietnamese fishing boats for operating in waters near the Spratlys.

Yet even though many in Vietnam regard China as a threat and resent its encroachments, Vietnamese leaders have found it necessary to accommodate China. Since 1988 and especially since the collapse of the Soviet Union in 1991, they have often downplayed the perception of China as a great power pursuing hegemony and have instead looked to it as a savior of socialism, despite its rejection of Vietnam's proposal to form a socialist alliance.[25] For these leaders, following the collapse of Communist regimes in Eastern Europe, the danger of peaceful evolution far outweighed the threat of China's growing regional hegemony: in their view, the prevailing trend that led to the collapse of Communism in Eastern Europe presented an immediate danger to Vietnamese Communism. Building a socialist alliance with China took precedence over the publicly announced policy of openness, diversification, and multilateralization in foreign relations. While worried about and regularly protesting Chinese moves in the South China Sea, Vietnamese officials argued that one can change friends, but one cannot change geography.[26] Every time

---

[25] Chinese leaders told Vietnamese leaders that they were "comrades but not allies." Alexander L. Vuving, "Changing Synthesis of Strategies: Vietnam's China Policy Since 1990" (paper presented at the conference "Regenerations: New Leaders, New Visions in Southeast Asia," Council for Southeast Asia Studies, Yale University, New Haven, November 11–12, 2005), 11.

[26] Author's interviews, conducted in Hanoi in summer 2006.

it prepared to make a move toward the United States, Vietnam had to cast an anxious look toward China.

There are, however, limits to Vietnam's patience. Tension rose after the May 2009 deadline to submit claims to the UN Commission on the Limits of the Continental Shelf. China drew a "U-shaped line" (also called the nine-dash line) to delineate its maritime boundaries, staking a claim to 80% of the South China Sea and encroaching on Vietnam's 200-mile exclusive economic zone. China also began to aggressively assert its rights by unilaterally imposing fishing bans, sending boats to patrol disputed areas around both the Paracel and Spratly Islands, seizing Vietnamese boats, and harassing Vietnamese fishermen. The Vietnamese National Assembly began to discuss draft legislation establishing a People's Self-Defense Force to protect Vietnam's sea boundaries, and open letters to Vietnam's leaders by prominent Vietnamese intellectuals and anti-Chinese demonstrations in Hanoi and Ho Chi Minh City in 2011 and 2012, despite government repression and arrests, put huge pressure on the leadership to stand up to China.

In 2012, Vietnam became increasingly alarmed over China's aggressive behavior in the South China Sea territorial disputes. The Scarborough Shoal incident in May 2012 exposed the helplessness of the Philippines when it had to stand alone against China without the support of ASEAN. The disunity and disarray displayed during the July 2012 foreign ministers' meeting in Phnom Penh showed ASEAN's vulnerability to China's divide-and-rule tactic.[27] Vietnam responded in a keynote address by Prime Minister Dung on June 1, 2013, at the Shangri-La Dialogue. For the first time, a top Vietnamese leader indirectly but openly denounced China's behavior in a multilateral forum. While affirming that Vietnam's foreign policy was basically defensive and that it would not ally with any country against any other country, he suggested that ASEAN must be strengthened to play the role of an honest broker in building strategic trust and declared, in a nod to the United States, that Vietnam sought to form strategic partnerships with all permanent members of the UN Security Council.

Two months after Dung's hard-hitting speech, President Sang visited China and signed a number of agreements to implement a Vietnam-China "comprehensive strategic partnership." Yet apparently all was not well during the visit, because afterward the Vietnamese media began to publish articles

---

[27] For a detailed discussion of the Scarborough Shoal incident and its implications, see Nguyen Manh Hung, "ASEAN's Scarborough Shoal Failure?" *Diplomat*, June 16, 2012, http://thediplomat.com/asean-beat/2012/06/16/aseans-scarborough-failure.

highly critical of China.[28] In an unprecedented move, on July 12, the well-connected newspaper *Dat Viet* published an article that speculated on two possible scenarios involving a Chinese invasion and even described the ways in which Vietnam could "take revenge" despite Chinese technical superiority, warning that "the enemy will pay a heavy price."[29] A hasty visit was organized to bring Sang to the United States where he agreed with Obama to open a new phase of bilateral relations and form a comprehensive partnership to provide an overarching framework for advancing the relationship.[30] While the results of the trip were less than anticipated, there were some positive developments in U.S.-Vietnam relations. It appears that while Vietnamese distrust of U.S. intentions and staying power—and concern over Chinese sensibilities—could still push the two countries apart, China's aggressive behavior has drawn Vietnam closer to the United States.

Nonetheless, Vietnamese leaders are still not of one mind on this issue. Since 1989, the fall of Communist regimes in East and Central Europe has split the top leadership into two factions: reformers who want to open up to the United States and the West and conservatives who want to rely on China to save socialism. At present, few in Vietnam sincerely believe in Marxism-Leninism, but nominal adherence to socialism is a requirement for members of the ruling circle and those who want to be part of it.

The cumulative impact of China's aggressive behavior, fanned by the recent Chinese oil rig incident, seriously weakened and undermined the legitimacy of the pro-China conservatives within the CPV leadership. Prime Minister Dung criticized China by name for the first time for its "extremely dangerous action [that] is directly threatening peace and security" in the region and for "speaking one way and doing things another way." He vowed that Vietnam would never exchange national sovereignty and territorial integrity for "any sort of friendly and illusionary peace based on a relationship of dependency."[31] Outside the government, a chorus of voices argued for political reform, a *thoát Trung* or *thoát Hán* (liberation from China) policy, and the formulation of a

---

[28] See "Trung Quoc chiem va XD phi phap tren Da Chau Vien như the nao?" [How Has China Illegally Occupied and Built on Cuarteron Reef?], *The Thao Viet Nam*, June 28, 2013, http://thethaovietnam.vn/thoi-su-xa-hoi/201306/trung-quoc-chiem-va-xd-phi-phap-tren-da-chau-vien-nhu-the-nao-315072.

[29] "Vietnam's Electronic Warfare in the Defense of Spratlys," *Dat Viet*, http://www.baodatviet.vn/quoc-phong/vu-khi/tac-chien-dien-tu-viet-nam-trong-bao-ve-truong-sa-2350320.

[30] For more details of the context and results of Sang's trip, see Hung Nguyen and Murray Hiebert, "President Sang Seeks New Ties during Washington Visit," CSIS, CogitASIA, July 29, 2013, http://cogitasia.com/president-sang-seeks-new-ties-during-washington-visit.

[31] V. V. Thanh, "Khong doi chu quyen lay huu nghi vien vong, le thuoc" [Never Exchange Sovereignty for Illusionary Friendship, Dependency], *Tuoi tre*, May 23, 2014, http://tuoitre.vn/Chinh-tri-Xa-hoi/608819/khong-doi-chu-quyen-lay-hu%CC%83u-nghi%CC%A3-vien-vong-le-thuoc.html.

military alliance with the United States.[32] In an unprecedented development, an open forum on "How to Liberate [Vietnam] from China?" was allowed to take place in Hanoi on June 5, 2014. Hundreds of Vietnamese intellectuals signed an open letter criticizing the party for failing to stand up to Chinese expansionism and calling for the country to move toward democracy to get out of China's orbit.[33]

As Chinese pressure increased, Vietnamese leaders could not fail to notice clear manifestations of support from the United States. Secretary of State Kerry invited Foreign Minister Pham Binh Minh to the United States for "consultations on the full range of bilateral and regional issues" after the first-ever direct telephone call by Minh to Kerry in May 2014 to exchange views on the HD-981 crisis in the South China Sea.[34] Recently nominated U.S. ambassador to Vietnam Ted Osius joined this chorus by stating in his Senate confirmation hearing that it might be "time to begin exploring the possibility of lifting the ban" on weapons sales to Vietnam.[35] A flurry of visits by U.S. senators (Bob Corker, John McCain, and Sheldon Whitehouse), followed by the first visit to Vietnam since 1971 by the chairman of the Joint Chiefs of Staff, General Martin Dempsey, signaled the United States' increasing determination to "help Vietnam to protect its security and national sovereignty."[36] All of them told their hosts that they supported an easing of the ban on lethal weapons exports to Vietnam. General Dempsey assured his hosts that despite the fact that there were many events and many places

---

[32] See, for example, Hoang Mai, "Tieng goi cua non song: Thoat Han" [The Nation's Call: Escape from China], Bauxite Viet Nam, web log, May 23, 2013, http://boxitvn.blogspot.com/2014/05/tieng-goi-cua-non-song-thoat-han.html; Nguyen Van Dai, "Giai phap cho dang CSVN de bao ve chu quyen quoc gia" [A Proposed Solution for the CPV to Protect National Sovereignty], Radio Free Asia, May 16, 2014, http://www.rfa.org/vietnamese/in_depth/solution-f-communist-party-nvdai-05162014093204.html; "Xoa bo doc tai moi cuu duoc nuoc" [Ending Authoritarianism to Save the Country], Radio Free Asia, May 16, 2014, http://www.rfa.org/vietnamese/in_depth/itw-with-dr-cu-huy-ha-vu-05162014133903.html; To Van Truong, "Viet Nam khong phai la phien bang cua Trung Quoc" [Vietnam Is Not a Chinese Vassal], Bauxite Viet Nam, web log, May 22, 2014, http://boxitvn.blogspot.com/2014/05/viet-nam-khong-phai-la-phien-bang-cua.html; and Dinh Hoang Thang, "Giac ngo de thoat khoi kiem toa" [Wake Up to Escape from Chinese Control], Bo lap que choa, web log, May 22, 2014, http://bolapquechoa.com/giac-ngo-de-thoat-khoi-kiem-toa.quechoa.

[33] "Thu ngo ve tinh hinh khan cap cua dat nuoc" [Open Letter on the Emergency Situation in the Country], Bauxite Viet Nam, web log, June 30, 2013, http://boxitvn.blogspot.com/2014/05/thu-ngo-ve-tinh-hinh-khan-cap-cua-at.html.

[34] See Nguyen Manh Hung, "Oil Rig Crisis in the South China Sea Prompts Vietnam to Consider Stronger Ties with the United States," CSIS, CogitASIA, May 30, 2014; and David Brown, "Vietnam: Turning Points?" *Asia Sentinel*, June 2, 2014.

[35] See Matthew Pennington, "Envoy Nominee Open to Lifting Arms Ban to Vietnam," Associated Press, June 17, 2014.

[36] "Senator McCain: My san sang tro giup de Viet Nam bao dam an ninh va bao ve chu quyen," [Senator McCain: The United States Is Ready to Help Vietnam Defend Its Security and National Sovereignty], *Dan Viet*, August 8, 2014, http://danviet.vn/chinh-tri/my-san-sang-tro-giup-de-viet-nam-bao-dam-an-ninh-va-bao-ve-quyen-chu-quyen-468257.html.

in the world vying for his attention, Vietnam was his "top priority."[37] While secretary general of the CPV, Nguyen Phu Trong, told Senator McCain that Vietnam regarded the United States as its most important partner, McCain declared at a press conference in Hanoi that "in light of the recent events in the East Sea…it is time for Vietnam and the United States to take a giant strategic leap together."[38]

Thus, there is a convergence of strategic interest between the United States and Vietnam to work together to deal with the China problem. A strong bond between the countries that is mutually beneficial depends, however, on a clear and unmistakable determination of the Vietnamese leadership to pursue an independent foreign policy and abandon their belief and hope that the survival of socialism in Vietnam requires the protection and leadership of China. The struggle between China liberationists and China accommodationists will probably continue through the next party congress in 2016, but at the moment the China liberationists are in ascendance. This trend works in favor of closer U.S.-Vietnam relations.[39]

The Values Factor

In the short term, human rights issues—religious freedom, freedom of expression, freedom of information, freedom of association, and the right to form independent unions—have affected and will continue to affect the direction of U.S.-Vietnam relations. The issue of human rights occupies a significant place for several reasons: it reflects American values, Vietnam's economic and strategic importance to the United States is not yet significant enough to overwhelm human rights considerations, and many Americans who fought in the Vietnam War consider this an important issue and would like to see progress in Vietnam. Finally, many Vietnamese-American activists think that joining forces with dissidents inside Vietnam to campaign for human rights and democracy by peaceful means is a promising method for bringing about change in Vietnam.

Since the Carter administration, human rights have been an important part of the U.S. foreign policy agenda. Although in relations with many countries—including China, Egypt, Saudi Arabia, and Pakistan—human

---

[37] "Lanh dao My khang dinh tam quan trong cua Viet Nam" [U.S. Leader Affirms the Importance of Vietnam], *Dat Viet*, August 14, 2014, http://baodatviet.vn/quoc-phong/quoc-phong-viet-nam/lanh-dao-my-khang-dinh-tam-quan-trong-cua-viet-nam-3052423.

[38] John McCain, "Statement by Senator John McCain in Hanoi, Vietnam," Press Release, August 8, 2014, http://www.mccain.senate.gov/public/index.cfm/press-releases?ID=f5fd4b07-3d87-4a9f-a892-03018c779888.

[39] For a perceptive analysis of the impact of Vietnam's evolving strategic thought and the China factor on the development of U.S.-Vietnam defense relations, see Jordan, Stern, and Lohman, "U.S.-Vietnam Defense Relations."

rights sometimes have taken a backseat to economic and strategic interests, the issue has not gone away. President George W. Bush, in his second-term inaugural address, solemnly declared that "all who live in tyranny and hopelessness can know: the United States will not ignore your oppression, or excuse your oppressors. When you stand for your liberty, we will stand with you."[40] While Vietnamese leaders do not like outside interference, they certainly took this view into serious consideration when trying to get what they wanted from the United States. In 2006, during the preparations for the APEC summit in Hanoi and critical trade negotiations with the United States, there were visible improvements in Vietnam's treatment of human rights to the point that the U.S. State Department removed Vietnam from the list of "countries of particular concern." When Secretary of State Condoleezza Rice accompanied Bush to the APEC summit in November 2006, she even called on the leaders of Burma and North Korea to follow the example of Vietnam.[41]

Vietnamese dissidents took advantage of these developments to press their demand for political reforms and form political groups, such as Bloc 8406, which denounced the one-party political system and called for a boycott of the May 2007 National Assembly elections. Others soon followed, such as the 21st Century Democratic Party, the Vietnam Progress Party, the Farmers-Workers United Alliance, the Workers Independent Union, and the Alliance for Democracy and Human Rights. These groups demanded a multiparty system, published their own papers through the Internet, and made common cause with overseas Vietnamese to put pressure on the government. The government reacted by cracking down with a wave of arrests and trials in February 2007, jailing prominent democracy activists. This move caused tension between Washington and Hanoi during the much anticipated first visit of the new deputy prime minister and foreign minister Pham Gia Khiem to the United States in March 2007, prompting many leading U.S. legislators from both parties to react angrily, including those who previously had advocated improved relations between the two countries. Congressman Earl Blumenauer resigned from the chairmanship of the Congressional Caucus on Vietnam in protest, and introduced a resolution condemning the convictions of pro-democracy activists. Earlier, the House had overwhelmingly passed a resolution demanding Vietnam release all political prisoners and urging the U.S. government to consider blocking Vietnam's candidacy to become a nonpermanent member of the UN Security Council in 2008. Under these circumstances, the Bush administration was

---

[40] George W. Bush, "Second Inaugural Address," January 20, 2005, available at http://www.npr.org/templates/story/story.php?storyId=4460172.

[41] Condoleezza Rice (remarks at the APEC CEO Summit, Hanoi, Vietnam, November 18, 2006), http://2001-2009.state.gov/secretary/rm/2006/76277.htm.

forced to express its strong displeasure, and only last-minute concessions from Vietnam made it possible for the anticipated U.S. visit of President Nguyen Minh Triet to take place in June 2007 as scheduled. Human rights remained an issue when President Sang visited the United States in July 2013, and the "importance of protection and promotion of human rights" was part of the joint statement released by the two leaders.[42] Congressional leaders and U.S. human rights organizations continue to condemn abuses in Vietnam and press for the release of many activists and bloggers who have been arrested and tried for "abusing democratic rights" to harm national interests.

Vietnamese leaders themselves have become more familiar with the requirements of U.S. domestic politics and do not wish bilateral relations to be seriously damaged over the issue of human rights. Recently, they have tried to accommodate the United States as much as possible without endangering the survival of the regime. On the issue of religious freedom, they have to a large extent satisfied Washington's demands. They allowed embassy officials to visit the highlands where Protestants were alleged to be mistreated. High-ranking U.S. officials were also allowed to visit opposition Buddhist leaders. When members of the U.S. Commission on International Religious Freedom came to Hanoi in October 2007, they were assured by Prime Minister Dung that Vietnam was willing to talk with the United States about differences on religion. Commission members were also allowed to visit leaders of the banned United Buddhist Church of Vietnam and to visit and talk separately with some jailed political dissidents.

In 2009–10, the issue of human rights surfaced again as the government clashed with Catholic protesters over land issues, silenced and harassed bloggers, and arrested and tried democracy activists. While Human Rights Watch denounced Vietnam's violations of human rights and the Commission on International Religious Freedom demanded that Vietnam be put back on the list of "countries of particular concern," the U.S. State Department resisted this pressure. Then U.S. ambassador to Vietnam Michael Michalak admitted in a press conference on January 3, 2010, that there was a spike in human rights abuses, but he suggested that dialogue, rather than harsher measures, was the best way to respond. As relations between the United States and Vietnam have improved and become beneficial to both sides, the U.S. approach to the human rights issue tends to rely more on dialogue than sanctions.

Nevertheless, without a radical improvement in human rights in Vietnam, bilateral relations will remain at the level of a dialogue partnership. Undersecretary Robert Hormats made this point very clear in his speech in

---

[42] "Joint Statement by President Barack Obama of the United States of America and President Truong Tan Sang of the Socialist Republic of Vietnam."

Hanoi on April 12, 2010. He stated that "the United States is committed to strengthening our partnership with Vietnam as a key pillar of our presence in the region," but also insisted that "while the relationship between Vietnam and the United States has never been stronger, deeper, and more constructive, our differing views on human rights also have the potential to make progress in some areas more difficult."[43] The lack of human rights progress remains an impediment to a deeper partnership—lifting the embargo on lethal weapons sales to Vietnam, for example. The requirement for further progress in U.S.-Vietnam relations was effectively summed up in a remark by Ambassador David Shear. Following President Sang's 2013 visit to the United States, Shear stated that "the Vietnamese side has expressed an interest in lifting the restriction, and we will consider that request seriously," but "we also believe that in order to generate political support for lifting the restrictions…we will need to see some progress in human rights on Vietnam's side."[44]

The Strategic Importance of Vietnam for the United States

After the Vietnam War and especially after Vietnam's invasion of Cambodia, the United States viewed the country as an instrument of Soviet expansionism in Southeast Asia. However, as Vietnam reformed its economy, changed its foreign policy, and accelerated its integration into ASEAN, the U.S. view of Vietnam changed. Vietnam's role as ASEAN chair in 2008 and its competent performance as a nonpermanent member of the UN Security Council in 2010–11 further demonstrated the country's capability to be a useful U.S. partner in strengthening ASEAN and contributing to a desirable balance of forces in the Asia-Pacific region in the face of a rising China.

While it is in the interest of the United States to avoid unnecessary conflict with China, it is also in Washington's interest to encourage and support an independent Vietnam in order to facilitate strategic diversity and multipolarity in Asia and prevent any single country from dominating the region, especially the strategic sea lanes in the South China Sea. Chinese actions over the last two years—forcing the Philippines out of the Scarborough Shoal in May 2012, unilaterally declaring an ADIZ in the East China Sea over areas disputed with Japan in December 2013, blocking Philippine ships bringing supplies to troops at the Second Thomas Shoal in March 2014, and bullying Vietnam in the oil rig incident in May 2014—have forced the United States to face the danger of, in the words of the U.S. assistant secretary of state Daniel Russel, the "incremental effort by China

[43] Robert D. Hormats, "The U.S.-Vietnam Economic Relationship" (remarks given at Foreign Trade University, Hanoi, April 12, 2010), http://www.state.gov/e/rls/rmk/2010/140077.htm.

[44] Hookway, "Vietnam Rights Record Cools U.S. Ties."

to assert control over the [South China Sea].”[45] If successful, this would end U.S. naval supremacy in the western Pacific and drastically reduce the power and influence of the United States in one of the world's most strategically and economically important regions.

In this context, Vietnam's firm reactions to Chinese encroachment in the South China Sea are a welcome sign and show that Vietnam can be an important force contributing to the emerging security order in the Asia-Pacific.[46] Undersecretary Hormats referred to the strengthening of the United States' partnership with Vietnam as a "key pillar of our presence in…[the] region and of our involvement in multilateral institutions in the Asia-Pacific area.”[47] So far the U.S. desire to strengthen relations with Vietnam has varied in direct proportion with the aggressiveness of China's behavior and with the determination and capability of Vietnam to play an independent role in Asia. As discussed above, recent improvements in bilateral relations in the face of China's challenge prompted General Dempsey to state during his visit to Vietnam in August 2014 that Vietnam was a top priority, while Senator McCain has talked about the astounding progress in U.S.-Vietnam relations and called for the two countries to take "a giant strategic leap together."

Implications

U.S.-Vietnam relations must be seen in the wider regional context of a competition for supremacy and influence in the Asia-Pacific region between China, a rising power, and the United States, the reigning superpower.[48] While the United States prefers cooperation with China and is willing to accord China a regional and global status commensurate with its power, with a view of encouraging it to become a responsible stakeholder in the international system, it certainly does not want China to dominate Southeast Asia and the South China Sea. For the United States, a Chinese version of the Monroe Doctrine in Asia is not acceptable.

---

[45] Geoff Dyer, "China Training for 'Short, Sharp War,' Says Senior U.S. Naval Officer," *Financial Times*, February 20, 2014.

[46] In July 2015, Prime Minister Dung strongly accused China of "disregarding morality and law, and violating previous agreements between leaders of two countries" when it "blatantly moved the Haiyang Shiyou-981 oil rig into Vietnam's EEZ and continental shelf." He then vowed that Vietnam will "resolutely struggle to protect the country's sacred sovereignty, and will not accept or bend under any kind of pressure, threat, or dependency." See http://www.vietnamplus.vn/thu-tuong-vn-kien-quyet-dau-tranh-bao-ve-vung-chac-chu-quyen/268850.vnp.

[47] Hormats, "The U.S.-Vietnam Economic Relationship."

[48] For more details, see Nguyen Manh Hung, "Drawing a Line in the South China Sea: Why Beijing Needs to Show Restraint," *Global Asia* 7, no. 4 (2012).

In the short and medium term, China is seeking the role of a regional hegemon, while the United States is trying to encourage the emergence of a multipolar security structure in the Asia-Pacific. In this context, Vietnam plays a critical role. Because of geographic proximity and ideological compatibility, Vietnam is more important to China than to the United States. For the United States, Vietnam can be an important, if not critical, factor in building a regional security structure in which China's excessive ambitions can be managed. It is thus in the interest of the United States for Vietnam to be strong, independent, and capable of resisting China's influence. This, in turn, depends on two factors: the strength of Vietnam's economic and political systems and Vietnam's sincere desire and need for U.S. assistance. The United States cannot and should not help Vietnam if its leaders only want to use relations with the United States as a bargaining chip with China, because they are still afraid of U.S. plots to subvert the regime and prefer the low-risk policy of accommodating China.

Politically, the Communist Party of Vietnam is in control, but its leadership is divided over the speed of reform and the China challenge, and the regime is not as stable and strong as it once was. Tensions are brewing under the surface, as urban youth and intellectuals clamor for greater freedom and democracy. Peasants are angry over land confiscated without fair compensation. Many party members are disillusioned with the party and its outdated ideology.[49] On top of this, China's aggressive behavior has fanned Vietnamese nationalism against "Han hegemony" and the popular perception of the government's subservience to China, which seriously undermine the legitimacy of the CPV regime. Its two traditional instruments of political control—fear and information control— are becoming increasingly less effective against public protests and the widespread use of the Internet. Compared with Eastern Europe in the late 1980s, where demand for freedom and resentment against Soviet control led to the collapse of several Communist regimes, the regime in Vietnam is facing bigger challenges: demand for political reform in the cities, resentment against exploitation and injustice in the countryside, rampant corruption, a huge gap between the rich and the poor, and perceived

---

[49] In an open letter to the CPV on July 28, 2014, 61 Communist Party members accused the party of having led the people on the "wrong road of building a Soviet-style socialism," and demanded that the party self-correct and "take the initiative to change the party's political program, reject the wrong road of building socialism, and embrace nationalism and democracy, aiming basically at resolutely and peacefully transforming a totalitarian system into a democracy." See "Thư ngo gui BCH Trung ương va toan the dang vien Dang CSVN," Basam, web log, July 29, 2014, http://anhbasam.wordpress.com/2014/07/29/thu-ngo-gui-bch-trung-uong-va-toan-the-dang-vien-dang-csvn. Le Hieu Dang, a 45-year party veteran and former vice president of the Ho Chi Minh City's Vietnam Fatherland Front, published an open letter on August 12, 2013, urging the party to abandon its obsolete Communist ideology and party members to leave the party en masse to organize an opposition party to check the abuses and monopoly of power by the CPV.

government weakness against a traditional enemy. This is a combustible mixture ready to explode if the economy goes sour.

While the United States can do little about the state of Vietnamese politics without being accused of interfering in the country's internal affairs, it can do much more for the Vietnamese economy. The most serious flaw of the Vietnamese economy is the leading role of the state sector, which is dominated by incompetent and inefficient state-owned enterprises. This situation is aggravated by corruption and a poor banking system. The TPP presents Vietnam with an opportunity and incentive to reform its economy to be better able to compete in the global economy and benefit from globalization. The United States should find ways to include Vietnam in the TPP, provide technical advice to help Vietnam complete its move toward a market economy and open up its political system to create an environment conducive to increased U.S. investment, and help make Vietnam's economy less dependent on China. Vietnamese officials identify three areas that are critical for economic development and national power—infrastructure development, manpower training, and legal reform—and they think the United States is uniquely qualified to help in all these areas.[50]

As mentioned above, however, Vietnam's distrust of U.S. intentions, commitment, and staying power are impediments to closer U.S.-Vietnam relations. The United States could take a number of actions to allay this distrust and promote cooperation. First, the United States could explain fully, repeatedly, and in no uncertain terms that its strategic interest requires a strong and independent Vietnam, not regime change. A formal declaration that the U.S. government wants Vietnam to become more democratic and supports its declared goal of democratization, but does not seek regime change, would be welcomed by Vietnamese officials who want closer relations with the United States and would undermine the arguments of those who oppose closer U.S.-Vietnam relations.[51]

Second, the United States could explain to Vietnamese officials that, due to U.S. politics, strengthening bilateral relations requires a satisfactory management of the human rights issue. At the very least, Vietnam must prove that its human rights record is better than that of China. Progress on this issue

---

[50] Author's private conversations with Vietnamese officials.

[51] Prime Minister Dung himself, in his 2014 New Year's message, spoke of the need for "institutional reform." He asserted that "democracy is an inevitable trend in the development process of humankind" and that "democracy and [a] law-governed state are twins in a modern political institution." In addition, he promoted the concept of limited government when he stated, "The people have the rights to do anything they are not prohibited by law.... State agencies and civil servants are only allowed to do things stipulated by law. Every decision by [the] state must be transparent." "Thong Diep Nam Moi cua Thu Tuong Nguyen Tan Dung" [New Year Message of Prime Minister Nguyen Tan Dung], VGP News, http://baodientu.chinhphu.vn/Tieu-diem/Thong-diep-nam-moi-cua-Thu-tuong-Nguyen-Tan-Dung/190279.vgp.

could provide an additional benefit to Vietnam by enhancing its potential to play a leading role in ASEAN, closing the political gap between Vietnam and other members, and making ASEAN a more coherent bloc. Secretary of State Kerry, who as a U.S. senator blocked several House resolutions sanctioning Vietnam for human rights abuses and enjoys Vietnam's trust, is a perfect person to deliver this important message.

Third, the expansion of educational exchange programs to bring more Vietnamese students to the United States and train the next generation of Vietnamese leaders could help clear mistrust and promote understanding and cooperation between the two countries. With over 16,000 Vietnamese students already studying in the United States, Vietnam ranks first among Southeast Asian countries and eighth among all countries that send students to the United States. Many former exchange students have risen to the middle and top levels of the leadership in Vietnam.

Fourth, Vietnamese-Americans could play a role in bridging the gap and promoting mutual trust and friendship between the two countries. Professionals and youth can serve as goodwill ambassadors, projecting the image of a United States that is democratic, free, fair, prosperous, self-confident, and friendly. To this end, the United States should encourage and facilitate interaction between Vietnamese and Vietnamese-Americans by including, whenever possible, qualified Vietnamese-Americans in U.S. delegations dealing with Vietnam.

Furthermore, to allay Vietnam's concerns over U.S. commitment and staying power, the United States could, on a quid pro quo basis, enact the following measures:

- Washington could remove the embargo on the sale of lethal weapons and begin to sell defensive weapons to Vietnam. This sale may be accompanied by training and maintenance that require the presence of U.S. military personnel in Vietnam.[52]

- The United States could provide Vietnam with satellite surveillance information and assistance, as it already does for the Philippines, and/or sell Vietnam signals intelligence aircraft to enable it to better follow maritime activities in the South China Sea.

---

[52] For a technical discussion stemming from this recommendation, see Jordan, Stern, and Lohman, "U.S.-Vietnam Defense Relations."

- The United States could sell ships to Vietnam, provide training for its coast guard, and engage in joint exercises. Faced with assertive behavior by the Chinese coast guard in disputed areas of the South China Sea, Vietnam has begun to expand its own coast guard. This newly expanded force is still relatively free of vested financial and ideological interests that might obstruct full cooperation with the United States. Vietnam may also have an interest in acquiring shore-based missiles to improve its maritime defense capability.

- The United States could actively advise and help Vietnam in its search for a peaceful settlement of disputes in the South China Sea in general and in preventing the repeat of the 2014 oil rig crisis in particular. Joint and frequent patrols to enforce maritime law and perform rescue missions could be introduced.

- The United States could continue to press Vietnam for more ship visits to improve its naval presence as a possible deterrent to unilateral efforts to change the status quo.

- The United States could boost defense cooperation through third parties. Trilateral or multilateral meetings and joint exercises between the United States, Vietnam, and a U.S. military ally, such as the Philippines or Japan, could be more comfortably achieved than bilateral endeavors. In addition, UN peacekeeping missions and search and rescue operations are good opportunities for the U.S. and Vietnamese militaries to work together and promote further cooperation.

- The United States could help develop Vietnam's energy sector. The presence of U.S. oil and gas companies and their concrete accomplishments could be viewed by Vietnam as reflecting a serious U.S. commitment to engage the country.

- Washington could ratify UNCLOS in order to be in a legitimate position to champion its implementation in the South China Sea disputes.

In sum, because of Vietnam's sensitivity and its difficult relations with China, as well as the ambivalence of a divided leadership, the process of building an effective partnership between the United States and Vietnam requires patience, persistence, understanding, and frank talk from the U.S. side. The success of these efforts, however, also depends critically on the emergence of a Vietnamese leadership that is united behind a strong determination to implement the reforms necessary to tie Vietnam to the West and reduce the country's dependence on China economically, politically, and ideologically.

STRATEGIC ASIA 2014–15

SPECIAL STUDY

EXECUTIVE SUMMARY

This chapter analyzes the trend of Asian governments adopting hedging strategies and draws implications for U.S. policy toward the Asia-Pacific.

MAIN ARGUMENT:
Asian governments are being driven to pursue hedging strategies in their approaches to foreign policy. At issue is less whether strategic hedging is pervasive than what it means for stability and how long the trend is likely to endure. This is the case whether Asian states are pursuing greater economic integration with China, even as they pursue greater security cooperation with the United States; modernizing their militaries despite often lacking declared adversaries; or engaging in greater levels of security cooperation overall while eschewing both new alliances and rules-based regional institutions. This chapter, therefore, explores some of the policy and strategy implications of the strategic hedging trend by offering three system-level approaches to understanding it: power transition theory, multipolar neorealism, and network complexity.

POLICY IMPLICATIONS:

- U.S. policies relating to security cooperation should focus on brokering military cooperation among regional actors and enabling smaller powers to resist coercion by stronger powers.

- Continued active U.S. participation in Asia's many multilateral institutions, rather than either withdrawing from them or betting on only one, should promote stability by reassuring allies and partners and legitimizing cooperative diplomacy.

- Consensual multilateralism may be the only acceptable or functional model of security governance in Asia. As long as indicators of strategic hedging persist, any order-building project should eschew attempts to replicate a NATO-like structure in the region.

The Rise and Persistence of Strategic Hedging across Asia: A System-Level Analysis

Van Jackson

The evolving Asian security order offers strong incentives for national governments to adopt hedging strategies. The traditional order, defined by a network of bilateral security alliances originating during the Cold War, now also includes an array of consensual institutions lacking the rules-based structure found in Europe. The prospect of new alliances forming seems dim, yet existing ones have been reinvigorated. Whereas the United States once stood alone as the regional hegemon, scholars increasingly talk of its "relative decline," not just compared with China but also as a result of the "rise of the rest."[1] The pervasiveness of military modernization in Asia, alongside asymmetric strategies of conflict and coercion, lends support to arguments that power is somehow diffusing. And for foreign policy elites in the region, Cold War–era simplicity with regard to strategic alignment has given way to issue complexity; it is increasingly difficult to separate regional security issues from economic, cultural, and domestic political considerations, complicating

Van Jackson is a Visiting Fellow at the Center for a New American Security and a Council on Foreign Relations International Affairs Fellow. He can be reached at <vanallenjackson@gmail.com>.

Portions of this chapter originally appeared in Van Jackson, "Power, Trust, and Network Complexity: Three Logics of Hedging in Asian Security," *International Relations of the Asia-Pacific* 14, no. 3 (2014). The views expressed in this chapter belong solely to the author and in no way reflect those of the U.S. Department of Defense or U.S. government.

---

[1] See, for example, Richard N. Haass, "The Age of Nonpolarity: What Will Follow U.S. Dominance," *Foreign Affairs*, May/June 2008; Fareed Zakaria, *The Post-American World* (New York: W.W. Norton & Company, 2008); and Barry R. Posen, *Restraint: A New Foundation for U.S. Grand Strategy* (Ithaca: Cornell University Press, 2014).

policymaker calculations of where and when to make bets in support for or opposition to the foreign policy initiatives of other states.

Within this evolving order, national governments are aligning economically with China and one another even as they look for the United States to offer various forms of security. Asian governments are assiduously avoiding balancing or bandwagoning in any overt form and are building up military capabilities, despite lacking a declared adversary in most instances. Asian foreign policy elites lack an appetite either for the legalistic multilateral institutions of Europe or for new bilateral alliances, while nevertheless demonstrating a preference for stable expectations enshrined in international norms and, in some cases, extant international law. These are all indicators of strategic hedging and can be variously explained in terms of power, mistrust, and network complexity. If the United States is to successfully navigate the evolving Asian security order, it will need to understand the emergence and persistence of strategic hedging.

This chapter offers three different system-level lenses through which to interpret strategic hedging. The first lens, power transition theory, focuses on the rise of China in the context of U.S. hegemony and expects Asian states to align themselves with the preeminent regional power. Strategic hedging is seen through this lens as a function of uncertainty about which state will be the dominant power in the future. The second lens, multipolarity in an anarchical security environment, draws attention to the persistent inability of states to trust the intentions of one another, particularly amid military buildups. Seen through this lens, Asian states are expected to establish new alliances or military investments as ways of balancing against threats. Such hedging strategies are rational responses to pervasive mistrust about the intentions of others when threats are ambiguous. The third lens integrates insights from the network analysis and complex interdependence literatures, pointing to the fluid and complex web of relations that define the region. From this perspective, states are expected to employ hedging strategies because incentives for alignment are unclear and likely to change from issue to issue. By demonstrating that a state's decision to strategically hedge can be plausibly explained in multiple ways, and that each way emphasizes different approaches to thinking about strategy, this chapter will maintain that debates about the Asian security order can embrace the complexity of the regional security environment rather than focusing only on questions of the United States' staying power and the rise of China.

The remainder of the chapter consists of three parts. The first provides a brief introduction to power transition theory, mistrust under multipolarity, and the uncertainty of network complexity in contemporary international relations as three distinct ways of viewing the regional order and explaining the strategic hedging trend. The second part considers evidence that substantiates each of these perspectives on the regional order. The third part discusses the implications that logically flow from each of these three perspectives for U.S. strategy and policy toward Asia.

Three Perspectives on Strategic Hedging

Regardless of whether Asian governments are willing to acknowledge it, a region-wide trend of strategic hedging has emerged in the last decade. National governments are seeking to avoid overt balancing and bandwagoning.[2] There is a strong desire for cooperative diplomacy but little appetite for a rules-based institutional order. Governments are increasingly enmeshing themselves economically with China even as they seek enhanced forms of security cooperation with the United States. And arms buildups are occurring even without declared adversaries in most cases. This chapter proposes that the emergence of these activities collectively constitutes a broader phenomenon described as "strategic hedging," which can be understood as a way of coping with uncertainty by mitigating or avoiding the downside risks of alignment behavior.[3] The extreme ideal types of alignment behavior are balancing and bandwagoning.

Explanations for Strategic Hedging

Why is strategic hedging on the rise? There are at least three ways to explain it (see **Table 1**). The logic of power transition holds that when a weaker power begins overtaking the strongest power in terms of material capabilities, the likelihood of conflict will become a function of the extent to which the rising power is dissatisfied with its status quo in relation to the stronger power.[4] For more than a decade, Asia scholars have applied this theory to the United States and China, contributing to debates about whether China would overtake the United States, as well as whether China

---

[2] Bandwagoning is the strategic alignment of one state with another. Balancing is alignment of one state against another and can take at least two forms: internal (accumulation of military power) and external (alliances and military cooperation). For a discussion of these ideal types of alignment, see Randall L. Schweller, "New Realist Research on Alliances: Refining, Not Refuting, Waltz's Balancing Proposition," *American Political Science Review* 91, no. 4 (1997): 927–30.

[3] David A. Lake, "Anarchy, Hierarchy, and the Variety of International Relations," *International Organization* 50, no. 1 (1996): 1–33; and Brock Tessman and Wojtek Wolfe, "Great Powers and Strategic Hedging: The Case of Chinese Energy Security Strategy," *International Studies Review* 13, no. 2 (2011): 214–40.

[4] A.F.K. Organski and Jacek Kugler, *The War Ledger* (Chicago: University of Chicago Press, 2008).

TABLE 1   Three ways to explain strategic hedging in Asia

	Power transition theory	Multipolarity	Complex networks
Cause of hedging	Hierarchical ambiguity, uncertainty about who will become the regional hegemon	Intentions of other states, uncertainty about whom to trust	High sensitivity, fluid alignment incentive structures, issue complexity/heterarchy
Observable indicators	Arms buildups, strengthened relations with the two greatest powers	Arms buildups, dissolution of alliances, avoiding new alliances, avoiding institutional commitments	Arms buildups, multiplicity of consensual networks, avoiding new alliances, avoiding institutional commitments
Disconfirming evidence	Balancing or hedging after only one great power remains	Persistent alliances, rules-based institutions	Clear balancing or bandwagoning, rules-based institutions

has revisionist intentions.[5] In recent years, however, scholars have argued that the trajectory of power distribution between China and the United States is unclear. Ambiguity about whether China will overtake the United States, whether China will seek to change the regional order if it overtakes the United States, and whether the United States has the wherewithal to maintain primacy in the Asia-Pacific has provided motivations for East Asian states to hedge.[6] Implicit to this line of thinking is the assumption that if only the

---

[5] In the context of China, the term "revisionist intentions" refers specifically to China's long-term intention to upend the existing international order in favor of some other international arrangement, presumably in accord with its preferences. Steve Chan, *China, the U.S., and the Power-Transition Theory: A Critique* (New York: Routledge, 2007); and Jeffrey W. Legro, "What China Will Want: The Future Intentions of a Rising Power," *Perspectives on Politics* 5, no. 3 (2007): 515–34.

[6] Dennis Roy, "Southeast Asia and China: Balancing or Bandwagoning?" *Contemporary Southeast Asia* 27, no. 2 (2005): 305–22; Evelyn Goh "Southeast Asian Perspectives on the China Challenge," *Journal of Strategic Studies* 30, no. 4 (2007): 809–32; Evelyn Goh, "Hierarchy and the Role of the United States in the East Asian Security Order," *International Relations of the Asia-Pacific* 8, no. 3 (2008): 355–57; P.M. Cronin et al., "The Emerging Asia Power Web: The Rise of Bilateral Intra-Asian Security Ties," Center for a New American Security, June 2013; Vibhanshu Shekhar, "ASEAN's Response to the Rise of China: Deploying a Hedging Strategy," *China Report* 48, no. 3 (2012): 253–68; and Yuen Foong Khong, "Coping with Strategic Uncertainty: The Role of Institutions and Soft Balancing in Southeast Asia's Post–Cold War Strategy," in *Rethinking Security in East Asia: Identity, Power, and Efficiency*, ed. J.J. Suh, Peter J. Katzenstein, and Allen Carlson (Stanford: Stanford University Press, 2004).

future trajectory of a rising China and U.S. staying power were clear, Asian states would know whether they should be balancing or bandwagoning.

Another way to interpret the hedging trend is through the lens of multipolarity in an anarchical security environment. Like power transition theory, multipolarity emphasizes the distribution of military and economic power when determining the incentives that states have to make alignment decisions such as balancing and bandwagoning.[7] But whereas power transition theory principally applies to a world in which there is one great power and one up-and-coming challenger, multipolarity describes an environment defined by the existence of three or more significant powers. For more than two decades, scholars have argued that multipolarity is coming to Asia, and some have argued that Asia is already multipolar in structure.[8] That the U.S. National Intelligence Council claims that multipolarity and the diffusion of power is already a reality only cements multipolarity as a kind of conventional wisdom.[9] In a multipolar system, alliances are fleeting, the balance of power can change quickly because of the ease with which alliances form and fade, and institutions cannot be relied on for security.[10] Hedging is rational in such an environment: because states can never be certain about the intentions of others,[11] they are incentivized not to wed themselves to a single great power or coalition.[12]

A third system-level perspective on strategic hedging takes a complex network approach. Fundamentally, networks are nothing more than representations of linkages (relationships) among nodes (actors).[13] The density and regularity of the pattern of interaction among nodes serves as a measure of the strength of the linkage. Networks are structures, meaning they

---

[7] Kenneth N. Waltz, "The Emerging Structure of International Politics," *International Security* 18, no. 2 (1993): 44–79.

[8] Aaron L. Friedberg, "Ripe for Rivalry: Prospects for Peace in a Multipolar Asia," *International Security* 18, no. 3 (1993): 5–33; and Kenneth N. Waltz, "Evaluating Theories," *American Political Science Review* 91, no. 4 (1997): 913–17.

[9] Office of the Director of National Intelligence, *Global Trends 2030: Alternative Worlds* (Washington, D.C., 2012).

[10] John J. Mearsheimer, "The False Promise of International Institutions," *International Security* 19, no. 3 (1994): 5–49.

[11] It should be noted that in the Waltzian tradition multipolarity is expected to produce balancing coalitions, but this is an assertion of expectation, not an observation of fact. The logic of multipolar anarchy should be just as likely to produce hedging.

[12] Mearsheimer, "The False Promise of International Institutions"; and Barry R. Posen, "Emerging Multipolarity: Why Should We Care?" *Current History*, November 2009, 349.

[13] Networks can also be viewed as purposive actors, such as transnational activist networks that connect for some specific purpose, but purposive networks have a separate and distinct ontology. For a discussion of networks in both senses, see Miles Kahler, "Networked Politics: Agency, Power, and Governance," in *Networked Politics: Agency, Power, and Governance*, ed. Miles Kahler (Ithaca: Cornell University Press, 2013), 1–20.

provide a context within which actors make decisions; structures "shape and shove" actor decisions in a certain direction but do not necessarily determine them. As Kenneth Waltz explained, states are "free to do any fool thing they care to, but they are likely to be rewarded for behavior that is responsive to structural pressures and punished for behavior that is not."[14] The key point of differentiation between a network structure and the traditional, Waltzian understanding of structure is that complex networks define structure in terms of linkages among nodes; a network structure is inherently derived from relationships, which are by their nature fluid, multidimensional, and sometimes interdependent. A useful illustrative example of the importance of a relational approach to structure can be seen in the case of relations between the Republic of Korea (ROK) and Japan. Despite having a common great-power ally (the United States) and no large power disparity between them, the ROK and Japan continually demonstrate mistrust and a corresponding inability to undertake meaningful cooperation with one another. The foreign policy of each toward the other is constrained by the nature of this relationship, which is defined in terms of conflicting historical memory.[15] In this way, relationships and patterns of interaction among nodes are potentially much more revealing than simply knowing the distribution of power among actors.

Why Do Complex Networks Produce Hedging?

The complex network structure of the region pressures Asian states to adopt hedging positions. Three attributes in particular encourage this response: sensitivity, fluidity, and heterarchy.[16] Yet it is not only the presence of these three attributes but also the interaction among them that generates powerful incentives for nodal agents in Asia's complex network to hedge.

National governments today have become highly sensitive to the foreign and domestic policies of other states. Sensitivity refers specifically to the extent to which one state is affected by the actions of another.[17] During the Cold War, the division into two clear camps—with the non-Communist camp

---

[14] Waltz, "Evaluating Theories," 915.

[15] Van Jackson, "Getting Past the Past: Korea's Transcendence of the Anti-Japan Policy Frontier," *Asian Security* 7, no. 3 (2011): 238–59.

[16] Complex networks, as opposed to simpler lattice or binary networks, are strictly defined in terms of the number of nodes and linkages making up the network. The attributes described here are specific to the definition of a complex network as applied to Asia. Not all complex networks are, for example, heterarchical; many networks are peer-to-peer or simply hierarchical. For a discussion of the attributes of a complex network in mathematical terms, see M.E.J. Newman, "The Structure and Function of Complex Networks," *SIAM Review* 45, no. 2 (2003): 167–256.

[17] Robert O. Keohane and Joseph S. Nye, *Power and Interdependence: World Politics in Transition* (Boston: Little Brown, 1977).

being defined entirely in terms of the U.S.-led "hub-and-spoke" model (itself a simplified network)—meant that Asian states were not highly sensitive to the moves of one another; any sensitivity one "spoke" might have had with regard to another was mediated through the U.S. "hub," insulating a state from the political movements of other states.[18] Even states outside the hub-and-spoke network, like China and India, arguably benefited from the clarity of relationship alignments because it simplified their geopolitical calculations. Yet, as Dennis Blair, former commander of U.S. Pacific Command, has observed, contemporary Asia is quite different.[19] Compared with only a decade ago, dramatically enhanced intraregional sensitivity has been abetted by the growth of intraregional trade and investment flows.[20] But economic connectivity is not the only, nor the most important, basis for heightened sensitivity. The other major enabler of heightened intraregional sensitivity in the last decade has been the development and diffusion of technology. Information and communication technologies (ICT) connect societies across national boundaries, for better or worse, even when national governments deliberately opt out of connectivity with other governments, such as during sanctions or diplomatic rows. The connectivity that ICTs foster heightens awareness by increasing both the speed at which information can flow and the volume of information available.[21] To put it simply, technology promotes linkages, linkages increase sensitivity, and sensitivity motivates hedging as a means of mitigating what would otherwise constitute vulnerabilities.

The second attribute that incentivizes hedging in a complex network is fluidity, which is closely intertwined with sensitivity. A fluid structure is a changing structure, which is to say it is not fixed or static.[22] During the Cold War, there were very few shifts in regional alignments among Asian governments. Today, it is more difficult for decision-makers to have confidence in the incentives and consequences of their decisions because they are operating in fluid structures rather than in rigid or fixed structures. The fluid structure of Asia's complex web of relations does not provide clear incentives for states to make long-term commitments to balance against or bandwagon with others. Trust among Asian states is generally low, so

---

[18] Victor D. Cha, "Powerplay: Origins of the U.S. Alliance System in Asia," *International Security* 34, no. 3 (2009/2010): 158–96.

[19] Dennis C. Blair and John T. Hanley Jr., "From Wheels to Webs: Reconstructing Asia-Pacific Security Arrangements," *Washington Quarterly* 24, no. 1 (2001): 7–17.

[20] United Overseas Bank of Singapore, "The Rise of Intra-Regional Trade in Asia," Report, 2012.

[21] Johan Eriksson and Giampiero Giacomello, "The Information Revolution, Security, and International Relations: (IR)Relevant Theory?" *International Political Science Review* 27, no. 3 (2006): 221–44.

[22] Nan Lin, *Social Capital: A Theory of Social Structure and Action* (Cambridge: Cambridge University Press, 2001), 38.

linkages among them will form consensually, not bindingly. Low trust makes binding ties less likely and consensual ties more likely because low trust engenders fluid relational structures. In this context, there is little reason for decision-makers to expect that the structural incentives for alignment today—if they can even be identified—will still be around tomorrow.

The third attribute that incentivizes hedging in a complex network is the presence of heterarchy, which refers to the coexistence of multiple hierarchies.[23] Hierarchy itself is a contingent set of relations in which the dominant actor exercises legitimate influence over others—without relying primarily on coercion—within a given domain.[24] Even if states felt comfortable embracing an order dominated by the United States or China, it seems implausible that domination could be pervasive across all aspects of political life. If one state willingly subordinates itself to the preferences of another state, such deference need not be universal but could instead be limited to one dimension of international affairs, such as foreign policy, weapons procurement, cultural affairs, or economic activity. Complicating matters further is the reality that Joseph Nye and Robert Keohane famously highlighted decades ago: over time, decisions are increasingly difficult to categorize as belonging to the "high politics" of national security or the "low politics" of economics or domestic governance; issue interdependence is becoming more the norm than the exception.

As foreign policy issues are increasingly multidimensional, states are incentivized to conform to multiple, and sometimes contradictory or competing, hierarchies, which equates to a hedge. When different aspects of a single issue—such as regional trade policy—are governed by multiple hierarchical relationships, rendering a decision is not so simple. This complexity makes it difficult for states to make broad, long-term alignment decisions. Instead, they prefer to hedge when making strategic decisions and address discrete, near-term decisions on a case-by-case basis, which may on occasion give the outward appearance that a state is pursuing contradictory policies or working at cross-purposes with itself. Under conditions of heterarchy with high degrees of issue interdependence, therefore, states will tend to myopically focus on the near term and make decisions nonstrategically. If they are willing or able to make a strategic alignment decision, it will tend toward hedging, not balancing or bandwagoning.

---

[23] Jack Donnelly, "Rethinking Political Structures: From 'Ordering Principles' to 'Vertical Differentiation'—and Beyond," *International Theory* 1, no. 1 (2009): 49–86.

[24] Goh, "Hierarchy and the Role of the United States," 355–57; David A. Lake, "Escape from the State of Nature: Authority and Hierarchy in World Politics," *International Security* 32, no. 1 (2007): 55; and Alexander Cooley and Hendrik Spruyt, *Contracting States: Sovereign Transfers in International Relations* (Princeton: Princeton University Press, 2009).

Assessing Evidence from the Region

How do the realities of the Asian security order appear through these three different lenses? This section shows that there is ample evidence from the region to support all three views; even though each lens reflects a different logic and emphasizes different assumptions, they all are potentially compatible.

Ambiguous Power Transition

A strong case exists for the assumption that the United States and China are in the midst of an uncertain power transition. Not only is it unclear whether China will ever surpass the United States in terms of military or economic capacity, but it is equally debatable what China's long-term intentions are likely to be. The belief that China will one day overtake the United States in terms of any measure of power requires assuming that U.S. power holds constant or declines while China's continues to grow at an astonishing pace for many years. China's domestic vulnerabilities call this assumption into question. Not only is government corruption pervasive, but economic inequality is large and the Communist Party's continued rule of China is frequently contested domestically by groups and individuals on religious, ethnic, and political grounds. And while some scholars have argued that a China-centric order will be relatively benign,[25] others envision a China-led regional order as one in which "might makes right" is the only rule.[26] Despite these ambiguities, China's rate of economic growth currently outpaces that of the United States. China's annualized growth in military spending also far outstrips the United States, though the latter admittedly has a large lead. Moreover, the lure of the Chinese economy has proved to be an attractive force in the region, as China is now either the largest or second-largest trading partner with each country in East Asia. **Table 2** summarizes some simple indicators suggesting that the United States and China are indeed on a power transition trajectory, even though the numbers themselves offer little in terms of understanding whether and how such a transition might unfold.

The power transition lens urges us to view the behavior of governments in the region in terms of the dynamics between the two greatest regional powers—the United States and China. In Northeast Asia, South Korea and Japan have simultaneously pursued security cooperation throughout Asia as a means of diversification away from the U.S. bilateral alliance structure,

---

[25] David C. Kang, "Hierarchy and Legitimacy in International Systems: The Tribute System in Early Modern East Asia," *Security Studies* 19, no. 4 (2010): 591–622.

[26] Aaron L. Friedberg, "The Future of U.S.-China Relations: Is Conflict Inevitable?" *International Security* 30, no. 2 (2005): 7–45; and Yves Heng-Lim, *China's Naval Power: An Offensive Realist Approach* (Vermont: Ashgate, 2014).

TABLE 2   U.S. hegemony v. rising China by the numbers

	United States	China
Defense spending in 2013 (in billions)	$618.68	$171.38
Defense spending growth in 2012–13	-8%	7%
GDP annual growth in 2013	1.88%	7.67%
Predicted GDP annual growth in 2019	2.22%	6.52%
Predicted GDP based on purchasing power parity in 2019 (in % of the world)	18.22%	18.48%

SOURCE: Stockholm International Peace Research Institute (SIPRI), Military Expenditures Database, http://www.sipri.org/research/armaments/milex/milex_database; and International Monetary Fund, World Economic Outlook Database, http://www.imf.org/external/pubs/ft/weo/2014/01/weodata/index.aspx.

even as those two alliances have strengthened considerably since the 2008 global recession.[27] Second, and rather overtly, South Korea and Japan have cooperated to establish trilateral mechanisms with the United States and with China, respectively, and both countries continue to integrate economically with China even as they have strengthened their respective security alliances with the United States.[28] South Korea, in particular, has voiced concerns about U.S.-ROK-Japan trilateral cooperation on the grounds that Beijing might incorrectly perceive it as a balancing coalition against China.[29] And even though South Korea has pursued closer alliance relations with the United States, it still avoids security behavior that might be seen as taking aim at China, which partially explains South Korea's reluctance to participate in a regional ballistic missile defense system.[30]

Southeast Asia has tended to follow a similar pattern of dual-track, proportionate engagement with the region's two greatest powers. Southeast Asia's increased integration with the U.S. military presence and posture in Asia—a form of cooperation that might otherwise be construed as balancing against China—has occurred simultaneously with a longer-term pursuit of

---

[27] Jae Jeok Park, "The U.S.-Led Alliances in the Asia-Pacific: Hedge against Potential Threats or an Undesirable Multilateral Security Order?" *Pacific Review* 24, no. 2 (2011): 137–58.

[28] For an early accounting of the evolution and limits of Japan and South Korea's joint connections with China, see ibid.

[29] Tae-hyo Kim and Brad Glosserman, eds., *The Future of U.S.-Korea-Japan Relations: Balancing Values and Interests* (Washington, D.C.: Center for Strategic and International Studies, 2004).

[30] Park Byong-su "Defense Minister Says He Wouldn't Oppose THAAD," *Hankyoreh*, June 20, 2014, http://english.hani.co.kr/arti/english_edition/e_international/643168.html.

economic and diplomatic enmeshment with China. This is one of the most familiar observations in the scholarly literature on interactions between China and the Association of Southeast Asian Nations (ASEAN).[31] One scholar describes this strategy as "omni-enmeshment," a deliberate effort to entangle China (and the United States) in a web of interdependent economic and diplomatic relations in the hopes of influencing and forestalling any aggressive intentions.[32] Various forms of Southeast Asian security cooperation with the United States have increased over the last decade. In the Philippines, the United States has formed a joint special operations task force to counter terrorist activity, and in 2014 the two countries signed the Enhanced Defense Cooperation Agreement (EDCA). Among other things, the EDCA will allow U.S. military forces to operate from Philippine military bases and enhance interoperability.[33] The United States and Thailand have reaffirmed their alliance treaty, and, with U.S. military support, Thailand is becoming a hub for humanitarian assistance and disaster relief operations. In addition, at ASEAN's invitation, the U.S. Department of Defense has become a major participant in the ASEAN Defence Ministers' Meeting-Plus (ADMM-Plus), the broader circle of multilateral defense ministry coordination in the region.[34] Many Southeast Asian countries—and others from throughout Asia—have also become key participants in Rim of the Pacific (RIMPAC), the largest U.S.-led maritime military exercise in the world.[35] Such outreach to outside powers is one way that Southeast Asian governments try to hedge against uncertainty about China's long-term intentions.[36]

While signs of greater security cooperation with the United States are evident in both Northeast and Southeast Asia, a different trend emerges when looking at patterns of economic cooperation, a domain in which China commands considerable loyalty. As **Table 3** shows, China is the top export destination for Australia, Japan, South Korea, Taiwan, and Thailand, the second-largest export destination for Indonesia and Singapore, and the third-largest for the Philippines. As seen in **Table 4**, the region also relies

---

[31] Goh, "Southeast Asian Perspectives on the China Challenge"; and Alice D. Ba, "Who's Socializing Whom? Complex Engagement in Sino-ASEAN Relations," *Pacific Review* 19, no. 2 (2006): 157–79.

[32] Evelyn Goh, "Great Powers and Southeast Asian Regional Security Strategies: Omni-Enmeshment, Balancing, and Hierarchical Order," Institute of Defence and Strategic Studies, Working Paper, no. 84.

[33] Cheryl Pellerin, "Hagel Praises 'Unbreakable' U.S.-Philippine Alliance," American Forces Press Service, August 30, 2013, http://www.defense.gov/news/newsarticle.aspx?id=120696; and "PH Primer on Military Pact with U.S.," *Rappler,* April 28, 2014, http://www.rappler.com/nation/56598-primer-enhanced-defense-cooperation-agreement.

[34] Mark Rolls, "Centrality and Continuity: ASEAN and Regional Security since 1967," *East Asia* 29, no. 2 (2012): 127–39.

[35] Donna Miles, "Locklear: RIMPAC Exemplifies PACOM's Multilateral Focus," American Forces Press Service, July 12, 2012, http://www.defense.gov/News/NewsArticle.aspx?ID=117089.

[36] Roy, "Southeast Asia and China."

TABLE 3   Key export destinations by country (2013)

Country	Primary export market	Secondary export market	% of exports to China
Australia	China	Japan	29.6%
India	EU	U.S.	5.1%
Indonesia	Japan	China	11.4%
Japan	China	U.S.	18.1%
Singapore	Malaysia	Hong Kong (China)	10.8%
South Korea	China	U.S.	24.5%
Taiwan	China	Hong Kong (China)	26.8%
Vietnam	EU	U.S.	11.2%
Philippines	Japan	U.S.	11.8%
Thailand	China	Japan	11.7%

SOURCE: World Trade Organization (WTO), Trade Profile Database, http://stat.wto.org/ CountryProfile/WSDBCountryPFReporter.aspx?Language=E.

NOTE: China is the third-largest export market for the Philippines and the fourth-largest export market for Vietnam and India.

heavily on China as a source of affordable imports, ranging from rare earth minerals and textiles to the manufacturing of technology components.

Mistrust in a Multipolar Environment

The aforementioned discussion makes the plausible case that Asian governments are hedging between alignment with China and the United States because of ambiguity about whether, when, and how a future power transition might occur between the two nations. But taking a broader view of the region, rather than limiting our focus to only the two strongest powers, reveals another observable region-wide pattern—military modernization, the diffusion of material power, and a regional trust deficit. The multipolarity lens highlights both the strengthening of military power and the mistrust intrinsic to a "self-help" international system—that is, a system in which states must provide for their own security—as key factors that incentivize hedging. If the United States and China were the only countries that mattered for the purposes of strategic calculations at the national level, then there would be no latent rivalries between, for example, Singapore and Malaysia

TABLE 4   Key sources of imports by country (2013)

Country	Primary import market	Secondary import market	% of imports from China
Australia	China	EU	18.4%
India	EU	China	11.1%
Indonesia	China	Singapore	15.3%
Japan	China	EU	21.3%
Singapore	EU	Malaysia	10.3%
South Korea	China	Japan	15.5%
Taiwan	Japan	China	15.1%
Vietnam	China	South Korea	25.5%
Philippines	U.S.	China	10.9%
Thailand	Japan	China	14.9%

SOURCE: WTO, Trade Profile Database.

NOTE: China is the third-largest import market for Singapore.

or Australia and Indonesia. Yet mistrust regarding the intentions of other states is pervasive in the region and is not limited only to concerns about Chinese intentions. Likewise, security competition exists across a surprising number of relationships in Asia beyond the obvious tension between North Korea and South Korea.

Some observers of Asian defense spending have rightly pointed out that defense budgets in Asia are not growing across the board.[37] As others have correctly argued, though, Asian security competition tends not to follow the strict logic of arms racing and instead reflects a certain asymmetry in capability development.[38] This latter insight suggests that numerical figures might be less of a leading indicator of military modernization than observations of qualitative improvements in payload capacity, range, technological complexity, doctrine, and overall asymmetry relative to the militaries of potential competitors.

---

[37] See, for example, David C. Kang, "A Looming Arms Race in East Asia?" *National Interest*, May 14, 2014, http://nationalinterest.org/feature/looming-arms-race-east-asia-10461.

[38] Rod Lyon, "Gamechangers in Asia," *Strategist Online*, March 12, 2014, http://www.aspistrategist.org.au/gamechangers-in-asia.

China's dramatic press for military modernization is well documented, but an obsession with China misses the broader trend.[39] Taiwan is undergoing a comprehensive military modernization program ranging from upgraded point missile defense to procuring new minesweepers, attack helicopters, and naval surface vessels.[40] Similarly, the Philippines has 24 modernization projects underway, including new multipurpose attack vessels, upgraded fighter aircraft, and improved maritime surveillance capabilities.[41] The Indonesian military is allocating roughly one-third of its entire defense budget for the fiscal period 2010–14 to wholesale modernization across all warfighting domains.[42] Australia and Singapore are both moving in the direction of advanced fighter aircraft procurement with their respective decisions to pursue the F-35. Vietnam has increased investments in maritime patrol craft and begun acquiring fast attack submarines from Russia.[43] Myanmar, which has focused most of its military effort internally in recent decades, is looking to produce the Sino-Pakistani JF-17, a multirole fighter aircraft that is a better fit for fighting foreign militaries than domestic rebellions.[44] And Japan, despite being the only nation with a constitution that forswears war, has increased its role in Asian security and "collective defense," alongside maintaining its regional superiority in ballistic missile defense, upgrading its fighter aircraft to the F-35, increasing investments in antisubmarine warfare, and beginning amphibious landing exercises with the United States.[45]

The gradual militarization of the region as described above looks much more like a security dilemma than a security community. Fitting with a security dilemma image is the trust deficit that exists, even though most Asian nations lack declared adversaries. One survey of foreign policy elites in

---

[39] For an official assessment of China's military modernization, see Office of the Secretary of Defense, *Annual Report to Congress: Military and Security Developments Involving the People's Republic of China 2013* (Washington, D.C., 2013).

[40] "Taiwan's Force Modernization: The American Side," *Defense Industry Daily*, June 4, 2014, http://www.defenseindustrydaily.com/taiwans-unstalled-force-modernization-04250.

[41] Richard Jacobson, "Modernizing the Philippine Military," *Diplomat*, August 22, 2013, http://thediplomat.com/2013/08/modernizing-the-philippine-military.

[42] Tiarma Siboro, "Indonesia, U.S. Deepen Defense Ties amid Exercises and Arms Deals," *Defense News*, September 30, 2013, http://www.defensenews.com/article/20130930/DEFREG03/309300033/Indonesia-US-Deepen-Defense-Ties-Amid-Exercises-Arms-Deals.

[43] Daniel Bodirsky, "Vietnam's Naval Modernization Threatens to Destabilize Region," *Global Risk Insights*, April 1, 2014, http://www.globalriskinsights.com/2014/04/01/vietnams-naval-modernization-threatens-to-destabilize-region.

[44] Zackary Keck, "Burma to Purchase Chinese-Pakistani JF-17 Fighter Jets," *Diplomat*, June 25, 2014, http://thediplomat.com/2014/06/burma-to-purchase-chinese-pakistani-jf-17-fighter-jets.

[45] Greg Waldron, "In Focus: China Crisis Adds Urgency to Japanese Air Force Modernisation," *Flight International*, October 8, 2012, http://www.flightglobal.com/news/articles/in-focus-china-crisis-adds-urgency-to-japanese-air-force-377060; and James Hardy, "Japan's Navy: Sailing Towards the Future," *Diplomat*, January 21, 2013, http://thediplomat.com/2013/01/japans-navy-steaming-towards-the-future.

Southeast Asia found that 59.8% of respondents claimed that ASEAN states could not be trusted to be "good neighbors." When asked whether ASEAN neighbors could be trusted, 37.5% of respondents answered in the affirmative, but 36.1% were unsure and 26.4% answered that they could not trust all their neighbors.[46] Some observers of Southeast Asian politics have pointed to this combination of mistrust and military investment as indicative of intra-ASEAN military competition.[47] In Northeast Asia, meanwhile, the lack of trust in Korea-Japan relations has prevented even modest information-sharing agreements from being implemented.[48]

The Uncertainty of a Complex Network

The third perspective that accounts for the strategic hedging trend—the uncertainty of decision-making in a complex network structure—also anticipates arms buildups but focuses on additional indicators of hedging. Two such indicators are evident by their absence: the first is governments avoiding institutional commitments, and the second is governments avoiding new alliances. The network perspective also delivers a different explanation for the trend of Asian states gravitating toward China economically while simultaneously moving closer to the U.S. security orbit.

Alliances often form in order to cope with a shared external threat, though the persistence of shared threats is not necessary to sustain them.[49] Because alliances create binding commitments between states, each must enter into the commitment with some expectation about the role or interest that the alliance would potentially serve in the future in order for a country to justify tying its fate to another. It thus follows that if decision-makers in the region are unclear about the incentives for an alliance, they will be keen to avoid committing to one. By all indications, such is the state of Asian international relations today. Although existing treaty allies are quick to reaffirm and even strengthen their commitments in the face of a complex and uncertain decision-making environment, there is no demand

[46] Chris Roberts, "Ideas and Institutions: Building an ASEAN Community?" (paper presented at the ASEAN 40th Anniversary Conference, S. Rajaratnam School of International Studies [RSIS], Singapore, 2007); and Chris Roberts, "The ASEAN Community: Trusting Thy Neighbour?" RSIS, RSIS Commentaries, no. 110, 2007.

[47] Richard A. Bitzinger, "A New Arms Race? Explaining Recent Southeast Asian Military Acquisitions," *Contemporary Southeast Asia* 32, no. 1 (2010): 50–69.

[48] Yul Sohn and Won-Taek Kang, "South Korea in 2012: An Election Year under Rebalancing Challenges," *Asian Survey* 53, no. 1 (2013): 198–205.

[49] Robert O. Keohane, *International Institutions and State Power: Essays in International Relations Theory* (Boulder: Westview Press, 1989), 3; and Celeste A. Wallander, "Institutional Assets and Adaptability: NATO after the Cold War," *International Organization* 54, no. 4 (2000): 705–35.

for new alliances coming from any state in the region. There are debates about regional institutional constructs and how the Cold War–era alliance system fits in the context of Asia today,[50] but there is no discourse around new alliance formation.

The same story applies to the creation of rules-based institutions. If institutions are defined as "persistent sets of rules (formal and informal) that prescribe behavioral roles, constrain activity, and shape expectations,"[51] ASEAN, the ASEAN Regional Forum, the Asia-Pacific Economic Cooperation (APEC), the East Asia Summit, ADMM-Plus, and other multilateral bodies demonstrate that institutions are an important part of Asia's security landscape. But all these institutions are of a certain type, involving free association and consensus-based decision-making. States participate in Asia's institutional forms freely, every participant has veto power over institutional decisions, the decisions of these institutions are not legally binding, and there are no enforcement mechanisms if the rules of the institutions are violated. Contrast this situation with the Western experience, in which the legal-contractual institutional design of the European Union and NATO rely heavily on binding rules and enforcement mechanisms.[52] It has been argued that the binding commitments of rules-based institutions found in Europe are incompatible with either the identities or the prevailing norms in Asia. Yet this may not be the only reason rules-based institutions do not arise in Asia and seemingly will not arise anytime soon. For states that seek to hedge by avoiding "locking in" to long-term alignment decisions, it should not matter whether the lock-in takes the form of commitment to an alliance or commitment to an institution. Viewed in this way, Asia's soft form of consensual multilateral institutions is resilient and garners broad participation because such institutions offer at least the possibility of doing what stricter institutions do (benchmarking intentions, reducing transaction costs, socializing norms, and facilitating collective action) without posing much of a threat to any member nation's interests.

Finally, the network perspective's embrace of heterarchy provides a different way of accounting for what appears to be China's considerable attraction within the economic sphere and the parallel appeal of the United States within the security sphere. The examples cited in the power transition section serve as evidence that Asian international relations are heterarchical. At a minimum, there exists an economic hierarchy, a security

---

[50] See, for example, Amitav Acharya, "The Emerging Regional Architecture of World Politics," *World Politics* 59, no. 4 (2007): 629–52.

[51] Keohane, *International Institutions and State Power*, 3.

[52] Christopher Hemmer and Peter J. Katzenstein, "Why Is There No NATO in Asia? Collective Identity, Regionalism, and the Origins of Multilateralism," *International Organization* 56, no. 3 (2002): 575–607.

hierarchy, and an ambiguous values or cultural hierarchy. Although the United States remains the most critical security partner in the region, China—not the United States—is the top trading partner with nearly every East Asian country. China has called for a new regional architecture that seeks to jettison U.S. alliances as a Cold War relic,[53] yet U.S. allies in the region have across the board strengthened their security ties with the United States. And the U.S.-touted Trans-Pacific Partnership (TPP), a values-laden regional trade pact, has struggled to gain accession from the region's largest economies, including China, Taiwan, South Korea, Japan, and Vietnam, at least partly because of disagreement with certain U.S. expectations relating to environmental and labor requirements. At the same time, the Regional Comprehensive Economic Partnership (RCEP) promoted by China, which is a potential regional trade pact alternative that explicitly excludes the United States and has so far implied greater flexibility on regulations and labor standards, has not yet supplanted TPP efforts.[54] The fact that these regional issues remain unresolved makes sense when accepting that regional relations are structured as an informal heterarchy.

Strategic and Policy Implications

Accounting for trends in the design of strategy is crucial because it allows us to cope with an uncertain future analytically. The above discussion laid the conceptual groundwork necessary to understand the trend of strategic hedging that has emerged in Asia over the past several years because trust in the region is generally low and uncertainty (of various types) is generally high. Given the rise and persistence of this trend and the three different ways of understanding it offered above, what does the power of this trend mean for U.S. strategy and policy toward the region? The U.S. record of taking advantage of regional trends in Asia is mixed and has had dramatic consequences in the past.

Consider one example of success and one of failure in this regard: Sino-U.S. rapprochement and the Vietnam War. As the Cold War proceeded into the 1960s, it became increasingly clear that Communism was no monolith. Instead, a trend had taken hold: the Communist bloc was fissuring into what looked like Chinese and Soviet camps, creating opportunities

---

[53] Shannon Tiezzi, "At CICA, Xi Calls for New Regional Security Architecture," *Diplomat,* May 22, 2014, http://thediplomat.com/2014/05/at-cica-xi-calls-for-new-regional-security-architecture.

[54] For a comparison of the TPP and RCEP, see the transcript from the Brookings Institution conference "TPP and RCEP: Competing or Complementary Models of Economic Integration?" held on February 11, 2014. The transcript is available at http://www.brookings.edu/events/2014/02/11-asia-pacific-economic-integration.

for smaller powers like North Korea to take advantage of the Sino-Soviet split by playing one Communist power off of the other and maintaining an equidistant position between them.[55] Over time, the geopolitical trend of Sino-Soviet enmity was hard not to acknowledge. Neither the Soviet Union nor China commanded the consistent loyalty of smaller Communist nations in Asia, and Nikita Khrushchev and Mao Zedong harbored ill will toward one another. By the time Richard Nixon took office in 1969, the Sino-Soviet split had erupted into a string of firefights between the two sides.[56] Nixon and Henry Kissinger's controversial but ultimately successful rapprochement with China had the effect of isolating the Soviet Union—a gambit that was only possible because they recognized a major geopolitical trend.[57]

By contrast, in the 1950s and 1960s a different trend emerged in Asia involving nationalist anticolonial movements for independence. In Vietnam, Ho Chi Minh's highly nationalist form of Communism enabled him to mobilize the Vietnamese people against the colonial government, ejecting the French from Vietnam by 1954. Even though Vietnam represented only one of many anticolonial movements in Asia emerging at the time, the United States failed to recognize it as such, viewing it instead as part of the steady march of Communism, the advance of which had to be stopped.[58] The Vietnam War had many causes, but a crucial assumption in U.S. decision-making before and during the conflict was that the United States was fighting a Communist affront, not a nationalist movement.[59] The regional policy failure that the Vietnam War represented was partly made possible by a U.S. failure to recognize a regional trend.

How, then, can the United States adapt to the era of strategic hedging in Asia? How does this trend affect different aspects of U.S. strategy and policy toward the region? The remainder of this chapter explores the implications of strategic hedging in three specific areas: competition and interoperability, security cooperation, and multilateralism.

---

[55] Bernd Schaefer, "North Korean 'Adventurism' and China's Long Shadow, 1966–72," Woodrow Wilson International Center for Scholars, Cold War International History Project, Working Paper, no. 44, October 2004.

[56] U.S. Department of State, "USSR/China: Soviet and Chinese Forces Clash on the Ussuri River," Intelligence Note, no. 139, March 4, 1969, available from George Washington University, National Security Archives, http://www2.gwu.edu/~nsarchiv/NSAEBB/NSAEBB351/Doc006.pdf.

[57] Evelyn Goh, *Constructing the U.S. Rapprochement with China, 1961–1974: From "Red Menace" to "Tacit Ally"* (Cambridge: Cambridge University Press, 2005).

[58] For a discussion of the anticolonial movements in Asia during this period, see Benedict Anderson, *The Spectre of Comparisons: Nationalism, Southeast Asia and the World* (New York: Verso, 1998).

[59] For further discussion, see Yuen Foong Khong, *Analogies at War: Korea, Munich, Dien Bien Phu, and the Vietnam Decisions of 1965* (Princeton: Princeton University Press, 1992), chaps. 4 and 6.

Competition and Interoperability

Security dilemmas in international relations are typically conceived in terms of one state's perception of another. As state A tries to secure itself against state B, its defensive actions and investments are perceived by state B as threatening, causing state B to pursue further armaments itself, which further undermines state A's feelings of security.[60] As long as strategic hedging continues to manifest as military modernization and increased defense spending, all states in the region will have the continuing incentive to do the same, if only to be able to avoid binding alliance or institutional commitments. As a result, security dilemmas may now come not only from an individual state's concerns about a single state but also from an individual state's need to keep up with region-wide militarization.

The response of Asian governments to this problem of a diffuse—rather than only dyadic—security dilemma raises an interoperability risk for the United States in two ways: as an operational barrier to cooperation with the United States and as an enabler of others to cooperate with potential U.S. competitors to the exclusion of the United States.[61] As Asian governments engage in force modernization, there is a risk that their demand for newer, better, and more extensive military equipment—from naval frigates and intelligence collection to unmanned aerial vehicles (UAV) and cruise missiles—will compel them to either indigenously develop military systems or import these systems from non-U.S. competitors (both in the defense-industrial sense and the geostrategic sense). These paths to force modernization make it more likely that the military equipment others develop or acquire will not be able to work together with U.S. equipment and U.S. forces. Even interoperability between the United States and South Korea—underwritten by a 60-plus year alliance, a combined military command, and a strong history of security cooperation—continues to face challenges that can mean the difference between victory and defeat on the battlefield.[62]

To illustrate the problem, even though Japan and South Korea share in common the United States as ally and military patron, the two governments'

---

[60] Robert Jervis, *Perception and Misperception in International Politics* (Princeton: Princeton University Press, 1976); and Shiping Tang, "The Security Dilemma: A Conceptual Analysis," *Security Studies* 18, no. 3 (2009): 587–623.

[61] Interoperability refers to the operational ability of one military's equipment, organizational procedures, and command and control to function together with those of another military for the sake of achieving a common purpose. This point is often taken for granted in discussions of cooperation between governments in international relations theory; when two governments express a political will to cooperate, it is assumed they will.

[62] Kurt E. Van Slooten, "Army's Top Communicator Visits Korea's Combined Military Headquarters," U.S. Army, Press Release, April 27, 2014, http://www.army.mil/article/124793/Army_s_top_communicator_visits_Korea_s_combined; and John Di Genio, "U.S. Forces in Korea Face Unique Challenges," *Signal Online*, October 2001, http://www.afcea.org/content/?q=node/489.

militaries are largely unable to work together at present, politically or operationally.[63] Large multilateral exercises that include both countries have helped bridge the interoperability gap between them. However, such exercises harmonize organizations and practices but cannot in themselves resolve hardware and software compatibility issues that stem from possessing, for example, Cold War–era Soviet military platforms or indigenously designed systems.[64] If, hypothetically, Japanese and South Korean politicians decided to pursue full military cooperation, there would still be many years of work and expense needed to align their respective commands and capabilities.

Japan and South Korea help illustrate the larger point: the ability of foreign militaries to engage in combined operations with the United States depends not only on political will but also on interoperable weapons systems and organizational practices. As more foreign militaries procure weapons systems from non-U.S. sources, it may become more difficult for them to engage in combined operations with the United States. To the extent that foreign militaries primarily operate Russian or Chinese equipment, they will be much better optimized to cooperate militarily with those countries than with the United States. And to the extent that governments develop indigenous military capabilities, they will in all likelihood be poorly optimized to work together with any potential partner at the operational level.

It should also be noted that strategic hedging represents a structural trend, which means that while it creates incentives for Asian states to favor some decisions and strategies over others, such hedging does not actually deprive Asian governments of agency. This is crucial because to the extent that China is or becomes an overtly revisionist power, its behavior should compel neighboring states to reluctantly abandon hedging in favor of a firmer approach. If contemporary signs of Chinese assertiveness endure or worsen, they could disrupt what appears at present to be a powerful, if uneasy, equilibrium that has heretofore reinforced regional stability. The same principle would likewise apply to a dramatic decision by any Asian state, such as a decision by South Korea to acquire nuclear weapons or by Japan to adopt a policy of preventive conflict.

Building Partner Military Capacity

The strategic hedging trend is also instructive for how the United States should go about building the military capacity of foreign partners through weapons exports, collaboration on R&D, training, and the socialization

---

[63] "U.S. Wants 'Interoperable, Integrated' Missile Defense with S. Korea: Official," Yonhap, May 31, 2014.

[64] Ankit Panda, "Chinese Navy Will Participate in RIMPAC Exercise for First Time," Diplomat, May 8, 2014, http://thediplomat.com/2014/05/chinese-navy-will-participate-in-rimpac-exercise-for-first-time.

of U.S. values with foreign partner military organizations. When it comes to building partner capacity (BPC), each of the three lenses on strategic hedging suggests a somewhat different (though not irreconcilable) approach.

Viewed through the power transition lens, U.S. BPC strategy should explicitly attend to states' ability to fight a larger, more powerful, high-end adversary such as China in a way that minimally disturbs the rising state's preference for disrupting the security *status quo ante* in the region. Because hedging strategies in Asia are being caused by uncertainty both about whether China will surpass the United States and about China's overall intentions, an optimal BPC strategy would need to enable Asian militaries to resist Chinese military force while not exacerbating China's dissatisfaction with the region's current equilibrium. If this became the principal concern of U.S. BPC efforts, the United States would need to deprioritize ground forces capacity and counterterrorism training in favor of naval mining and antisubmarine warfare capabilities, maritime surveillance, air and missile defense, attack helicopters, and cruise missiles. These are the ideal emphases of BPC from a military perspective, but they would need to be tailored to avoid making a revisionist China inevitable. Complicating this approach further is the reality that this shopping list of capabilities and skills is likely to face some resistance in nations with long traditions of disproportionate investment in (and privilege to) ground forces.

However, if one principally believes that the structure of Asian international relations is anarchical and increasingly multipolar—that China is not the only regional actor of potential concern—then diffuse mistrust becomes an important factor to which U.S. BPC strategy should be attuned. The challenge of BPC becomes one of enhancing the armaments of the United States' closest allies and partners—again with a focus on air, naval, and amphibious capabilities—so that they can keep up with military modernization norms in the region, while still managing security dilemmas and eschewing an arms-racing dynamic. The difference in BPC approach called for in this scenario versus the power transition scenario exists only to the extent that the tailored capabilities necessary to hedge against China differ from the capabilities required for a country to defend against its neighbors.

Finally, to the extent that the United States takes cues about an optimal BPC strategy from the network perspective on Asian international relations, the key considerations are those that socialize countries toward both restraint and U.S.-preferred values, preserve the United States' status as the security partner of choice in the region, and enable the United States to serve as a trust-building bridge between distant actors.[65] To socialize countries to U.S. values through BPC, export policy would be relaxed to allow the transfer of advanced weapons systems such as UAVs and cruise missiles to more partners in the region. The United States should also introduce behavioral constraints in the form of end-use agreements and perhaps follow-on, U.S.-based systems training. Because the United States' BPC is a finite resource, a network perspective would prioritize assistance in the form of capabilities and training that promote trust and interoperability among uncooperative partners through U.S. efforts as a bridge, as well as efforts to increase U.S. influence with governments with which Washington has historically had few ties. In practice, this would likely mean emphasizing capabilities such as regional missile defense, maritime surveillance, and humanitarian assistance and disaster relief cooperation between countries like Japan and South Korea or Indonesia and Australia. It would also mean using BPC resources to build U.S. connectivity to countries that have associated more closely with China than the United States in the past, including continuing support to Myanmar, as well as military connectivity with countries even less connected to the United States, such as Cambodia and North Korea. Because trust with these nations is so low, cooperation and assistance might not emphasize weapons systems but instead logistics and organizational interoperability.

Although some of these measures are admittedly difficult to implement, the principle of operating in a network system holds that connectivity is a basic prior condition for influence. If, years from now, the Sino-U.S. relationship takes an unfortunate turn and evolves into an openly competitive relationship, the United States would only be able to disrupt or co-opt China's relations with some of its traditional client states if the United States has preexisting network ties to them. The United States and the region would be better off avoiding a repeat of the Cold War, but if it happened, the United States would be better positioned to shape regional relations with ties to these states than without them. The United States would also be seen as more crucial to regional stability if it were the principal bridge that connected politically or strategically distant nations. This is the role that the United States

---

[65] These factors in a network-centric strategy are nontechnical descriptions of a different way to think about power, placed in the vocabulary of complex networks, which correspond to the concepts of homophily (influence by cooperation made possible by norming actors toward having common attributes), network centrality (influence by being crucial for the existing connections between others), and bridging structural holes (influence by making possible connections that did not exist previously).

played during much of the Cold War, and, according to some, it is the role that is currently being implicitly renegotiated in contemporary Asia.[66]

Multilateralism and Regional Integration

All three perspectives on the strategic hedging trend augur against the United States trying to replicate the institutional successes of Europe in Asia. A multilateral alliance structure akin to NATO or a supranational community like the European Union would not fit well with either the Asian experience or the region's trajectory based on any of the three theoretical perspectives offered here. If the focus of our analysis is Sino-U.S. relations, conceived primarily as a contest for regional supremacy, institutions can be viewed as a means of perpetuating the preferences of the hegemon. There would be no need for a collective security arrangement if regional stability rested on adhering to the preferred order of the hegemon. If, by contrast, we primarily take the view that power is diffusing, multipolarity is around the corner, and states are largely incapable of trust, then binding, rules-based security institutions are incompatible with what is actually achievable in the region. Asian states would resist such constructs, and if the United States somehow were to manage to impose them anyway, the lack of trust would inhibit the ability of these institutions to promote stability. Finally, if we view Asian international relations as a complex web of relations with a high degree of sensitivity, issue complexity, and multiple hierarchies, rules-based institutions run contrary to regional preferences for avoiding new commitments, whether to new alliances or multilateral institutions.

The implications of strategic hedging extend beyond the security domain as well. The United States has put considerable effort toward gaining region-wide support for the TPP but has met with limited success in gaining as signatories some of the most important economies in the region. From the power transition perspective, the TPP is unlikely to gain full regional support as long as states are unclear about how Sino-U.S. relations will be resolved. In the unlikely event that either China or the United States were to unambiguously become the dominant power in the region, such an outcome would determine the fate of the TPP. The multipolarity perspective is concerned primarily with the high politics of national security rather than the low politics of political economy, which generally makes multipolarity an insufficient basis for answering economic questions. Still, the multipolar perspective suggests that the TPP may face challenges for reasons of

---

[66] Evelyn Goh characterizes the U.S. leadership role—including as the region's connective bridge during the Cold War—as continuously contestable and negotiable. See Evelyn Goh, *The Struggle for Order: Hegemony, Hierarchy, and Transition in Post–Cold War East Asia* (New York: Oxford University Press, 2013).

pervasive mistrust.[67] And from the complex network perspective, the TPP is incompatible with the heterarchical realities of Asia: the TPP largely reflects U.S.-preferred values related to human rights, environmental regulations, and labor standards, yet Asia's economies align more closely with China's preference for disentangling economic transactions from normative judgments, which has argued for the RCEP as an alternative to the TPP. In this way, the complex network perspective views the TPP as simply dissonant with the structural incentives of Asian international relations.

Regardless of one's perspective, then, viewing the strategic hedging trend from the system level suggests that the TPP is likely to continue as an uphill battle in the near term. Because conclusion of the TPP is in the U.S. interest, the challenges facing the TPP do not imply that U.S. diplomats and trade negotiators should simply abandon the trade pact. These challenges do, however, suggest that it may be imprudent to make the TPP a presidential priority or the cornerstone of the U.S. policy of rebalancing to Asia.

Conclusion

There are layers of incentives for Asian states to adopt hedging strategies, each obeying a distinct logic but potentially reinforcing each other. As the United States continues its policy of rebalancing to the Asia-Pacific, it must account for these drivers of regional behavior. At a basic level, states may be uncertain about a potential power transition between China and the United States, leading them to hedge because they are uncertain about with whom to align. Asian states also seem to be uncertain about the intentions of other states, and it is no longer only the United States and China to which they must be attuned. The region may have only two "great powers," but power is diffusing and the ability of smaller states (and nonstate actors) to influence international outcomes is growing. Uncertain about whom to trust, states cope by hedging as long as threats remain undeclared and beneath the surface. At the same time, the complex patchwork of Asian international relations is a web of relationships of varying degrees of strength and with a wide range of purposes. In a security environment structured in this way, states are inclined to avoid balancing and bandwagoning and are similarly inclined to avoid submitting themselves to rules-based institutions. The network perspective tells us that states should be inclined to hedge because the complex structure of the regional order makes it difficult to assess the future consequences of present-day commitments.

---

[67] For a discussion of security definitions and high-low politics, see David A. Baldwin, "The Concept of Security," *Review of International Studies* 23, no. 1 (1997): 5–26.

Every Asian government has its own domestic concerns and geopolitical imperatives, but there is a common set of incentives encouraging Asian states to adopt hedging strategies, illuminated by the three lenses introduced here: power transition, multipolarity, and complex networks. As some states pursue military modernization as part of hedging strategies, other states are encouraged to follow suit in order to keep up, which risks perpetuating mistrust and creating a region-wide security dilemma. As this sort of asymmetric arms racing proceeds, there is an added risk for the United States posed by challenges to military interoperability. The United States must ensure maximum interoperability with trusted allies and partners if it is ever expected to actually work cooperatively in a military sense, and that is best achieved by co-developing and cooperatively developing capabilities, training together, and establishing the United States as the partner of choice for military systems acquisitions. The recently signed EDCA with the Philippines provides a blueprint for how security cooperation can be structured to achieve these ends.

As the United States seeks to build the military capacity of foreign partners as part of its announced strategy to be engaged globally, it should de-emphasize BPC focused on ground forces and counterterrorism in favor of developing maritime capabilities, improving surveillance, and building bridges between historically uncooperative actors. Although BPC receives little attention in the broader discourse on foreign policy, it is vital. In Asia, U.S. BPC strategy faces the dual challenge of enabling allies and partners to be capable of resisting coercion by stronger powers while not exacerbating feelings of insecurity throughout the region. Finally, the United States should remain active in Asia's array of consensually oriented multilateral institutions and continue to eschew order-building of the kind now found in Europe; there can be no NATO in Asia as long as hedging strategies remain pervasive. Similarly, the United States should not invest too much of its policy resources in convincing others in the region to conclude TPP negotiations in the near term, even though doing so seems like an intuitive suggestion given the potential benefits to the United States and the region.

Yet although hedging is a long-term trend, and arguably the new state of equilibrium in Asia, this does not mean deviations are impossible. Major changes based on the decisions of regional states, such as a Chinese shift from assertiveness to outright aggression or a Japanese shift from a defensive footing to an offensive one, would surely transition the region from the current state of strategic hedging to a more conflict-ridden one that is tragically more familiar. Because the current state of affairs is what is creating common incentives for Asian states to seemingly all adopt hedging strategies, a dramatic shift in the regional structure would change the decision-making incentives. Ultimately, U.S. and Asian policymakers are free to do "any fool thing they like"—they need not act according to the incentives of the existing regional structure. But the trend of strategic hedging suggests that some strategies and policies toward Asia are more likely to be successful than others.

STRATEGIC ASIA 2014–15

TRENDS AND INDICATORS

TABLE OF CONTENTS

Strategic Asia Trends and Indicators

The past year witnessed significant evolution in Asia's geopolitical environment. The region has become ever more central to the long-term strength and prosperity of the United States. This reality is reflected in the continued progress of the Obama administration's rebalance to Asia, where greater focus in 2014 was devoted to the diplomatic and economic elements of the initiative.

While the most significant development in the Asia-Pacific continues to be the economic and geopolitical rise of China, other trends are of potentially great strategic importance. Crises in Central Europe and the Middle East, combined with continued restrictions to the U.S. defense budget, have raised questions in some quarters about the long-term capabilities and commitment of the United States in the Asia-Pacific. These concerns have led some regional powers—many of them U.S. allies and partners—to enhance their relationships with the United States and to adopt more active defense policies in the face of an increasingly complex regional security environment.

At the same time, Asia is becoming ever more economically integrated. This past year saw substantial progress on a number of major intra- and inter-regional trade deals that will further cement the region's status as the engine of global economic growth in the 21st century.

The following pages contain short essays on these and other major events and strategic trends that are likely to have lasting implications for the Asia-Pacific. Each piece was written by a member of the NBR team. Collectively, the essays explore some of the more prominent regional developments over the past year. The editors would like to thank Clara Gillespie, R. Lincoln Hines, Ildiko Hrubos, Tiffany Ma, Matthew Portwood, Clare Richardson-Barlow, Laura Schwartz, Kunihiro Shimoji, Ved Singh, Alison Szalwinski, and Jonathan Walton for their excellent contributions.

The U.S. Rebalance to Asia

Now in its third year, the U.S. rebalance to Asia remains a work in progress. While the focus on the United States' engagement in the Asia-Pacific reaffirms the region's ever-growing importance to U.S. national interests, competition for Washington's attention and resources continues to raise questions about the credibility and sustainability of the rebalance.

In the face of an increasingly complex security environment, the rebalance calls for modernizing and strengthening U.S. alliances that undergird the regional security order. The U.S.-Japan alliance, which remains the cornerstone of regional peace and stability, is poised to rise to new levels of cooperation. Following the Shinzo Abe government's historic reinterpretation of Japan's constitutional ban on "collective self-defense," Washington and Tokyo have pledged to complete a review of the bilateral defense cooperation guidelines—the first review in almost two decades. Elsewhere in the region, the United States took notable steps in 2014 to strengthen other alliances, including the signing of a 10-year military pact with the Philippines and a 25-year agreement to continue U.S. Marine rotations through Darwin, Australia. The long-planned deployment of an additional U.S. Army battalion to South Korea to increase combat readiness was similarly lauded as an affirmation of the rebalance. Likewise, Washington has worked to shore up long-term strategic partnerships with Singapore and New Zealand as well as solidify informal ties with Taiwan.

In addition to alliances and partnerships, the rebalance also prioritizes deepening ties with emerging powers to diversify U.S. engagement in Asia. The United States made strides in 2014 with the easing of an arms embargo on Vietnam and upgrading of relations with Malaysia to a "comprehensive partnership." U.S.-India relations were likewise reinvigorated with the change of government in New Delhi. India's potential as an economic and strategic partner underscores its dynamic role in the U.S. rebalance.

On the other hand, the rebalance has achieved limited success toward the goal of a constructive relationship with Asia's other giant, China. Tensions mounted in 2014 due to China's assertive maneuvers in the East and South China Seas and the fallout from continued Chinese cyberattacks against the United States. Meanwhile, the rebalance continues to exacerbate Beijing's suspicions that the United States and its allies seek to encircle and contain China. Despite efforts toward trust and confidence building—including China's inaugural participation in the annual Rim of the Pacific (RIMPAC) exercises—and the promise of a "new type of major-power relationship," significant disagreements and tension remain a major aspect U.S.-China relations.

Beyond improving the quality of bilateral relationships, the rebalance seeks to advance U.S. interests in a cooperative and prosperous Asia. The diplomatic arm of the rebalance has embraced Asia's multilateral organizations with the establishment a new permanent mission and appointment of an ambassador to the Association of Southeast Asian Nations (ASEAN). In 2014 the informal U.S.-ASEAN Defense Forum was hosted on U.S. soil for the first time. The United States has also utilized "minilaterals"—such as meetings between high-level officials from the United States, Australia, and Japan—as effective mechanisms for cooperation and coordination on security strategy and policy.

While the rebalance has created significant diplomatic momentum, progress on the economic front still faces significant hurdles. The success of the U.S. economic pivot has come to be measured by negotiations over the Trans-Pacific Partnership (TPP). The future of economic integration as envisioned by this Pacific Rim agreement not only ensures U.S. access to commerce and trade in Asia but also reinforces the United States' economic leadership in Asia. However, negotiations stalled in 2014 due to an impasse between Washington and Tokyo on access to agricultural markets and automobile tariffs, and President Barack Obama's inability to secure the authorization by Congress for trade promotion authority continues to hamper the rebalance as well.

Although U.S. allies and friends in the region have welcomed the rebalance, questions about the United States' credibility remain. In 2014, unanticipated crises in the Middle East and Eastern Europe preoccupied policymakers in Washington, while shrinking budgets continued to call into question the United States' ability to sustain the rebalance. Reductions in defense spending may impose constraints on force posture and procurement, with long-term repercussions. Although the United States has pledged to deploy 60% of naval and air forces to the Asia-Pacific by the year 2020, some analysts have expressed skepticism that this will produce a real increase in assets due to reduced force size. In the foreseeable future, fiscal austerity will necessitate prioritization and trade-offs—not just in the Pacific theater but also elsewhere in the world.

Despite these challenges, however, the United States remains the dominant power in the region. Its dynamic economy and its military might remain unrivaled in both breadth and capability, and its network of alliances and partnerships has firmly integrated the United States into the fabric of the Asia-Pacific. The challenge for the United States is not preventing a loss of power but maintaining its ability to effectively wield that power in the world's most geopolitically significant region. The overall success of the rebalance will depend on Washington's ability to push forward a comprehensive agenda across military, diplomatic, and economic dimensions.

Asia's Maritime Disputes

Over the past year, Asia's disputed waters have roiled with increasing tension and greater potential for crisis. China's unilateral declaration of an air defense identification zone (ADIZ) over the East China Sea and its general assertiveness in disputed waters along its periphery have dramatically increased regional uncertainty about the country's so-called peaceful development and intensified regional interest in greater interaction with the United States.

China's assertiveness in the East and South China Seas has taken place against the backdrop of its growing maritime capabilities, both civilian and military. Beijing has concentrated on developing a formidable blue water navy, announcing plans to build several new aircraft carriers to add to its sole existing carrier, *Liaoning*. According to the U.S. Department of Defense's annual report on the Chinese military, China's $119.5 billion defense budget for 2013 continues a trend of annual defense spending increases that has persisted for over two decades.

While much attention has been focused on China's naval advancements, such as the modernization of both its conventionally powered and its nuclear submarines, moves to consolidate the Chinese coast guard and utilize paramilitary vessels have become a key aspect in China's maritime dispute playbook. China's previously disparate civilian maritime forces have become the primary enforcers in disputes throughout the South and East China Seas, while imposing navy vessels have generally kept their distance during incidents. Using fishing vessels and civilian patrol vessels is a critical component of what some call a "salami-slicing" strategy meant to incrementally gain control of contested areas without inciting a major conflict.

China's dispute with Japan in the East China Sea over the Senkaku/Diaoyu Islands, remains an area of high tension and has witnessed multiple minor flare-ups. In November 2013, China expanded its sovereignty claims in the East China Sea from the sea to the air by declaring the aforementioned ADIZ that encompasses the disputed islands. Viewed by much of the international community as an unnecessary provocation, the move led to a range of responses. The United States flew two unarmed B-52 bombers through the zone (though U.S. officials claimed that such flights were unrelated to the ADIZ declaration), Japan rejected the claim outright, and South Korea raised concerns about China's inclusion of areas also claimed by Seoul. Continuing to shore up the United States' commitment to the U.S.-Japan alliance, President Obama reaffirmed U.S. support for Japan against external aggression while visiting Tokyo in April 2014 and, in the first such statement by a U.S. president, asserted that the U.S.-Japan security treaty covered the disputed Senkaku Islands.

The maritime disputes in the South China Sea have also seen significant activity this year. In an ongoing attempt to find a legal mechanism to settle its maritime dispute with China in the South China Sea, the Philippines submitted materials to the United Nations Court of Arbitration under the UN Convention on the Law of the Sea (UNCLOS), arguing that China's claim is invalid. China has refused to participate in the arbitration, and any ruling the court hands down will be largely symbolic. Beyond the outcome of the court's ruling, the case forms an important component of the Philippines' strategy against China by raising the profile of the dispute and giving the Philippines a chance to legitimate its claim and influence international public opinion.

While largely ignoring the UNCLOS case, Chinese leaders remain confident in China's growing ability to coerce and win escalatory conflicts with smaller neighbors in the region, and have sought to change the status quo incrementally in China's favor. For example, reports circulated this year that China was beginning to build structures on and artificially expand low-tide features in the Spratly island chain, raising alarm across the region. By building their own islands, China may hope to establish a firmer claim to the surrounding features, as well as create a base for surveillance and other operations throughout the South China Sea. Further escalating tension, China placed an exploratory oil rig near the disputed Paracel Islands in May 2014, touching off violent anti-Chinese protests in Vietnam. While China removed the oil rig ahead of its announced schedule, the combination of these more aggressive tactics has caused growing distrust in China's intentions in Southeast Asia, a perception that China had previously sought to prevent.

Despite increasing concern over China's maritime activities, ASEAN has been unable to come to an agreement on a Code of Conduct (CoC) to establish a legal framework for resolving rival maritime claims. Twelve years after signing the Declaration on the Conduct of Parties in the South China Sea that called for the negotiation of a CoC, ASEAN nations are not much closer to overcoming sensitive issues, such as national sovereignty, that impede progress toward a final agreement. Since Beijing finally signaled a willingness to begin negotiations on a CoC last year, the parties have met several times without any tangible results.

Given the success of its salami-slicing strategy in the South China Sea, China will likely continue to use relatively aggressive and asymmetrical tactics to make gains in its various maritime disputes. Although ASEAN continues to work on positive mechanisms to resolve differences among member states—most notably, by creating a CoC—China shows little willingness to reach an agreement. In the East China Sea, tensions between Japan and China remain a constant source of concern to stakeholders in the region. These factors indicate that maritime disputes will continue to be an important issue to watch in the years to come.

Abe's Reforms of Japan

Under the leadership of Prime Minister Shinzo Abe, Japan is undertaking a seismic change in its foreign and domestic policies. Having spent the first two years of his administration laying out his plans for reform, Abe is now approaching the phase where he will need to put those plans into action. The outcomes of these reforms will have critical implications for Japan's domestic affairs and for security and economic prosperity in Asia.

The security environment surrounding Japan has become increasingly tense. Tokyo is growing concerned about Beijing's continued military development and its assertive actions challenging Japan's territorial claims over the Senkaku Islands in the East China Sea (known as the Diaoyu Islands in China). Indeed, Japanese leaders worry that current tensions could escalate into open conflict. Meanwhile, North Korea poses an ever-present danger to the region, having engaged in further provocative actions by launching several short-range missiles toward the Sea of Japan and threatening to conduct additional nuclear tests.

This tense environment has led Abe to take steps to firm up Japan's national security. Central to these efforts has been Japan's shift in defense policy to enable the country to make a "proactive contribution to peace," a policy that reflects the administration's view that Japan's national security is dependent on its broader engagement in shaping the external security environment and contributing to international stability.

Under this new national defense policy, Abe has established two lines of focus. The first centers on strengthening the U.S.-Japan alliance as the key factor in developing a favorable strategic environment in the Asia-Pacific. To this end, Abe has announced ambitious new policies and reforms, including a nearly 3% increase to the defense budget, the establishment of a National Security Council, passage of the national secrecy law, the introduction of Japan's first-ever National Security Strategy, the cabinet decision to reinterpret Article 9 of the "peace constitution" to allow Japan to engage in collective self-defense, and a plan to revise the U.S.-Japan Guidelines for Defense Cooperation. While this process of "normalization" has raised concerns domestically and internationally due to Japan's historical militarism, Abe has emphasized that these changes will not move Japan away from its traditional pacifism and are intended to show its commitment to the alliance, which he and his U.S. counterparts believe is the cornerstone of regional peace and security.

The second line of Japan's new national defense policy focuses on deepening ties with like-minded nations in order to achieve peace and stability in the Asia-Pacific. In the past year, Abe emphasized strengthening bilateral and multilateral ties with maritime Asia, including with Australia and India. Furthermore, he has stressed the importance of working side by side with members of the Association of Southeast Asian Nations (ASEAN) to achieve a stable maritime domain given the area's importance to Japan's economic future. In particular, Japan has directed significant investment into Southeast Asia and is contributing to a number of infrastructure projects in the region, while also revising the charter on overseas development assistance, to allow Japanese funds to be directed toward military assistance.

Abe's ambitious national security policies, and his broader objective to revitalize Japanese power, cannot be achieved without the parallel success of his strategy to rejuvenate Japan's stagnant economy. The latter outcome will depend on the ultimate success of Abe's tri-fold economic policy known as Abenomics, as well as the completion of the Trans-Pacific Partnership (TPP). Concerns about Abe's economic reforms, however, skyrocketed when Japan's national growth rate fell to -6.8% in the second quarter of 2014, indicating that the policies are failing to meet their targets. Furthermore, TPP negotiators from the twelve participating countries are encountering difficulties reaching broad agreement on a number of issues. To make matters worse, the United States and Japan, the two largest economic parties to the TPP negotiations, are at loggerheads over several outstanding issues, including agricultural market access.

Domestic politics will also greatly affect Abe's ambitious policy agenda. In 2014, his approval rating fell from a high of 61% in early 2013 to below 50%. This recent dive is principally the result of the public's frustrations over Japan's uncertain economic recovery, Abe's plan to introduce another tax increase in 2015, and his defense policy reforms, including the reinterpretation of Article 9. As Abe moves forward in implementing these various reforms, he must overcome this recent dip in popularity. While many in Japan appreciate Abe's strong leadership, even while they may disagree with some of his specific reforms, the prime minister will need to demonstrate results if he seeks to sustain public support.

Since becoming prime minister, Abe has sought to lead Japan in a new direction by rejuvenating its economy, initiating major reforms to its national security approach, and demonstrating a renewed commitment to the U.S.-Japan alliance. In order to successfully complete his defense and security policy reforms, Abe will need to pursue a path that bolsters Japan's still-struggling economic recovery and allays domestic and international concerns. Without the success of these two factors, Japan risks a diminution in its regional power, reducing its ability to shape the future geopolitics of the Asia-Pacific. While Japan certainly has the wherewithal to sustain and build upon its remarkable postwar record of peace, economic development, and international engagement, it will be incumbent on Abe and his successors to realize the country's tremendous potential.

The Ukraine Crisis and East Asia

Russia's annexation of Crimea and its subsequent assertiveness against Ukraine have prompted concerns over the impact of unrest in Europe on U.S. strategic interests in East Asia. Russia's actions have challenged international norms, resulting in short-term geopolitical maneuvering, and have raised concerns about whether the United States will uphold its security commitments in East Asia. At this time, however, the tangible long-term implications of the Ukraine crisis for East Asia are unclear.

The financial, political, and strategic costs of President Vladimir Putin's gambit against Ukraine are growing for Russia. The United States has retaliated against Russian aggression with increasingly targeted, coordinated, and robust economic sanctions. Europe, once reluctant to follow suit because of its close energy and economic ties with Moscow, is also sanctioning Russia in coordination with the United States. As a result, Russia is now faced with further diplomatic isolation and economic pressure. The need to diversify its energy exports and place political pressure on European economies gives Moscow an added impetus for improving its relationships with East Asian countries. However, many of these countries have a stake in condemning Russia's flagrant violation of international norms and are now under diplomatic pressure from the United States to join the growing sanctions regime against Russia.

Consequently, the crisis in Ukraine has complicated bilateral relations between Russia and some of its East Asian neighbors, particularly Japan. Japanese prime minister Shinzo Abe has been seeking closer relations with Russia in order to resolve the two countries' territorial dispute over the Northern Territories (known as the Kuril Islands in Russia) and to diversify Japan's energy imports. However, Tokyo also has a keen interest in upholding international norms against unilateral territorial annexation, given its territorial disputes with China in the East China Sea. Moreover, it is now under pressure from the United States to join the expanding sanctions regime against Russia and is following the group of seven (G-7) partners in sanctioning Russia, though mostly through token measures. Russia has retaliated by holding military drills on the disputed islands of Etorofu and Kunashiri. The duration of Russia-Japan tensions, however, is questionable. The Ukraine crisis could improve or Japan could decide that the sanctions are too inimical to its trade and energy interests with Russia.

Meanwhile, the crisis has seemingly enhanced Sino-Russian relations. In May 2014, Beijing and Moscow signed a $400 billion deal to build a pipeline providing natural gas to China for the next 30 years. Though negotiations for this energy deal lasted over a decade, the timing of this announcement may be seen as symbolic—a gesture that Russia is not exclusively dependent on the Western market for its energy supplies. Moreover, Putin may see China as a potentially useful means to distract the United States' attention away from his actions in Eastern Europe, or at least as a means to complicate U.S. calculations in responding to Russian assertiveness.

China and Russia have long made gestures of forming a closer partnership. Yet they also have long been suspicious of each other's intentions and have actively competed for influence in the resource-rich region of Central Asia. Furthermore, as China continues to rise in economic and military power, Russia may become increasingly uncomfortable with being the lesser partner in this relationship. However, even though a truly robust partnership between Russia and China may never materialize, the specter of a close relationship between the two serves as a powerful political tool.

Apart from the impacts of the Ukraine crisis on Russia's bilateral relationships in East Asia, the crisis has also raised concerns regarding U.S. security commitments in the region and its ability and will to rebalance to Asia. To some observers, the Obama administration's response to Russia's annexation of Crimea was tepid, potentially encouraging Chinese adventurism and raising concerns among U.S. allies about whether or not the United States would uphold its security commitments in the event of a similar crisis in the Asia-Pacific. To others, Ukraine demonstrated the danger of economic dependence on a territorially aggressive neighbor without enjoying the protection of an alliance with the United States.

Nevertheless, the perception that the United States is declining and the weakening of fundamental international norms are harmful to U.S. security interests and should be countered in word and deed. Although U.S. policy toward Ukraine has not placed tangible, material constraints on the rebalancing effort to Asia, the United States' credibility in the region has been called into question in some quarters. These concerns about the U.S. response in Crimea are understandable, as the Crimea crisis has occurred within the larger context of U.S. budget constraints, reduced defense spending, and continued setbacks in the Middle East.

However, it is also important to not overstate the net effect of the Ukraine crisis for U.S. credibility in Asia. Chinese policymakers could conclude that the United States would have similar difficulty intervening in the event of an armed conflict in the Taiwan Strait or the South and East China Seas, but these disputes are incomparable to Crimea. Ukraine is not an ally, does not receive security guarantees from the United States, and is a much smaller trading partner to the United States than any of its Asian allies. Therefore, the credibility of U.S. power in Asia is not being tested in Ukraine.

Overall, the Ukrainian crisis has produced limited tangible consequences for the Asia-Pacific. China-Russia relations are temporarily enhanced, but Russia's relationship with Japan has become more complicated. At the same time, Washington's ability and will to maintain its security commitments in Asia remain unchanged. Perceptions of U.S. credibility, however, have been damaged at least for the short term by the crisis. The longer-term implications will likely hinge on the disposition of Ukraine and the rest of Eastern Europe. If U.S. allies come under a direct and real threat, the United States' credibility in Asia will certainly be tested. Until then, regional countries—both friends and adversaries—will likely continue to watch and wait.

The Complicated Relationship between Japan and South Korea

2015 marks the 50th anniversary of the normalization of relations between Japan and the Republic of Korea (ROK). In 1965, Japan established diplomatic relations with South Korea, offering $800 million in grants and low-interest loans. Five decades later, however, historical and political disputes have cast a chill on bilateral relations.

Unresolved historical tensions continue to complicate the Japan-ROK relationship: Seoul demands that Tokyo apologize for the treatment of

Korean "comfort women" before and during World War II, while Japan insists that the 1965 Treaty on Basic Relations already delivered apologies as well as reparations. A 2014 study by a Japanese government panel of the 1993 Kono Statement, which apologized to former comfort women and acknowledged the culpability of the Japanese military in their abuse, found that the statement had been developed through frequent exchanges with the South Korean government—a finding that Seoul rejects.

Further exacerbating tensions, in December 2013 Japanese prime minister Shinzo Abe made an unapologetic visit to the controversial Yasukuni Shrine, which memorializes Japan's war dead, including several Class A war criminals from the occupations of South Korea and China during World War II. Abe and other government officials were also widely criticized for statements that seemed to minimize Japanese culpability for aggression and human rights violations before and during the war.

Adding more fuel to the fire is a centuries-old territorial dispute over small rocks in the Sea of Japan, known as the Dokdo Islands in South Korea and the Takeshima Islands in Japan. In August 2012, Lee Myung-bak became the first South Korean president to visit the disputed islands, igniting nationalist passions on both sides, as this dispute often serves as a symbol of a more fundamental antagonism and competition between the two nations.

Given persistent tension over their shared wartime past, Korean president Park Geun-hye raised the specter of Japanese militarism following Abe's 2014 reinterpretation of Japan's peace constitution. In order to enable Abe's doctrine of "proactive pacifism," Japan's cabinet chose to reinterpret Article 9 of the constitution to allow the exercise of the right of collective self-defense. This decision would allow Japan's military capability to expand and enable enhanced military cooperation between the United States and Japan throughout the Asia-Pacific. It further allows Japan to militarily assist a foreign country with which it has a close relationship, provided that the attack threatens Japan's survival and poses a clear danger to the rights of the Japanese people. While Abe assured the world that Japan's capabilities would remain limited and inherently peaceful, the language utilized includes a great deal of ambiguity.

At the national level, significant elements of the Japanese and South Korean polities are fiercely nationalistic. For example, when Lee considered signing the General Security of Military Information Agreement and the Military Acquisition and Cross-Servicing Agreement in June 2012 to bolster military cooperation with Japan, he encountered such significant domestic backlash that he put the two agreements on hold. This contributed to a chilling of diplomatic relations that persists to this day: Japan and ROK leaders have not held a formal bilateral meeting since Yoshihiko Noda and Lee met in May 2012.

Despite the current level of political animus, Japan and South Korea have maintained robust working-level ties in multiple spheres. In the summer of 2014, Japan and the ROK joined 21 other countries for the Rim of the Pacific (RIMPAC) exercise, the world's largest international maritime exercise. In July 2014, Japan, the ROK, and the United States jointly conducted the Search and Rescue Exercise (SAREX) off the southern coast of the Korean Peninsula. In addition, U.S. secretary of defense Chuck Hagel, ROK minister of national defense Kim Kwan-jin, and Japanese defense minister Itsunori Onodera met in Singapore on the sidelines of the Shangri-La Dialogue in May 2014 to discuss North Korea and Asia-Pacific regional security.

In terms of economic relations, South Korea, and Japan have tabled their historical differences to pursue a trilateral free trade agreement (FTA) with China. The FTA will stimulate the three countries' economic growth and encourage regional integration. Bilaterally, South Korea has recently increased its smartphone exports to Japan, and Japan has increased its investments in South Korea's raw materials sector.

The United States has a significant interest in encouraging cooperation between Japan and the ROK for several reasons: First, Washington wants its two allies to support each other; divisions between allies are detrimental to the Obama administration's policy of rebalancing to Asia and the United States' larger goals in the region. Second, if a situation on the Korean Peninsula were to require U.S. intervention, Japan would serve as a critical launch, surge, and evacuation point. Third, Japan-Korea cooperation is needed to respond to the North Korean threat and China's growing influence in the Asia-Pacific, especially as Kim Jong-un continues to test missiles and develop a viable nuclear weapons program and tensions continue to rise in the South and East China Seas.

In an effort to improve relations between Washington's two closest allies in Asia, President Obama convened with Abe and Park for a trilateral discussion on the sidelines of the Nuclear Security Summit in March 2014. Although Abe and Park were cautious in their first meeting since either leader took office, they agreed that strong U.S.-Japan-ROK relations were necessary to roll back the North Korean nuclear threat. In a positive step, Park agreed to reopen discussions—on hold since 2012—regarding the trilateral sharing of military intelligence. Continued effort from the United States will be required, however, for Japan and the ROK to put their historical differences aside and work together. Only then can the United States, Japan, and the ROK more seriously address the significant challenges confronting the region.

The Consolidated Leadership of Xi Jinping

The members of the Central Committee of the Chinese Communist Party are named every five years and meet for a total of seven plenary sessions over their five-year term. The third such plenary session, or "Third Plenum," has historically been a chance for the leadership to unveil new reforms—the 1978 Third Plenum launched China's "reform and opening" and the 1993 Third Plenum introduced additional economic reforms. Consequently, expectations were high for the Third Plenum of November 2013, which was the first real chance for President Xi Jinping to articulate his vision for China's future.

Both leading up to and in the months after the plenum itself, popular, scholarly, and official discussions of potential reforms were closely intertwined with speculation about Xi's agenda. Much attention was paid to Xi's efforts to consolidate his personal authority within the Communist Party, where factionalism, rule-by-committee, and heeding the words of retired party elders is often the norm. Compared with his predecessor Hu Jintao, Xi has moved much more rapidly and forcefully than expected to sideline his political opponents and assert his own power independent of other major players. However, it is unclear if Xi will be able to successfully convince, cajole, coerce, or outmaneuver the significant entrenched political and economic interests that his reforms will inevitably confront. While Xi certainly has a greater degree of authority than several of his predecessors, questions remain about whether he is powerful enough to put China on a different course.

In the months prior to the Third Plenum, Xi announced multiple campaigns purportedly aimed at strengthening discipline, reducing waste, and combatting corruption within the Communist Party. Officials were encouraged to live simply, conduct government affairs in an economical fashion, travel with only a small entourage, cease issuing reports with no real content, and otherwise improve the quality of governance and reduce criticism from Chinese citizens by combating formalism, bureaucracy, hedonism, and extravagance.

Building on this effort, an anticorruption campaign was launched to investigate and remove officials who had unfairly profited from their positions, including multiple "tigers" or high-level targets connected to China's state-run oil companies. The biggest of these tigers was former security czar Zhou Yongkang, who previously served on the all-powerful Politburo Standing Committee. While the investigation of Zhou was not officially announced until summer 2014, he was previously criticized for being a supporter of Bo Xilai, the purged and imprisoned former party secretary of Chongqing.

Controversy remains over whether the intent behind these campaigns is truly to reduce corruption and waste or rather to strengthen unity and Xi's own position within the top leadership. He likely has multiple goals in mind, and these objectives are not mutually incompatible. The investigation of Zhou has not necessarily signaled the apex of Xi's efforts in this regard, though some party elders have signaled that they do not want these campaigns to turn into an unchecked witch-hunt in the manner of Mao-era "rectification" purges that caused great suffering, significant domestic turmoil, and damage to the party's legitimacy.

Though not as ambitious as rumors had suggested prior to the Third Plenum, the economic and policy reforms announced in November 2013 are still the most comprehensive since the beginning of the reform and opening period in 1978. They include letting markets play a stronger role in the economy; major revisions to the household registration system, tax system, and property rights; strengthening the regulation of state-owned enterprises; abolishing China's system of work camps for accused criminals; major reforms to the structure of China's military; a loosening of some aspects of the one-child policy; strengthening the legal system; re-examining and restructuring the way the Chinese government handles both internal and international security; and enacting social, medical, and health reforms to better support the country's aging population.

While this list of reforms is impressive, their implementation will likely be highly difficult. A number of "leading small groups" that are directly accountable to the top leadership have been tasked with enacting these reforms, but many of the institutions involved—including the military and state-owned enterprises—are notoriously resistant to large-scale changes and have previously been the target of proposed reforms that were never fully implemented. However, some changes are already underway, and Xi's significant personal authority and mandate from the rest of the party's leadership may give him and the rest of the Politburo Standing Committee the ability to push through reforms that have been stymied before.

While China is an authoritarian state with a centralized system for monitoring and directing lower-level officials, it is not likely that significant and controversial initiatives can be enacted quickly and easily. The most probable result is that the announced reforms will usher in significant changes, but will not be fully realized or necessarily have all the intended effects. Initiatives from the top will have to be negotiated and implemented at the local level, and local experiments will lead to specific proposed efforts being revised or canceled outright. A few major initiatives may prove to be impossible because of intense resistance from local officials or vested economic and political interests that stand to lose power if these reforms are enacted. Concerns about domestic stability and international security may trump other efforts to loosen certain controls. Some reforms may lead by necessity to a cascade of other unexpected changes—a prospect that raises serious concerns in Beijing about a general loss of control and legitimacy by the Chinese Communist Party.

Reform will not come easily to China. The seven members of the Politburo Standing Committee will next be reshuffled following the 19th National Congress of the Chinese Communist Party in 2017, which should also launch Xi's second five-year term in charge and provide a platform for analyzing the process of reform up to that point. The results of the next few years will thus help determine the composition and orientation of China's future leadership, as Xi continues to face an incredibly complex web of political and economic interests, traditions, and ideologues as he seeks to guide China into the 21st century.

Changing Energy Dynamics in the Asia-Pacific

Dramatic shifts in the Asia-Pacific are reshaping world energy markets, with significant economic, geopolitical, and environmental implications. As of 2014, the Asia-Pacific accounts for the majority of both the world's leading energy producers and its leading energy consumers, with China and the United States among the top five on both lists. Meanwhile, as global energy demand rises by 33% through 2035, nearly two-thirds of that growth will come from developing Asia alone. This growth will also feature a prominent role for coal in fueling Asia's continued development. The policy community and industry are increasingly making sustainable and cleaner development a top priority in both national and regional dialogues on energy security. Yet leaders across the Asia-Pacific also face significant market and policy uncertainties, suggesting a need for ongoing, innovative discussion of how to best address common concerns in an evolving regional context.

An important element of this regional picture are the revolutionary changes underway in North America, particularly in the United States. As NBR has previously noted, since 2006, hydraulic fracturing and horizontal drilling technology have reversed a historical decline in U.S. oil and gas production. Consequentially, U.S. dependence on oil imports peaked in 2005, and China ultimately surpassed the United States as the world's largest oil importer in 2013. Developments in gas markets have been even more dramatic, with the United States emerging as the world's top global producer of natural gas, a status that BP estimates the country will retain through at least 2035.

These trends are having far-reaching impacts on market outlooks by freeing up supplies of oil and gas in global markets and reducing the relative use of coal in the U.S energy mix. Yet for most countries in the Asia-Pacific, the energy narrative is still one of perceived scarcity. As noted by the Asian Development Bank, by 2035 most Asian countries will produce less than half the energy that they consume, and many will produce only a tiny fraction. As a result, policymakers and industry leaders across Asia must address growing and quite varied questions about adapting to increasing dependence on energy imports.

Yet such soaring Asian demand, coupled with rising North American production, suggests an incredible opportunity for closer energy ties to benefit both sides of the Pacific. Currently, the United States is revisiting many of its existing energy policies, with key implications for Asia. Of particular importance is the future role of the United States as an exporter of gas, coal, and potentially even crude oil to the region. However, uncertainty in U.S. policy—as evidenced by the positive yet slow growth in liquefied natural gas export agreements and the contentious debates in the Pacific Northwest surrounding coal exports—poses significant questions regarding when, and how, this trans-Pacific potential will be realized.

More broadly, Asian policymakers are also rethinking their overarching approaches to energy policy and security. Over the course of the last year, China, Japan, South Korea, and Taiwan all announced new national energy policies. These policies attempt to not only address issues for specific sectors, such as increasing the reliable use of nuclear energy, but also implement larger overhauls of national energy security strategy, such as in China's efforts to reshape its energy mix to manage demand, decrease the use of coal, and minimize import dependence.

Ultimately, increasing energy supplies is vital to sustaining the region's economic growth. Yet if current trends continue, the Asian Development Bank has estimated that carbon dioxide (CO_2) emissions in Asia and the Pacific will more than triple by 2050—resulting in significant harm to public health and the environment. To address these challenges, China and the United States are both looking to set targets across a range of environmental and energy-related issues, including tackling vehicle emissions, developing carbon capture and storage technology, and increasing energy efficiency. As the two largest CO_2 emitters in the world, and as countries with many shared energy and environmental concerns, the United States and China will need to work toward playing a greater and more cooperative global leadership role on these issues.

The Challenges Confronting India's Modi Government

In May 2014, Narendra Modi and his Bharatiya Janata Party (BJP) emerged victorious from the largest democratic election in world history. Modi's victory marked a major change in the political landscape in India, as it was the first time in 30 years that a single party won a majority in the Lok Sabha (the lower house of India's parliament) and was therefore able to form a government without needing to rely on coalition partners. This decisive margin of victory gives Modi enormous leeway in pursuing his policy agenda, which includes reviving the Indian economy, strengthening India's ties with its South Asian neighbors, revitalizing its partnership with the United States, and managing its relationship with China.

To revitalize India's economy, the Modi government has proposed to lift the cap on FDI in the defense and insurance sectors from 26% to 49% and placed a renewed emphasis on the manufacturing sector. In an effort to improve India's infrastructure, the government has plans to build one hundred "smart cities" and promote investment in factories, roads, and ports, among other measures. It also has pledged set up a committee to review the country's retrospective tax policy, which has caused great concern among foreign investors.

Modi has linked these efforts to strengthen the Indian economy with his foreign policy. He has emphasized the importance of economic diplomacy to strengthen trade ties and invite foreign investment into the country. Ambitions for India to regain its standing within South Asia have led Modi to make regional engagement a central pillar of his foreign policy, resulting in his robust engagement in the BRICS summit (which includes Brazil, Russia, India, China, and South Africa), where he announced with leaders of the other member states the creation of a BRICS development bank. As part of his strategy of engagement with India's neighbors, Modi invited the leaders of all the South Asian Association for Regional Cooperation (SAARC) member countries to his inauguration ceremony. Modi's visits to Bhutan and Nepal, along with other developments, such as India's acceptance of a United Nations tribunal's ruling in a decades-long maritime dispute with Bangladesh, and proposals for increased foreign aid packages to India's neighbors, also signal the new government's commitment to improving ties with fellow South Asian nations.

The only exception to this engagement strategy remains Pakistan. Modi's meeting with Pakistani prime minister Nawaz Sharif, after his inauguration ceremony, marked a promising start to the normalization of ties between India and Pakistan. However, India's decision to cancel high-level diplomatic talks between the two sides after Pakistan's envoy in New Delhi met with Kashmiri separatists and the current domestic political crisis in Pakistan have led the Modi government to take a harder line by giving the Indian forces deployed along the border a free hand in dealing with the Pakistani forces that India claims are violating the ceasefire both countries had signed in 2003.

India's relationship with the United States, which was at its apex after the signing of a civil nuclear agreement in 2008, has plateaued as a result of diplomatic spats and trade disputes. Modi's acceptance of President Barack Obama's invitation to visit the United States, despite Modi having previously been denied a U.S. visa over his alleged role in communal riots in Gujarat when he was chief minister of the state, is a welcome step toward reviving U.S.-India ties.

As part of its efforts to engage with the Modi government, the Obama administration used the fifth U.S.-India Strategic Dialogue to discuss the five pillars of the strategic partnership identified by both governments in 2009: strategic cooperation; energy and climate change; education and development; economics, trade, and agriculture; and science and technology, health, and innovation. Secretary of Defense Chuck Hagel subsequently visited New Delhi and sought to improve defense ties by exploring opportunities for greater cooperation and collaboration across a wide range of security issues. These high-level U.S. visits, which were followed by Modi's visit to Washington in September 2014, signal an ongoing commitment on both sides to the U.S.-India partnership.

India's interest in trade and cooperation with China is moderated by lingering security concerns and intensifying geopolitical competition. Although Modi called for stronger economic ties with China during his meeting with President Xi Jinping ahead of the 2014 BRICS summit, India is increasingly concerned over China's clout in South Asia and its assertiveness in their long-simmering border dispute. In response, Modi has announced his intentions to expedite projects to build the infrastructure needed to support a new mountain strike corps along the border. He has also worked to strengthen India's growing ties with Japan on both the economic and security fronts, as reflected in his successful visit to Japan.

As prime minister, Modi thus confronts the challenge of implementing an ambitious domestic and foreign policy agenda. In order to succeed on the foreign policy side of his agenda, he will need to be successful on the domestic policy front. This will require him to set into motion the reforms necessary to bring back the foreign investment that India's lagging economy needs and to fulfill his campaign promises on the development front. Just as Modi's goals are primarily domestic, so too are his challenges: controlling India's notoriously complicated bureaucracy will pose a particularly difficult problem, as will managing the many parochial interests that stand in the way of necessary reform. Modi's success in addressing these challenges will shape the future of Asia's rising democratic giant.

Myanmar's Political and Economic Development

Myanmar's political and economic reforms have opened a window for enhanced engagement with the United States, the Association of Southeast Asian Nations (ASEAN), and the Asia-Pacific more generally. The reforms initiated during 2011–12 included measures to relax the censorship of the press, implement a national human rights commission, increase financial regulation, and establish labor laws. By bringing the country one step closer to meeting standards set by its neighbors and trading partners, these measures have provided an impetus for increased international engagement and are viewed as opening the door for future reforms.

As an acknowledgment of its progress, Myanmar was named chair of ASEAN for the first time in its seventeen-year membership—a major role for a country freshly re-emerging onto the international and regional scene. Myanmar chose "Moving Forward in Unity to a Peaceful and Prosperous Community" as the 2014 ASEAN theme and set an ambitious agenda that prioritized implementation of the ASEAN Economic Community by developing the visions of regional economic integration and unity. The difficulties that ASEAN faces in achieving this goal are similar to the challenges Myanmar itself faces as an authoritarian state moving slowly toward democracy. Political will and capability must align with the interests of multiple parties. In Myanmar's case, the interests of political groups, leaders, and citizens must align, while in the case of ASEAN, the interests of member states and regional powers like China and the United States must align. Myanmar's own internal struggles and gradual democratic accomplishments provide an example of steady, incremental success for ASEAN and the rest of the Asia-Pacific region.

Myanmar's ASEAN chairmanship has seen very few hiccups, mostly related to capacity and effectiveness in following an agenda. While the establishment of the ASEAN Economic Community is hardly complete, the debates surrounding increased economic engagement among partners have been useful and have advanced Myanmar's own positive engagement with its ASEAN neighbors. Over the longer term, a Myanmar that is more regionally engaged will be better positioned to address critical regional and domestic issues, including: ASEAN's unity and relevance; regional economic integration; democracy and human rights issues related to interfaith engagement, the status of women, and the management of cross-border ethnic minorities (such as the Rohingya); environmental and natural resource issues, including the development and production of oil and gas, timber, and minerals; and military engagement and cooperation on issues of mutual interest like humanitarian assistance and disaster relief.

Although none of these issues have been entirely resolved during Myanmar's leadership of ASEAN, the completion of the ASEAN Foreign Ministers' Meeting in early August was a good sign of progress. Discussions on territorial disputes in the South China Sea were said to be positive and moving toward a peaceful resolution, and those in attendance stated that progress was made toward the realization of the ASEAN Economic Community by 2015 and increasing trade and economic development. Whether Myanmar can become an active member of ASEAN and continue to drive progress in the region following the conclusion of its chairmanship will be an equally important appraisal of its advancement.

Looking beyond Myanmar's ASEAN chairmanship, it is clear that the importance of the country's parliament will continue to increase. There are potentially great benefits from continuing to expose Myanmar's political leadership to strong engagement with foreign and U.S. government offices, businesses, civil society organizations, universities, and executive branches. Additionally, there is much room for analysis of how emerging domestic political and economic dynamics stand to alter Myanmar's regional position, with a particular focus on the combined economic, diplomatic, and military impact of its opening on the broader Asia-Pacific. Indeed, any indication that progress on political and economic reform has stalled, or even slid backward, would pose a fundamental challenge to Myanmar's ability to continue to enhance its relations with the United States and the rest of the international community. All of these issues will intensify leading up to the 2015 presidential election, as the country focuses inward to assess the status of political and economic developments that are only a few years old.

Myanmar's increased engagement on domestic political and economic issues will greatly enhance its development prospects and the overall stability and prosperity of Southeast Asia, significantly enhancing ASEAN's credibility as a political and economic force with increasing interregional support. Myanmar's ASEAN chairmanship has set the groundwork for continued political and economic growth, but the country will need to address several internal challenges to keep the reform process moving forward.

Deepening Economic Integration along Different Models

The Asia-Pacific is marked by incredible economic dynamism and opportunity. U.S. efforts to rebalance toward the region have highlighted the geopolitical significance of economic engagement, and significant progress has been made in negotiating key multilateral trade agreements, including the Trans-Pacific Partnership (TPP). Additionally, 2014 witnessed a number of developments in trade negotiations and dispute rulings that highlight the region's importance to major economies both in the Asia-Pacific and beyond.

Negotiations on the TPP—an ambitious, high-level trade agreement that involves the United States, Japan, and ten other countries on both sides of the Pacific—grabbed numerous headlines. The TPP is both economically and strategically significant for the United States, as it provides an opportunity to encourage greater regional economic integration based on the rule of law and the principles of economic liberalism while deepening the United States' ties to the region. However, the agreement's ambitious goals, which involve complex issues such as e-commerce, intellectual property, environmental standards, and consumer protection, have complicated negotiations. Another obstacle has been the goal to not exclude any sensitive sector from the lowering of trade barriers. For example, Japan has long protected its agricultural sector against the effects of foreign influence, and Tokyo's perceived inflexibility on this point may threaten recent progress in the negotiations. Similarly, in the United States, the dairy industry and other agricultural sectors have threatened to pull support for the agreement if their needs are not met. Negotiators have called for increased activity to surmount the remaining hurdles to the agreement.

A key element that will affect the success of the TPP in the United States is Congress's ability to grant the president trade promotion authority (TPA). TPA legislation would give President Obama authority to negotiate the specifics of the TPP and force Congress to conduct a simple up or down vote, without amendment, at the end of the agreement's negotiations and consultations. The passage of TPA would strengthen the United States' position in TPP negotiations by reassuring other countries that the final agreement will be passed, despite the divisive political atmosphere in the United States. However, TPA remains contentious, as some U.S. lawmakers and observers worry that it embraces opaque procedures and sacrifices the opportunity for debate on the ultimate agreement.

Many hope that the TPP will set an example for future trade agreements in the Asia-Pacific, but the exclusion of major economies such as China and India will temper the immediate effects of the ultimate agreement. Some critics have seen the United States' promotion of and leadership in negotiations as a means to contain China, and Beijing has responded in part by throwing its weight behind the Regional Comprehensive Economic Partnership (RCEP). RCEP aims to knit together numerous existing free trade agreements among the members of the Association of Southeast Asian Nations (ASEAN) as well as Australia, China, India, Japan, South Korea, and New Zealand. RCEP is less ambitious than the TPP in a number of ways, choosing to embrace flexibility and acknowledge differing levels of development among the potential signatories. RCEP's relatively narrow focus on the standard goals of conventional free trade agreements makes it more attractive to countries like China and India, which would struggle to meet the requirements of the TPP. This flexibility, however, limits the potential impact of the agreement, as does the exclusion of the United States.

ASEAN is also working toward regional economic integration through the planned ASEAN Economic Community (AEC). The top five economies within ASEAN (Indonesia, Malaysia, the Philippines, Thailand, and Vietnam) achieved an average of 6% GDP growth in 2012, which is particularly impressive considering the residual effects of the 2008 financial crisis seen in many other economies. Proponents of the AEC believe that greater economic integration will further propel growth among ASEAN nations. However, ASEAN comprises a diverse group of member nations with differing needs, desires, and resources, which inevitably complicates plans for broad integration. Although considerable progress has been made toward securing the foundation of the AEC, there remains much to be accomplished before the planned implementation deadline of 2015.

The first half of 2014 also included a number of dispute rulings by the World Trade Organization (WTO), including several featuring China and the United States as principal participants. A case brought by the United States, the European Union, and Japan yielded a ruling against China's restrictions on rare earth exports, in spite of China's argument that the restrictions were necessary to address legitimate environmental concerns. The WTO also sided with the United States in a complaint against Chinese tariffs on U.S. cars, while in July, U.S. duties on Chinese and Indian steel exports were found to be in violation of WTO rules. In recent years, the increased use of the WTO's dispute settlement procedure by the United States and China has led some observers to express fears of a trade war between the two countries. Other observers argue that the use of these channels is evidence that the WTO system is working as it should.

This flurry of activity in the Asia-Pacific is indicative of the region's significance in the world economy. Progress in TPP, RCEP, and AEC negotiations, as well as ongoing WTO talks, will have profound effects on economic interactions within the Asia-Pacific. Embracing and understanding the complexities of these overlapping initiatives will be important for the United States as it continues its rebalance to the Asia-Pacific and develops its economic engagement with the region.

About the Contributors

Greg Chaffin is a Project Manager with the Political and Security Affairs group at The National Bureau of Asian Research (NBR), where he manages the Strategic Asia, Strengthening the Asia-Pacific Order, Strategic Assistance, and Korea Studies programs. Prior to joining NBR, Mr. Chaffin worked for the University of London's Centre for International Studies and Diplomacy and as a consultant on international security affairs for several private firms in Washington, D.C. Mr. Chaffin holds a BA in Political Science from the University of Rochester and is pursuing an MA in Security Studies at Georgetown University's Edmund A. Walsh School of Foreign Service.

Catharin Dalpino is a Contract Course Chair at the State Department's Foreign Service Institute and an Adjunct Professor at Seton Hall University. She has taught Southeast Asian Studies at the Johns Hopkins University's School of Advanced International Studies, George Washington University, and Georgetown University. From 2005 to 2010, Professor Dalpino was Director of Thai Studies at Georgetown University. She was a Deputy Assistant Secretary of State (1993–97) and has been a fellow at the Brookings Institution, Carnegie Endowment for International Peace, and the Atlantic Council.

Abraham M. Denmark is Vice President for Political and Security Affairs at The National Bureau of Asian Research (NBR). Mr. Denmark has significant experience both inside and outside government. He previously worked as a Fellow at the Center for a New American Security and served in the Pentagon as Country Director for China Affairs in the Office of the Secretary of Defense. Mr. Denmark also is a Senior Advisor at the Center for Naval Analyses and serves on the Advisory Council of the Emerging Science and Technology Policy Centre. He is a member of the National Committee on United States–China Relations, the U.S. Naval Institute, and the International Institute for Strategic Studies, and was named a 21st Century Leader by the National Committee on American Foreign Policy. Mr. Denmark is widely published and has been featured in major media outlets in the United States and Asia, including the *Financial Times*, *Foreign Policy*, the *Global Times*, the

New York Times, Newsweek, Time, and the *Washington Quarterly*. He holds an MA in International Security from the Josef Korbel School of International Studies at the University of Denver and a BA in History with Honors from the University of Northern Colorado, and studied at China's Foreign Affairs University and Peking University.

Richard J. Ellings is President and Co-founder of The National Bureau of Asian Research (NBR). He is also Affiliate Professor of International Studies in the Henry M. Jackson School of International Studies, University of Washington. Dr. Ellings is the author of *Embargoes and World Power: Lessons from American Foreign Policy* (1985); co-author of *Private Property and National Security* (1991); co-editor (with Aaron Friedberg) of *Strategic Asia 2003–04: Fragility and Crisis* (2003), *Strategic Asia 2002–03: Asian Aftershocks* (2002), and *Strategic Asia 2001–02: Power and Purpose* (2001); co-editor of *Korea's Future and the Great Powers* (with Nicholas Eberstadt, 2001) and *Southeast Asian Security in the New Millennium* (with Sheldon Simon, 1996); founding editor of the *NBR Analysis* publication series; and co-chairman of the *Asia Policy* editorial board. He also established the Strategic Asia Program and AccessAsia, the national clearinghouse that tracks specialists and their research on Asia. Previously, he served as Legislative Assistant in the U.S. Senate, office of Senator Slade Gorton. Dr. Ellings earned his BA in Political Science from the University of California–Berkeley and his MA and PhD in Political Science from the University of Washington.

Bates Gill is CEO of the United States Studies Centre at the University of Sydney, a position he has held since 2012. Prior to this, he was Director of the Stockholm International Peace Research Institute from 2007 to 2012, held the Freeman Chair in China Studies at the Center for Strategic and International Studies, and was Senior Fellow in Foreign Policy Studies and inaugural Director of the Center for Northeast Asian Policy Studies at the Brookings Institution. Dr. Gill is author, co-author, or co-editor of seven books, including *Rising Star: China's New Security Diplomacy* (2007, revised edition 2010), *Governing the Bomb: Civilian Control and Democratic Accountability of Nuclear Weapons* (2010), and *Asia's New Multilateralism* (2009). In 2013, he received the Royal Order of the Commander of the Polar Star, the highest award bestowed upon foreigners by the Swedish monarch, for his contributions to Swedish interests.

Sheena Chestnut Greitens is an Assistant Professor of Political Science at the University of Missouri and a Nonresident Senior Fellow at the Center for East Asian Policy Studies at the Brookings Institution. She is also an Associate in Research at the Harvard Fairbank Center for Chinese Studies and a Fellow with the National Committee on U.S.-China Relations' Public Intellectuals Program. Her work focuses on East Asian politics and international relations, particularly issues of security, authoritarian politics, illicit networks, and the impact of state-society relations on foreign policy. Her research has been published in academic journals and edited volumes in English, Chinese, and Korean, and has appeared in *Newsweek*, Huffington Post, *Foreign Policy*, the *International Herald Tribune*, and the *New York Times*. Dr. Greitens holds a PhD from Harvard University; an MPhil from Oxford University, where she studied as a Marshall Scholar; and a BA from Stanford University.

Russell Hsiao is a Nonresident Senior Fellow at the Project 2049 Institute and a National Security Fellow at the Foundation for Defense of Democracies. Prior to joining the Project 2049 Institute, he was the Editor of *China Brief* at the Jamestown Foundation from 2007 to 2011. Before that, he worked as a Special Associate in the International Cooperation Department at the Taiwan Foundation for Democracy. Mr. Hsiao is a JD candidate at the Catholic University of America's Columbus School of Law. He received a BA from the American University's School of International Service and the University Honors Program.

Van Jackson is a Visiting Fellow at the Center for a New American Security and a Council on Foreign Relations International Affairs Fellow. He is also a Visiting Scholar in Georgetown University's Asian Studies program in the School of Foreign Service. From 2009 to 2014, Dr. Jackson held positions in the Office of the Secretary of Defense as Advisor for Asia-Pacific Strategy, Senior Country Director for Korea, and Working Group Chair of the U.S.–Republic of Korea Extended Deterrence Policy Committee. From 2011 to 2013, he was also a Nonresident James A. Kelly Fellow in Korean Studies with the Pacific Forum at the Center for Strategic and International Studies. In addition, Dr. Jackson teaches courses on Asian security and grand strategy at Georgetown University and the Catholic University of America. His research has appeared in *International Relations of the Asia-Pacific, Asian Security, Comparative Strategy, Contemporary Security Policy*, and *Far Eastern Economic Review*. He holds a PhD in World Politics from the Catholic University of America and was formerly selected as one of the "Top 99 under 33" foreign policy leaders by *Diplomatic Courier* magazine.

Ann Marie Murphy is an Associate Professor in the School of Diplomacy and International Relations and founding Director of the Center for Emerging Powers and Transnational Trends at Seton Hall University. She is also a Senior Research Scholar in the Weatherhead East Asian Institute at Columbia University and an Associate Fellow in the Asia Society. Dr. Murphy has been a Visiting Scholar at the Centre for Strategic and International Studies in Jakarta, Indonesia, and at the Institute for Security and International Studies in Bangkok, Thailand. Her research interests include international relations in Asia, political development in Southeast Asia, U.S. foreign policy toward Southeast Asia, and the rise of transnational issues such as climate change and global health. With the support of a grant from the Smith Richardson Foundation, Dr. Murphy is currently researching and writing a book on the impact of democratization on Indonesian foreign policy. She holds a PhD in Political Science from Columbia University.

Nguyen Manh Hung is a Professor Emeritus of Government and International Relations at George Mason University and a Nonresident Senior Associate at the Center for Strategic and International Studies (CSIS). Dr. Nguyen has participated in major policy working groups on Vietnam and Indochina, including the Indochina Policy Forum of the Aspen Institute, the Indochina Study Group of the Council on Foreign Relations, and the Southeast Asia Working Group of Georgetown University's CSIS. He is the author of several books and book chapters and has published articles in journals such as *Amerasia Journal*, *Asia Pacific Bulletin*, *Asian Survey*, *Global Asia*, *International Security*, *Journal of Asian Thought and Society*, *Pacific Affairs*, and *World Affairs*. His recent publications include "ASEAN's Scarborough Failure?" (2012), "Drawing a Line in the South China Sea: Why Beijing Needs to Show Restraint" (2012), and "Vietnam–United States Relations: A Thirty-Five-Year Retrospective" (2010).

Scott Snyder is a Senior Fellow for Korea Studies and Director of the Program on U.S.-Korea Policy at the Council on Foreign Relations (CFR). Prior to joining CFR, he was a Senior Associate in the International Relations Program of the Asia Foundation, a Senior Associate at Pacific Forum CSIS, an Asia Specialist at the United States Institute of Peace, and Acting Director of the Contemporary Affairs Program at Asia Society. Mr. Snyder is the co-editor with Kyung-Ae Park of *North Korea in Transition: Politics, Economics, and Society* (2013) and co-author with Brad Glosserman of *The Japan–South Korea Identity Clash: East Asian Security and the United States* (2015). He holds degrees from Harvard University and Rice University.

Matthew Shannon Stumpf is Director of the Washington, D.C., Office of the Asia Society Policy Institute. He has worked in the U.S. government and leading U.S. NGOs to deepen cooperation between the United States and Asia. Mr. Stumpf has served as Special Assistant to the Administrator at the U.S. Agency for International Development (USAID) and in the Bureau of International Security and Nonproliferation at the U.S. Department of State. He was also Program Officer for International Peace and Security at the John D. and Catherine T. MacArthur Foundation. Mr. Stumpf received his MPP from the Kennedy School of Government at Harvard University and his BA from the Elliott School of International Affairs at the George Washington University.

Nicholas Szechenyi is a Senior Fellow and Deputy Director of the Japan Chair at the Center for Strategic and International Studies (CSIS). His research focuses on U.S.-Japan relations and U.S.–East Asia relations. In 2009, he was selected as an Inaugural Fellow of the U.S.-Japan Network for the Future program established by the Maureen and Mike Mansfield Foundation. Prior to joining CSIS in 2005, he was a news producer for Fuji Television in Washington, D.C., where he covered U.S. policy in Asia and domestic politics. Mr. Szechenyi co-authors a triannual review of U.S.-Japan relations in *Comparative Connections*, an electronic journal on East Asian bilateral relations. His other publications include "Japan-U.S. Relations" (with Michael J. Green) in *The Routledge Handbook of Japanese Politics* (2011) and "A Turning Point for Japan's Self Defense Forces," published in the *Washington Quarterly* (2006). He holds an MA in international economics and Japan studies from the Johns Hopkins University School of Advanced International Studies and a BA in Asian studies from Connecticut College.

Ashley J. Tellis is a Senior Associate at the Carnegie Endowment for International Peace, specializing in international security, defense, and Asian strategic issues. He is also Research Director of the Strategic Asia Program at The National Bureau of Asian Research (NBR) and co-editor of eleven volumes in the annual series. While on assignment to the U.S. Department of State as Senior Adviser to the Undersecretary of State for Political Affairs (2005–8), Dr. Tellis was intimately involved in negotiating the civil nuclear agreement with India. Previously, he was commissioned into the Foreign Service and served as Senior Adviser to the Ambassador at the U.S. embassy in New Delhi. He also served on the National Security Council staff as Special Assistant to the President and Senior Director for Strategic Planning and Southwest Asia. Prior to his government service, Dr. Tellis was a Senior Policy Analyst at the RAND Corporation and Professor of Policy Analysis at the RAND Graduate School. He is the author of *India's Emerging Nuclear Posture* (2001) and co-author of *Interpreting China's Grand Strategy: Past, Present, and Future* (2000). His academic publications have also appeared in many edited volumes and journals. Dr. Tellis holds a PhD in Political Science from the University of Chicago.

Daniel Twining is Senior Fellow for Asia at the German Marshall Fund of the United States, where he leads a sixteen-member team working on the rise of Asia and its implications for the West through a program of research and convening focused on India, China, Japan, Pakistan, and the future of the liberal order. He is also an Associate of the U.S. National Intelligence Council. He previously served as a Member of the Secretary of State's Policy Planning Staff responsible for South Asia, where he worked on the U.S.-India strategic partnership, Pakistan's transition from military to civilian rule, and the future of Afghanistan. Dr. Twining has taught a graduate-level course on South Asian security studies at Georgetown University and regularly teaches a seminar on South Asian security to U.S. military personnel. He holds a doctorate in international relations from Oxford University, where he was the Fulbright/Oxford Scholar from 2004 to 2007.

About Strategic Asia

The Strategic Asia Program at The National Bureau of Asian Research (NBR) is a major ongoing research initiative that draws together top Asia studies specialists and international relations experts to assess the changing strategic environment in the Asia-Pacific. The program combines the rigor of academic analysis with the practicality of traditional policy analyses by incorporating economic, military, political, and demographic data and by focusing on the trends, strategies, and perceptions that drive geopolitical dynamics in the region. The program's integrated set of products and activities includes:

- an annual edited volume written by leading specialists

- an executive brief tailored for public- and private-sector decision-makers and strategic planners

- briefings and presentations for government, business, and academe that are designed to foster in-depth discussions revolving around major public-policy issues

Special briefings are held for key committees of Congress and the executive branch, other government agencies, and the intelligence community. The principal audiences for the program's research findings are the U.S. policymaking and research communities, the media, the business community, and academe.

To order a book, please visit the Strategic Asia website at http://www.nbr.org/strategicasia.

Previous Strategic Asia Volumes

Now in its fourteenth year, the *Strategic Asia* series addresses how Asia is increasingly functioning as a zone of strategic interaction and contending with an uncertain balance of power.

Strategic Asia 2013–14: Asia in the Second Nuclear Age examined the role of nuclear weapons in the grand strategies of key Asian states and assessed the impact of these capabilities—both established and latent—on regional and international stability.

Strategic Asia 2012–13: China's Military Challenge assessed China's growing military capabilities and explored their impact on the Asia-Pacific region.

Strategic Asia 2011–12: Asia Responds to Its Rising Powers—China and India explored how key Asian states and regions have responded to the rise of China and India, drawing implications for U.S. interests and leadership in the Asia-Pacific.

Strategic Asia 2010–11: Asia's Rising Power and America's Continued Purpose provided a continent-wide net assessment of the core trends and issues affecting the region by examining Asia's performance in nine key functional areas.

Strategic Asia 2009–10: Economic Meltdown and Geopolitical Stability analyzed the impact of the global economic crisis on key Asian states and explored the strategic implications for the United States.

Strategic Asia 2008–09: Challenges and Choices examined the impact of geopolitical developments on Asia's transformation over the previous eight years and assessed the major strategic choices on Asia facing the new U.S. president.

Strategic Asia 2007–08: Domestic Political Change and Grand Strategy examined internal and external drivers of grand strategy on Asian foreign policymaking.

Strategic Asia 2006–07: Trade, Interdependence, and Security addressed how changing trade relationships affect the balance of power and security in the region.

Strategic Asia 2005–06: Military Modernization in an Era of Uncertainty appraised the progress of Asian military modernization programs.

Strategic Asia 2004–05: Confronting Terrorism in the Pursuit of Power explored the effect of the U.S.-led war on terrorism on the strategic transformations underway in Asia.

Strategic Asia 2003–04: Fragility and Crisis examined the fragile balance of power in Asia, drawing out the key domestic political and economic trends in Asian states supporting or undermining this tenuous equilibrium.

Strategic Asia 2002–03: Asian Aftershocks drew upon this baseline to analyze changes in these states' grand strategies and relationships in the aftermath of the September 11 terrorist attacks.

Strategic Asia 2001–02: Power and Purpose established a baseline assessment for understanding the strategies and interactions of the major states within the region.

Research and Management Team

The Strategic Asia research team consists of leading international relations and security specialists from universities and research institutions across the United States and around the world. A new research team is selected each year. The research team for 2014 is led by Ashley J. Tellis (Carnegie Endowment for International Peace). Aaron Friedberg (Princeton University, and Strategic Asia's founding research director) and Richard Ellings (The National Bureau of Asian Research, and Strategic Asia's founding program director) continue to serve as senior advisors.

The Strategic Asia Program has historically depended on a diverse base of funding from foundations, government, and corporations, supplemented by income from publication sales. Major support for the program in 2014 comes from the Lynde and Harry Bradley Foundation. In addition, the Smith Richardson Foundation provided support for the research of several of the chapters in this year's volume.

Attribution

Readers of *Strategic Asia* and visitors to the Strategic Asia website may use data, charts, graphs, and quotes from these sources without requesting permission from NBR on the condition that they cite NBR and the appropriate primary source in any published work. No report, chapter, separate study, extensive text, or any other substantial part of the Strategic Asia Program's products may be reproduced without the written permission of NBR. To request permission, please write to:

NBR Publications
The National Bureau of Asian Research
1414 NE 42nd Street, Suite 300
Seattle, Washington 98105
publications@nbr.org

Index